$3400

D1537410

reading problems

DIAGNOSIS AND REMEDIATION

Margaret Ann Richek
Northeastern Illinois University

Lynne K. List
Professor Emeritus-College of the Virgin Islands

Janet W. Lerner
Northeastern Illinois University

WiLLiAM TEALE
SHiRley BRicé HEATH
DonAiD HoiDAWAY

June.
August 11. 1987

2 Articles.
2 Summarie
1 presentation.

PRENTICE–HALL, INC., ENGLEWOOD CLIFFS, N.J. 07632

Library of Congress Cataloging in Publication Data

Richek, Margaret Ann.
  Reading problems.

  Includes indexes.
  1. Reading disability. 2. Reading—Remedial
teaching. I. List, Lynne K., (date)   . II. Lerner,
Janet W. III. Title.
LB1050.5.R53   1983   428.4′2   82–16486
ISBN 0-13-755173-8

To our parents, our first and most loving teachers . . .

Editorial/production supervision and interior design by A.G. Roney
Cover design by Miriam Recio
Manufacturing buyer: Ron Chapman

Printed in the United States of America

10 9 8 7 6 5 4 3 2

ISBN 0-13-755173-8

Prentice-Hall International, Inc., *London*
Prentice-Hall of Australia Pty. Limited, *Sydney*
Editora Prentice-Hall do Brasil, Ltda., *Rio de Janeiro*
Prentice-Hall Canada Inc., *Toronto*
Prentice-Hall of India Private Limited, *New Delhi*
Prentice-Hall of Japan, Inc., *Tokyo*
Prentice-Hall of Southeast Asia Pte. Ltd., *Singapore*
Whitehall Books Limited, *Wellington, New Zealand*

CONTENTS

List of Test Inventories

PREFACE

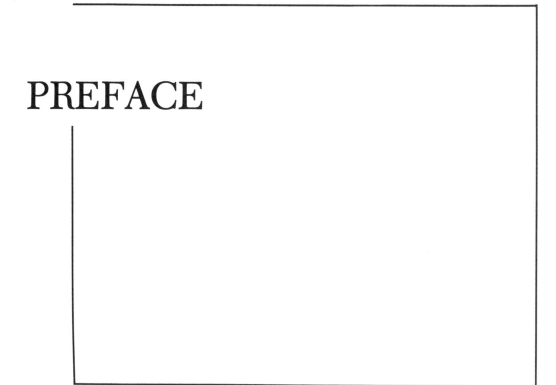

This book is concerned with helping the many children, adolescents, and adults who encounter difficulty with reading. Without appropriate help, these individuals remain handicapped in many ways. As a primary cause of school failure, poor reading leads to a lowered self-esteem and consequent emotional problems. Reading disability prevents individuals from reaching desired career goals, and it robs them of the opportunity to read for pleasure and enjoyment. Illiteracy is associated with many social problems, and therefore society as a whole suffers the consequences of poor reading among its citizenry.

Many remedial teaching techniques have a long-established tradition and have been widely used for many years. It is important for today's teachers to be familiar with and to develop competencies in the traditional diagnostic and teaching methods. Important recent innovations and changes in the field of reading, however, have had a profound effect on the diagnosis and teaching of disabled readers. The field of remedial reading must be updated to bring it into modern educational thought. Teachers working with disabled readers must learn about the new research findings and current trends and ways of thinking in order to synthesize them with the traditional diagnostic and remedial methods. This book brings the old and the new together in a workable and practical way.

The field of remedial reading has been updated with contributions from (a) linguistics, which offer a better understanding of the nature of spoken and written language systems; (b) the psycholinguistic perspective of reading, which shows how the student's language base affects reading and learning to read; (c) special education, which provides important legal ramifications for working with handicapped students; and (d) learning disabilities, which contributes a perspective on the important role of prerequisite skills for students with intrinsic learning problems. This book merges traditional diagnostic and remedial methods with newer perspectives and insights to provide an effective remedial reading program.

The book is divided into four parts. Part I is an introduction and examines the field of remedial reading and the consequences of reading problems.

Part II deals with the diagnosis of reading disability and the correlates associated with reading problems. It includes general principles of diagnosis (Chapter 2); ecological (or environmental), emotional and physical correlates (Chapter 3); and the correlates of intellectual potential and language (Chapter 4). Chapters 5 and 6 present methods of assessing reading achievement and the components of reading: formal diagnostic methods, including commercial tests (Chapter 5); and informal diagnostic methods, including informal reading inventories, miscue analysis, observation, and teacher-made tests (Chapter 6).

Part III presents methods for treating reading problems and offers many practical suggestions and activities. It includes general principles of remediation (Chapter 7); characteristics of severely disabled readers (Chapter 8); and teaching strategies for severely disabled readers (Chapter 9). The balance of Part III deals with ways to improve reading ability: improving word recognition through sight words and phonics (Chapter 10); improving word recognition through context, structural analysis, and holistic strategies (Chapter 11); improving reading comprehension (Chapter 12); and improving meaning vocabulary, reading-study skills, and reading rate (Chapter 13).

Part IV presents organizational aspects of remedial reading: important laws and their effect on reading and special education teaching (Chapter 14); and the keeping of reports and records (Chapter 15).

The Appendixes provide information to help in remedial reading instruction: materials for remedial reading (Appendixes A and B); a sample form for a diagnostic report (Appendix C); and a complete informal reading inventory (Appendix D).

The various forms, checklists, and tests throughout the book, including the Informal Reading Inventory, are designed to be reproducible for teacher use.

Many people helped us in the development of this book. We owe a special debt of gratitude to several graduate students at Northeastern Illinois University. Elizabeth Conner, Ursula Jonas, Jeanne Moisan, Mary Margaret Rappe, and Susan Samuels developed the inventories of commercial tests and the descriptions of reading materials. Sherrill Lynn Crivellone modified and validated the informal reading inventory. The Department of Learning Services at Northeastern Illinois

University, and especially artist David W. Morrow, were responsible for many of the fine illustrations and diagrams. Mr. Stephen Peters helped in the manuscript preparation and was a valuable asset in the editing process.

The authors have many others to thank for the development of this book. As remedial reading teachers in elementary and secondary schools, we learned much from the children we had the privilege of teaching. As college instructors and directors of reading clinics, we learned from our students who were teachers or prospective teachers. As long-time members of the reading profession, we learned from authors of journal articles, publishers of research reports, presenters at conferences, and discussions with our colleagues. Perhaps most important in the development of this book has been our continuing dialogue with other experienced practitioners, who provided an invaluable sounding board for our ideas.

Margaret Ann Richek
Lynne K. List
Janet W. Lerner

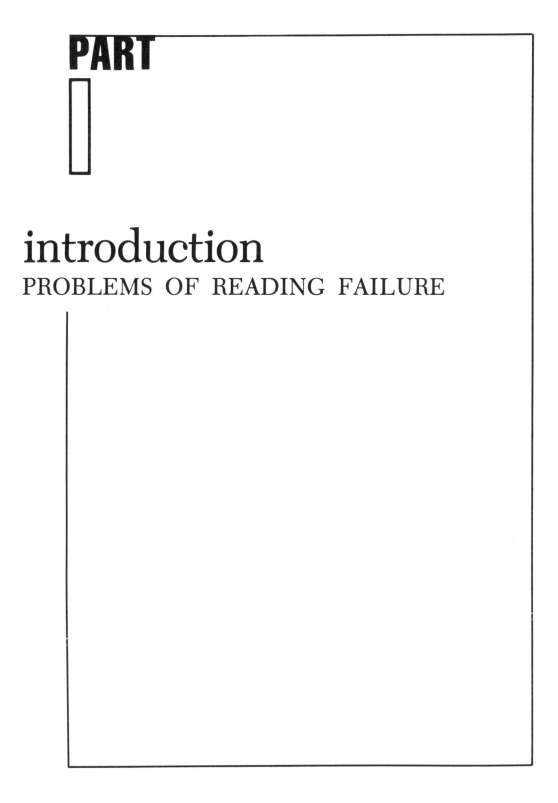

PART

introduction
PROBLEMS OF READING FAILURE

1

READING DISABILITIES
a personal and national dilemma

A newspaper story of an attempted burglary reported that a would-be robber handed this note to a bank teller:

I GOT A BUM. I ALSO HAVE A CONTOUR. I'M GOING TO BLOW
YOU SKY HEIGHT. I'M NO KILLEN. THIS IS A HELD UP.

Unable to decipher the note, the teller asked the robber for help in reading it. By the time the robber told the teller what the words were, the police arrived and arrested the bank robber. The police were also able to trace the robber to other bank holdups in which the same errors were made. This news report of a thwarted bank holdup illustrates the point that literacy is required in most occupations today—even to be a successful bank robber (*Miami Herald*, 1980).

The individual who cannot learn to read is the concern of educators, parents, physicians, and psychologists, as well as society in general. The field of remedial reading is dedicated to serving the needs of such people. Established in the early part of the century, the current field of remedial reading is a distillation of a half-century of research, theory, and clinical practice.

Students with reading problems can be found throughout our schools. Some of these poor readers are served through remedial reading programs; some are served through special education programs; still others receive instruction solely in the regular classroom (see Figure 1.1).

The incidence of reading disability in American schools is about 15 percent (Harris, 1981). To help all these students effectively, classroom teachers, reading teachers, and special education teachers need certain skills and knowledge about the study and treatment of reading difficulties. A thorough knowledge of remedial reading is needed by all teachers who have the responsibility of understanding and helping reading disabled students. This book conveys important concepts, methods, research, and practices from the field of remedial reading. The issues discussed in this first chapter include (1) the impact of poor reading upon the individual and on society, (2) the definition of reading, (3) the field of remedial reading, and (4) an overview of the book.

THE IMPACT OF READING PROBLEMS
UPON THE INDIVIDUAL
AND SOCIETY

Studies reporting the literacy level in our nation are alarming. A large-scale national assessment showed that 10 percent of the nation's seventeen-year-olds are unable to read even simple materials (National Assessment of Educational Progress, 1981). Another study shows that over 50 million adults in the United States are functionally illiterate, and that one in every seven individuals has reading difficulties requiring special attention at some time in their lives (Rosner et al., 1981).

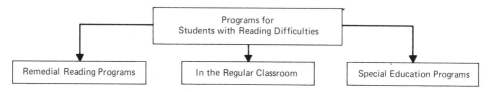

Figure 1.1   School Programs for Serving Students with Reading Difficulties

The consequences of these reading problems upon the individual and society can be devastating. Illiteracy has personal, political, and economic implications. Disabled readers often suffer intense feelings of shame and inadequacy. They may be unable to handle the demands of their schools, their jobs, and their personal lives. Poor reading can also affect an individual's social life and acceptance of responsibilities as a citizen.

Inability to read is a primary cause of school failure. Such failure may occur in any subject since the ability to read is essential for all types of academic success. For example, students with reading problems, even if they are superior in mathematical computations, often have difficulty solving word problems. Emotionally, the strain of being unable to read in school may cause the individual to feel lost and frightened and to experience rejection and defeat. In the case of failing students, there is no escape. They are forced to face their inadequacies day after day in school and to be subjected to degradation or grudging tolerance by others (Roswell and Natchez, 1977). A variety of emotional symptoms may result, ranging from diminished self-concept to serious emotional disturbances. Frequently, students with reading handicaps display overt disruptive behaviors, or they may simply "give up," convinced that they are not capable of doing any better.

The poor reader finds that doors are closed for personal growth and career opportunities. Reading is the key tool for acquiring and maintaining employable skills. With the rapidity of change in today's world, old jobs become obsolete, and there is need for continual retraining. In our technological society, individuals in every occupational area will have to prepare for new jobs many times during their work careers. Automation has caused the elimination of many jobs that once were filled by unskilled or semiskilled workers, and the number of jobs for uneducated workers is diminishing. When workers are functionally illiterate, they are likely to become chronically unemployable.

Reading problems of individuals also affect society in general. Many of the ills of our society have been related to poor reading. The unemployed, school dropouts, juvenile delinquents, and criminals in our prisons tend to have very poor reading skills. Examinations of the problem of our schools, of poverty, of the concerns of troubled parents all seem to show some association with poor reading.

A trilogy of watchwords seems to dominate the existence of individuals with severe reading problems. They must learn to *cope, compensate,* and *conceal* in an attempt to function as normally as possible. Coping involves dealing successfully with the situation. Compensating requires that the individual "make up

"Read me my report card, Dad."

for" the deficiency. Concealing involves hiding the handicap. One man coped by accepting his menial work status and income as inevitable. He rationalized that his father and grandfather before him had held the same station in life and that he should be content with his lot. A school-aged youngster convinced herself that she was stupid and that she just could not do any better. Interviews with psychologists revealed that she sincerely believed she was "dumb." Her failure was, therefore, easy to accept, since she did not have to blame herself. Both these individuals had learned to cope with their reading handicap.

A young boy with a severe reading problem learned to compensate by reading with one eye shut. In this way he could more clearly discern the letters. Since he did not realize that he was suffering from a visual problem, he compensated in the best manner he knew how. A woman compensated by devoting her energies to the development of her artistic abilities. The recognition and acceptance that she achieved through her talent overshadowed her lack of ability to read even the newspaper.

The act of concealing has stimulated some ingenious behavior. Some people have mastered the art so well that their close associates never suspect the truth. For example, an elderly widowed gentleman, who was caught up in the social dating whirl, would enter a restaurant with his lady friend, put down the menu, and exclaim, "Please order for us both, dear. Whatever you select will please me." When this same gentleman explained that he hired professionals to handle all his personal matters, including his checkbook, his friends attributed his actions to wealth; they never suspected a lack of reading ability. A nonreading adolescent spent hours listening to the news on television and radio so that he could converse with his friends. He pretended to have read the information in newspapers and magazines, successfully concealing his reading handicap.

A poignant letter written to newspaper columnist Ann Landers (1979) vividly reveals the desperate and tragic plight of the nonreader:

I went with this man for six months. He grew up on a farm in Vermont, loves nature and animals . . . and is very kind and considerate. We have a good marriage . . . I began to notice he never read a newspaper, magazine or book and had trouble with signs, directions and even labels. His excuse was he couldn't see the small print.

Yesterday John admitted the truth. He can't read. He was so ashamed he cried when he told me. How can I help him? Now that I know, I feel it is our problem.*

THE DEFINITION OF READING

For many years, reading specialists have attempted to define reading. No one interpretation, however, has as yet been entirely acceptable to all. This lack of agreement is due to the many different perspectives within the field of reading itself. In general, reading is the ability to gather meaning from printed symbols. To some, however, recognizing words is the essential ingredient. Others stress literal comprehension of the printed word, sentence, and paragraph. Others emphasize the important role of prediction and judgment in reading.

In practice, teachers must define reading to meet the instructional levels and educational needs of their particular students. For students at the beginning stages of reading, recognizing words and comprehending literal meaning are important components of the definition. For students at intermediate reading levels, the definition of reading is extended to include a deeper understanding of passages. As reading ability matures, the definition of reading broadens to include interpretation and critical evaluation.

The purpose of reading also affects the definition. For the severely mentally retarded child, for example, the ability to recognize the word *poison* on a bottle can be considered reading. For a student at the junior high school level, reading might mean studying a social studies text. For millions of people, reading is a means of recreation and enjoyment. In the world of work, reading enables people to perform their jobs effectively. Automobile mechanics, chefs, accountants, and physicians all use reading in the daily tasks required by their jobs.

Reading, thus, is not one task, but a variety of complex tasks. It serves many functions for society and the individual. In general, reading can be thought of as the ability to gather meaning from printed symbols, taking into account both the individual's level of reading and purpose for reading.

THE FIELD
OF REMEDIAL READING

Remedial reading can be viewed within the context of a broader field—that of *remedial education*. Remedial education designates programs for individuals who are having difficulty in learning in any of several academic areas: reading, spelling, arithmetic, or writing (Otto and Smith, 1980).

* Reprinted with the permission of Ann Landers and the Field Newspaper Syndicate.

While the term "remedial education" refers to teaching in several academic areas, the greatest attention is directed toward failure in the area of reading. Remedial reading designates programs for individuals who are not learning to read in the normal fashion for a variety of reasons. Remedial reading is but one segment of a much broader discipline—that of reading. In addition to remedial reading, the field of reading consists of many other special-interest areas including developmental reading, adult reading, reading methods and materials, the reading process, and evaluation of reading.

The roots of remedial reading can be traced back to the period of the 1920s when standardized tests first began to be used widely (N.B. Smith, 1965). The results of these tests revealed that thousands of children were failing to make normal progress. By the 1930s, remedial reading had become established as a professional endeavor; the number of research studies increased, and reading clinics were organized in schools and universities. In the 1940s, a major effect of World War II was the shocking discovery that thousands of young men in the military services could not read well enough to follow simple printed instructions for camp life. Ways of teaching reading to young men in army camps was a product of the war years and another impetus to the development of remedial reading (Kirk, Kliebhan, and Lerner, 1978). Interest in remedial reading has continued to grow over the years and the field has now become a vital subspecialty of its own.

The remedial reader is a student who is not reading up to an expected level. One definition views the remedial reader as having a discrepancy between potential for reading and actual reading achievement. According to another definition, the remedial reader cannot read well enough to perform school and life tasks in a satisfactory manner. The various definitions of a remedial reader are discussed further in Chapter 4.

A variety of factors are associated with poor reading. They include educational, psychological, social, cultural, cognitive, and physical factors. For some students, it appears that many of these factors contribute to the reading problem. The nature and assessment of these factors are discussed in Chapters 3 and 4.

Remedial and Developmental Reading

Remedial reading is often differentiated from *developmental reading*. Developmental reading is concerned with the normal growth of the reading process, as well as with materials and methods to enhance this growth. In contrast, remedial reading concentrates on those students who have difficulty in learning to read. Despite this difference in focus, many reading authorities see basic similarities between remedial and developmental reading. For example, Bond, Tinker, and Wasson (1979, p. 15) state that

> Remedial instruction in reading is essentially the same as good classroom teaching, but is individualized. . . . The teacher works with the child using regular teaching methods but concentrates on the skill in which the child is deficient.

Similarly, Harris and Sipay (1980, p. 333) believe that

> In many ways remedial [reading] teaching resembles good classroom teaching. Both are aiming toward the same desired outcomes of reading skills and interest. Both try to apply or induce effective motivation. Both utilize many of the same materials. Both involve application of the same basic principles of learning.

Thus, there are many parallels between remedial and developmental reading. Principles, methods, and techniques that hold true in one are appropriate for the other. The major differences are that (1) there is more individualization in remedial reading; (2) highly specialized nondevelopmental techniques, which are not used in the regular classroom, are used for students with very severe and particular types of problems; and (3) reading instruction is based on a careful diagnosis of the problem.

Corrective and Remedial Reading

Some reading specialists have found it helpful to divide remedial instruction into two categories according to the severity of the problem. They differentiate *corrective reading* from *remedial reading*. Corrective reading describes programs for students with relatively mild reading problems, and instruction takes place in the regular classroom or in small groups. Remedial reading describes programs for students with more severe problems. This instruction is likely to take place on an individual basis in a special setting, such as a reading room or a reading clinic. Instruction is usually provided by a reading specialist. Despite these differences, corrective and remedial reading have much in common in terms of diagnosis and treatment. Therefore, in this book, both corrective and remedial reading are viewed together, and both are referred to as remedial reading.

The Role of Remedial Reading in Special Education Programs

Since many students in special education programs are poor readers, classroom teachers and reading teachers must participate in the evaluation and treatment of exceptional students. It is important, therefore, for teachers who deal with reading problems to understand the structure of special education. The field of special education consists of several categories of atypical individuals, that is, individuals who deviate from the norm in some way—physically, developmentally, emotionally or in the ability to learn. Special education can be defined as instruction that is designed specifically to meet the unique needs of exceptional students. This means that special materials, special teaching techniques, special equipment, or special facilities may be required (Hallahan and Kauffman, 1978).

THE SCOPE OF SPECIAL EDUCATION.   Approximately 4 million handicapped children in the United States, ages three to twenty-one, are receiving special education and related services. This is about 9.5 percent of the students enrolled in schools (U.S. Department of Education, 1980). Twenty years ago, many of these students would not have been recognized or identified as handicapped. They might have been ignored in the classroom or excluded from school altogether. The responsibility of educating the handicapped was relegated completely to parents or institutions. In today's world, the education of the handicapped is considered among the responsibilities of the public schools.

Special education students are classified under several handicapping conditions. The categories of handicap under Public Law 94–142 include deaf, deaf-blind, hard-of-hearing, mentally retarded, multihandicapped, orthopedically impaired, other health-impaired, seriously emotionally disturbed, specific learning-disabled, speech-impaired, and visually handicapped students. The definition of each of these conditions appears in Chapter 14. About 63 percent of all handicapped students need remediation in reading, or in oral or written language (U.S. Department of Education, 1980).

Reading problems are especially evident in *mildly handicapped* students. Some authorities suggest that three types of handicaps seem to form a cluster: (1) learning disabilities, (2) emotional disturbances, and (3) mental retardation. Since these three categories have many commonalities in diagnostic and instructional procedures, these authorities recommend that *mildly handicapped* students be placed together for educational services (Blackhurst, 1981; Hallahan and Kauffman, 1976). It should be noted that many professionals in special education do not agree that these three categories of handicapped students form a viable cluster for instruction purposes. Whatever their instructional placement, most "mildly handicapped" students are in need of special instruction in reading.

RELATION OF REMEDIAL READING TO LEARNING DISABILITIES. The special education category that is allied most frequently with the perspectives and procedures used in remedial reading is that of learning disabilities. About 3 percent of the school population has been identified as learning disabled (U.S. Department of Education, 1980). While only a small minority of students with reading problems are classified as having learning disabilities (Harris and Sipay, 1980), about 80 percent of learning-disabled students have reading problems (Kirk and Elkins, 1975). In fact, it is sometimes difficult to determine whether a student with a reading problem should be served by the school's remedial reading or learning disabilities programs. Whatever the placement, the primary objective should be to improve the student's reading ability.

Reading teachers and classroom teachers play increasingly important roles in the identification, evaluation, and treatment of learning-disabled students with reading problems. For this reason, all teachers should be familiar with basic concepts of learning disabilities and laws governing special education. Since most students in learning disabilities programs have reading problems, it is also imperative for learning disabilities teachers to know about the teaching of reading. It is evident that specialists need information from both fields to build an effective interdisciplinary team that will succeed in helping students. Despite this obvious need for professional communication and cross-disciplinary knowledge, Harris and Sipay (1980) report that unfortunately many learning disabilities teachers know little about remedial teaching of reading, and many reading specialists know little about learning disabilities.

OVERVIEW OF THIS BOOK

This book presents theoretical and practical information about remedial reading. Both diagnostic and remedial procedures are surveyed from beginning reading levels through advanced levels. Part I is an introduction, and Chapter 1 examines the field of remedial reading and the consequences of reading disabilities upon the student and society.

Part II deals with the diagnosis of reading problems. It includes a discussion of the factors associated with reading disability and methods of evaluation and assessment. Chapter 2 deals with some general principles of diagnosis. In Chapter 3, ecological (or environmental), emotional, and physical factors associated with reading difficulty are examined. In Chapter 4, intellectual and language factors that affect reading are analyzed.

Chapters 5 and 6 present methods of assessing both reading achievement and the components of reading ability. Formal diagnostic methods, including commercial tests, are analyzed in Chapter 5. In Chapter 6, informal diagnostic tools, including informal reading inventories, miscue analysis, observation, and teacher-made tests, are analyzed.

In Part III methods for treating reading problems are examined, and many practical suggestions and activities are given. In Chapter 7, general principles of remediation are presented. Chapters 8 and 9 deal with severely disabled readers, the small percentage of students most resistant to remedial treatment. In Chapter 8, the characteristics of severely disabled readers are discussed; in Chapter 9, special remedial methods are presented.

Chapters 10, 11, 12, and 13 deal with ways to improve reading ability. Chapter 10 examines methods for teaching students to recognize words, including sight words and phonics. Chapter 11 continues with ways of teaching word recognition using context, structural analysis, and holistic strategies. Chapter 12 discusses the challenging topic of teaching reading comprehension. Chapter 13 deals with the acquisition of meaning vocabulary, the use of reading-study skills, and ways of improving reading rate.

Part IV presents some organizational aspects of the remedial reading program. Chapter 14 reviews laws that affect programs for students with reading problems. Chapter 15 is concerned with the necessary process of keeping reports and records. In addition to general record-keeping forms in remedial reading, the record-keeping requirements and forms for special education are discussed.

Appendices A and B describe materials that may be of value to teachers of remedial readers. Appendix C presents a sample form for a diagnostic report. Appendix D contains an informal reading inventory for testing students.

SUMMARY

A reading handicap can be devastating to the individual and to society. It can lead to emotional problems, prevent persons from completing their education, and block career opportunities. Illiteracy leads to problems for society.

In defining reading, one must take into account several factors. Reading is the ability to gather meaning from printed symbols. However, the level of the person's reading ability and the individual's purpose for reading must also be considered.

Remedial reading is one concern of remedial education. The field of remedial reading is one subspecialty within the broader area of reading. Remedial reading designates programs for individuals who are not learning to read in a normal fashion.

Many students in special education programs also have reading problems. Both regular teachers and reading teachers instruct special education students. Specifically, since about 80 percent of the students with learning disabilities have reading problems, it is especially important for classroom and reading teachers to be familiar with this field.

This book provides practical and theoretical information needed to treat remedial readers. The major sections of this book are (1) introduction, (2) diagnosing reading, (3) remediation of reading problems, and (4) organizing the reading program.

PART II

diagnosis
of reading problems

Part II deals with the diagnosis of reading problems. In Chapter 2, general information about diagnosis is provided. In Chapters 3 and 4, some factors related to reading problems are discussed, and methods of assessing these factors are given. Chapter 3 contains a discussion of ecological factors (the environments of home, school, and culture), emotional factors, and physical factors. In Chapter 4, intelligence and language factors are discussed. Chapters 5 and 6 concentrate upon the diagnosis of reading levels and skills. Measures for diagnosing reading are divided into formal tests of reading (Chapter 5) and informal reading measures (Chapter 6).

2
OVERVIEW
OF DIAGNOSIS

A careful and objective reading diagnosis can be a turning point in a student's academic career or even total life. The reading diagnosis is conducted to gather pertinent information about a reading problem and to analyze and synthesize this information in making crucial decisions about teaching. The diagnosis includes the investigation and analysis of the student's reading performance, as well as other factors that may contribute to the reading problem. A productive diagnosis should enable the teacher to learn enough about the failing reader to develop a viable teaching plan. The depth of the reading diagnosis depends upon the nature of the problem and on the available time, facilities, and resources. Therefore, reading diagnoses vary in form, comprehensiveness, and level of intensity. Although the diagnosis is generally conducted prior to instruction, diagnostic probing continues throughout the teaching process as well.

THE PURPOSES
OF THE READING DIAGNOSIS

It is useful to consider the purposes of a reading diagnosis within the context of the broader framework of *educational assessment.* Educational assessment is concerned with all types of data collection for educational decision making. The reading diagnosis is concerned specifically with the analysis of a student's reading problems, including the contributing factors and strategies for improvement. Both, however, are conducted for similar reasons. Five purposes of both the reading diagnosis and educational assessment are screening, determining placement, instructional planning, measuring student progress, and evaluating the program (Salvia and Yssyldyke, 1981).

Screening

The screening process identifies those individuals who may be in need of special attention. In some cases, screening procedures are designed to prevent possible future problems. For example, a screening procedure can be used for early identification of high-risk preschoolers so that an intervention program can be implemented to prevent the predicted failure from occurring. In the reading diagnosis, the survey-level diagnosis (discussed later in this chapter) is often used to screen students. Group or classroom tests are usually used for this purpose. In addition, remedial readers are sometimes screened to see if there is a need for further referral to other professionals, such as medical specialists. For example, a student's vision can be screened to see if referral to an eye care specialist is needed.

Determining Placement

Assessment information can lead to a student's classification or assignment to a class or a program. Placement decisions depend upon many factors, including the nature and severity of the problem, facilities and personnel available in the school, the input of the parent, needs of the student, and legal requirements for placement (especially in the case of special education students). Information gathered in a reading diagnosis helps the teacher to decide if the poor reader can best be taught in the classroom or in a small group or through individual remedial instruction.

Instructional Planning

Assessment information also provides the basis for developing a plan of instruction. This is, in fact, the most important purpose of a reading diagnosis. Based on diagnostic findings, the teacher selects instructional strategies, methods, and materials for teaching reading. *Instructional planning is the heart of the reading diagnosis.*

Measuring Student Progress

The progress of a student or a group of students can be monitored by using educational assessment information. The end-of-the-year achievement tests often given in classrooms are common ways to measure the progress of students. In the reading diagnosis, information is gathered which can provide a baseline to measure later progress. Improvement in reading can be gauged by comparing the later measures with the level at which the student began. It is important to continue to measure reading growth and progress throughout the teaching process.

Evaluating the Program

Finally, assessment information can be used to evaluate an entire curriculum or educational program. For example, judgments about the success of an organizational plan (such as a nongraded school), or specific teaching materials (such as a particular mathematics series), or a teaching method (such as finger math) can be based on this type of assessment information. In the reading diagnosis, this purpose is achieved as teachers monitor the ongoing reactions of a number of students to teaching methods and materials.

THREE LEVELS OF DIAGNOSIS

Reading diagnoses range from relatively simple measures of reading achievement to intensive, in-depth evaluations. The depth of the diagnosis need not be the same for every student. Rather, the amount of diagnostic information obtained should be tailored to the needs of the particular situation. Typically, the diagnosis conducted by a teacher with limited time and resources will be less extensive than the diagnosis conducted by a specialist.

Most reading specialists agree that it is useful to think about three levels of diagnosis. These levels can be classified as (1) the survey level, (2) the specific level, and (3) the intensive level (Bond, Tinker, and Wasson, 1979; Otto and Smith, 1980).

The purpose of the *survey-level diagnosis* is to screen those individuals who require further attention. Usually, the survey-level diagnosis is conducted by the classroom teacher who uses sources of information such as achievement tests and cumulative record folders.

In the *specific-level diagnosis*, areas of reading difficulty are analyzed carefully, using individual formal and informal tests. The teacher identifies specific areas of critical weaknesses in a student's reading performance.

The *intensive-level diagnosis* level is reserved for severe cases of reading disability that are complicated by other factors which interfere with learning. Severely disabled readers often need this type of full case study. The intensive diagnosis sometimes requires input from specialists in other disciplines. Such information can give a more complete picture by providing further information about the student and suggesting possible courses of treatment. For example, an audiologist or otologist might be called upon for additional information about a student with a hearing impairment.

PHASES OF THE DIAGNOSTIC PROCESS

There are several phases in the process of conducting a reading diagnosis. Because the diagnosis varies according to the needs of different students, the exact sequence of the diagnostic process may also vary. At times, several phases are accomplished at the same time. Occasionally, the teacher must go back to an earlier phase. Nevertheless, there is general agreement that a reading diagnosis proceeds from more general to more specific concerns (Harris, 1969). The sequential phases of the diagnosis, as shown in Figure 2.1, serve as a general guide. These phases are most likely to be used in the intensive-level diagnosis, the most complete type of diagnosis. When the survey level or specific level diagnosis is used, some phases may be omitted or covered in less detail.

Determining the Existence
of a Reading Problem

It is important at the outset to decide if the student has a reading problem. Objective evidence is needed to substantiate the existence of a disability. In some instances, students are referred for remedial reading instruction, but further investigation reveals that they are reading as well as can be expected or that their primary problems are not in the area of reading. Time for diagnosis is limited and resources for remediation are in short supply. Therefore, it is important, as an initial step, to decide which students are most likely to benefit from remedial help.

Several procedures can be used to determine the existence of a reading disability. In one procedure, the teacher compares the student's performance on a test of potential ability or intelligence with performance on a reading achievement

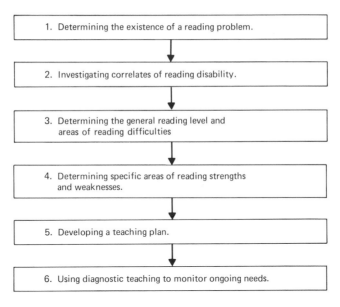

1. Determining the existence of a reading problem.

2. Investigating correlates of reading disability.

3. Determining the general reading level and areas of reading difficulties

4. Determining specific areas of reading strengths and weaknesses.

5. Developing a teaching plan.

6. Using diagnostic teaching to monitor ongoing needs.

Figure 2.1   Phases of the Reading Diagnosis

test. In another procedure, the student's ability to function in the current classroom situation is examined carefully. Teachers may use several procedures, depending upon the level of the diagnosis. Techniques for judging if the student has a reading disability are presented in Chapter 4.

Investigating Related Factors

Reading disabilities are often accompanied by related problems known as *correlates*. Correlates of reading disability are non-reading factors that may impinge upon learning to read. These include ecological (environmental), emotional, physical, intellectual, and language factors. An investigation and analysis of these correlates can deepen the teacher's understanding of a student's reading problem. However, the relationship of a correlate to an individual's reading problem is quite complex. In any individual case, it is difficult to determine the precise relationship between a factor and the reading problem. Therefore, teachers should be cautious about interpreting a correlate as the *cause* of a reading problem. Cautions that should be noted before making such judgments are discussed later in this chapter.

General Reading Diagnosis: Determining the Reading Level and the General Areas of Reading Difficulties

An important phase of the reading diagnosis is assessing the student's present level of reading performance. How well can the student read and understand what is read? It is also important to note the general area of reading in which the student is experiencing difficulty. Remedial students have trouble with one or more of the major areas of reading, which are (1) word recognition, (2) comprehension, (3) meaning vocabulary, (4) study skills, and (5) reading rate.

As students improve in reading, different areas of reading take on importance in the diagnosis. For remedial readers at the beginning levels, the diagnosis must concentrate on word recognition, the ability to identify words. As the remedial reader progresses, the diagnosis of meaning and vocabulary comprehension assumes greater importance. Remedial readers at the advanced levels may need an assessment of their study skills and reading rate.

During this phase of the diagnosis, the teacher also looks at affective behaviors such as the student's motivation for reading, anxiety about reading, reading choices, and purposes for reading. These are important because the ultimate success of instruction is strongly affected by the reader's attitudes. For example, students who view reading as a meaningful activity will be more highly motivated than those who view reading merely as a school requirement.

Specific Reading Diagnosis: Determining Areas of Reading Strengths and Weaknesses

Once the general areas of reading difficulty are noted, the teacher tries to pinpoint specific areas of reading strengths and weaknesses. It is very important to assess abilities (or strengths) as well as disabilities (or weaknesses). What the student *can* do is as essential to the diagnosis as what the student *cannot* do. Even students with the most severe reading problems will have some areas of strength.

This phase involves the detailed analysis of the student's reading abilities. For example, the teacher might already know that a student is poor in the general area of word recognition but now needs more specific information. To gather this information the teacher (1) gives diagnostic tests to determine the precise skill abilities and needs in word recognition and (2) analyzes the strategies the student is using to read materials. The measurement tools for determining specific reading strengths and weaknesses include diagnostic tests, observations, informal probing tests, and trial teaching.

Developing a Teaching Plan

After all the information gathered in the diagnostic process is analyzed and synthesized, a plan for teaching is developed. The teaching plan includes the areas of reading to be taught; the appropriate level of reading for instruction; the materials to be used in the teaching; the instructional methods; and time, frequency, and duration of the teaching.

Using Diagnostic Teaching to Monitor Ongoing Needs

Even after the formal diagnosis is concluded, the teacher should remain sensitive to changing needs. Ideally, remedial teaching continues to be diagnostic in nature. This may imply, for example, changing instructional plans when necessary, based upon student responses. The essence of good remedial teaching is constant diagnostic questioning and decision making.

WAYS OF GATHERING INFORMATION

Tests are one source of diagnostic information, but there are several other excellent ways to obtain diagnostic data. Each method provides a different type of insight. The use of multiple sources creates an opportunity to corroborate findings. For example, the parents of 13-year-old Jean stated that she loved to read and that she was an avid reader at home. However, observations of Jean in the classroom and library, and informal conversations with her, indicated that she did not enjoy reading, that she did not read frequently, and that she generally avoided reading activities. In this case, the different sources provided contradictory information, consequently further investigation was needed. Several methods for collecting assessment data are noted briefly in this section. However, each is also discussed more fully elsewhere.

Formal Tests

There are two types of formal tests. (1) *Standardized tests* compare the student's performance with that of other students of comparable age and grade levels. (2) *Criterion-referenced tests* determine directly if the student has mastered specific reading skills.

Informal Tests

Informal tests include teacher–made tests and other nonstandardized measures. Informal tests permit the teacher to gather information in an unconstrained and relaxed manner. Although these tests have not been normed on a large population, they often provide information which is not available in formal tests.

Interviews

An interview involves discussions with parents, teachers, or the student. The purpose of the interview is to gain a more comprehensive picture of the student's attitudes and behaviors.

Reports from Related Professionals

Often, other professionals have useful information to contribute. Such information may come from sources such as medical reports, psychological reports, or speech and language reports. The related professionals can give information on the student from the perspective of these related specialities.

Cumulative Records

Cumulative records are kept by the school and present an overview of a student's school history. These records contain attendance records, changes of schools, report card grades over the years, grade repetitions, age of beginning school, and so on. Cumulative records might show, for example, that 10-year-old Alice was absent for two months of the fall term in first grade due to an automobile accident. During this time, Alice missed some vital reading instruction, a factor which contributed to her later reading disability.

Observations

Observing the student's behavior in a variety of settings provides important assessment information. By observing students in a classroom situation, the teacher can note their ability to attend to a task, their level of frustration, and the frequency of disruptive behaviors. Observations in the lunchroom or at recess show how students interact with peers in social situations.

Sample Teaching Lessons

This method refers to the use of work samples in which students are given an instructional task for the purpose of gathering diagnostic information. By actually trying out an instructional technique during the diagnostic period, the teacher gains valuable information about the student's likelihood of success using that particular strategy. For example, Barbara was taught six words using a sight word approach to see if she learned well using this method.

Each of these methods contributes valuable information to the diagnosis. Familiarity with these assessment sources enables teachers to select those most appropriate for a specific student.

SOME GENERAL PRINCIPLES OF DIAGNOSIS

Conducting a diagnosis is an exciting intellectual challenge. In a way, the process is rather like solving a mystery. The teacher is confronted with the mystery of a student who has a reading problem. Like the famous detective Sherlock Holmes going about his work, the mystery is solved by using clues gathered from many sources. Sources in the reading diagnosis include: the student, parents, classroom teachers, cumulative school records, observations, sample teaching lessons, and tests. The alert diagnostic teacher pulls together the entire picture to solve the mystery. The following general principles serve as guidelines for conducting the reading diagnosis.

The Diagnosis Is
a Decision Making Process

It is important to remember that a diagnosis is not merely testing; rather, it is a decision-making process. Although the diagnosis involves the administration of tests, they are only one vehicle for making judgments about the student's reading problem. However, the decisions should not be limited to information generated from test scores but should include other types of information as well.

Decision making involves searching for patterns in the student's behavior. For example, Jim, a nine-year-old boy, was observed to yawn while reading orally. Upon questioning, his mother reported that he generally yawned when under stress. When the teacher observed Jim, he seemed uncomfortable in the classroom when doing schoolwork but not on the playground. When he was given an intelligence test, he scored particularly poorly on subtests that were timed and required working under pressure. Combining all these clues, the teacher hypothesized that the pressure of schoolwork was making Jim nervous.

Sometimes one test or observation can be used in several ways. For example, an oral reading inventory is usually used to determine the level of a student's reading. But careful observation during the oral reading can also reveal the strategies that the student uses to recognize words.

The Diagnosis Evaluates
the Student Objectively

For many students, the reading diagnosis is the only attempt ever made to counsel their educational and personal problems. For this reason, it is important that the teacher remain as objective as possible. For example, the teacher should realize that information from classroom teachers or parents can be subjective. Students with reading problems often acquire negative "reputations" in their schools and homes and even with themselves. The diagnostician owes the student a fresh, unbiased look.

The Diagnosis Considers
the Whole Individual

Reading is but one part of the student's life. The teacher must consider the student's past experiences, future plans, likes and dislikes, fears, and interests. Every attempt should be made to perceive the student as an entire person—not just as someone who is failing in reading.

Diagnosis and Remediation
Are a Continuous Process

Diagnosis and remediation are not independent processes, but are highly interrelated. Since the plan of action changes as teachers and students work together, diagnosis continues through the instructional process. In a very real sense, the diagnostic process never ends. The teacher must continuously adjust instruction to the student's changing needs. This type of teaching is known as "diagnostic teaching." Sometimes only a minimum amount of initial diagnosis is done, allowing the use of diagnostic teaching at the earliest opportunity.

CORRELATES OF READING DISABILITY

In the following discussion, the factors, or correlates, contributing to reading disability are reviewed briefly; each is discussed in further detail in Chapters 3 and 4. These correlates include the areas of ecology (environment), emotional status, physical well-being, intelligence, and language. Knowledge of these contributing factors may help the teacher to determine effective treatment.

Cautions of Interpreting Correlates

Knowledge of contributing factors may help the teacher to understand the student's reading problem and to plan effective treatment. However, these factors relate to reading in multiple and complex ways. For this reason, the term correlates, rather than causes, is used. Several cautions should be observed in interpreting the impact of these correlates:

1. Precise causes of reading difficulty may be extremely difficult to determine. A reading disability and a correlate may occur together. This does not mean, however, that one causes the other. For example, the appearance of storks near a Caribbean Island correlated highly with an increase in the birth rate. This does not mean that the storks caused the increase in the birth rate!

2. People are affected differently by their handicaps. Thus, not every student with poor vision will have reading difficulties. Some learn to work around their visual problems, whereas others may find a similar visual problem insurmountable.

3. Reading failure is often the product of several interacting factors. In a classic study of the causes of reading disability, Robinson (1946) concluded that poor reading was generally the result of several causes, all interacting with each other.

4. Even when a specific cause can be identified, it is sometimes impossible to alleviate the situation. For example, specific family difficulties may be identified as the causal factor of a reading problem, but the school cannot control the home situation. The situation must be accepted while the teacher concentrates on dealing with the reading problem.

Despite these limitations, it is important to investigate correlates of reading problems. Often they provide a key element in the understanding and successful remediation of the reading problem.

Correlates Affecting Reading

ECOLOGICAL FACTORS.   Each human being functions in many complex environments (or ecological systems). A student may be uncomfortable in the school environment and therefore unable to learn effectively. Problems at home or in social settings may also affect learning. The social or cultural group can influence the importance of reading for the student (see Chapter 3).

EMOTIONAL FACTORS.   Many students with reading problems have accompanying emotional problems. In some cases, the emotional problem is the root of the learning difficulty. In other cases, reading problems trigger the emotional distress. In either case, the teacher must try to understand the emotional problem and provide a warm, supportive environment (see Chapter 3).

PHYSICAL FACTORS.   A variety of physical factors can contribute to reading disability. These include visual and auditory impairment and general health problems. In addition, physical factors can include subtle neurological problems and perceptual deficits (see Chapter 3).

INTELLIGENCE.   Intellectual abilities are related to reading ability. In fact, remedial readers are sometimes defined as students who are reading below the level predicted by intelligence tests. However, true intelligence is difficult to measure, and the relationship between reading ability and intelligence is imperfect (see Chapter 4).

LANGUAGE.   Reading is one form of language. If language abilities are not well developed, poor reading may result. For example, students who lack a language base of rich vocabulary and sentence structure will find it difficult to acquire higher-level reading skills. The role of language in the reading process is underscored by the *psycholinguistic* view of reading discussed later in this book (see Chapters 4 and 6).

SUMMARY

A reading diagnosis is one form of educational assessment. The purposes of both the educational assessment and the reading diagnosis include (1) screening, (2) determining placement, (3) instructional planning, (4) monitoring progress, and (5) program evaluation. Instructional planning is the most important in a reading diagnosis.

A diagnosis may take place on three different levels: survey, specific, and intensive.

There are a number of elements in a reading diagnosis. They include (1) determining the existence of a reading problem, (2) investigating related factors, (3) determining the reading level and general areas of reading difficulties, (4) determining specific areas of reading strengths and weaknesses, (5) developing a teaching plan, and (6) using diagnostic teaching to monitor ongoing needs.

Assessment methods include formal tests (standardized and criterion-referenced tests), informal tests, interviews, reports from related professionals, cumulative records, observations, and sample teaching lessons. Although each of these methods can provide valuable information, the teacher should select those methods that are the most appropriate for the particular situation.

Several general principles are useful for the teacher to keep in mind during the reading diagnosis: the diagnosis is a decision making process, the diagnosis should consider the student objectively, the diagnosis should consider the whole individual, and diagnosis and remediation are a continuous process.

Factors contributing to a reading disability are called correlates. A correlate cannot be assumed to be the cause of a reading problem. Correlates of a reading disability include ecological, emotional, physical, intelligence, and language factors.

3
CORRELATES OF READING DISABILITY I
ecological, emotional, and physical factors

Three factors that are related to a student's ability to read are discussed in this chapter: (1) ecological factors (the various environments in which the student operates), (2) emotional factors (the social and psychological factors that affect learning), and (3) physical factors (vision, hearing, neurological, and other health factors).

As noted earlier, such factors are referred to as correlates of reading disability (rather than as causes) because the exact nature of the cause-and-effect relationship cannot be known with certainty. Nevertheless, most reading authorities agree that, it is important to investigate these correlates and evaluate their relevance to the student's reading problem.

ECOLOGICAL FACTORS

The different environments in which students live and grow have a strong impact on their desire and ability to learn. The term *ecological systems* describes the many environments within which students operate: the home, the school, the social group, and the cultural milieu. This term, originally used in biology, also goes beyond a description of the different environments of the student to include the interactions of these environments and the student's effect on the environments.

The ecological perspective recognizes the complexity of the interrelationship between the individual and each of the environmental settings. For example, teachers know that students often behave differently in a clinical or testing situation than they do in the classroom. In fact, the description of the student in a clinical setting is often so different from that of the classroom that one wonders if the same individual is being described. Formal testing usually takes place in an unnatural situation—one that is divorced from the usual environment. In contrast, ecological assessment requires the use of other methods that take into account the natural environment.

The Home Environment

The home environment is the child's first ecological system. Early formative years in the home are the foundation for tremendous growth and development. Environmental experiences during these crucial first five or six years are a powerful influence upon cognitive growth and intelligence. Language development is greatly influenced by the child's home experiences with a parent (Bloom, 1964, 1976; White, 1975).

Parents provide emotional well-being as well as intellectual stimulation. The crucial period known as "bonding" takes place during the early months of infancy and becomes the basis for later emotional health. Bonding depends upon a successful interactive relationship between the mother (or primary parent figure) and the infant (Bowlby, 1969). The early development of the ego and self-concept are also dependent upon the support and encouragement of parents. Studies that compare good and poor readers show that the good readers are more likely to have had a favorable home environment (Abrams and Kaslow, 1977).

The parent also provides a role model for the child. Through activities such as doing recreational reading, going to the library, and reading stories aloud, parents teach children to value reading. Experiences with a parent are a very important factor in stimulating good reading and a love for reading. The parents' role continues to be crucial after the child enters school. Students who experience difficulty learning to read are in special need of satisfying family relationships.

Children are profoundly affected by what happens to parents. In today's society, children are often dramatically touched by changes in the family, moves to new locations, divorce or separation of the parents, death of relatives, or leave-taking of older siblings. Parents and teachers can often work reciprocally to help the student cope with these changes. However, teachers should not automatically assume that the home situation is the sole cause of the reading problem.

In recent years, an unprecedented number of students have been affected by the divorce or separation of their parents. Nearly 25 percent of American children are living with one parent or with a parent who has remarried (Monmeith, 1981). Understandably, these children may be under stress, particularly if the family change is recent. Teachers can provide considerable help to such students. They can help students through these trying times through the use of several techniques.

1. Talking to students and allowing them to express their feelings. Teachers should try to be nonjudgmental about the family situation.
2. Temporarily lessening academic and behavioral demands in the classroom or clinic.
3. Being sensitive to the student's living and legal custody arrangements. Teachers should make sure that the appropriate parent receives communications. With permission from the custodial parent, both parents can be informed of the student's progress.

PARENTS' ROLE IN READING.   Parent cooperation can be an invaluable asset to the remedial teacher. For example, teachers can learn much about a child's reading problem by talking to the parents, who can relate important information about their child. Parents can also alleviate some of the psychological and emotional consequences of reading failure by what they do in the home environment.

Sometimes very concerned parents believe that they must provide direct reading instruction by themselves, even though the student is already receiving remedial help. However, parents may lack sufficient training or they may be so deeply involved in their child's welfare that they are not effective teachers. We believe that parents should not be expected to teach their own child to read. Of course, each individual parent and child is different. Some parents may be effective in providing certain kinds of instruction. In our reading clinic, for example, some mothers learned how to review sight words successfully with their child on a regular basis. Most important, however, is that teachers encourage parents to provide other kinds of supportive help to enhance reading progress.

SUGGESTIONS FOR PARENTS.   Parents can do much to help their children improve in reading without actually teaching reading. Some suggestions that teachers can give to the parent are:

1. *Share in the child's success.* Children enjoy the experience of reading material that they have mastered to the parent. The parent should be an enthusiastic listener.
2. *Provide a reading model in the home.* Parents can surround their children with books in the home and demonstrate the value of reading. They can also take trips to the library and bring home materials that the child selects.
3. *Read to the child.* It is important to read stories aloud from the time the child is a toddler. This activity promotes language learning, stresses the value of the printed word, and encourages a close relationship between parent and child.
4. *Accept the child as he or she is.* It is often difficult to admit that one's own child has a problem. When parents deny that the problem exists or hold unrealistic expectations, children are sensitive to their parent's disappointment. This situation may trigger a poor parent-child relationship.
5. *Help the child to feel secure and confident.* Look for ways in which the child can succeed and encourage those activities. Help the child to be happy and healthy in the home environment.
6. *Share in the excitement of reading success.* Every bit of reading acquisition is an important step for the disabled reader. Parents, as well as teachers, should emphasize and enhance successful learning experiences.

A final word of caution is in order. Often well-meaning parents are taken aback by their child's sudden transition to becoming a successful reader. They may be unprepared for the adjustments that success requires. The wise teacher will prepare the parents for this happy change in reading and the difference that it may bring to the student and the parent.

The School Environment

Children and adolescents spend a substantial portion of their waking hours in school. Their experiences and relationships in this ecological system can profoundly affect their lives.

INTERACTIONS WITHIN THE SCHOOL.   Social unpopularity has been found to accompany school failure. A sizable body of evidence shows that poor achievers tend to be rejected by their classmates in school (Siperstein, Bopp, and Bale, 1977; Bruininks, 1978).

Encounters with adults (such as teachers, diagnosticians, teacher aides, and principals) also are an integral part of the school experience. Studies show that poor achievers tend to be perceived negatively by the adults in their educational environment. Adults form negative impressions of students with learning problems based on very short observations. Bryan and Perlmutter (1979) and Bryan and Sherman (1980) found that adults made relatively harsh judgments of low-achieving students after viewing them on videotapes for only a few minutes.

Classroom teachers tend to show strong disapproval of students who have learning problems (Good and Brophy, 1973). In one study, Keogh, Tchir, and Windeguth-Behn (1974) found that teachers associate characteristics such as aggressiveness and lack of self-discipline with failing students. Other investigators have found that low-achieving students receive both less praise and acknowledgment from teachers and are more likely to be criticized (Goldenberg, 1969; Good and Brophy, 1970).

In her book, *Teachers Pets, Troublemakers, and Nobodies*, Gouldner (1978) summarizes an extensive anthropological study of kindergarten and primary classrooms. Gouldner concludes that teachers concentrate their energies and the bulk of their interactions on only a few children, generally high-achieving girls. This pattern is established early in the first grade and is maintained in subsequent years. Other students become "nobodies." They tend to be ignored by teachers and do not develop normal patterns of classroom social interactions. By the fifth or sixth grade, these "nobodies" may be ignored almost totally.

These findings have serious implications for students with reading problems. It seems that the school does not provide a satisfying environment for them.

Instructional Factors in Reading Disability.   In many cases, the reading problem is related to poor or inappropriate instruction; sometimes immature children are given formal reading instruction before they can profit from it. As a result, the child is initially frustrated, achieves poorly, and eventually develops a substantial lag behind classmates. In other cases instruction is not geared to the needs of a student. For example, a teacher may routinely use reading material which does not meet the needs of a specific child. This practice may result in failure and a negative attitude about reading (Brown, 1982). It is important to remember that teachers may unintentionally provide inappropriate instruction because of the difficulty they encounter in meeting the needs of 25 to 35 students.

Clinicians should look into past instructional practices that may have contributed to the reading problem. The school history reveals such information. Questions that may be investigated include:

1. Was the student given initial reading instruction before he or she was ready?
2. Was a method of instruction inappropriate to the student's needs used?
3. Were the student's initial school experiences positive and successful?
4. When did the reading problem begin?
5. Were there frequent moves or transfers which resulted in changes in instructional methods and materials?

The Social Environment

The student's social environment is another important ecological system. Social relationships and interactions with friends and peers provide an environment in which students grow and develop socially, emotionally, and cognitively. Successful interaction with friends provides many satisfactions, and opportunities to gain confidence. For some disabled readers, however, the social sphere is another area of dismal failure. Such students present social interaction problems and exhibit poor social perception skills (Bryan and Bryan, 1978; Kronick, 1978; Moore, 1979; Yarrow, 1979).

When children develop normally in the social sphere, they learn social skills in a casual and informal manner. Through incidental experiences, they learn appropriate ways of acting with people: what to say, how to behave, and how to give and take in a human situation. However, some individuals are not socially perceptive. They are not sensitive to social nuances in everyday living, and they may be unaware of how their actions and behavior are interpreted by others.

Research studies on social correlates show that students with reading and learning disabilities tend to have poor social skills. Chandler (1977) suggests that such students are unable to accommodate themselves to another person's point of view. Because they fail to consider the needs of other people, their chances for successful social interaction with peers are reduced. Bryan et al. (1976) found that disabled students were not aware of the need to give additional instructional statements to young children when they were teaching them games. The research of Wong and Wong (1980) showed that learning-disabled students, particularly girls, were less able than normal students to adopt an alternative point of view in judging a series of events suggested by cartoons. These authors suggest that role-playing games, in which a person is made to adopt the viewpoint of another person, may help to improve social relationships. A study by Bruininks (1978) showed that, in contrast to normal children, learning-disabled children overestimate their popularity. These students do not seem to be able to perceive their own social shortcomings. Thus, research evidence substantiates that students in remedial and special education programs often have difficulty relating to peers in a social setting.

The Cultural Environment

The population of our nation is a composite of hundreds of different ethnic and cultural traditions. In today's society, we see ever-changing patterns of immigration and movement as new groups of individuals add their cultural diversity and richness to our schools. A few decades ago, it was assumed that Americans would all be assimilated into the "melting pot" of the dominant culture. Since then, we have witnessed a new awareness of the value of different cultural traditions and the importance of maintaining them. One of the greatest challenges of our schools has been the education of students from all cultures, whatever their geographical origin, socioeconomic status, or language.

Poverty can produce certain cultural effects. Since a significant portion of American families live below a specified poverty level, it is important for reading teachers to be aware of the effects of poverty on students' academic performances. Although individuals with incomes below the poverty level come from diverse backgrounds, they tend to have certain similarities. Because they are necessarily concerned with basic survival needs, parents are likely to have less energy to devote to their children's intellectual and cognitive development. As a consequence, children from these families often must learn to care for themselves at a very young age. These children often come to school with relatively limited background experiences. For example, Deutch (1965) found 65 percent of the poor children in his study had never been more than 25 blocks from their homes.

Sometimes these students reject the traditional values of the school. They may identify, instead, with subcultures in which values work against education. This trend is particularly evident when adolescents join "gangs." In a study of reading performance, Labov (1969) showed how the values of a gang conflict with successful school performance. In his study, the reading achievement of gang members fell substantially below that of other boys, despite the fact that the researchers evaluated gang members as possessing a high degree of verbal skills, leadership qualities, and intelligence. Cultural differences, particularly those arising from a culture of poverty, may lead to intense suspicion and discomfort with those individuals perceived to be in the dominant culture.

These generalizations do not, of course, hold true for all low income students. In many families, education is cherished, the values of the school are upheld, and family members are encouraged to read and achieve. The opportunity to progress from poverty to economic security is a fundamental promise of democratic nations such as the United States.

Assessment of Ecological Factors

Informal strategies that the teacher of reading can use to assess ecological environments include *behavioral observation*, the *interest inventory*, and *interviewing*. These methods are discussed in the paragraphs that follow.

BEHAVIORAL OBSERVATION.   Systematic observation is a useful method of assessing student behavior and interaction with the environment. Even short observations can provide invaluable information, since they provide objective evidence to substantiate information from other sources. The key to behavioral observation is to identify and describe clearly behaviors that are being observed. The observation should not consist of value judgments, such as "Amy misbehaved." A written observation is a careful recording of what is actually observed. For example, "Amy walked up to Mary's desk and tore up Mary's spelling paper." The cumulative records of many observations provide a base for making diagnostic decisions and planning remediation.

Many different systems can be used for observing behavior (Wallace and Larsen, 1978). Three methods of observation are: time sampling, event sampling, and the anecdotal record.

1. *Time sampling.* This method enables the teacher to observe the length of time a student persists in certain behaviors. Generally, one type of behavior is

chosen for analysis. The teacher records the number of times the behavior occurs and the length of time it persists during the observation period. Table 3.1 illustrates a time sampling observation for Chet, a student whose attention in class was a matter of concern.

2. *Event sampling.* Here, a specific type of event is chosen for recording. In event sampling, the observer tries to record the event in as much detail as possible each time it is observed. Table 3.2 illustrates event sampling for Billy, a student who was thought to have problems getting along with peers.

3. *The anecdotal record.* This method is also known as a continuous recording. Anecdotal recording is not limited to one type of event. The student is observed throughout the day, and all incidents of particular interest are described in as much detail as possible. Many different types of activities can be recorded in the anecdotal record, since it is meant to give the "flavor" of a student's activities.

THE INTEREST INVENTORY.   The interest inventory is a valuable tool for all remedial reading students. It serves to establish rapport with the student, it provides insight into the student's areas of interests, and it gives the teacher a way to motivate a desire to read. A negative attitude toward reading can often be overcome if the teacher captures the student's personal interests. A strong positive relationship has been found between student interests and reading preferences (Hunt, 1970; Estes and Vaughan, 1973).

In an interest inventory, students respond to specific questions regarding their interests and activities. Topics include hobbies, play and sports preferences, television viewing, comics, and movie attendance, as well as reading preferences. The sample interest inventory, given in Table 3.3, is a suggested format. The

Table 3.1   Time Sample Observation

Reason for observation:	Chet was thought to be inattentive during class lessons at school.	
Setting:	Chet was observed during a group remedial lesson by a teacher aide.	
Time frame:	Observed during two thirty-minute lessons, from 10:00 A.M. to 10:30 A.M.	
Behavior observed:	Inattention to the teacher or to class lesson was noted.	
Observations:		
Day 1	10:04–10:10	Chet looked around room.
	10:15–10:20	Chet talked to another student.
	10:25–10:28	Chet listened to his radio using an earphone.
Day 2	10:05–10:12	Chet wrote a note to another student.
	10:15–10:20	Chet talked to another student.
	10:25–10:29	Chet looked at his papers and "daydreamed."
Conclusion:	Chet attended to less than half the lessons.	

Table 3.2   Event Sample Observation

Reason for observation:	Billy was thought to be an aggressive student.
Setting:	Observed in the classroom by teacher.
Time frame:	One school day.
Behavior observed:	All conflict situations were noted and described.
Observations:	

8:45 A.M.   On way to classroom, Jimmy A. accidentally bumped Billy. Billy kicked him; Jimmy did not respond.

10:00 A.M.   Bob made a face at Billy during group lessons; Billy returned it.

11:30 A.M.   Billy kicked Lynn in the lunch line. Lynn says she did nothing. Billy says he doesn't know why he did it.

1:00 P.M.   (Report, not observation)   Billy and Joe were reported for fighting. They said they had not been fighting.

2:00 P.M.   While standing in line, Bob called Billy "a rat" (overheard by teacher). Billy started to punch him.

Conclusions: Four hostile incidents were observed, and one was reported to teacher. They involved three boys and one girl and physical and verbal abuse. Billy seems to initiate some hostilities; other students initiate others.

Table 3.3   Sample Interest Inventory

Name: _____ Age: ___ Date: _____

I. Hobbies (circle the hobbies you pursue)

photography	collecting postcards	knitting
painting	crocheting	carpentry
dancing	making models	raising plants
collecting stamps	collecting coins	collecting matches
acting	singing	sewing
raising animals (pets)	other _____	

What hobby do you think you would enjoy doing?

II. TV (circle the kind of TV programs you enjoy most)

comedies	sports	news
cartoons	mystery	documentaries
monster shows	science fiction	movies
westerns	variety shows	adventure
other _____		

What are the names of the TV shows you like best? _____
Least? _____

III. Sports (circle the sports you enjoy doing)

baseball	golf	handball
basketball	bowling	ice skating
football	volleyball	roller skating
jogging	soccer	swimming
bicycling	hockey	boxing
fishing	tennis	wrestling
other _____		

Now go back and put a check next to the sports you do not do yourself but you enjoy watching.

IV. Reading (circle what you like to read)

comic books	animal stories	magazines
mystery	humor	newspapers
romance	stories about people	"how to" books
adventure	history	other_____

What is the name of the best book you've ever read? _____

The worst book? _____ What is your favorite comic book? _____

V. Miscellaneous

1. How do you spend your time after school? _____
2. How do you spend your time on weekends? _____
3. What toys do you enjoy most? _____
4. What do you like to do best? _____
5. What do you like to do least? _____
6. Who is your favorite real-life hero? _____
7. Who is your favorite fiction/make-believe hero? _____
8. What is your favorite game? _____
9. What is your favorite movie? _____

VI. School

1. What is your favorite subject in school? _____
2. What subject do you like least in school? _____

VII. Interests (check things you would like to know more about)

_ auto mechanics	_ fairy tales	_ history	_ health
_ famous people	_ electricity	_ electronics	_ radio
_ television	_ woodwork	_ printing	_ aviation
_ art	_ music	_ adventure	_ dancing
_ mystery	_ foreign lands	_ poetry	_ current events
_ riddles	_ comic strips	_ cartoons	_ animals
_ insects	_ science	_ transportation	_ soap box derby
_ race cars	_ football	_ cars	_ baseball
_ basketball	_ other sports	_ cooking	_ monsters
_ stories about people	_ geography	_ myths and legends	_ jokes
_ comic books	_ Indians	_ reptiles	_ circus
_ detectives	_ zoo	_ nations	_ space travel
_ cowboys	_ astronomy	_ singers	_ other_____

teacher may wish to modify the content depending upon the age, sex, and geographic location of the student. For example, a pupil in Colorado might be asked about an interest in skiing, whereas one in California might have an interest in surfing.

While the interest inventory can be administered at any time during the diagnostic procedure, it is usually given early. It can also be used during a long or strenuous testing period to provide a break or change of pace. The interest inventory may be given in a written form to students whose reading level is sufficient to read the inventory and write the answers. For more disabled readers, it may be necessary for teachers to read the questions aloud and record oral responses. Teachers should be aware that some students hide their true feelings and misrepresent their actual interests. Those who are seeking approval answer questions in a way that they believe will be acceptable.

Information on interests can also be derived from several other sources: discussions with the student, the parent interview, and student observations. Frequently, further interests are revealed after reading instruction has begun and students have confidence that the teacher will be responsive to their preferences.

The importance of using a pupil's interests to plan the instructional program cannot be overemphasized. Often students have been exposed to years of unmotivating and difficult instruction. The use of student interests personalizes the reading program and assures students that their needs and concerns are important. Such assurance can be a powerful motivational tool.

THE INTERVIEW.   Interviews with informed and concerned people yield information about the student that cannot be obtained in any other way. Parents are often interviewed as part of the reading diagnosis. The personal and informal atmosphere of the interview encourages parents to share valuable information about their child. Interviews are best conducted by the teacher responsible for the student's remedial instruction. The interview serves many important purposes:

1. An interview provides an opportunity for parents to express themselves freely to a sympathetic but objective party whose sole purpose is to help their child. In addition, the interview reveals the parents' perceptions and attitudes about their child's reading problem.

2. The interview can also aid in the development of teaching strategies by rounding out the picture of the student. For example, if the interview reveals that the student is interested in old cars, the lessons and materials can center on this interest.

3. The interview provides an avenue for obtaining information that would be difficult to discover through other evaluation techniques. Data about early illnesses, accidents, birth history, school history, family relationships, and developmental milestones can be collected readily. Parents often do not remember all the relevant information during the initial interview, but with continued parental contact, they may add additional background information at a later time. We have found that parents are usually eager to share information about their child.

The following basic principles of interviewing should be helpful.

1. Begin by telling parents that this information will be used to help their child and will be kept confidential.
2. Strive for an amiable, open atmosphere, yet one in which the conversation follows a directed plan.
3. Avoid indicating disapproval of parent responses or actions.

There are important legal and moral considerations involved in conducting an interview. The interview must be kept confidential. If the teacher wishes to tape the interview, parents or guardians must give their consent. The presence of another individual during the interview, also requires the consent of parents or guardians. Finally, information shared at an interview or any other part of the diagnostic procedure cannot be released to another agency without parental permission. A sample interview form is presented in Table 3.4 as a guide for questions that might be included. Teachers can copy this form in developing an interviewing instrument.

Although the interview often reveals intriguing information, the teacher should remember that the interview is only one source of diagnostic data. Interviewers should refrain from drawing conclusions until sufficient information is collected from several sources and integrated with the interview information.

EMOTIONAL FACTORS

Poor readers, particularly those with a long history of reading failure, often have accompanying emotional problems that impede learning. Spache (1981) estimates that emotional problems are experienced by at least three out of four disabled readers; moreover, these problems are likely to increase as the youngster enters teenage and adult years.

It is often difficult to determine whether the reading disorder results from an emotional problem or whether the emotional problem develops because of reading failure. There are two points of view. The first is the psychological approach to remediation, which focuses on the student's emotional health. The premise of this perspective is that reading failure is the result of a primary or existing emotional disturbance. As a consequence, the remedial treatment is designed to eliminate the interfering emotional problem. Techniques for remediation focus upon psychotherapeutic methods and materials that build confidence, establish self-esteem, and capture the pupil's interest. A primary concern of the psychological perspective, then, is the elimination of the emotional problems that impede learning to read.

The second viewpoint is the direct teaching approach. This assumes that the emotional problems result from the primary reading difficulty. It is, therefore, unnecessary to eliminate emotional problems before teaching reading. The

Table 3.4 **Sample Interview Form**

Student's Name: _____ Age: ___ Grade: ___ Sex: ___
Birthdate: _____ Birthplace: _____
Home Address: _____
            Street   City   State   Zip

Telephone: _____
School: _____ School Address: _____
Interviewer: _____ Interviewee: _____
Date of Interview: _____

A. Members of Immediate Family in Present Home

	Name	Age	Birthplace	Occupation
Father	_____	__	_____	_____
Mother	_____	__	_____	_____

Siblings

	Name	Age	Birthplace	Occupation
1.	_____	__	_____	_____
2.	_____	__	_____	_____
3.	_____	__	_____	_____
4.	_____	__	_____	_____

Others in Home

1. _____
2. _____

Family Members Not in Home

1. _____
2. _____

Have any members of the family had reading or learning difficulties? _____
If yes, give details: _____
Languages Spoken at Home: _____

Previous Diagnoses of Student

	Professional/Agency	Date	Conclusions
1.	_____	_____	_____
2.	_____	_____	_____

B. Educational History

1. Did student attend nursery school? _____ No. of years: ___ Age: ___
2. Did student attend kindergarten? _____ Age: ___
3. Age of entering first grade: ___
4. Has student repeated any grades? _____ If yes, indicated grades and reasons for
   retention: _____
   _____

5. Schools attended by student

Name and Location	Grades	Dates	Reasons for Withdrawal
_____	____	____	_____
_____	____	____	_____
_____	____	____	_____
_____	____	____	_____

6. Summer school private tutoring: _____
7. Special placement or special help in school: _____
8. Have there been periods of frequent or extended absence?_____ If so, give
   reasons: _____
9. How is student functioning in school at present? _____
   _____
10. Level of general achievement. Good: _____ Average: _____ Poor: _____
11. At what age did a reading problem develop? _____
12. What may have contributed to the development of this problem? _____
    _____
13. How does student do in academic areas other than reading? _____
    _____
    _____

C. Physical Health

1. Pregnancy, delivery, and early birth history: _____
   _____

2. General health: _____
   _____

3. Illnesses (include dates and temperatures): _____
   _____

4. Accidents (describe injury, whether unconscious, and give age): _____
   _____

5. Has student ever been unconscious? _____
   _____

6. First walked: _____ Talked (single words): _____ (sentences): _____

7. Disabilities (indicate age of initial observation and treatment): Speech problems:
   _____
   Hearing defects: _____
   Physical disability: _____
   Others:_____
8. Vision. When was student's vision last tested? _____ (results)
   Does student wear glasses? _____ If yes, how long? _____

D. Reading Environment

1. What are the reading materials in the home? _____
   _____

2. What are the attitudes of the parents toward reading?
   Father: _____
   Mother: _____

3. What are the reading activities in the home?
   Oral reading: _____
   Story telling: _____

4. What are student's attitudes?
   Toward reading: _____
   Toward school: _____

E. Ecological Environment

1. Describe the student's relationship with parents: _____
   _____

2. Describe student's relationship with siblings: _____
   _____

3. What are the student's interests? _____
   _____

4. How does student spend leisure time? (TV, hobby, work) _____
   _____

5. How does student get along with peers? _____
   _____

F. Emotional Climate

1. How does student feel about the reading problem? _____
   _____

2. Is there any evidence of emotional tension, fear, irritation, or lack of confidence
   in student's behavior? _____ If yes, please describe: _____
   _____
   _____
   _____

3. In comparison with other children of this age, would you describe the student's
   general development as average____, above average____, below average____.

4. List three (3) positive things or characteristics your child possesses: _____
   _____
   _____
   _____

From Reading Clinic, Northeastern Illinois University

premise of the direct teaching approach is that, with successful remedial reading experiences, the student's emotional problems are likely to lessen and, it is hoped, be overcome.

Types of Emotional Problems
That Affect Reading Achievement

No one personality type describes all poor readers. While some disabled readers evidence no emotional problems, others display a variety of disordered psychological behaviors. Some of the psychodynamic symptoms seen in poor readers are reviewed by Medrano (1977) and Gardner and Sperry (1974).

LEARNING BLOCK.   If learning has been a painful experience, the student may develop a block which prevents learning. The student builds a defense mechanism to keep pain and distress out of the reach of consciousness. Learning blocks often can be overcome when reading is taught in interesting and non-threatening ways and students begin to enjoy learning.

In one case, nine-year-old Lorraine developed an emotional block against books. Whenever the teacher brought out a book, her response was "I told you I can't read a book." In this case the teacher took all the words out of one picture book and taught them, one word at a time, without showing Lorraine the source. After all the words were mastered, the teacher presented the book to Lorraine who, of course, at first refused to read it. However, when the teacher demonstrated that Lorraine could read any word in the book, she overcame the learning block and went on to read that book, and others.

HOSTILITY-AGGRESSIVE BEHAVIOR.   Reading-disabled pupils may become hostile and overly aggressive to compensate for feelings of inadequacy. Such students may appear to be tough, ready to fight, and even delinquent in their behavior. Actually, they may be seeking a sense of accomplishment that they are unable to find in the classroom setting.

Antisocial behavior can be a manifestation of students' anger and frustration experienced because of failure in academic areas, as well as the failure of others to understand them. Often such students display less hostility when they are taught in small groups, or individually, and when their problems receive earnest attention from teachers.

PASSIVE-WITHDRAWN BEHAVIOR.   Learning to read is an active process. It requires assertiveness, self-confidence, and some degree of risk taking. The student who is insecure, self-conscious, and overly dependent may find learning to read a very forbidding task. The personality structure of such students is described as "passive-withdrawn" by psychiatrists and psychologists.

These students avoid areas of stress, such as reading, through withdrawal and apathetic behavior. They may refuse to engage in reading activities, claiming that they do not wish to read or that they do not need reading. In effect, the learner becomes emotionally unavailable. These students need to be encouraged to take risks, to guess at words they are not sure of, and to learn that a certain amount of failure is an unavoidable and acceptable part of living. When instructing such students, it is wise to tell them what they will be learning and why they are learning it. Also, encouraging and rewarding students for "guessing" may be helpful.

Low Self-Esteem and Depression.   Understandably, students who have been subjected to continual failure develop a low opinion of themselves. They display a negative self-image, poor ego development, and a lack of confidence. The problem often deepens when students become older and realize that they are not meeting society's expectations.

A self-defeating "what's the use" attitude may result in an overall depression. Such students need to know that they are accepted as they are, and that the teacher understands the problem, and has confidence that the student can learn. Every instructional success must be emphasized for the student who displays low self-esteem.

Anxiety.   Anxiety is another reaction to academic stress and failure in the learning situation. Anxious students are never sure of their abilities and are afraid of making a mistake and being reprimanded. A state of pervasive anxiety clouds their lives, which in turn drains their energy and ability to concentrate on learning. Anxious students need reassurance that they can learn; they need to feel comfortable in the learning situation.

Assessing Emotional Status

The primary aim of the teacher of reading is to help students read more effectively. To accomplish this goal, information about the student's emotional status is often useful in understanding more fully the student's reading problem.

While informal assessment of emotional factors is usually sufficient for the purposes of the reading diagnosis, sometimes it is necessary to make a referral to specialists such as psychiatrists, psychologists, or social workers, to give a more formal assessment. (Formal tests of ecological and emotional factors are described in Test Inventory 3.1 at the end of this chapter.) A referral is considered when the emotional problems appear to be severe and interfere with reading progress and the student has made little progress over a long period of reading instruction.

An informal measure that teachers can use is the sentence completion test. In addition, information from the interview (described in the previous section) also provides data on emotional status.

Table 3.5 Sample Sentence Completion Form

1. I like _____
2. Eating _____
3. I am happiest when _____
4. School is _____
5. My greatest fear is _____
6. I wish I could _____
7. There are times _____
8. My mother _____
9. My father _____
10. Sometimes I wish _____
11. I sleep _____
12. When I dream _____
13. My greatest ambition is _____
14. I am most annoyed _____
15. Sometimes I hope _____
16. I think I will never _____
17. Compared with other people, I am _____
18. My greatest asset is _____
19. I dislike _____
20. I feel sorry for people who _____
21. My mind _____
22. Most of the time _____
23. I try to _____
24. I think of myself as _____
25. My greatest regret is _____

THE SENTENCE COMPLETION ACTIVITY.   The sentence completion activity is a series of beginning sentence fragments that the student completes. Examples are "I like to _____" and "Reading is _____." By completing these sentences, students often provide revealing insights into their thoughts and feelings. Like the interest inventory, the sentence completion activity can be administered in an oral or written fashion. A sample sentence completion form is given in Table 3.5. In interpreting the sentence completion activity, bear in mind that it is only an informal measure. While it may suggest ideas about student attitudes, these hypotheses should be verified further through interview, observation, and perhaps the administration of formal measures.

PHYSICAL FACTORS

Many physical factors affect the student's ability to learn reading skills. These include hearing problems, visual problems, neurological dysfunction, as well as other physical problems. Some students with reading difficulties may be receiving medical or biomedical treatment. Tests of physical factors are described in Test Inventory 3.2 (at the end of this chapter).

Since the ability to acquire reading skills may be severely affected by even moderate or temporary hearing loss, it is recommended that pupils be screened for possible hearing impairment. It should be noted that the ability to *hear sounds* (auditory acuity) is different from the ability to *distinguish between sounds* (auditory discrimination). (See Chapter 8 for a discussion of auditory discrimination.)

Hearing loss has several causes: (1) childhood diseases, such as scarlet fever, meningitis, mumps, or measles; (2) environmental conditions, such as repeated exposure to loud noises; (3) congenital conditions, such as malformation of, or injury to, the hearing mechanism; or (4) temporary or fluctuating conditions, due to allergies, colds, or even a buildup of wax in the ears; (5) maternal prenatal infection (including rubella); (6) middle ear infection or problems; (7) certain medications (such as *amino glycosides* and some *diuretics*).

SCREENING FOR HEARING IMPAIRMENT.   Hearing acuity is measured by testing the ability to hear in two dimensions: frequency and intensity. *Frequency* refers to the ability to hear different pitches or vibrations of a specific sound wave. The pitches are actually musical tones; and the higher the tone, the higher the frequency. Since different sounds of our language have different frequency levels, a person may be able to hear sounds clearly at one frequency level but miss sounds at another.

Intensity refers to the loudness of a sound and is measured in terms of *decibels.* The louder the sound, the higher the intensity or decibel level. Hearing loss is measured in terms of a decibel loss. How loud does the sound (or decibel level) have to be before the subject can hear it? A person with a decibel loss of 0 to 10 decibels, for example, has excellent hearing. If the student cannot hear sounds at a 30 decibel level, then he or she is likely to encounter difficulty in school learning.

The audiometer is an electronic instrument for measuring hearing acuity. In screening for a hearing loss, students wear headphones and sit with their backs to the examiner. The examiner sounds tones and asks the subject to raise a hand when a tone is heard. For screening, the audiometer is set at one intensity level and the student is tested at several frequency levels. The right and left ears are tested separately. Also, several intensity levels can be tested at each frequency level.

An audiogram showing the results of an audiometric hearing test is illustrated in Figure 3.1. Students who cannot hear frequency sounds at the preset level of 30 decibels at one or more frequencies should be referred to a hearing specialist for further testing. The eight-year-old pupil whose audiogram appears in Figure 3.1 showed a 40 decibel loss at 2000 frequencies and 4000 frequencies in the right ear and was therefore referred to a hearing specialist.

If auditory screening indicates a hearing problem, students should be referred to an audiologist (a nonmedical specialist in hearing) or to an otologist or otolaryngologist (medical specialists in hearing). Although the audiometer is an ex-

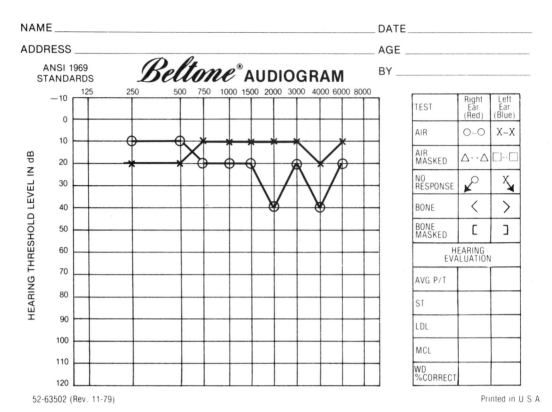

NAME _____ DATE _____

ADDRESS _____ AGE _____

Beltone® AUDIOGRAM   BY _____

ANSI 1969
STANDARDS

Figure 3.1   A Sample Audiogram

Reprinted with the permission of Beltone Electronics Corporation.

cellent device for screening for hearing loss, only a specialist trained in measuring and treating hearing difficulties can make a final determination of the extent and nature of the possible hearing impairment.

SYMPTOMS OF HEARING PROBLEMS.   A teacher may suspect the student has a hearing impairment based on such symptoms as

1. Slurred speech, monotone speech, or articulation problems.
2. Frequent minor ear problems such as infections or pain.
3. Turning the head to one side when listening.
4. Apparent inability to be attentive or to follow directions.
5. Frequent requests for repetitions.
6. Lack of response when being addressed.

Even moderate loss of the ability to hear may substantially affect the ability to learn reading. A hearing loss impedes effective communication with teachers and peers. It also places a burden on students when phonics methods are used because they have difficulty hearing certain sounds. A low-frequency hearing loss,

46

of, for example, 500–1500 Hz (cycles per second) means that students may have difficulty distinguishing vowel sounds. High-frequency losses (2000–4000 Hz) indicate the student might have difficulty with consonant sounds that continue, such as *s, z, f, v, th, sh,* and *ch.*

Sometimes students pass the audiometric screening test, yet have hearing problems. For example, one little girl had a sporadic hearing loss due to allergies. Her visits to the pediatrician came after the allergy season so the hearing problem was undetected for years. Although the problem was eventually cleared up, she had a hearing impairment during much of her early reading instruction, and her problems in reading continued in the later grades.

The most devastating effect of a hearing loss is that it prevents normal language development. When children cannot hear adequately, they are deprived of the communication necessary for normal language acquisition and growth. Their vocabulary, grammar, and verbal thinking processes often remain poorly developed and their language skills may be inadequate to acquire higher-level reading skills.

Visual Impairment

The ability to see clearly is obviously critical to the reading process. However, the relationship between reading and vision is complicated. A particular visual impairment impedes reading development in one individual, while another person with a similar impairment may be able to read effectively.

FACTORS IN VISION.   There are several types of visual impairment of concern to the reading teacher. These include myopia, hyperopia, astigmatism, binocular vision problems, and color perception.

1. *Myopia or nearsightedness.* This refers to the inability to see objects at a distance. Myopia is caused by an elongated eyeball that focuses visual images in an improper way. Although the problem of myopia has not been found to be highly related to reading difficulty (Robinson 1946), myopia can make it difficult to see farpoint objects, such as the blackboard. A substantial portion of the population is myopic, and the condition tends to begin between the ages of nine and twelve. Myopia is usually correctable with eyeglasses.

2. *Hyperopia or farsightedness.* This refers to the inability to see objects clearly at nearpoint (that is, 13 inches or less). In children, it is often caused by an eyeball that is too short to permit focusing in the proper place. Children are typically hyperoptic until they reach the age of seven or eight; thus, primary-grade textbooks generally contain large print. If hyperopia is a continuing problem, it can be corrected with glasses. Since reading is done at nearpoint, hyperopia can affect the ability to read.

3. *Astigmatism.* Astigmatism refers to the blurring of vision because of irregularities in the surface of the cornea. This condition is generally correctable with eyeglasses.

4. *Binocular difficulties.* Binocular vision, the ability to focus both eyes on the same object, is one of the most complicated of visual functions. Both eyes focus together easily on an object that is far away, but as the object moves closer, the eyes must turn inward to maintain their focus. If the eyes cannot focus together, a double image (diplobia) may result. This condition is not tolerated well by the brain, and the image of one eye may be suppressed, possibly leading to a deterioration of that eye. In severe cases, the eyes appear to be crossed. Binocular vision problems may blur vision and also cause the reader to become easily fatigued. Binocular difficulties appear to interfere with reading (Spache, 1981).

Unfortunately, binocular vision is not as easily correctable as are other visual problems. Three strategies are used to correct binocular problems: (1) surgery (often used to correct a "cross-eyed" condition), (2) corrective lenses in eyeglasses, and (3) visual exercises to strengthen eye muscles. Opinions differ among eye specialists about the value of visual exercises as a treatment in overcoming binocular difficulties.

5. *Color perception.* A small portion of the population is unable to perceive color. Males are more often affected by this condition, and the colorblindness may be limited to a few colors.

SCREENING FOR VISUAL IMPAIRMENT. Students with reading problems should be screened for possible visual difficulties. As with the hearing tests that are used by the reading teacher, the visual tests are intended only for screening purposes. Students who do poorly on the visual screening test should be referred to an ophthalmologist (a physician who specializes in eye problems) or to an optometrist (a non-medical eye specialist) for further testing. A description of the three most widely used visual screening tests is given in Test Inventory 3.2. The *Orthorater* and the *Keystone Vision Screening Test for Schools* are particularly useful for the reading specialist, since they test a variety of visual functions, including binocular vision.

Teachers can observe students for symptoms of possible visual problems (Optometric Extension Program Foundation, 1968):

1. Losing place while reading.
2. Avoiding close work.
3. Poor sitting posture and position while reading.
4. Positioning print at an unusual angle.
5. Holding reading material closer than normal.
6. Frowning excessively, squinting, scowling.
7. Excessive head movements while reading.
8. Tilting head to one side.
9. Rubbing eyes frequently.
10. Covering one eye during reading.

The act of reading is a complex human task, requiring an intact and well-functioning brain and central nervous system. It is not surprising that a dysfunction in a student's central nervous system can interfere with many aspects of learning, including the process of learning to read.

Professionals in the fields of medicine, psychology, and education were first alerted to the possibility that a child's learning problems might be related to brain dysfunction by the publication of the book, *Psychopathology and Education of the Brain-Injured Child* (Strauss and Lehtinen, 1947). These authors reported on their studies of children who had been identified as mentally retarded or emotionally disturbed. The children under study exhibited behavior patterns that were similar to those of soldiers who had received brain injuries during World War II. Both had perceptual problems, displayed extreme hyperactivity, and had other similar behaviors. Strauss and Lehtinen concluded that, like the soldiers, these children had incurred brain damage. They further surmised that subtle damage to the central nervous system was the source of the children's learning problems. The children could have sustained the brain damage before, during, or after birth. These concepts were subsequently applied to children with severe reading and learning problems.

In practice, however, the term "brain injury" has proven to be difficult for educators to use in a functional way. A variety of alternative terms have been suggested to describe this type of student. "Minimal brain dysfunction" (MBD), an alternative recommended by Clements (1966), was adopted by many medical specialists, including pediatricians, neurologists, and child psychiatrists. However, a medical diagnosis of minimal brain dysfunction in children is very difficult to make with certainty. In most cases, the central nervous system dysfunction must be inferred from observation of behavioral manifestations, such as hyperactivity, perceptual problems, motor awkwardness, and the inability to learn.

Therefore, the medical profession has recently suggested that the term "attention deficit disorders" (ADD) be used instead of "minimal brain dysfunction" (*Diagnostic Statistical Manual*, 1980). (See Chapter 8 for a further discussion of ADD.) In the field of special education, the term "learning disabilities" is commonly used to identify this type of student (Lerner, 1981).

Research on brain dysfunction and its relationship to learning problems continues to be an important priority for the scientific community (Geschwind, 1979; Rie and Rie, 1980). Recent medical research strongly indicates that different areas of the brain control different aspects of the reading process and that damage or insult to brain tissue affects learning. For example, there is evidence that stroke patients who have had brain injury in one area of the brain can name letters but cannot read words. Other stroke patients, with injury in another area, can read words, but not identify letters (Albert et al., 1973; Hecaen and Kremlin, 1976). While the implications of brain research for the teaching of reading are not clear at this time, optimism about the eventual application of brain research for teaching remains high.

Perceptual difficulties are thought to be a symptom of a neurological dysfunction. The discussion of treatment for students with perceptual disorders appears in Chapters 8 and 9.

Sex Differences

For reasons that are not entirely clear, more boys than girls exhibit reading problems in American schools. In fact, boys commonly outnumber girls by more than four to one in remedial reading programs (Asher, 1977). At least two reasons have been proposed for the preponderance of boys in remedial reading: maturation and the school environment.

(1) Maturation. Since boys are less physically mature than girls at the age of beginning reading instruction, they may not have developed certain skills that aid in reading, such as the ability to pay attention and the ability to manage pencils and books.

(2) School environment. The school environment may affect boys and girls differently. The primary classroom is traditionally female oriented, employing women teachers and rewarding behaviors such as being neat and quiet. In some cultures, boys actually exhibit superior reading ability (Preston, 1979; Gross, 1978), suggesting that sex differences may be due to cultural factors or other factors in instruction rather than maturational differences. Since more boys than girls are likely to be in remedial reading classes, it is important to make these boys feel welcome and happy in the reading environment.

Other Physical Problems

Good physical health is an important basic condition for learning. Learning is an active process that requires the student to be alert, energetic, and concentrate for long periods of time. The pupil who is listless, tires easily, and cannot maintain attention may have an underlying medical problem. Prolonged illness, especially accompanied by high fevers and long periods of absence from school, can also contribute to a reading problem.

GENERAL HEALTH AND NUTRITION.   Nutrient deficiency in infancy or early childhood has been shown to result in anatomical and biochemical changes in the brain. Early malnutrition impairs growth, both of the body in general and the central nervous system in particular (Martin, 1980). Health concerns include problems of nutrition, rheumatic fever, asthma, lack of sleep, biochemical imbalances, and endocrine problems. A general physical examination is often recommended as part of a complete assessment for reading problems.

MEDICAL AND BIOCHEMICAL TREATMENTS.   Many students with reading problems receive medical or medically related treatments. Since teachers may be asked to provide feedback to physicians or parents about students, it is important to be aware of both the underlying conditions and the therapies.

1. *Hypoglycemia.* One theory of the cause of learning problems is a medical condition known as hypoglycemia. This condition is due to a deficiency in the level of blood sugar. Treatment consists of control of sugar in the student's diet (Runion, 1980).

2. *Allergy.* Allergies, which are caused by both the diet and the environment, are the basis of another theory of the cause of learning and reading difficulty. The treatment consists of the removal of the element causing the allergy (Crook, 1977; Rapp, 1979). The precise relationship of allergies to the learning process is yet to be determined.

3. *Drug therapy.* Many students with reading disabilities are prescribed medication intended to control their hyperactivity, increase attention span, and reduce impulsive and aggressive behavior. Widely used medications include Ritalin, Dexedrine, Librium, and Cylert. There is some difference of opinion about the effectiveness and safety of these drugs. It is very important to monitor their effects closely. Teachers are an important resource for providing essential feedback to physicians on the effectiveness of the medication and the behavior of the patient.

4. *Food additives.* The concept that food additives and some food substances can adversely affect learning and behavior is the basis for another medically related treatment. One of the most widely discussed and controversial theories on the effect of food additives is that of Feingold (1975), who points out that artificial flavors, colors, and preservatives are used increasingly in the American diet. Feingold's treatment consists of the control of diet and the removal of foods that contain additives, as well as certain natural foods. Research is still inconclusive on the effectiveness of this treatment for learning problems, although a recent research report suggests that it might be effective in certain cases (Swanson and Kinsbourne, 1980).

SUMMARY

Correlates of reading problems are factors that are related to reading disability, but the precise cause and effect relationship cannot be specified. Correlates discussed in this chapter include ecological factors (environments), emotional factors, and physical factors.

Ecological factors are the environments in which a student lives and grows. The home environment is the child's first ecological system. The parents play a crucial role in the home environment. The school environment is another important ecological system for the student, one that is often difficult for students with reading problems. Reading disabled students also have difficulty in their social environments. The cultural environment is another ecological system that affects attitude and interest in reading. Methods for assessing ecological systems include behavioral observation, interest inventory, and the interview.

Emotional problems also influence reading achievement. Opinions differ about the need to treat emotional problems prior to the treatment of reading problems. Among the emotional problems exhibited by remedial readers are emotional blocks, hostility-aggressiveness, passive-withdrawn behavior, low self-esteem, depression, and anxiety. Emotional factors may be informally assessed using the sentence completion activity. Interview data also provides emotional insights.

Physical factors are also related to reading disability. Hearing impairment, including a mild or temporary hearing loss, can affect language learning and learning to read. The audiometer is used to screen for a hearing loss. Teachers can also note symptoms of hearing problems by carefully observing students in the classroom.

Visual impairment is also related to reading disability. Visual problems include myopia, hyperopia, astigmatism, and poor binocular vision. There are several instruments for screening for visual impairment, and teachers can learn to observe symptoms of visual difficulty.

Neurological problems and perceptual disorders are another factor for some remedial readers. Central nervous system dysfunctions can impede the learning of reading.

Reading difficulties are more common in boys than girls. Causes may be maturational or cultural.

Other physical problems related to reading are health and nutrition. Many disabled readers receive medical and medically related treatments, including drug therapy, control of food additives, and treatment for hypoglycemia and allergies. Teachers should be aware of such conditions and the students who are receiving such treatment.

Test Inventory 3-1   Tests of Ecological and Emotional Factors

---

Children's Apperception Test (CAT)
Western Psychological Services, 1974   *Ages: 3-10 years*

Consists of a series of ten pictures of animals in various situations to which students react verbally. Personality disturbances are classified through assessment of such topics as relations to authority figures, sibling rivalry, relationship to parents, and fantasies about aggression. No norms are given. Individual administration: 10–15 minutes. Usually given by a trained psychologist who interprets results.

**Devereux Adolescent School Behavior Rating
Scale (DASB)
Devereux Elementary School Behavior Rating
Scale (DESB)**
Devereux Foundation, 1967   *Ages: 5-12, 13-18 years*

Teachers rate individual students from 1 to 7 on forty-seven items broken into eleven factors: classroom disturbance, impatience, defiance, external blame, achievement anxiety, external reliance, comprehension, inattentiveness, irrelevant responsiveness, creative initiative, and dependence on teacher. Yields scores for factors, standard scores.

Individual test.

The Piers-Harris Children's Self-Concept Scale

Counselor Recordings and Tests, 1969   *Grades: 3-12*

Student reads such statements as "I am a happy person" and "I cause trouble to my family" and responds "yes" or "no" to each. Statements may be read by teacher. Six factors assessed include behavior, intellectual status, physical appearance, anxiety, popularity, and happiness. Yields percentile and stanine scores.

Group or individual test: 20 minutes.

The Pupil Rating Scale

Grune & Stratton, 1971 (1st edition)   *Grades: K-6*

Students rated 1 to 5 on several teacher-observed behaviors including auditory comprehension, spoken language, orientation, coordination, and social behavior. Yields verbal, nonverbal, and total learning scores.

Individual test: 10–15 minutes.

The Rorschach Technique

Grune & Stratton, 1951   *Ages: 3 years–adult*

Projective test has students reveal feelings by telling what they see in ten inkblot pictures. Used to assess personality disturbances. No norms given.

Individual test: 1 hour. Must be administered and interpreted by psychologist.

Thematic Apperception Test (TAT)

Harvard University Press, 1971   *Ages: 4 years–adult*

Projective test has students reveal feelings by telling a story about each of nineteen pictures and one blank card. Used to assess personality disturbances. No norms.

Individual test administered in two sittings: 2 hours total. Trained psychologist must administer and interpret.

Vineland Social Maturity Scale

American Guidance Service, 1965   *Ages: birth to maturity*

Assesses social and independent living skills. Individual familiar with student provides ratings on the major categories of self-help, self-direction, locomotion, occupation, communication, and social relations. Yields age scores and social quotient.

Individual administration: 30 minutes.

Test Inventory 3-2   Tests of Physical Factors

Audiometer

Beltone Electronics Corporation
Maico Hearing Instruments

Instruments screen a subject's hearing threshold for a series of tones, or frequencies, at various decibel levels. Left and right ears are tested separately. The subject raises a hand to indicate when a tone is heard. Both air and bone conduction can be tested. Hearing threshold is graphed on an audiogram in decibels of loss.

Individual test: 10–20 minutes.

Keystone Vision Screening for Schools
Keystone View Company

Instrument screens fourteen basic skills including eye posture and binocular imbalance, binocular depth perception, color discrimination, usable binocular vision, and nearpoint and farpoint acuity. Eyes can be tested separately. Ratings of unsatisfactory, retest, and satisfactory are received.

Individual test: 10–15 minutes.

The Orthorater
Bausch and Lomb

Instrument contains twelve subtests that screen for the binocular action of the eyes, nearpoint and farpoint vision, depth perception, and color discrimination. Norms are available for job-related activity, and an adapted version may be used with children.

Individual administration: 15–20 minutes.

Snellen Chart
American Optical Company

A method of screening visual acuity using a wall chart consisting of rows of letters gradually decreasing in size in each descending row. The letters are to be read at a distance of twenty feet. The test is a limited visual screening method since it does not assess nearpoint (reading) vision or binocular vision. Only nearsightedness (myopia) is detectable.

Individual administration: 2–3 minutes.

Spache Binocular Reading Test (BRT)
Keystone View Company, 1955

Student orally reads passages from cards inserted into Telebinocular machine. Some words appear only to left eye, others only to right eye. By noting word omissions, examiner can see if one eye is suppressed during reading. Lower level contains pictures rather than words. Informal norms provide basis for visual referral.

Individual test: 2–4 minutes.

A Teacher Rating Scale for Use in Drug Therapy with Children (Hyperkinesis Index)
Abbott Laboratories, 1975   *Ages: 6–12 years*

Questionnaire assesses the effectiveness of drug therapy. One set of questions is for the parent and one for the teacher. The questions cover behavior of child, group participation, attitude toward authority, and family. A rating of 1 to 3 is given to each item. Questionnaire is given before student is placed on drugs and again periodically to assess effects of drugs. No norms available. Scores obtained at different times are compared.

Individual administration: 10–15 minutes. No special training required.

4

CORRELATES OF READING DISABILITY II

intellectual potential and language development

In this chapter, two correlates of reading achievement are discussed: (1) intelligence (the potential or capacity to learn) and (2) language abilities. Both factors play critical roles in the reading process.

INTELLIGENCE: THE POTENTIAL FOR LEARNING

Intelligence refers to an individual's potential ability to learn. Intelligence plays an important role in the reading diagnosis because it gives the teacher an idea of whether students have the capability to read better than they do at present.

A person's intelligence cannot be observed directly. What we call intelligence is an inferred construct, which is used to explain differences among people in their present behavior and to predict differences in their future behavior. One definition of intelligence is

> The capacity of an individual to understand the world about him and his resourcefulness to cope with its challenges. (Wechsler, 1975, p. 139)

Paradoxically, intelligence tests do not measure the construct defined as intelligence—innate capacity. The hypothetical construct of intelligence is much richer than what is actually measured through intelligence tests. While there are many factors that could be considered intelligence (such as mechanical ability, street knowledge, creativity, social skills), most intelligence tests simply predict whether the individual is likely to do well in schoolwork, especially in learning tasks with highly verbal content (Anastasi, 1976; Sattler, 1974; Salvia and Ysseldyke, 1981; Bryan and Bryan, 1978). Therefore, intelligence tests can be best regarded as measures of scholastic aptitude.

Intelligence tests are often called "IQ tests." The letters IQ originally were an abbreviation for "intelligence quotient." The term now refers to the score obtained in an intelligence test.

The limited nature of many intelligence tests has been a matter of great concern to educators and psychologists. During the 1950s and 1960s attempts were made to develop culture-free IQ tests that would not penalize culturally disadvantaged children. Following this same way of thinking, some contemporary psychologists believe that an intelligence test should measure general level of life functioning as well as academic potential. For example, can the student communicate with peers and handle money? Tests like the SOMPA have attempted to measure life-functioning skills. See Test Inventory 4.1 at the end of this chapter.

Certain issues about intelligence and intelligence testing have been debated since the tests were first developed at the turn of the century. In recent years, however, the intelligence testing debate has spread from sedate academic discussions among professionals to heated open argument among concerned citizens, advocate groups, and legislators. In fact, public concern about intelligence testing has become so intense that it has affected many of the assessment procedures, including such basic decisions as whether or not intelligence tests may be used. Laws passed in some school districts prohibit the use of intelligence tests for certain purposes. For example, the Chicago Board of Education voted to discontinue the use of intelligence tests for assigning children to some special education classes for the mentally handicapped (*Chicago Tribune*, 1981). Teachers who are responsible for diagnosing a reading problem should be aware of issues concerning intelligence and intelligence testing.

Heredity Versus Environment

The issue of whether intelligence is determined by heredity (the result of biological makeup) or the environment (the result of personal experiences) has been researched by the scientific community for many years. Events in recent years have brought this debate to the public, engendering much controversy. What is the nature of the heredity-environment debate?

THE ENVIRONMENTAL PERSPECTIVE.   Studies supporting the environmental perspective show that mental abilities can change under favorable conditions. Environmental factors which influence an individual's intellect include the home, the school, social experiences, and the level of health care and nutrition.

Research has shown that the IQs of young children are highly modifiable. Several studies have examined the effect of placing young children, who had been identified as mentally retarded, in a nurturing environment. In each study the favorable environment increased children's intelligence test scores, as well as their ability to live successful and independent lives. Some of these children even earned college degrees (Skeels, 1942; Kirk, 1958; and Heber et al. 1972).

More recently, Feuerstein (1979) has demonstrated that the cognitive functioning of adolescents, as well as children, can be increased. Feuerstein worked in Israel with disadvantaged and mentally retarded adolescents who functioned at a very low level. By using specifically designed "mediated learning experiences," Feuerstein succeeded in teaching such individuals to perform higher-level cognitive tasks. His research showed that identified cognitive deficits can be remediated through a formal instructional program in which the teacher literally shows the student how to think. Feuerstein's work indicates that the human organism is open to modifiability at all ages and stages of development.

A widely watched large-scale educational experiment, the Head Start program, tested the effects of the environmental experiences on the intelligence and learning ability of young children. Head Start was designed to provide early education to four- and five-year-old children from disadvantaged populations. The intent of Head Start was to offer these young children compensatory education so that they could have the kinds of environmental experiences that middle-class children were thought to have. Although the early reports of the results of Head Start were somewhat disappointing (Bissell, 1972), measures of long-term effects are very encouraging. Two studies followed up students ten to fifteen years after they had been in the Head Start program. Lazar (1979) showed that fewer Head

Start pupils than pupils in a control group were placed in special education classes, fewer were left back a grade or more, and more Head Start students finished high school by age eighteen. The Perry Preschool Project (Schweinhart and Weikart, 1980) showed that preschool education led to improvement in cognitive ability, greater success in school, and more commitment to schooling. By the eighth grade, the Head Start group scored a full grade-level higher in reading, arithmetic, and language achievement than did similar groups who did not have the Head Start experience. Further, the students who had been in Head Start were more likely to find and hold jobs and to continue on to college and were less likely to be on welfare.

Thus, it appears that environmental experiences, such as those provided by the Head Start programs, are successful in making important and significant long-term changes in the learning ability of young children.

THE HEREDITY PERSPECTIVE.   The heredity viewpoint presents another perspective of the nature of intelligence. According to this view, a person's intelligence is largely inherited and is not very amenable to modification by environmental experiences. A major advocate of this position, Jensen (1969, 1979), gathered evidence suggesting that heredity establishes the limits of a person's intelligence. From his research data, Jensen concluded that compensatory education programs that assumed that environment could "create" intelligence with disadvantaged children were doomed to failure. The most controversial portions of Jensen's conclusions are that early tests predict later educational abilities of racial populations and that educational efforts cannot greatly change this prediction. Jensen's findings have been questioned by many other authorities concerned with the nature of intelligence. In addition, some research which formed part of the rationale for the hereditary perspective has recently come under serious question (Gould, 1981).

THE PERSPECTIVE OF THE TEACHING PROFESSION.   The teaching profession has much at stake in the heredity-environment debate. The professional actions of teachers are based on the conviction that educational intervention can make a difference. After analyzing much research on the environment versus heredity issue, Anastasi (1976) concluded that environment and instruction do affect intelligence and learning:

> An individual's intelligence at any one point in time is the end product of a vast and complex sequence of interactions between heredity and environmental factors, and because each interaction in turn determines the direction of subsequent interactions, there is an ever-widening network of possible outcomes. The connection between the genes an individual inherits and any of his behavioral characteristics is thus highly indirect and devious. (Anastasi, 1976, p. 354)

Thus, the evidence seems to show that, although heredity may account for much of the variance in intelligence, the environment also contributes a substantial portion. The contributions of environment to intelligence are extremely important and teachers can play a vital role in this process.

Another important factor in considering intelligence test scores is that different tests give varying estimates of intelligence. Different kinds of questions are asked on different intelligence tests. Therefore, students' scores vary from one intelligence test to another. The IQ score reflects the relationship between the kinds of questions asked and the environmental background of the student.

Teachers should remember that we cannot predict what an individual's true intelligence might be or the ultimate amount that an individual might be able to achieve. A person's IQ is not fixed and unchanging; rather, it is amenable to modification by environmental interventions, including educational experiences. Thus, while intelligence tests may be useful tools in the reading diagnosis, they must be used in a judicious manner. Intelligence tests merely measure current potential for learning; future potential may be affected by many factors.

General Intelligence Versus Specific Mental Abilities

Another controversial issue about intelligence is its composition. Is intelligence a single overriding capacity that underlies individual abilities? Or is it comprised of many different and separate subabilities? Initially, intelligence was conceptualized as a single, general factor. Indeed, statistical validity and predictability is much greater for general measures of intelligence than it is for measurements of separate abilities (Anastasi, 1976). The current trend, however, is to conceptualize intelligence as comprised of separate abilities. This is sometimes referred to as the "component" theory of intelligence (Sternberg, 1981).

In addition to providing an overall general score (or IQ score), some tests of intelligence contain subtests that measure separate abilities of mental functions. These tests are particularly useful in the reading diagnosis because they help in the clinical analysis of the student's component mental abilities.

One intelligence test that is particularly useful for measuring component subskills of intelligence is the *Wechsler Intelligence Scale for Children-Revised* (WISC–R). (The WISC–R is described in detail in Test Inventory 4–1, which is given at the end of this chapter.) This test yields a verbal IQ score, a performance IQ score, and an overall IQ score. There are twelve subtests: six verbal subtests and six performance subtests.

WISC-R SUBTESTS

VERBAL SUBTESTS	PERFORMANCE SUBTESTS
Information	Picture Completion
Comprehension	Picture Arrangement
Similarities	Block Design
Arithmetic	Object Assembly
Vocabulary	Coding
Digit Span*	Mazes*

* Digit Span and Mazes are alternate tests.

The WISC–R provides a score for each of the twelve subtests. By comparing the various subtest scores, the clinical teacher tries to detect a pattern in the components of mental functioning. When there is a great deal of variance (or difference among the scores), this is referred to as a "scatter" pattern. Scatter in the subtest scores of the WISC–R can reflect strengths and weaknesses in mental functioning. Students with learning problems are thought to exhibit more scatter than normal learners.

Kaufman (1981) reviewed a number of studies concerning the scatter of the subtest scores of the WISC–R. The studies indicated that even normal readers have quite a bit of scatter in their WISC–R subtest scores. However, the scatter produced by readers with learning problems was somewhat greater than it was for the normal population. In addition, students with reading problems tend to have higher performance IQ's than verbal IQ scores (Moore and Wielan, 1981).

"... I can't go bowling tonight, Freddie, I'm cramming for an IQ test tomorrow..."

Another test that measures separate abilities is the *Illinois Test of Psycho-linguistic Abilities* (ITPA). Although not an IQ test, this test was designed to provide discrete subtest scores that would be useful for analyzing component mental functions, particularly in the area of language processes. The ITPA and other tests of cognitive processes are discussed in Chapter 8.

Although the analysis of subtest scores is a fairly common diagnostic procedure, measurement specialists urge caution in the use of WISC–R subtest scores in diagnosing a student (Anastasi, 1976; Kaufman, 1981; Tabachnick, 1979; Salvia and Ysseldyke, 1981). The theory that subabilities of mental functions can be identified and measured separately is still an unproven concept. In fact, the separate scores on intelligence tests such as the WISC–R were not designed for this kind of diagnostic analysis. It should be noted that even highly reliable tests with well-established validity do not yield sufficiently precise results for individual diagnosis. Moreover, individual subtest scores are far less reliable than is the total score.

Nevertheless, many teachers, diagnosticians, and psychologists do find it helpful to consider component subtest scores of tests such as the WISC–R in the reading diagnosis. Since the clinical analysis of remedial readers requires multiple sources of data, the analysis of subtest sources can contribute useful information. However, teachers should analyze subtest scores knowing the limitations of this procedure. If the teacher guards against overgeneralization from subtest scores, this information contributes a rich harvest of leads for further exploration.

> As long as such instruments serve primarily to suggest leads for the skilled clinician to follow up, their use can be justified. There is danger, of course, that a relatively inexperienced and overzealous clinician, unmindful of the limitations of the instrument, may place more confidence in its results than is warranted. (Anastasi, 1976, p. 464)

The Relationship Between Reading and Intelligence

A statistically positive relationship exists between intelligence test scores and reading ability. Verbal intelligence test scores have a higher correlation with reading comprehension than do nonverbal or performance tests. The verbal correlations range from .60 to .85, whereas the nonverbal correlations range from .20 to .56. As students mature, the correlations between reading achievement and intelligence scores become stronger (Spache, 1981; Harris and Sipay, 1980; Savage and Mooney, 1979). Although the relationship between intelligence and reading scores is positive, intelligence tests typically do not even predict half of the relationship of reading test scores (Harris and Sipay, 1980; Brown, 1982). Therefore, intelligence tests should *not* be considered infallible predictors of reading achievement.

Intelligence tests given to very young children are not highly predictive of early reading success (Savage and Mooney, 1979; Kirk, Kliebhan, & Lerner, 1978). This may be due to the fact that tests for preschool children usually assess nonverbal areas, which have a lower correlation with reading.

Neville (1965) found that poor readers score significantly higher on individually administered intelligence tests than they do on tests administered to a group. Average readers, however, score about the same on both individual and group tests; good readers score better on group tests than they do on individual tests. This is because many group intelligence tests require the student to read.

Some reading authorities suggest that the assessment of intellectual capacity should not be limited to the administration of standardized IQ tests. For example, Lawson et al. (1975) examined the relationship between reading scores and Piaget's stages of cognitive development. These tasks, developed by the Swiss psychologist Jean Piaget, identify the developmental sequence of thinking processes that children use in solving problems. The Piagetian measures are different from IQ scores because they measure the "process" of thinking rather than the "product" of learning. Lawson's study showed that there was a high, positive correlation between the reading test scores of high school students and their performance on ten Piagetian tasks.

Teachers using IQ tests or receiving IQ scores on students should remember that the content of these tests and the validity of their scores has come under serious question. An IQ test provides much valuable information, but it cannot give a definitive or permanent rating of a student's mental ability. Thus, teachers should be alert to the many other sources of information about students, including behavior in class, independence in living, and interests and accomplishments outside the school setting.

Interpreting Intelligence Test Scores

Several technical terms used in reporting scores on intelligence tests are important for teachers to know. Two of the most important are mental age (MA) and intelligence quotient (IQ).

MENTAL AGE. Mental age (MA) refers to the age-level score of a student's performance on an intelligence test when compared with the norm population. (The norm population is the large number of students who initially took the test to establish norms.) For example, if a student receives an MA of 15 on an intelligence test, that student's performance is equivalent to the performance of the average fifteen-year-old subject. If the student receives an MA score of 7–6, this means that the student's performance was equivalent to that of the average student of age seven years, six months who took the test. Although early intelligence tests used the concept of MA scores extensively, many recent test developers believe that the concept of the MA may be misleading (Wechsler, 1975).

IQ SCORES. There are two ways to report an IQ score: (1) the ratio IQ and (2) the deviation IQ. In the *ratio IQ*, a ratio is taken between *mental age* and *chronological age.* For example, if a student has a mental age of eight years and a chronological age of ten years, an IQ score of 80 indicates that the student learns eight-tenths as fast as a student of similar age with a score of 100. Students with scores over 100 would then be expected to learn faster than the student with the score of 100. The rate of learning would depend upon the relationship of the student's score with the norm score of 100.

The second type of IQ score is the *standard deviation IQ.* Here, the student is compared only with others of the same age who were in the norm group. The standard deviation IQ score is based upon the concept of a normal curve, as shown in Figure 4.1. An IQ of 100 is designated as the mean for each age group. As shown in Figure 4.1, approximately 34 percent of the population will fall within one standard deviation below the mean and 34 percent of the population will fall within one standard deviation above the mean. To illustrate, on the WISC–R, one standard deviation is 15 points. Therefore, 34 percent of the population will score between 85 and 100, and 34 percent of the population will score between 100 and 115. Figure 4.1 illustrates the distribution of IQ scores on a normal curve.

Intelligence ranges for the WISC–R (Weschler, 1974) are shown below. Teachers will find them useful for reporting results of this IQ test to parents. If tests

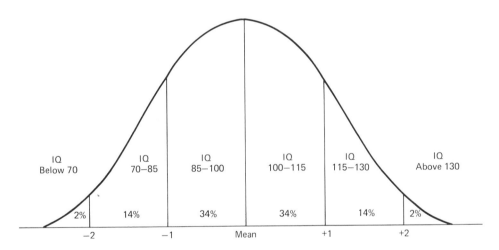

Figure 4.1   Distribution of IQ Scores on a Normal Curve*

* Scores are clustered around the mean, which is the highest point. A standard deviation (SD) is a number (e.g., in the WISC–R it is 15). A child scoring one standard deviation above the mean, if the mean is 100 and the standard deviation is 15, would score 115. A child scoring two standard deviations above the mean would score 130. The percentages show what percent of the population is included in any standard deviation. For example, 34 percent of the people score between zero and one standard deviations below (or above) the mean. Two percent of the population scores between two and three standard deviations below (or above) the mean.

other than the WISC–R are used, the test manual should be consulted for the IQ ranges for those tests.

130 and above	Very superior
120–129	Superior
110–119	High average (bright)
90–109	Average
80– 89	Low average (dull)
70– 79	Borderline
69 and below	Mentally deficient

Determining the Existence of a Reading Disability

As noted in Chapter 2, a critical first step in the reading diagnosis is to decide if the student actually has a reading disability. In the process of selecting students for remedial instruction, teachers often find that some students who have been referred do not, in fact, have a reading disability. In addition, more students are usually referred for special reading instruction than time and resources permit to be helped. Selecting students for special reading instruction is a complex and demanding task—one that entails serious consequences for the student. Criteria must be established for selecting students most in need of remedial instruction.

There are two ways to identify students with reading disabilities: the "practical" approach (which looks at how well the student functions in the reading environment) and the "discrepancy" approach (which compares intellectual potential to current reading achievement).

PRACTICAL CRITERIA FOR DETERMINING A READING DISABILITY. A practical way to select students for special reading instruction is to look at how well they are adapting academically to their school environment. In this approach, the teacher considers how students function in the school and with their peers. The teacher investigates the student's ability to cope within the classroom situation and also takes into account such factors as the degree of reading retardation in relation to the peer group and the student's need for special assistance in order to cope in the classroom. The following criteria may be considered.

1. *Students cannot function in school and reading activities as well as peers.* Disabled readers cannot function well academically with peers in the educational setting, and they are unable to participate fully in reading tasks with their age or peer group. This criterion suggests that "national" norms are not applicable to all segments of the population. To apply national norms without discretion is considered discriminatory and unfair to the students (Spache, 1981).

2. *Students have a consistent pattern of poor reading.* The disabled reader shows poor reading performance consistently over a period of time. That is, the

reading problem is not temporary. Further, the disabled reader requires extensive intervention rather than a minor correction for a specific area of reading.

3. *The amount of reading retardation meets guidelines set for the grade level.* The school should set guidelines to help determine the amount of reading retardation needed for eligibility for reading assistance. However, adjustment can be made for each particular situation. Many remedial reading programs use the following guidelines:

Primary grades	Over 0.5 years
Intermediate grades	Over 1.0 years
Junior high school	Over 1.5 years
Senior high school	Over 2.0 years

DISCREPANCY CRITERIA FOR DETERMINING A READING DISABILITY.   The second approach to deciding if a student has a reading disability is to use discrepancy criteria. The teacher determines if a significant discrepancy exists between reading expectancy (determined partially by the IQ score) and the student's current reading performance. That is, does the student read as well as predicted by measures of potential? The discrepancy concept of reading disability is widely accepted and used. For example, the American Psychological Association (*Diagnostic and Statistical Manual*, 1980) defines a reading disorder as a reading level that is significantly below the student's intellectual capacity.

STEPS IN DETERMINING A READING DISCREPANCY.   There are three steps in determining a reading discrepancy. It should be noted that each has certain inherent problems that have been the source of professional debate and disagreement.

1. *Estimating reading expectancy.* This refers to a judgment of how well a student is potentially capable of reading. Methods of estimating reading expectancy use IQ, MA, listening levels, or arithmetic achievement grade level.

2. *Estimating current reading level.* This refers to the level at which a student is currently reading. Reading survey tests, individual reading tests, or oral reading tests are used to make this estimate.

3. *Determining the discrepancy between reading expectancy and reading achievement.* This refers to the size of the gap between the level at which the student is capable of reading and the level at which the student is currently reading. Opinions differ about how much of a discrepancy is required before a student is eligible for remedial reading services. Some experts suggest using the criteria based upon time (e.g., the student is retarded in reading by six months, one year, two years, and so on). If time criteria are employed, the guidelines in the previous section can be used. Other reading authorities suggest using a reading quotient. For example, the quotient would tell us that Patty is reading at 60 percent of what she is capable of reading or that Jeffery is reading at 95 percent of what he is capable of reading; in these cases, Patty would be considered to have a reading disability and Jeffery would not.

EXPECTANCY FORMULAS. Determining the reading discrepancy requires that the teacher first estimate the student's reading expectancy. Several formulas have been developed to aid in this process. One of the most widely used methods for estimating reading expectancy is *the reading discrepancy age method* (Harris and Sipay, 1980):

$$\text{REA (reading expectancy age)} = \frac{2\text{ MA} + \text{CA}}{3}$$

In this formula, MA (mental age) and CA (chronological age) should be expressed in years and tenths (rather than years and months). The formula gives a reading expectancy age. To convert from an expectancy *age* to an expectancy *grade*, subtract 5.2.

To illustrate the reading age expectancy formula, Marion is 10–0 years old, and she has an IQ of 120 and a MA of 12.0 years. Using this formula, she has a reading expectancy age of 11.3 and a reading grade expectancy of 6.1 (11.3 – 5.2). If Marion's current level of reading is 3.0, she would have a 3.1-year discrepancy.*

$$\text{REA} = \frac{2(12.0) + 10.0}{3} = 11.3 \quad \text{REG (grade)} = 11.3 - 5.2 = 6.1$$

Another widely used formula is the *years-in-school formula* suggested by Bond, Tinker, and Wasson (1979):

$$\text{REG (reading expectancy grade)} = \frac{\text{years in school} \times \text{IQ}}{100} + 1.0$$

To illustrate, if Marion is now in the middle of the fifth grade, she has been in school 4.5 years (grades one, two, three, four, and half of the fifth). Using this formula, Marion has a reading expectancy grade of 6.4.

$$\text{REG} = \frac{4.5 \times 120}{100} + 1.0 = 6.4$$

If she has a current reading level of 3.0, she would have a discrepancy of 3.4 years.

As is apparent, these two methods give different estimates of reading expectancy, resulting in different estimates of discrepancy. These two formulas, along with several others, were studied by Dore-Boyce et al. (1975) to determine which best predicted reading achievement. Using fourth and fifth grade students, their findings indicate that the years-in-school method was not as good a predictor of reading achievement as was the reading expectancy age method. Further they found that the reading expectancy age formula proved to be most useful with fourth and fifth graders who had IQs of 90 or better.

To avoid doing calculations in assessing reading expectancy, a table such as that shown in Table 4.1 is a helpful aid. If a teacher knows the IQ and CA of a stu-

---

* To obtain MA from the IQ, use the formula:

$$\text{MA} = \frac{\text{IQ} \times \text{CA}}{100}$$

Table 4.1 Reading Expectancy Grade Table*

IQ SCORE

Chronological Age	70	75	80	85	90	95	100	105	110	115	120	125	130	135	140	145
6-0	—	—	—	—	—	—	—	1.0	1.2	1.4	1.6	1.8	2.0	2.2	2.4	2.6
6-3	—	—	—	—	—	—	1.0	1.2	1.5	1.7	1.9	2.1	2.3	2.5	2.7	2.9
6-6	—	—	—	—	—	1.1	1.3	1.5	1.7	2.0	2.2	2.4	2.6	2.8	3.0	3.2
6-9	—	—	—	—	1.1	1.3	1.6	1.8	2.0	2.2	2.4	2.7	2.9	3.1	3.4	3.6
7-0	—	—	—	1.1	1.3	1.6	1.8	2.0	2.3	2.5	2.7	3.0	3.2	3.4	3.7	3.9
7-3	—	—	1.1	1.3	1.6	1.8	2.0	2.3	2.5	2.8	3.0	3.2	3.5	3.7	4.0	4.2
7-6	—	1.0	1.3	1.6	1.8	2.0	2.3	2.6	2.8	3.0	3.3	3.6	3.8	4.0	4.3	4.6
7-9	1.0	1.3	1.5	1.8	2.0	2.3	2.6	2.8	3.1	3.3	3.6	3.8	4.1	4.4	4.6	4.9
8-0	1.2	1.5	1.7	2.0	2.3	2.5	2.8	3.1	3.3	3.6	3.9	4.1	4.4	4.7	4.9	5.2
8-3	1.4	1.7	2.0	2.2	2.5	2.8	3.0	3.3	3.6	3.9	4.2	4.4	4.7	5.1	5.3	5.5
8-6	1.6	1.9	2.2	2.4	2.7	3.0	3.3	3.6	3.9	4.2	4.4	4.7	5.0	5.3	5.6	5.8
8-9	1.8	2.1	2.4	2.7	3.0	3.3	3.6	3.8	4.1	4.4	4.7	5.0	5.3	5.6	5.9	6.2
9-0	2.0	2.3	2.6	2.9	3.2	3.5	3.8	4.1	4.4	4.7	5.0	5.3	5.6	5.9	6.2	6.5
9-3	2.2	2.5	2.8	3.1	3.4	3.7	4.0	4.4	4.7	5.0	5.3	5.6	5.9	6.2	6.5	6.8
9-6	2.4	2.7	3.0	3.4	3.7	4.0	4.3	4.6	4.9	5.2	5.6	5.9	6.2	6.5	6.8	7.2
9-9	2.6	2.9	3.2	3.6	3.9	4.2	4.6	4.9	5.2	5.5	5.8	6.2	6.5	6.8	7.2	7.5
10-0	2.8	3.1	3.5	3.8	4.1	4.5	4.8	5.1	5.5	5.8	6.1	6.5	6.8	7.1	7.5	7.8
10-3	3.0	3.3	3.7	4.0	4.4	4.7	5.0	5.4	5.7	6.1	6.4	6.8	7.1	7.4	7.8	8.1
10-6	3.2	3.6	3.9	4.2	4.6	5.0	5.3	5.6	6.0	6.4	6.7	7.0	7.4	7.8	8.1	8.4
10-9	3.4	3.8	4.1	4.5	4.8	5.2	5.6	5.9	6.3	6.6	7.0	7.3	7.7	8.1	8.4	8.8
11-0	3.6	4.0	4.3	4.7	5.1	5.4	5.8	6.2	6.5	6.9	7.3	7.6	8.0	8.4	8.7	9.1
11-3	3.8	4.2	4.6	4.9	5.3	5.7	6.0	6.4	6.8	7.2	7.6	7.9	8.3	8.7	9.0	9.4
11-6	4.0	4.4	4.8	5.2	5.5	5.9	6.3	6.7	7.1	7.4	7.8	8.2	8.6	9.0	9.4	9.8
11-9	4.2	4.6	5.0	5.4	5.8	6.2	6.6	7.0	7.3	7.7	8.1	8.5	8.9	9.3	9.7	10.1
12-0	4.4	4.8	5.2	5.6	6.0	6.4	6.8	7.2	7.6	8.0	8.4	8.8	9.2	9.6	10.0	10.4
12-3	4.6	5.0	5.4	5.8	6.2	6.6	7.0	7.4	7.9	8.3	8.7	9.1	9.5	9.9	10.3	10.7
12-6	4.8	5.2	5.6	6.0	6.5	6.9	7.3	7.7	8.1	8.6	9.0	9.4	9.8	10.2	10.6	11.0
12-9	5.0	5.4	5.8	6.3	6.7	7.1	7.6	8.0	8.4	8.8	9.2	9.7	10.1	10.5	11.0	11.4
13-0	5.2	5.6	6.1	6.5	6.9	7.4	7.8	8.2	8.7	9.1	9.5	10.0	10.4	10.8	11.3	11.7
13-3	5.4	5.8	6.3	6.7	7.2	7.6	8.0	8.5	8.9	9.4	9.8	10.2	10.7	11.1	11.5	12.0
13-6	5.6	6.0	6.5	7.0	7.4	7.8	8.3	8.8	9.2	9.6	10.1	10.6	11.0	11.4	11.9	12.4
13-9	5.8	6.3	6.7	7.2	7.6	8.1	8.6	9.0	9.5	9.9	10.4	10.8	11.3	11.8	12.2	12.7
14-0	6.0	6.5	6.9	7.4	7.9	8.3	8.8	9.3	9.7	10.2	10.7	11.1	11.6	12.1	12.5	13.0
14-3	6.2	6.7	7.2	7.6	8.1	8.6	9.0	9.5	10.0	10.5	11.0	11.4	11.9	12.4	12.8	13.3
14-6	6.4	6.9	7.4	7.8	8.3	8.8	9.3	9.8	10.3	10.8	11.2	11.7	12.2	12.7	13.2	13.6
14-9	6.6	7.1	7.6	8.1	8.6	9.1	9.6	10.0	10.5	11.0	11.5	12.0	12.5	13.0	13.5	14.0
15-0	6.8	7.3	7.8	8.3	8.8	9.3	9.8	10.3	10.8	11.3	11.8	12.3	12.8	13.3	13.8	14.3

Chronological Age (in years and months)

* This table gives reading expectancy grade level. If the intelligence score or chronological age falls between two values, use the closest one. For students over fifteen years of age, use the 15.0 chronological age value.

dent, the reading expectancy grade can then be found by noting the intersection of the chronological age with IQ. For students over fifteen years of age, use 15.0 as the chronological age. If the CA and IQ fall between two values on a table, use the closest value. Table 4.1 is based on the reading discrepancy formula of Harris and Sipay. To aid the teacher, the expecting *grade* level (rather than age) is reported directly.

Tests of Intelligence or Potential Ability

Instruments that assess intelligence can be divided into two types: group tests and individual tests. Group tests are designed to be given to several students (or a class) at one time. However, they can also be given to students individually. In contrast, individual tests must be given to one student at a time. Some individual tests require that the examiner have special training for administration. One problem with group intelligence tests is that taking the test requires the subject to read and, therefore, the IQ is dependent upon reading ability. In general, more credence is given to scores obtained on individual intelligence tests than those from group tests.

Since a reading diagnosis typically includes an estimate of intellectual potential, teachers should be familiar with major tests in this area. Widely-used tests of intelligence and potential are presented in Test Inventory 4.1 (at the end of this chapter). This inventory describes both group and individual tests. A detailed description of the important Wechsler tests (WISC–R, WAIS–R, and WPPSI) are useful features of the test inventory.

There has been a growing interest in measuring potential ability through assessment of everyday living skills, such as independent living, personal financial budgeting, and personal mobility. This trend is reflected in tests such as the SOMPA and the *Adaptive Behavior Scales*, also described in Test Inventory 4.1.

LANGUAGE DEVELOPMENT

Reading is language expressed in written form. The ability to express and receive thoughts through language is, therefore, fundamental to being able to read. The individual's underlying language structures profoundly affect the ability to acquire reading skills. It is not surprising that many disabled readers have language difficulties. As noted earlier, reviews of research on the *Wechsler Intelligence Scale for Children* show that pupils with reading problems have significantly more difficulties with verbal subtests than with the performance subtests (Spache, 1981; Moore and Wielan, 1981).

The Nature of Language

Teachers who deal with reading problems should have an understanding of the structure of language. Although it is easy to distinguish people who use language effectively from those who do not, it is difficult to define exactly what effective language usage is. To answer this question, many facets of language have been studied by scholars.

A broad perspective of language includes both the oral form (listening and speaking) and the written form (reading and writing). These four components of language have an interdependent relationship.

TWO SIDES OF ORAL LANGUAGE: RECEPTIVE AND EXPRESSIVE. Measures of oral language distinguish between receptive oral language (listening) and expressive oral language (speaking). Usually, people have greater abilities in receptive oral abilities than they do in expressive. That is, they understand more words than they use in speaking. This distinction is important in measuring the language skills of students. Sometimes teachers conclude erroneously that students have low-level language abilities because the students are observed to engage in little conversation or give one-word replies to the teacher's questions. However, measures of expressive language are influenced by factors such as the student's comfort in the classroom, clinic, or testing situation or conditions such as speech defects. These factors may only affect the student's expressive abilities, leaving receptive abilities functioning adequately. Therefore it is important to assess both aspects of oral language.

COMPONENTS OF LANGUAGE. To help understand the nature of language, linguists identify several different language systems: (1) phonology (the sounds of language), (2) morphology (meaningful elements within words), (3) syntax (the grammatical aspects of language), and (4) semantics (the vocabulary of language). Remedial readers may have difficulties with any of these language systems.

1. *Phonology.* The sound system of our language is called phonology. Language consists of a stream of sounds one after the other. The sounds of English speech do not reflect directly the letters of the English alphabet. For example, the letter "c" represents two different sounds as in the words "city" and "cat." The sound "sh" is composed of two letters, but it represents only one English sound. Although English has only twenty-six letters in the alphabet, the average American English dialect contains forty-four sounds.

Each of the individual sounds is called a phoneme. There are major differences in the phoneme sounds of English and those of other languages. For example, the sounds "y" and "j" are pronounced differently in English as in "yellow" and "jello," but the Spanish speaker may hear them as the same sound and confuse these words. These differences between English and other languages make the mastery of English difficult for students whose native language is not English (just as Spanish or French is difficult for native English speakers).

Phonology refers only to the sounds produced in speech. The term "phonics," which is used by reading teachers, refers to the system that relates letters to sound equivalents in written language.

Young children have difficulty in producing certain phonemes. Not all English speech sounds have been acquired by the time the average child enters first grade. Table 4.2 shows the average ages at which children are able to produce the consonant sounds of the English language. This table reflects the language acquisition of children who are native-born speakers of Standard English. The table does not apply to the child whose dialect or native language does not contain all these phoneme distinctions.

In addition to hearing sounds, students must learn to distinguish sounds that are spoken by others. "Auditory discrimination," the ability to hear distinctions between phoneme sounds is an area of great difficulty for some disabled readers (Wiig and Semel, 1976) (see Chapter 8).

2. *Morphology.* The term morphology refers to meaningful units (or morphemes) that are contained within words. For example, the word "walked" contains two morphemes: "walk" and "ed," a morpheme that signals the past tense. Other examples of morphemes are "s" (game*s*) and "re" (*re*wind). Many students with reading disabilities have deficits in morphological development (Wiig and Semel, 1976; Vogel, 1975; and Brittain, 1970–1971).

When pupils are tested on oral language abilities, they usually are tested on suffixes (which are attached to the end of a word). For example, the pupil is asked to make plurals or possessives. (Here is one dog. Here are two _____.) In the field of reading, morphology is referred to as structural analysis (see Chapter 11).

3. *Syntax.* Syntax (or grammar) refers to the principles that govern the formation of appropriate sentences in a language. The rules of English syntax tell us, for example, that a well-formed sentence has a subject and a verb (e.g., "Jane walks"). Further, we can combine sentences using conjunctions such as "Jane walks *and* Jane runs." The rules of English also tell us that we can delete certain elements; for example, "Jane walks and runs." Extensive study has gone into the

Table 4.2 Ages When Consonant Speech Sounds Are Normally Acquired

CONSONANT	AGE OF ACQUISITION	CONSONANT	AGE OF ACQUISITION
p	1.5–3	ng (si*ng*)	2 –5
m	1.5–3	r	3 –6
h	1.5–3	l	3 –6
w	1.5–3	ch (*ch*air)	3.5–7
n	1.5–3	sh (*sh*ow)	3.5–7
b	1.5–4	j	3.5–7
k	2 –4	th (*thy*)	4.5–7
g	2 –4	s	3 –8
d	2 –4	z	3.5–8
f	2.5–4	v	4 –8
y	2.5–4	th (*thigh*)	4 –8
t	2 –5	zh (plea*s*ure)	6 –8.5

From B. Y. Wellman et al., *Speech Sounds of Young Children* (Iowa City: State University of Iowa, 1931); M. Templin *Certain Language Skills in Children* (Minneapolis: University of Minnesota Press, 1975).

description of the syntax of English and its acquisition by children. Psycholinguistic research indicates that children do not acquire syntactic ability passively. Rather, they recreate syntactic rules for themselves. Children who say "he dided that" are using the rule that the past tense is formed by the addition of "ed"; however, they are overgeneralizing this rule. Although most basic syntactic structures are acquired by the age of six, some growth in syntax continues through the age of ten (C. Chomsky, 1969). The development of the ability to understand very complex or difficult sentence patterns may continue even throughout the high school years. Since the development of syntactic abilities continues through the school years, teaching sentence comprehension is important to reading instruction. Table 4.3 presents examples of difficult sentence types.

4. *Vocabulary (semantics)*. Compared with other languages, English has a very large vocabulary. The historical development of English helps to explain its complexity and variety. English vocabulary comes from two language roots: the Germanic and the Romance languages. The Germanic strand dates back to the original Anglo-Saxon language in old England. The Romance strand (which is related to French, Latin, Spanish, and Portuguese) was merged with the Anglo-Saxon when William the Conqueror invaded England from France in 1066. Words in English today reflect both historical strands. Examples of word pairs that originate in these two sources include mad-furious, deer-venison, father-paternal. The first of each pair is Germanic in origin; the second comes from the Romance

Table 4.3   Difficult Sentence Types

Category	Example
Passive sentences: reversible°	John was given the pen by Mary.
Out-of-order time sequences*	Move a yellow bead, *but first* move a red one.
	Move a yellow bead *after* you move a red one.
Relative clause construction	John, *who is in the second grade*, is learning to read.
	The man *standing on the corner* is nice.
Appositives	Mr. Smith, *the postman*, is very nice.
Complement structures	*The fact that* Steve is silly worries Meg.
	Steve's being silly worries Meg.
	For Steve to be silly worries Meg.
	Steve asked Meg *what was worrying her.*
Delayed reference in sentences†	John promised Mary to go.
	John asked Mary what to feed the doll.
Anophoric, or reference, structures	John saw Mary and *he* said hello.
	John saw Mary and said hello.
Sentence connectives	*If* you don't do this, I will go.
	Unless you do this, I will go.

° The nonreversible sentence *The ball was dropped by the boy* would be easier.

* The construction *Move the yellow one and then the red* would be simpler because it occurs in time order.

† In these cases, *John* does the action of going or feeding the doll. In a sentence such as *John told Mary what to feed the doll*, *Mary* feeds the doll. The latter type of sentence is easier to comprehend.

languages. The complex and rich variety of English makes the mastering of English vocabulary a lifelong task.

A student's vocabulary knowledge is considered to be highly related to reading abilities. Good readers have large vocabularies. In assessing vocabulary development, important considerations include

a. *Size of vocabulary.* This means the number of words that students can use or understand.

b. *Knowledge of multiple meanings of words.* For example, the words "plane" and "cold" each have several meanings.

c. *Accuracy of vocabulary meaning.* The student may overextend or underextend the meanings of words. For example, a small child may call all four-legged animals "dogs." Developing the accuracy of vocabulary is referred to as horizontal vocabulary growth (McNeil, 1970).

d. *Accurate classification of words.* For example, "red," "blue," and "green" all belong in the classification of "colors". The development of this system is referred to as vertical vocabulary growth (McNeil, 1970). Piaget (1926) also discusses the ability to classify objects into categories as an important aspect of language and cognitive development.

e. *Relational categories of words.* Relational words include prepositions (under, over, besides, to, from); comparative terms (good-bad, better-worse, lighter-darker); time elements (yesterday-today-tomorrow), and terms of human relationship (mother, father, aunt, uncle).

Limited vocabulary development can seriously hamper reading. In an extensive review of the literature, Anderson and Freebody (1981) found that vocabulary is highly related to reading achievement.

Language Problems and Reading

Since reading is based on language abilities, problems with language can affect the ability to read. In this section, two types of language problems are discussed: speech defects and language disorders.

SPEECH DEFECTS.   There are three kinds of speech problems: (1) articulation problems (the inaccurate production of sounds), (2) voice disorders (improper pitch or intonation), and (3) stuttering (breath or rhythm problems). Although there is a somewhat higher incidence of speech defects among poor readers, speech defects do not necessarily lead to reading failure. However, students who exhibit speech difficulties should be referred to the speech-language specialist for further evaluation and therapy, if needed. In addition, since hearing impairment is a possible cause of speech defects, hearing acuity should be tested. It is important to remember, however, that the average child does not complete full articulation development until the age of about eight, as shown in Table 4.2. Students with speech defects are often embarrassed when asked to read orally, and therefore this type of assignment should be avoided.

LANGUAGE DISORDERS AND READING. Language disorders refer to a slower or atypical development of receptive and expressive oral language. The child with a language delay is slow at talking, poor in vocabulary development, and may have difficulty in learning to formulate sentences. Language delay appears to be a forerunner of later difficulty in reading for many pupils (Vogel, 1974, 1975; Wiig and Semel, 1976). If the teacher suspects an underlying language disorder, the speech-language pathologist can provide further evaluation and treatment.

Assessing Language Development

Impressions about students' oral language can be gathered by observing them during conversation. More objective methods are given below.

TESTS OF LANGUAGE. Some of the widely used tests to assess expressive and receptive language ability are described in Test Inventory 4.2 (at the end of this chapter). There are several problems in obtaining objective measures of language. If the pupil does not know the examiner, the student tends to produce less language and therefore scores poorly. Language output can be increased if the examiner strives to develop rapport before testing. This can be accomplished by talking to the student for a short period of time or playing a game with the student prior to the testing session (Cazden, 1970). Another shortcoming of language tests is that many are not designed for students past age ten; there are relatively few language tests for older students.

MEASURING LISTENING LEVEL. The ability to comprehend what is heard is sometimes used as an informal measure of a student's receptive language abilities. If remedial students are reading below their listening comprehension level, this means that they are reading below their level of language comprehension. The listening level provides an idea of how well the student might read once the reading disability is overcome. If reading and listening levels are both low, further instruction for language development may be needed.

A student's listening level is sometimes used as a measure of potential for understanding the written word. Listening abilities can be compared with other estimates of a student's reading potential. The difference between instructional reading level and the listening level indicates the degree of reading disability. If a fifth-grader's instructional level is second grade and the listening level is fifth grade, the student can be estimated to have a three-year discrepancy between actual and expected levels. Of course, listening tests can be influenced by such factors as the ability to pay attention.

The procedure involved in determining the listening level consists of reading selections aloud to a student and then asking comprehension questions based on the material. Several commercial tests contain subtests which measure listening level.

1. *The Durrell Analysis of Reading Difficulty.* This test contains a subtest for measuring listening level. A graded story is read and comprehension questions are asked.
2. *Standard Reading Inventory.* This test contains a section for measuring listening level. Stories are read aloud to the child, followed by comprehension questions.
3. *Stanford Achievement Series.* This test contains a listening test for the primary I through the intermediate II levels.
4. *Durrell Listening-Reading Tests.* These group tests cover primary through elementary grades. At each level, they contain standardized tests of listening and reading on both vocabulary and comprehension.

In addition to these tests of listening, an informal reading inventory (IRI) can be used to evaluate listening level. (See Chapter 6 for a discussion of the IRI and Appendix D for a sample IRI.) After the frustration level of the IRI has been established, the teacher reads aloud passages at and above the frustration level and asks the student comprehension questions. The highest level at which the pupil can maintain a comprehension score of 70 is the listening level (see Chapter 6).

LANGUAGE DIFFERENCES AND READING

Many students in our schools use language forms that are different from the standard language of the textbook or of school instruction. These language forms are alternatives rather than deficit forms, and they are not inferior. However, because differences in language usage can affect reading instruction, teachers need to understand them. In this section, dialect-different students and bilingual (or second-language) students are discussed.

Use of Nonstandard Dialect

A dialect is a language pattern used by a subgroup of the speakers of a language. There are many dialects in American English. For example, speakers from New York City, Boston, Montreal, or certain Southern states often speak a characteristic regional dialect. Some students raised in certain specific cultural groups speak a dialect of English used in their environment, such as Appalachian or a dialect referred to as Black English Vernacular (BEV). To illustrate the differences between one such dialect of English and the dialect that is generally considered to be "Standard English," the features of BEV are given in Table 4.4.

American dialects have been studied by several linguists (McDavid, 1976; Wolfram, 1969; Labov et al., 1968). These linguists conclude that all dialects, regardless of their cultural associations, are logical, rule-based systems of English. They also have found that, while dialects may seem to be different, all English speakers share common underlying language forms. Students who speak nonstandard English can learn to read texts in Standard English without changing their speech patterns.

When assessing and teaching students with reading difficulties who speak

Table 4.4 Features of Black English Vernacular

PHONOLOGICAL OR SOUND CHANGES

Category	Examples
When two or more consonants are at the end of a word, one may be omitted.	*Test* is pronounced like *tes*.
"R" may be omitted.	*Bump* is pronounced like *bum*.
"L" may be omitted.	*Fort* is pronounced like *fought*.
Short "i" and short "e" are pronounced the same before some consonants.	*Toll* is pronounced like *toe*.
	Pin is pronounced like *pen*.

SYNTACTIC OR GRAMMATICAL CHANGES

Category	Examples
The possessive may be omitted.	That's Molly('s) book.
The verb to be may be omitted.	He('s) downstairs; they('re) there.
The past-tense ending may be omitted.	He walk(ed) to the store yesterday.
The third-person-singular ending may be omitted.	She think(s) he is very nice.
Contractions signaling the future may be omitted.	He('ll) be there soon.
A "be" construction to indicate ongoing action may be inserted.	I *be* going there on Thursdays.

---

nonstandard dialects, teachers should be aware of several pitfalls. Since reading is a language process, constant correction of the students' oral language may be very destructive. Such correction of dialect patterns makes students feel that their speech is unacceptable. If the student feels uncomfortable with the teacher, verbal output will be reduced in the classroom, and a barrier between the student and teacher can result. Dialect differences should not be mistaken for cognitive deficits or defective language development.

Bilingual and Foreign Language Students

An increasing number of students in our schools cannot speak the language of instruction fluently. Often, these students present reading problems and are placed in special reading or language programs. Although these students come from many different backgrounds and ways of life, they may be divided into two groups: (1) recent immigrants and (2) students whose families have been living in the country for several generations but maintain a separate language and cultural identity.

FACTORS IN SECOND-LANGUAGE LEARNING. Among factors which influence a person's ability to learn a second language are the age of acquisition, the role of language in the culture, the exposure to a second language, and the relationship of the first and second language. These topics are each considered in the paragraphs that follow.

Second languages are learned better at earlier ages, with children showing more facility than adolescents and adults. Lenneberg (1967) believes that the ability to acquire a foreign language with native fluency disappears at about the age of fourteen. Before this, the language will be acquired fully; after this, the speaker will tend to have a "foreign accent."

Language learning is also influenced by cultural values. If a second language is perceived positively in the student's environment, learning will be enhanced. Unfortunately, this is not always the case. Often, a second language is only used in school and thus is of little value in everyday life. Or a second language may be associated with people who are hostile. The more knowledge and empathy a teacher possesses of a student's personal background and cultural heritage, the more effective second-language instruction will be.

Exposure to a second language is important. If students use it frequently, they will learn it more easily. We have observed that students tend to learn a second language more quickly when only a few of their classmates speak their native language. Students benefit most from exposure to people who communicate fluently and naturally in the language to be learned.

Finally, the relationship between the native and second language must be considered. If the two languages are related closely, the second language will be easier to learn. For example, learning English presents fewer problems to the Spanish-speaking student than to a speaker of Cantonese. By knowing about the student's native language, teachers can anticipate possible difficulties in learning English. Because there are many Spanish speakers in our schools today, teachers may need to know about the differences between Spanish and English. These are presented in Table 4.5.

APPROACHES TO SECOND-LANGUAGE LEARNING. Three distinct approaches to second-language learning are (1) the TESL approach, (2) the bilingual approach, and (3) the immersion approach. Each is based on different assumptions, and each has certain advantages.

The acronym TESL stands for "teaching English as a second language." In the TESL approach, students learn by carefully controlled oral repetition of selected second-language patterns. The patterns are repeated, practiced, and memorized. Although attempts are made to make language learning meaningful by using whole sentences, the assumption of TESL is that languages are learned by practicing correct language habits. TESL programs ensure exposure to good second-language models and help students to avoid repeating language mistakes. However, the repetition method may emphasize the correct form of language at the expense of meaningful communication. The TESL model is particularly useful when teaching students of many different language backgrounds.

In the *bilingual* approach, students use their native language for part of the school day and a second language for the remaining portion. An important

Table 4.5 Differences Between Spanish and English

PHONOLOGY OR SOUND CHANGES

In English there are five vowel sounds; in Spanish there are over fourteen; thus Spanish speakers may confuse some English vowels.
The following consonant substitutions may be made:

"j" may become	"ch" as in "chair"
"th" may become	"d" as in "dis" or "s" as in "sigh"

"Voiced" consonants may become unvoiced:

"z" becomes	"s"
"b" becomes	"p"
"d" becomes	"t"
"v" may become	"b"
"use" and "yellow" may become	"juice" and "jello"
"w" in "way" may become	"guay"

SYNTACTIC OR GRAMMATICAL CHANGES

"Not" may become "no."	"He is no going."
Negative auxiliaries may be omitted.	"They no did that."
The progressive tense may become the present tense.	"I am going" becomes "I go."
"It" may be omitted from a sentence.	"It is Tuesday" becomes "Is Tuesday."
Sometimes "to be" is replaced by "to have."	"I have hunger." "I have twenty years."
"Does" and "do" may not be used to form questions.	"Does she have a job?" becomes "She has a job?"

aspect of bilingual programs is strengthening the native language so that it will provide a firm basis for learning a second language (Feitelson, 1979). Thus, academic subjects are taught in the native language, and the second language initially receives only oral practice. Bilingual programs motivate students by respecting their language and culture and by building upon the foundation of their native-language competence. However, the approach is only feasible where large groups of students share one native language and suitable teachers can be found. Since students interact mainly with speakers of their native language, exposure to the second language may not be sufficient for mastery. Bilingual programs have received support through federal funding (see Chapter 14).

In the *immersion* method, students are "immersed" in, or receive extensive exposure to, a second language. In fact, where there is no formal instruction, most individuals simply learn through this type of repeated exposure. Adults who wish to quickly acquire a second language often enroll in commercial programs where they must speak the language for several hours a day. Immersion was formalized as an instructional method for schoolchildren in Canada, where it is used to teach French to English-speaking children by enrolling them in French-speaking schools. The immersion method is most feasible where there are only a few foreign-language speakers who can be exposed easily to fluent second-language speech. The method gives the language learner wide exposure in learning. On the other hand, the immersion method may be uncomfortable for the student, is often unstructured, and does not incorporate the native language and culture.

READING AND THE BILINGUAL STUDENT.   As with other students in our schools, the foreign-language student is expected to learn to read the dominant language, English. Yet, since reading a language depends upon understanding it, teaching reading often presents many problems (Ching, 1976).

A distinction should be drawn between students who can read fluently in their native language and those who cannot. Students who are fluent readers simply need to learn English and then can transfer the reading knowledge they already possess to English. However, if students cannot read in any language, they must learn both to speak English and to read it. Students who come from countries where education is not universal often face these dual tasks.

A controversy exists as to whether reading instruction should be done in the student's native language or in the second language. If students cannot read and do not speak English fluently, reading instruction is often done in the native language. This approach is used widely in bilingual programs. Advocates of the native-language approach feel that, since learning to read is a difficult process, it should first be done in the strongest language. After the student has learned to read, the knowledge can be transferred to the second language, resulting in better long-term effects for academic learning in both languages. Many experimental studies have investigated this approach. Although, in general, teaching reading in the native language has shown positive effects, not all studies have supported this viewpoint. Relevant research is summarized by Engle (1975), Gamez (1979), and Mondiano (1974).

In the immersion approach, students are given reading instruction in the second language. It is assumed that students do not need to be fully fluent in a second language in order to read it and that reading skills and language learning can reinforce one another. Although research on learning to read in this way is not extensive, some studies have shown immersion programs to have positive cognitive and educational effects (Gamez, 1979; Hornby, 1980).

Often, of course, the language of reading instruction is determined by available resources rather than by philosophy. Where there are many students from one language group, reading instruction in the native language is feasible. When students come from many different language backgrounds, or there are only a few foreign-language speakers, English is generally used for reading instruction.

Whatever language is used for instruction, authorities agree that students must have *some* understanding of a language before they can read it effectively. For example, in the immersion approach, students are provided with oral teaching of a second language for one year before it is used in reading instruction. Teachers of students who are learning to read in a second language can help to assure understanding by practicing words and sentences in conversation before students are asked to read them. Perez (1981) found that oral English activities prior to reading a selection significantly improve the reading achievement of students whose native language is Spanish.

SUMMARY

Chapter 4 deals with two correlates of reading: intelligence and language.

Intelligence in the reading diagnosis means the potential for learning to read. Intelligence tests tend to measure scholastic aptitude.

One issue involving intelligence is whether it is most influenced by heredity or environment. The environment perspective, supported by several research studies, maintains that intelligence can be dramatically influenced by environmental conditions. The heredity perspective maintains that intelligence is inherited and is not amenable to environmental modification. In general, the teaching profession assumes that the environment, including teaching, can make a difference.

Another issue concerning intelligence is its composition. Some psychologists believe that intelligence is a general single factor. Others believe it to be composed of component or separate abilities. Some intelligence tests, especially the WISC–R (*Wechsler Intelligence Scale for Children*), have subtests that are useful for gathering information about subabilities.

There is a positive relationship between reading ability and intelligence. Although this relationship holds true for the general population, in individual cases the relationship may not exist.

In interpreting intelligence test scores, several technical terms are used, including *MA* (mental age) and *IQ*. Two kinds of IQs are the *ratio IQ* and the *standard deviation* IQ.

Two ways of determining if a student has a reading disability and should receive special reading instruction are (1) the practical method and (2) the reading discrepancy method.

It is important to assess language ability in a reading diagnosis. Many disabled readers have poor language skills. Oral language includes two modes: oral receptive language (listening) and oral expressive language (speaking).

Linguists have identified four language systems: (1) *phonology* (the sound system of language), (2) *morphology* (the system of expressing meaning through word parts), (3) *syntax* (the sentence structure or grammar form of language), and (4) *semantics* or vocabulary (the words in language). Studies show that some students with reading disabilities have difficulty with one or more of these language systems.

Language problems that can affect reading include speech impairment and language disorders.

Language differences can also affect reading. These include both a nonstandard dialect as well as a different language. Language differences should not be interpreted as language inferiority. The approaches to teaching students a second language include *TESL,* *bilingual instruction,* and *immersion.* Some authorities feel that students should first learn to read in their native language.

Test Inventory 4.1 *Tests of Intelligence and Potential*

AAMD Adaptive Behavior Scale
(Public School Version)
American Association on Mental Deficiency, 1975   *Grades: 2–6*

Determines intellectual aptitude based on tests of total life functioning. Considered more accurate for determining mental deficiency or need for special placement than traditional IQ tests (WISC, Stanford-Binet). While interviewing an informant, an assessment is made of (1) development, including, independent functioning, economic activity, domestic activity, and socialization; and (2) maladaptive behaviors, such as violence, withdrawal, and odd mannerisms. Percentile scores allow for comparison of students in five different school placements.
  Individual administration: 15–20 minutes.

Cognitive Skills Assessment Battery
The Psychological Corporation, 1981 (2nd edition)   *Grades: K–2*

Measures students' mastery of concepts needed for success in primary grades such as, up-down, story comprehension, and parts of the body.
  Oral and individual administration: 15–20 minutes.

California Short-Form Test
of Mental Maturity
California Test Bureau, 1963 (revised)   *Ages: preschool–adult*

Consists of multiple-choice items measuring such things as opposites, analogies, and number problems. Eight levels available. Yields IQ, mental age, standard scores, stanines, and percentiles as well as language and nonlanguage scores.
  Group test: 40–50 minutes.

Culture-Fair Intelligence Tests
Bobbs-Merrill, 1961   *Ages: 8 years–adult*

Nonverbal tests requiring four types of operations: (1) completing a pictorial series, (2) finding a picture that is different, (3) finding the missing part of a pictorial figure, and (4) determining picture relationships. Yields IQ and percentile rank.
  Group test: 25 minutes. Level I for ages 8–14 years; level II for ages 14 years–adult. Two forms available for each level.

The Goodenough-Harris Drawing Test
Harcourt Brace, 1963   *Ages: 3–15 years*

Nonverbal test in which mental ability is assessed through an analysis of the characteristics included in three student drawings: a man, a woman, and a self-portrait. Yields standard scores and percentile ranks.
  Group test: 10–15 minutes.

Hiskey-Nebraska Test of Learning Aptitude

Marshall S. Hiskey, 1966   *Ages: 3-17 years*

Nonverbal test of mental ability often used with mentally retarded, speech-handicapped, bilingual, and deaf students. Two sets of norms, one for pantomimed directions with deaf subjects. Yields learning age scores and learning quotient.
Individual test: 45–60 minutes.

Kuhlman-Anderson Intelligence Tests

Personnel Press, 1967   *Grades: K-12*

Multiple-choice format used to measure IQ. Scores given for verbal, quantitative, and total intelligence. Eight levels available.
Group test: 45 minutes–1 hour.

The Leiter International Performance Scale (LIPS)

Stoelting Company, 1969   *Ages: 2-18 years*

Nonverbal test where student places items on a tray to correspond with picture on stimulus card. Assessment includes the ability to judge the relationship between two events, spatial imagery, and immediate recall. Yields MA score.
Individual test: 1–1$\frac{1}{2}$ hours. Training needed in administration.

Lorge-Thorndike Intelligence Tests

Houghton Mifflin, 1964   *Grades: 3-13*

Measures general intelligence through verbal and nonverbal assessments. Yields an IQ, an age equivalent, grade equivalent, and a grade percentile.
Group test: 1 hour. Two forms available.

The McCarthy Scales of Children's Abilities (MSCA)

The Psychological Corporation, 1972   *Ages: 2 $\frac{1}{2}$-8 $\frac{1}{2}$ years*

Particularly appropriate for young children. Test contains eighteen subtests grouped into six categories: (1) verbal scale, (2) perceptual-performance, (3) quantitative scale, (4) memory scale, (5) motor scale, and (6) general cognitive index. Yields scaled scores and general cognitive index or IQ.
Individual test: 45–60 minutes.

Peabody Picture Vocabulary Test-Revised (PPVT–R)

American Guidance Service, 1981   *Ages: 2 $\frac{1}{2}$-40 years*

Tests verbal ability. Examiner says a word and subject chooses one of four pictures that represents that word. Test yields standard score (distributed as is done for IQ score), age equivalent, percentile, and stanine.
Individual test: 10–20 minutes.

Otis-Lennon School Ability Test (OLSAT)

The Psychological Corporation, 1979   *Grades: 1-12*

Multiple-choice measures of verbal, figural, and numerical reasoning abilities. Two forms (R and S) and five levels are available. Yields an age percentile and stanine score, a grade percentile and stanine score, and a School Ability Index, which has the same statistical properties as an IQ score.
Group test: primary levels, 80 minutes; 4 upper levels, 45 minutes.

Raven Progressive Matrices

STANDARD PROGRESSIVE MATRICES, 1965

COLOURED PROGRESSIVE MATRICES, 1947

ADVANCED PROGRESSIVE MATRICES, 1962

H. K. Lewis and Company　　　　　　　　　　　　　　　　　*Ages: 8–65 years*

Nonverbal tests assessing mental ability through problem solving using abstract figures and designs. The subject is asked to complete visual patterns. The Standard Progressive Matrices are for ages 8–65 years; the Coloured Progressive Matrices are for ages 5–11 years and defective adults; the Advanced Progressive Matrices are for adolescents and adults. Set I is for average ability and Set II is for above-average ability. All tests yield percentile scores.

　　Group or individual administration: approximately 30 minutes needed, but tests are untimed.

Slosson Intelligence Test (SIT)

Slosson Educational Publication, 1981　　　　　　　　　　*Ages: birth–adult*

Based on Stanford Binet IQ Test. A cognitive test that can be administered by teachers. Verbal and some performance items; no reading required. Yields an MA and an IQ score.

　　Individual test: 20–40 minutes.

SRA Primary Mental Abilities Test (PMA)

Science Research Associates, 1965　　　　　　　　　　　　*Grades: K–12*

Assesses five primary mental abilities or factors: (1) verbal meaning, (2) number facility, (3) reasoning, (4) perceptual speed, and (5) spatial relations. Multiple-choice, written format. Yields IQ and mental age. Five levels.

　　Group test: first two levels untimed; remaining levels from 34 to 52 minutes.

Stanford-Binet Intelligence Scale

Houghton Mifflin, 1973　　　　　　　　　　　　　　　　　*Ages: 2 years–adult*

A widely used test representing an adaptation of the first edition in 1916. Consists of a series of subtests each at an age level. Subtest levels begin with two years and end with superior adult III. Each subtest contains six short items assessing cognitive abilities. Items include word meanings, maze tracing, obeying simple commands, and identifying essential differences between two things. Test yields MA and IQ score. One form.

　　Individual test: 1–1$^1/_2$ hours. Specialized training required to administer.

System of Multicultural Pluralistic Assessment (SOMPA)

The Psychological Corporation, 1977　　　　　　　　　　　*Ages: 5–11 years*

An assessment "system" rather than a test. Determines intellectual level and functioning based on a wide variety of measures. Separate norms available for black, Hispanic, and white American students.

　　There are two main parts: the parent interview and the student assessment. The interview contains (1) Sociocultural Scales (information about the family); (2) Adaptive Behavior Inventory for Children (ABIC) (questions about the student's activities); and (3) Health History Inventories. The assessment contains (1) Physical Dexterity Tests, (2) the Bender Visual Motor Gestalt Test, (3) the Wechsler Intelligence Scale for Children-Revised, (4) Weight by Height, (5) Visual Acuity, and (6) Auditory Acuity.

　　Individual administration: about 3 hours. Specialized training required for administering some parts.

Wechsler Intelligence Scales

WECHSLER PRESCHOOL AND PRIMARY SCALE
OF INTELLIGENCE (WIPPSI), 1967   *Ages: 4–6.6*
WECHSLER INTELLIGENCE SCALE
FOR CHILDREN–REVISED (WISC–R), 1974   *Ages: 6–16*
WECHSLER ADULT INTELLIGENCE
SCALE–REVISED (WAIS–R), 1981   *Ages: 15–Adult*

The Psychological Corporation

These scales, along with the Stanford-Binet, represent the most widely used tests of intelligence. Each of the three levels is divided into a verbal and a performance scale. These two scales combine into a total scale. Three scores are available, verbal, performance, and total IQ.

WISC–R: AGES 6–16 YEARS

Verbal scale:
1. Information—answering informational questions.
2. Similarities—noting how two things are alike.
3. Arithmetic—solving timed problems.
4. Vocabulary—defining words.
5. Comprehension—dealing with everyday situations and abstract issues.
6. Repeating Digits—supplementary test.

Performance scale:
1. Picture Completion—determining missing items.
2. Picture Arrangement—sequencing pictures to "tell a story."
3. Block Design—duplicating pictoral design with red and white blocks.
4. Object Assembly—fitting puzzle pieces together.
5. Coding—matching and writing symbols with numbers.
6. Mazes—finding way through a maze (supplementary).

WAIS–R: AGES 16–74 YEARS

Verbal scale: Same as WISC with all six tests required.
Performance scale: Same as WISC but mazes omitted.

WPPSI: AGES 4–6½ YEARS

Verbal scale: Same as WISC but digit span is replaced with sentence repetition.
Performance scale:
1. Picture Completion, Block Design, and Mazes are the same as on the WISC.
2. Animal Houses—matching the color of the animal's house to the animal.
3. Geometric Design—duplicating a design on paper.

Items in arithmetic and all performance subtests are timed. Each subtest is scored individually, allowing for patterns of development to be obtained if manual directions on interpretation are followed. Tests yield IQ scores.

Individual administration: about 45 minutes. Special training needed for administration.

Woodcock-Johnson Psychoeducational Battery
Teaching Resources Corporation, 1977   *Ages: preschool to geriatric*

Evaluates cognitive level through twelve subtests: (1) picture vocabulary, (2) spatial relations, (3) memory for sentences, (4) visual-auditory learning, (5) blending, (6) quantitative concepts, (7) visual matching, (8) antonyms and synonyms, (9) analysis synthesis, (10) numbers reversed, (11) concept formation, and (12) analogies.

Only tests 1 through 6 are used at preschool level. The battery also contains ten achievement subtests and five interest subtests. Yields mental age and grade percentile scores.

Individual test: 1 hour for cognitive tests; complete battery about 2 hours.

Test Inventory 4.2   Tests of Language Development

Brown-Carlsen Listening Comprehension Test
Harcourt Brace, 1955   *Grades: 9–13*

Orally administered sixteen-item test includes assessments of immediate recall, following directions, recognizing transitions, recognizing word meanings, and lecture comprehension. Percentile and standard scores yielded. Forms Am and Bm.

Group test: 50 minutes.

Carrow Elicited Language Inventory
Learning Concepts, 1974   *Ages: 3–7 years*

Grammatical structures are measured by sentence repetition. Errors are tallied according to type (substitutions, omissions, reversals) and grammatical category. Age equivalents, percentiles, and mean are obtained.

Individual test: 10–15 minutes. Usually administered by speech or language therapist.

Carrow Test for Auditory Comprehension of Language
Learning Concepts, 1973   *Ages: 3–6, 6–11 years*

Test assesses receptive comprehension in vocabulary, morphology, and syntax. English and Spanish versions of the test are available. The test yields age equivalent, percentile, and age group scores.

Individual test: 20 minutes. Usually administered by speech or language therapist.

Clinical Evaluation of Language Functions (CELF)
Charles E. Merrill, 1980 (1st edition)   *Grades: K–12.*

Consists of a screening test and a diagnostic battery. The screening test has an elementary (K–5) and an advanced (5–12) level. It measures productive and receptive (called "processing") language. Elementary format is adaptation of "Simon Says"; advanced uses playing cards.

Diagnostic battery contains thirteen tests, including word association, model sentences, and spoken paragraphs. The test yields a percentile rank only.

Individual administration: screening test 15 minutes; diagnostic tests $1\frac{1}{2}$ hours.

Durrell Listening-Reading Series (DLRS)

DURRELL–SULLIVAN READING CAPACITY AND ACHIEVEMENT TESTS

The Psychological Corporation, 1970   *Grades: 1-9*

Tests both reading and listening levels to determine degree of reading retardation. Vocabulary and comprehension assessed in both reading and listening administration. Three levels, two alternate forms. Yields differential scores, percentiles, grade levels, and stanines.

Group test: 2–3 hours.

Goldman-Fristoe Test of Articulation

American Guidance Service, 1972   *Ages: 6-16+ years*

Articulation test measuring sound production in (1) words, (2) sentences, and (3) repetition format. Concentrates on consonant sounds. Yields percentile scores.

Individual test: 10–15 minutes. Usually administered by speech or language therapist.

Northwestern Syntax Screening Test (NSST)

Northwestern University Press, 1971   *Ages: 3-8 years*

Test consists of two parts: receptive and expressive. Yields percentile score.

Individual test: 15 minutes. Usually administered by speech or language therapist.

Picture Story Language Test

Grune & Stratton, 1965   *Ages: 7-17 years*

A developmental scale for written language. Students write a story about a picture and are scored for productivity, syntax, and abstraction of word meanings. Yields mean age score.

Group or individual administration: 20–30 minutes.

Templin-Darley Tests of Articulation

University of Iowa Press, 1969   *Ages: 3-8 years*

Test consists of a screening and diagnostic section measuring production of specific phonemes. Yields means for different ages.

Individual administration: 15–30 minutes. Usually given by speech or language therapist.

Test of Language Development (TOLD)

Pro Ed, 1977   *Ages: 4-11 years*

Five tests assess semantics and syntax in receptive and expressive language. Two supplementary phonology tests assess word discrimination and word articulation. Test yields a language age, scaled score, and linguistic quotient.

Individual administration: 40 minutes.

Utah Test of Language Development (UTLD)

Communication Research Associates, 1967   *Ages: 9 months-16 years*

Test includes receptive and expressive language and some perceptual skills. Yields a language age equivalent and a language quotient.

Individual administration: 30–45 minutes.

85

Woodcock Language Proficiency Battery
ENGLISH FORM
SPANISH FORM

Teaching Resources, 1982   *Ages: 6-13*

This test assesses oral language, reading, and writing. The English test contains eight subtests of the *Woodcock Johnson* (see Test Inventory 5.2). These tests have also been translated into Spanish, and if both the English and Spanish tests are administered, provisions are made for determining the student's dominant language. The subtests can also be used diagnostically. The three oral language subtests are picture vocabulary, antonyms-synonyms, and analogies.

5
ASSESSING READING ACHIEVEMENT I
formal methods

This chapter and Chapter 6 deal with the assessment of reading achievement. This chapter considers formal reading tests, and Chapter 6 discusses informal measures of assessing reading. In addition to the discussion of formal tests of reading, this chapter also describes a two-level framework for assessing reading achievement.

A FRAMEWORK FOR ASSESSING READING ACHIEVEMENT

The sequential phases of the comprehensive reading diagnosis were described in Chapter 2. As noted in that discussion, two essential components within the diagnosis are finding out how well the student can read and determining specific areas of reading strengths and weaknesses. This two-level framework is a useful way of organizing diagnostic information about the student's reading performance. The two assessment levels are (1) general reading assessment and (2) specific, or diagnostic, reading assessment. To assess reading achievement or performance, the teacher first gathers general information on the student's reading ability. Then, a search is made for more specific diagnostic information about the reading problem. This two-level framework, which provides an overall perspective for both Chapters 5 and 6, is illustrated in Table 5.1.

General Reading Assessment

General reading assessment relates to the evaluation of (1) the student's current reading level and (2) the student's performance in the major areas of reading. Major areas of reading include word recognition, comprehension, meaning vocabulary, and, for advanced students, study skills and reading rate. At the completion of the general reading assessment, the teacher should know both how well the student reads and the major areas of reading difficulty. For example, Steve, an eighth grade student, is reading at the sixth grade level, and he shows strengths in word recognition and vocabulary but a weakness in reading comprehension.

Table 5.1 Two Phases for Assessing Reading Abilities

	PHASE 1	PHASE 2
Purpose	General Reading assessment	Diagnostic Reading assessment
Type of information	Level at which student can read	Performance in specific skills
	Performance in major areas of reading	Observation of pupil's strategies and patterns

The purpose of the diagnostic level of reading assessment is to gather more specific information in order to develop an effective teaching plan. Information obtained in the general reading assessment guides the direction of the diagnostic phase. In Steve's case, the diagnostic assessment would probe his specific reading comprehension abilities in greater depth. Assessment in this phase also includes detecting the strategies that Steve uses to gather meaning from the text and determining what instructional comprehension strategies would be most effective.

OVERVIEW OF FORMAL
READING TESTS

There are several types of formal reading tests, each offering a different type of information. To obtain an accurate picture of the pupil's abilities, it is desirable to use a variety of assessment procedures, including formal as well as informal methods (Farr, 1969). Information obtained from one source can corroborate, check, or supplement that from another. The diagnostician's skill consists of analyzing and coordinating all of the diagnostic data to formulate a coherent set of conclusions and recommendations.

Ways of collecting information about reading can be divided into two broad classifications: formal measures (discussed in this chapter) and informal measures (discussed in Chapter 6). In formal testing, the teacher tries to assess the student's reading performance as accurately as possible. Formal testing may rely upon standardized tests (which enable the teacher to compare a student's reading level with that of other students) or commercially published criterion-referenced tests (which enable the teacher to know which specific reading skills the student possesses and which are lacking). In contrast, informal testing concentrates upon observation and the determination of reading strategies. Tests and procedures used in informal testing need not be constructed as stringently or administered according to standardized directions. However, the flexibility allowed in informal testing has the advantage of enabling the teacher to pursue "hunches" and gather a wide variety of information.

By formal tests, we mean commercially prepared, formally developed instruments. Many of these tests are *norm-referenced* or "standardized" tests. By using norm-referenced tests, the scores of a student being tested can be compared with the scores of the sample of students who were used to standardize the test (the "norm sample"). Norm-referenced tests have generally been developed carefully with a large number of students who are representative of the general population. To assure that a student's scores can, in fact, be compared with the norm sample, it is essential that procedures for test administration, scoring, and interpretation be followed strictly.

Other formal instruments are called *criterion-referenced* tests, and these are constructed from a different theoretical base. Rather than comparing students with one another, a criterion-referenced test determines whether a student has mastered certain competencies. Criterion-referenced tests are generally used to assess student mastery of reading skills.

The following discussion of formal tests is organized according to the two-phase framework for assessing reading achievement: (1) formal tests that are used to assess *general* reading abilities (group survey tests, individual survey tests, oral reading tests, and literacy tests) and (2) formal tests that are used for the *specific* or *diagnostic* reading assessment (diagnostic reading batteries and diagnostic tests of specific skills).

TESTS OF GENERAL READING ASSESSMENT

Tests of general reading assessment are used to assess a student's general level of achievement as well as the areas of reading strengths and weaknesses. Types of tests that are used in the general reading assessment phase include (1) group survey tests, (2) individual survey tests, (3) oral reading tests, and (4) literacy tests.

Group Survey Tests

Survey tests are norm-referenced tests that are used to assess the student's reading level. Both group survey tests and individual survey tests are used for this purpose.

Group survey tests are often used by classroom teachers to assess reading (as well as other academic areas) at the end of the year. Examples of group survey tests include the *Stanford Achievement Test* and the *Iowa Test of Basic Skills.* Although they are designed for group testing of developmental readers, they are also useful for testing remedial readers in individual settings. The remedial reader's scores on the group survey test can be compared with those of the norm sample.

The total score on the group survey reading test is usually computed from at least two subtests: (1) a measure of reading vocabulary and (2) a measure of paragraph comprehension. Scores on these subtest sections may be compared to determine the major areas of reading difficulties. For example, a comparison of 12-year-old Katie's vocabulary grade equivalent subtest score of 6.1 with her comprehension subtest score of 3.2 shows a weakness in comprehension in relation to vocabulary. Survey tests for advanced students also measure study skills and reading rate.

A useful feature of most survey tests is that they have more than one form (e.g., Form A and Form B). The two forms are normed similarly and therefore can be compared readily. Progress can be monitored by giving Form A during the diagnosis and Form B after a considerable amount of instruction is completed.

Despite their excellent statistical properties, survey tests have some limitations for use with remedial readers. (1) Generally, the survey test given varies with the grade level of the student. Since most remedial readers read well below grade level, it is difficult to know which level of the survey test to give. For example, should an eighth-grader reading at a third grade level receive the eighth grade level test or the third grade test? This problem is solved to an extent by the "out-of-level" norms provided by some publishers. (2) Some research indicates that scores on group survey tests tend to overestimate the student's reading ability by six months to a year (McCracken, 1962; Sipay, 1946; Jones and Pilusky, 1974).

Individual Survey Tests

Individual survey tests are used widely in assessing the reading level of remedial students. These achievement tests usually consist of one edition, which is suitable for a wide range of reading abilities. Since an individual test might cover levels 1 through 9, it would be suitable for an older reader who is reading at a primary grade level. Individual survey tests are usually standardized and permit valid comparisons with the norm sample.

Administering an individual survey test also allows the teacher to observe the strategies that a reader uses when arriving at answers. For example, in a test of word recognition, the teacher can note whether the student hesitates or recognizes words instantly and whether words are sounded out. Thus, an individual test enables the teacher to gather some diagnostic information in the process of the general reading assessment.

The actual reading tasks that students are asked to perform vary greatly from test to test. Often, test authors use considerable ingenuity to make their tests shorter or to make them conform to a multiple-choice format. Unfortunately, the resulting tests may not measure the ability to actually read. Before using a test, the teacher should inspect the actual items to determine exactly what the student is asked to do. The name of a test, or of its subtests, may not reflect the content.

The three most widely used survey tests are the *Wide Range Achievement Test (WRAT)*, the *Peabody Individual Achievement Test* (PIAT), and the *Woodcock Reading Mastery Test*. The *Wide Range Achievement Test* (WRAT) contains a reading test, consisting of a graded list of words for oral reading. A grade placement level is determined by having the student read this list. Although short and convenient to administer, this subtest does not present a comprehensive assessment of reading abilities. The WRAT also measures mathematics and spelling.

The reading sections of the *Peabody Individual Achievement Test* (PIAT) measure word recognition and comprehension. Word recognition is measured through oral reading on a list; in the reading comprehension subtest, students choose a picture that describes a reading paragraph. The PIAT also measures mathematics, spelling, and general information.

The *Woodcock Reading Mastery Tests* is a more complete individual survey test, allowing for comparisons of five subtests and covering reading levels 1 through 8. The test is standardized and yields three reading scores (independent, instructional, and frustration) for each subtest, plus a "confidence band" for each

INTERPRETATION OF TEST RESULTS / FORM A

SUMMARY OF SCORES

Subject's Grade Placement (G) _____

SPECIAL INSTRUCTIONS

1 Assume a mastery score of 173 for pupils reading at grade six or above who were not administered the Letter Identification Test.

2 Total reading score is based on the average mastery score for the five tests.

3 Double-check all arithmetic calculations.

4 Complete the Mastery Profile as follows:

  a) place dots within each bar to represent points E, R, and F

  b) draw a double-ended arrow (⟶) between each pair of E and F points to represent the instructional range

  c) record, above the bar, the percent of mastery for each E, R, and F point

  d) using a different color, place an "X" within each bar to represent point G

  e) record, below each bar, the percent of mastery at G.

		RAW SCORES AND MASTERY SCORES	READING GRADE LEVELS AND RELATIVE MASTERY LEVELS									PERCENTILE RANKS
TEST	Raw Score	(MS) Mastery Score TABLE I	(E) Easy Reading Level TABLE I	Relative Mastery at E	(R) Reading Grade Score TABLE I	Relative Mastery at R	(F) Failure Reading Level TABLE I	Relative Mastery at F	(MSG) Mastery Score at G TABLE II	(MS)−(MSG) Achievement Index (Indicate + or −)	Relative Mastery at G TABLE III	Percentile Ranks TABLE III
Letter Identification .... (45)	___	[ ]¹	___	96%	[ ]	90%	___	75%	___	___ ³	___ %	[ ]
Word Identification ....(150)	___	[ ]	___	96%	[ ]	90%	___	75%	___	___ ³	___ %	[ ]
Word Attack .... (50)	___	[ ]	___	96%	[ ]	90%	___	75%	___	___ **3**	___ %	[ ]
Word Comprehension .... (70)	___	[ ]	___	96%	[ ]	90%	___	75%	___	___ ³	___ %	[ ]
Passage Comprehension .... (85)	___	[ ]	___	96%	[ ]	90%	___	75%	___	___ ³	___ %	[ ]
	(Total)											
TOTAL READING² .... (Total ÷ 5)	___³	[ ]	___	96%	[ ]	90%	___	75%	___	___ ³	___ %	[ ]

Figure 5.1 Scoring Sheet for Woodcock Reading Mastery Tests

subtest. The scoring sheet is reproduced in Figure 5.1, which appears on page 92. During administration, the testing material stands upright on a table in an easel format, enabling the teacher to read directions from one side and students to read from the other. Three of the five subtests of the Woodcock have been questioned (Laffey and Kelly, 1979). First, the letter identification subtest does not seem appropriate past primary reading levels. Woodcock (1982) acknowledges this and states that the letter subtest is not statistically important in calculating scores past the primary level. Second, the vocabulary subtest consists of analogies rather than testing simply vocabulary knowledge. Third, the comprehension test uses a "cloze," (fill-in-the-blank) procedure. Thus, while the test has many strengths, the teacher must be aware of the specific tasks required of the reader. (Individual survey tests are further described in Test Inventory 5.1, which is located at the end of the chapter.)

Oral Reading Tests

Oral reading tests provide another excellent way in which to obtain a general reading assessment. These are individual tests consisting of graded passages for oral reading. Oral reading tests have two advantages for remedial assessment. First, the student's reading level is judged from actual samples of oral reading behavior, using a task that is actually used in the classroom. Second, the teacher can observe a student's reading closely and analyze the strategies that the student uses. In this way, considerable diagnostic information can be gathered. Because of these advantages, oral reading tests are used widely in the reading diagnosis.

Several tests of oral reading are available commercially. Some, such as the *Gilmore Oral Reading Test* and the *Gray Oral Reading Test*, are norm referenced. Others are nonnormed "informal reading inventories." Finally, some diagnostic reading batteries contain oral reading tests. Regardless of the form of the oral reading inventory, it is an excellent way to gain information about reading.

The analysis of oral reading behaviors and the rich diagnostic insights they provide are discussed in Chapter 6. Test Inventory 5.1, which is located at the end of the chapter, includes a description of published tests of oral reading.

Literacy Tests

Literacy tests are often used for the general reading assessment of older remedial readers who read at low levels. An increasing awareness of the problems of adolescent and adult illiterates has resulted in a number of tests that measure the ability to read functional material for everyday living. Material on these tests measure such skills as reading traffic signs, menus, and bills. These tests are often used in assessing minimal competencies for graduation requirements (see Chapter 14).

Some literacy tests are norm referenced; others are criterion referenced. Criterion-referenced tests are appropriate for use when the teacher wishes to determine whether or not a person possesses the skills to function in society. Literacy tests are described further in Test Inventory 5.1 at the end of this chapter.

TESTS FOR DIAGNOSING
SPECIFIC READING PROBLEMS

Diagnostic reading tests yield more specific information than general reading tests. They provide a more detailed analysis of specific reading strengths and weaknesses and often permit the teacher to assess student strategies in reading. Two kinds of diagnostic tests described in this section are (1) diagnostic reading batteries and (2) diagnostic tests of specific skills.

Diagnostic Reading Batteries

The diagnostic reading battery consists of a group of subtests, each of which assesses a different skill. It is therefore useful for obtaining a "profile" of the remedial student in several areas.

Diagnostic reading batteries evaluate such areas as oral reading, phonics, and sight vocabulary. Some contain complete oral reading tests, enabling the teacher to both administer an oral reading inventory and assess a wide variety of other skills. Areas such as spelling may be covered as well. While most batteries are individual tests, some are group tests (e.g., the *Botel Reading Inventory*). Many tests contain extensive teachers' manuals with information on interpretation of scores, error analysis, and provisions for culturally different students.

Although these batteries sample many skills, they are often better in the areas of readiness and word recognition than in comprehension and meaning vocabulary. Typically, diagnostic batteries are more suitable for lower-level readers.

Some caution must be used when giving a diagnostic battery. Although the tests are quite useful, they cannot substitute for teacher observation and analysis of the reading problem. The teacher may not wish to administer an entire test, but just give the sections relevant to that student. Finally, the teacher should examine the items on the subtests to ensure that they are actually testing the skills that are named.

Some diagnostic batteries are normed, whereas others (e.g., the *BRIGANCE®* Diagnostic Inventory) are criterion referenced. While norming is useful, the norms for diagnostic batteries are seldom constructed as carefully as are those of survey tests. Thus, teachers should inspect the norming procedures of batteries carefully before placing confidence in them.

The *Gates-McKillop-Horowitz Reading Diagnostic Test* is an illustration of a diagnostic battery. The eight distinct parts of the test are illustrated by the scoring sheet reproduced in Figure 5.2. The battery contains an oral reading inventory, several tests of word recognition and readiness, and an assessment of spelling and writing. The oral reading test consists of one continuous passage that increases in difficulty. Thus, there are only thirty words on any specific grade level. The grade placement score is based solely on oral reading, for no comprehension questions are asked. The many tests of sight vocabulary, phonics, and readiness require diverse tasks. Some involve primarily listening skills (such as the test of spoken

PUPIL RECORD BOOKLET

Gates • McKillop • Horowitz
READING DIAGNOSTIC TESTS

SECOND EDITION

ARTHUR I. GATES
Professor Emeritus of Education

ANNE S. McKILLOP
Professor of Education

ELIZABETH CLIFF HOROWITZ
Adjunct Assistant Professor of Education

TEACHERS COLLEGE, COLUMBIA UNIVERSITY

Pupil's Name _____ School _____ Date _____

Age____ Birthday_____ Grade_____ Examiner_____ Teacher_____

Age, Grade, Intelligence		**READING AND OTHER TEST SCORES**			**1** Raw Score	**2** Grade Score	**3** Ratings ( ) ( )
Chronological Age	_____						
Grade Corresponding to Chronological Age	_____	Name of Test		Date Given			
Actual Grade	_____	1 _____					
Intelligence Testing: Name of I.Q. Test	_____	2 _____					
Date Administered	_____	3 _____					
I.Q.	_____						

READING DIAGNOSTIC TESTS

	Raw Score	Grade Score	Ratings ( ) ( )		Raw Score	Grade Score	Ratings ( ) ( )
Oral Reading				**Knowledge of Word Parts: Word Attack**			
Analysis of Total Errors				Syllabication			
Omissions				Recognizing & Blending Common Word Parts			
Additions				Reading Words			
Repetitions				Giving Letter Sounds			
Analysis of Mispronunciations				Naming Capital Letters			
Directional Errors				Naming Lower-Case Letters			
Wrong Beginning				**Recognizing the Visual Form of Sounds**			
Wrong Middle				Vowels			
Wrong Ending				**Auditory Tests**			
Wrong in Several Parts				Auditory Blending			
Accent Errors				Auditory Discrimination			
Total Mispronunciation Errors				**Written Expression**			
Reading Sentences				Spelling			
Words: Flash				Informal Writing Sample			
Words: Untimed							

Figure 5.2 Scoring Sheet for the Gates-McKillop-Horowitz Reading Diagnostic Test

vowel sounds); others assess actual reading skills. The inclusion of spelling and writing subtests reflects new trends toward viewing reading in a broader context. This battery was standardized on only 600 students, a small sample compared with survey tests. In sum, the *Gates-McKillop-Horowitz* assesses a wide variety of skills in many different ways.

The BRIGANCE® Inventories are another widely-used set of diagnostic batteries. These include (1) the *Preschool Inventory* (yellow version), (2) the *Diagnostic Inventory of Basic Skills* for grades 1–6 (blue version), (3) the *Inventory of Essential Skills* for high school (red), and (4) the *Comprehensive Inventory of Basic Skills* for grades 1–9. We will describe the *Brigance Diagnostic Inventory of Basic Skills* (grades 1–6) here.

The *Brigance Diagnostic Inventory* is a criterion-referenced test containing no norms. It covers a wide range of skills in readiness, reading, language arts, and math. The topics covered by the reading section are reproduced in Figure 5.3. Section B contains graded oral reading passages in the form of an IRI.

A student's performance on any subtest of the *Brigance Diagnostic Inventory* can be *directly* translated into an instructional objective. For example, if students do not "pass" the Long Vowel Subtest of the *Brigance Diagnostic Inventory*, the test provides a specific objective for them to master.

> When presented with one syllable words having the patterns "consonant, vowel-consonant, and final e" or "consonant, double vowel, consonant," the student will pronounce the vowel(s) with a long sound. He will be able to perform this task for _____ (quantity) of the five vowels. (Brigance, 1977, p. 54)

Thus, performance on a subtest may be immediately transferred to a specific goal. This feature makes the *Brigance Diagnostic Inventory* valuable for writing the Individual Education Programs (IEP's) required for special education students. It also helps reading teachers to formulate direct instructional goals.

Despite the convenience of this test, it should be remembered that it has no developed norms or studies of reliability and validity. Thus, while the *Brigance Diagnostic Inventory* is diagnostically useful, the teacher cannot assume that it will place students at appropriate grade levels. (Diagnostic batteries are described further in Test Inventory 5.1 at the end of the chapter.)

Diagnostic Tests of Specific Skills

Unlike diagnostic reading batteries, tests of specific skills concentrate on the in-depth evaluation of a specific reading skill. The tests are particularly useful in gathering very detailed information about reading subskills, such as phonics. Diagnostic skills tests may be group or individual. Some provide norm-referenced scores, some provide criterion-referenced scores, and some provide both. Tests of specific skills include, for example, the *Instant Word Recognition Test* and the *Phonics Knowledge Survey*. Commonly used specific skills diagnostic tests are presented in Test Inventory 5.1.

II. READING

Test	Title
A.	**Word Recognition**
A-1	Word Recognition Grade Level
A-2	Basic Sight Vocabulary
A-3	Direction Words
A-4	Abbreviations
A-5	Contractions
A-6	Common Signs
B.	**Reading**
B-1	Oral Reading Level
B-2	Reading Comprehension Level
B-3	Oral Reading Rate
C.	**Word Analysis**
C-1	Auditory Discrimination

Test	Title
C-2	Initial Consonant Sounds Auditorily
C-3	Initial Consonant Sounds Visually
C-4	Substitution of Initial Consonant Sounds
C-5	Ending Sounds Auditorily
C-6	Vowels
C-7	Short Vowel Sounds
C-8	Long Vowel Sounds
C-9	Initial Clusters Auditorily
C-10	Initial Clusters Visually
C-11	Substitution of Initial Cluster Sounds
C-12	Digraphs and Diphthongs
C-13	Phonetic Irregularities

Test	Title
C-14	Common Endings of Rhyming Words
C-15	Suffixes
C-16	Prefixes
C-17	Meaning of Prefixes
C-18	Number of Syllables Auditorily
C-19	Syllabication Concepts
D.	**Vocabulary**
D-1	Context Clues
D-2	Classification
D-3	Analogies
D-4	Antonyms
D-5	Homonyms

©1976, 1977 Curriculum Associates, Inc.

Figure 5.3 BRIGANCE® Diagnostic Inventory of Basic Skills—Reading Sections

Reprinted with the permission of the publisher, Curriculum Associates, Inc., North Billerica, MA. 01862.

INTERPRETING SCORES
ON READING TESTS

The manuals of formal tests provide important information. This includes tables of test scores, information about the development of the test, and data about its standardization, validity, and reliability. Formal tests may be divided into norm-referenced tests and criterion-referenced tests.

Norm-Referenced Tests

As stated earlier, norm-referenced tests are standardized on representative samples of students. Using a norm-referenced test, a student's performance can be compared with other students of the same grade or age level.

Raw scores are converted into meaningful scores for interpreting reading performance. Scores on norm-referenced tests are reported in several ways. Types of scores include the reading grade score, reading age score, percentiles, and stanines. In addition, norm-referenced tests generally report standardization, validity, and reliability.

READING GRADE SCORE. This score indicates how well the student reads in terms of grade level. For example a score of 4.5 (fifth month of the fourth grade) indicates that the student correctly answered the same number of questions as the average pupil in the fifth month of the fourth grade. The International Reading Association (1981) warns about the misuse and misinterpretation of grade equivalent scores. Reading grade scores do not indicate an absolute performance; rather, they indicate how the student performed in relation to the students in the norm sample population.

READING AGE SCORE. This score is similar to a reading grade score except that the norms are developed according to the *age* of the pupils in the normed sample (rather than their grade levels). A score of 8–10 indicates that the student answered correctly the same number of questions as the average student in the norm sample of eight years, ten months of age.

PERCENTILES. Percentile scores, sometimes called centiles, describe the scores of the student in relation to the scores of others in the same age or grade. Percentiles can be understood as ranks in groups of 100, expressed in numbers from 1 to 99. A percentile score of 57 shows that the student scored higher than 57 percent of the comparison group and lower than 42 percent. The fiftieth percentile is the average, or median, for the age or grade group to which the student is being compared. The higher the percentile (the highest is 99) the better the student's performance.

Equal distances in percentiles, however, do not indicate equal differences in raw score points. Since many scores center near the mean, the difference between the fiftieth and sixtieth percentiles may be only a few raw score points, whereas the distance between the eightieth and ninetieth percentiles may be a great many raw score points on the test.

STANINES.   The stanine score ranks pupils of a given age or grade from 1 to 9. The lowest stanine score is 1, the median stanine is 5, and the highest is 9. Stanine scores are assigned so that the result represents a normal distribution. Thus, in an average class, most students will receive stanine scores of 4, 5, or 6, and few will receive stanine scores of 1 to 9.

The name "stanine" is a contraction of "standard nine" and is based on the fact that the score runs from 1 to 9. Stanines are normalized standard scores with a mean of 5 and a standard deviation of 2. Figure 5.4 shows the percentage of students in each stanine.

NORMAL CURVE EQUIVALENT SCORES (NCE).   NCE scores are similar to percentiles in that they have a range from 1 to 99 and a mean of 50. They differ from percentile scores because they have been transformed into equal units of reading achievement. For example, a difference of ten NCE units always represents the same difference in reading achievement.

STANDARDIZATION.   Teachers are often called upon to choose tests for remedial readers. Among the factors to be considered in judging the value of a norm referenced test are the test's standardization, validity, and reliability.

To standardize a test, it is given to a large representative group of students (the norm sample). Based on data derived from this norm sample, then, inferences are made about other students who take the test.

In making a judgment about the value of the test, the teacher can consider the characteristics of the individuals who comprised the norm sample. Was the sample size adequate? Was the makeup of the sample representative of the students who are being tested? If the norm sample population is not considered representative, some school districts develop their own local norms. The student being tested can then be compared with other students in the school district.

VALIDITY.   Validity refers to whether a test measures what it is supposed to measure. There are at least two types of validity: (1) content validity and (2) predictive validity. Content validity involves inspecting the test to see if the items seem valid for the testing purposes. For example, a valid reading comprehension

% in stanine

Figure 5.4   Percent of Students in Each Stanine.

test would probably contain paragraphs with questions. A comprehension test that required the student to match words would have questionable content validity.

Predictive validity refers to how the test compares with some other aspect of achievement. Most norm referenced reading tests provide information about the comparison of performance on the reading test with some aspect of school achievement (for example, grade point average). The comparison is usually done in the form of a statistical correlation. This correlation may range from +1.0 (a very positive correlation) to –1.0 (a very negative correlation). For acceptable predictive validity, the correlation should be positive and high (generally above + .70).

RELIABILITY.   Reliability refers to the constancy and stability of test scores. There are two forms of reliability (1) test-retest reliability and (2) internal reliability. In test-retest reliability, the test is given to a group of students two times. Then the scores are correlated to determine if individual students perform about the same on the first and second administrations.

In internal reliability, a student's performance on the items from one-half of the test is correlated with performance on the items from the other half of the test. For both types of reliability, the reliability correlation on an acceptable test should be above +.70. This type of reliability is often called "split half."

OUT-OF-LEVEL TESTING.   Remedial readers often must be given tests that are appropriate for their reading level but not for their age level. For example, George, an eleven-year-old student in the sixth grade, was given a third grade test because he could not read the sixth grade test. The problem encountered in "out-of-level" testing is that the third grade test was normed on an eight-year-old population (not with the scores of eleven-year-olds). George's score shows how he compares with eight-year-olds, not with eleven-year-olds. This is more of a problem for group tests, which are usually designed for developmental assessment of groups, than it is for individual tests, which are designed for assessment of individual remedial readers. Publishers of some group tests, such as the Gates McGinitie, provide tables for out-of-level norms, if requested.

Criterion-Referenced Tests

In contrast to norm-referenced tests, which compare students with a normed sample of other students, criterion-referenced tests offer a measure of the student's mastery of specific reading skills. For example, can the student recognize "ing" endings? Can the student find the main idea in a paragraph? To develop a criterion-referenced test, the test author must designate a hierarchy or ordered set of specific developmental reading skills. The student's reading ability is judged by how many of these sequential reading skills have been mastered.

An analogy can be drawn to another area of learning—swimming. In norm-referenced terms, a child can be tested in swimming and judged to swim as well as the average nine-year-old. In criterion-referenced terms, a child is judged as being able to do certain instructional tasks, such as putting one's face in the water, floating on one's back, and doing the crawl stroke. In other words, criterion-referenced tests measure mastery rather than grade level, or they *describe* rather than *compare* performance.

Criterion-referenced tests are useful because they provide a means of accountability. While it is often difficult to show that a student has improved in terms of percentiles, stanines, or even grade level scores, the teacher can show that the student has learned certain specific skills in terms of mastery of criterion-referenced measures.

Criterion-referenced tests have been criticized on the grounds that (1) they require a great deal of time in terms of record keeping, (2) students may pass the various skill tests but be unable to transfer the skills to reading situations, and (3) there is no agreed-upon sequence of reading skills.

Since criterion-referenced tests are being selected by many school districts as a measure for providing accountability, publishers are increasingly developing and marketing this type of instrument. Several criterion-referenced tests used in the reading diagnosis are listed in Text Inventory 5.1. In addition to these tests, publishers have developed large-scale criterion-referenced management systems for reading instruction. These include

- Diagnosis: An Instructional Aid (SRA)
- Fountain Valley Teacher Support System in Reading (Zweig)
- Individual Pupil Monitoring System (Riverside)
- Prescriptive Reading Inventory (CTB/McGraw-Hill)
- Skills Monitoring System-Reading (Psychological Corp.)
- System for Objective-Based Assessment (SRA)
- Wisconsin Tests of Reading Skill Development (National Computer Systems)

SUMMARY

This chapter discusses assessment of reading achievement through the use of formal tests. (Chapter 6 continues the discussion of the assessment of reading achievement through informal measures.)

A two-level framework for diagnosing reading problems is suggested. It consists of (1) general reading assessment and (2) specific diagnostic assessment. General reading assessment refers to the student's current level of reading ability and performance in the major areas of reading. Specific diagnostic assessment refers to the in-depth analysis of specific areas of reading.

Formal reading tests are commercially prepared instruments. They may be divided into norm-referenced tests (which compare students with a representative sample of other students) and criterion-referenced tests (which measure mastery of specific skills).

Many kinds of tests can be used for general reading assessment, including group survey tests, individual survey tests, oral reading tests, and literacy tests.

Tests for diagnosing specific reading problems include diagnostic reading batteries and diagnostic tests of specific skills.

When interpreting test scores, it is important to distinguish between norm-referenced and criterion-referenced tests.

The kinds of information reported in the manuals of norm-referenced tests include reading grade scores, reading age scores, percentiles, stanines, and normal curve equivalent scores. Validity and reliability statistics give the user information on the value of the test. Validity refers to whether a test measures what it says it is measuring. Reliability refers to the constancy of test scores. Out-of-level testing refers to cases in which poor readers take tests that are appropriate for their reading level, but are intended for younger students.

Several formal tests of reading ability are criterion-referenced. In addition, several criterion-referenced management systems for instruction have been published.

Test Inventory 5-1   Tests Commonly Used in the Reading Diagnosis

The tests listed in this table have been divided into the following categories.

- Survey tests
- Oral reading tests
- Informal reading inventories
- Oral reading miscue analysis
- Diagnostic batteries
- Diagnostic: Specific skills
- Literacy tests

If a test fits into more than one category, this is indicated. Dates of publication are for most recent editions of the tests.

Adult Basic Learning Examination (ABLE)   *Literacy Test*
The Psychological Corporation, 1974   *Ages: Adult*

For adults with limited reading skills. Measures oral vocabulary and reading comprehension. Also measures problem solving, spelling, and arithmetic computation. Two forms (A, B). Three levels: I, achievement, grades 1–6; II, grades 3–9; III grades 9–12.

Adult Basic Reading Inventory   *Literacy Test*
Scholastic Testing Services, 1966   *Grades: 6–12*

This analytic reading test for the functionally illiterate identifies severely illiterate adolescents and adults and those able to function at a fourth to fifth grade level. Contains (1) simple vocabulary where picture and word are matched, (2) test of matching dictated beginning sounds to printed words, (3) four lists of grade two to five vocabulary words to match with synonyms, (4) same words as part three read aloud to determine if listening vocabulary exceeds reading vocabulary, and (5) contextual material, stories, and questions on a third through fifth grade level.

Group test recommended for adult basic education classes: 60 minutes. One form.

Analytical Reading Inventory
Charles E. Merrill, 1981

Informal Reading Inventory

Grades: 1–9

Contains word recognition test (P–6) and oral reading passages for primer through grade nine. Six to eight comprehension questions following each passage: main idea, fact, terminology, cause and effect, inference, conclusion. Yields independent, instruction, frustration reading levels, listening, analysis of miscues, comprehension analyses. Longest passage is 339 words.

Individual test: 20–30 minutes. Three equivalent forms in one spiral notebook.

Basic Reading Inventory
Kendall/Hunt, 1978

Informal Reading Inventory

Grades: PP–8

Contains word recognition lists (PP–8) and reading passages from preprimer to grade eight. Five to eight comprehension questions following each passage: literal, critical, main idea, vocabulary. Uses facets of psycholinguistic miscue analysis in scoring. Yields independent, instructional, and frustration reading levels. Longest passage is 100 words.

Individual test: 20–30 minutes. Three forms.

Botel Reading Inventory
Follett, 1978

Diagnostic Reading Battery

Grades: 1–12

Used as a placement test, progress test, or test to check mastery. Includes a decoding test, spelling placement test, and a reading placement test. The first two tests diagnose the student's mastery of common syllable/spelling patterns. The word recognition test gives an estimate of oral reading abilities. The word opposites test gives an estimate of reading comprehension. The instructional level is the first level where score falls below 80 percent and remains below 80 percent.

Group test for spelling and word opposites. Individual test for word recognition.

Untimed: about 20 minutes. Two forms. Independent, instructional, and frustration levels determined.

BRIGANCE® Diagnostic Inventory of Basic Skills
Curriculum Associates, 1977

Diagnostic Battery

Grades: 1–6

Contains 141 criterion-referenced subtests for reading, readiness, and reference skills as well as for math, handwriting, spelling, and grammar. Used for assessing skill levels between grades one to six and very useful for remedial students. Subtests include twenty-four for readiness, six for word recognition, three for reading (oral reading level, comprehension, and oral reading rate), nineteen for word analysis, five for vocabulary, and nine for reference. Contained in easy-to-administer binder with student's copy and examiner's on opposite pages. Yields ratings of satisfactory/needs to improve for given grade level. Subtests coordinated with IEP rating system.

Individual test: 15–90 minutes. One form. (Also *Brigance Inventory of Essential Skills* for high school, *Brigance Preschool Inventory*, and *Comprehensive Inventory of Basic Skills* for grades 1–9.)

Classroom Reading Inventory (Silvaroli)
William C. Brown, 1979

Informal Reading Inventory

Grades: 1–8

Contains graded word lists (PP–8), graded oral paragraphs with five comprehension questions for grades preprimer to eight, and optional graded spelling survey. Yields independent, instructional, frustration reading levels, hearing level, rate, and analysis of oral reading errors. Longest passage 174 words.

Individual test: 12–20 minutes. Three forms in one spiral notebook.

Contemporary Classroom Inventory   *Informal Reading Inventory*
Gorsuch, Scarisbrick, 1980   *Grades: 2–9*

Contains graded word lists (P–6) and graded fiction, social studies, and science reading selections for primer through ninth grade. Five to eight comprehension questions following each passage: main idea, detail, inference, vocabulary, evaluation, and reasoning. Yields independent, instructional, frustration reading levels, listening level, analysis of oral reading errors. Also contains cloze selections for grades four through nine. Longest passage 316 words.

Individual test: 30–40 minutes. Three forms in one spiral notebook: (1) fiction, (2) social science, (3) science.

Corrective Reading System   *Diagnostic: Specific Skills*
Psychotechnic, 1976   *Grades: 1–6*

Tests sight words, phonics, and structural analysis as aid in individualizing instruction. Includes upper and lower case letter identification; basic sight word knowledge; phoneme knowledge of approximately eighty high-utility graphemes including consonants, vowels, digraphs, blends, dipthongs, "r"-controlled vowels, silent consonants, and sounds of "y"; word endings; vowel rules; syllabication principles; accent generalizations; contractions; suffixes; prefixes; and dictionary skills. Nonsense words used for testing. Criterion-referenced test. *No norms.*

Individual test: time varies. One form.

Diagnostic Reading Scales (Spache)   *Diagnostic Battery*
California Test Bureau, 1981   *(with informal reading inventory)*

Samples word recognition, passage reading, comprehension, and phonics knowledge through three graded word lists and two sets of graded selections containing eleven passages from levels 1.4 to 7.5, each followed by comprehension questions. Twelve supplementary tests of word analysis: initial consonants, final consonants, consonant digraphs, consonant blends, initial consonant substitutions, auditory recognition of initial consonant sounds, auditory discrimination, short and long vowels, "r"-controlled vowels, vowel dipthongs and digraphs, common phonograms, and blending. Phonics tests use nonsense words to fourth grade, then real words. Oral reading level called "instructional" level; silent reading level is higher and considered "independent." Yields independent (silent), instructional (oral), and frustration reading levels, listening level, and grade equivalent for phonics tests.

Individual tests: 20–30 minutes. Two forms of reading passages in one binder.

Doren Diagnostic Reading Test of Word Recognition Skills   *Diagnostic: Specific Skills*
American Guidance Service, 1973   *Grades: 1–3*

Measures twelve specific areas for remedial readers. Each skill is arranged from simple to complex. Subtests include letter recognition, beginning sounds, whole word recognition, words within words, speech consonants such as the difference between "ch" and "sh," ending sounds, blending, rhyming, vowels, discriminate guessing, spelling, and sight words. Criterion references with overlay correcting form for scoring. Remedial activities presented in manual. Individual skill profiles contain ratings for satisfactory/not satisfactory for each area.

Group test: 60–180 minutes. One form.

Durrell Analysis of Reading Difficulty

Diagnostic Battery
(with oral reading test)

The Psychological Corporation, 1980　　　*Grades: 1–6*

Contains (1) eight short, progressively harder paragraphs for oral reading from which rate and comprehension (using questions) are determined, (2) eight short paragraphs for silent reading from which reading rate and free recall are determined, (3) six paragraphs to determine listening comprehension, (4) two sets of isolated word lists to analyze instant recognition (tachistoscopic) and word analysis, (5) other subtests including listening vocabulary, visual memory for words, identifying sounds in words, sounds in isolation, phonic spelling of words, prereading phonics abilities, and spelling ability. Subtests administered vary. Yields grade equivalent scores.

　Individual test: 30–90 minutes. One form.

Ekwall Reading Inventory

Informal Reading Inventory

Allyn & Bacon, 1979　　　*Grades: 1–9*

Contains word recognition test (PP–9) and passages for oral and silent reading from preprimer through grade nine. Comprehension questions following passages: literal, inference, vocabulary. Oral and silent reading are presented alternately at each level. Testing continues in one mode if frustration level is reached in the other. Yields independent, instructional, frustration reading levels. Also contains El Paso Phonics Survey. Longest passage 202 words.

　Individual test: 20–30 minutes. Four forms available in one binder.

Gates-McKillop-Horowitz Reading Diagnostic Tests

Diagnostic Battery
(with oral reading test)

Teachers College Press, 1981　　　*Grades: 1–6*

Tests oral reading, sight knowledge, phonics, spelling, and writing. Contains (1) continuous set of graded short oral reading paragraphs; (2) four reading sentences with regular words; (3) flashwords presented with tachistoscope; (4) untimed word list for sight recognition or analysis; (5) tests of word attack using nonsense words: syllabication, recognizing and blending word parts, reading words, letter sounds, and naming capital and lowercase letters; (6) test of identifying spoken vowel sounds; (7) test of auditory blending and discrimination; and (8) spelling test and informal writing sample. Yields grade equivalent scores and informal ratings. Also analysis of oral reading errors, phonics.

　Individual test: 60–90 minutes. One form.

Gilmore Oral Reading Test, New Ed. (GORT)

Oral Reading Test

The Psychological Corporation, 1968　　　*Grades: 1–8*

Tests oral reading using ten graded paragraphs each followed by five comprehension questions. Yields grade equivalent, stanines, and percentiles for oral reading, comprehension, and rate.

　Individual test: 15–20 minutes. Four forms, each in separate booklet.

Gray Oral Reading Tests

Oral Reading Test

The Psychological Corporation, 1967　　　*Grades: P–12*

Measures oral reading through thirteen timed, graded reading passages each followed by four comprehension questions. Only errors in word pronunciation and rate count toward grade placement level. Test yields grade placement score. Separate norms for girls and boys. Checklist of oral reading habits and errors provided.

　Individual test: 15–20 minutes. Four forms, each in a separate booklet.

Group Phonics Analysis (GPA)   *Diagnostic: Specific Skills*
Dreier Educational Systems, 1971   *Grades: 1–3*

Criterion-referenced test assessing basic phonics skills that are presented in developmental order. Covers number reading, letter reading, consonant sounds, alphabetizing, recognizing long and short vowels, and the use of vowel sound rules. No norms.

Group test: 20–30 minutes. One form.

Informal Reading Assessment Tests   *Informal Reading Inventory*
Houghton Mifflin, 1980   *Grades: 1–12*

Contains word recognition tests (PP–8) and reading passages from preprimer through twelfth. Eight to ten comprehension questions following each passage: main idea, detail, sequence, cause and effect, inference, and vocabulary. Yields independent, instructional, and frustration reading levels, listening levels, oral reading error analysis, comprehension analysis. Longest passage: 217 words.

Individual test: 30 minutes. Four forms in one paperback binding.

Instant Word Recognition Test   *Diagnostic: Specific Skills*
Jamestown Publishers, 1971   *Grades: 1–3*

Self-scoring, criterion-referenced test of sight recognition of words selected from frequency count of words in reading materials. Two levels, lower and upper, are both contained on one page. Examiner reads twenty-four sentences at each level. Student selects one of five words for each sentence. The 600 instant words are presented in graded lists in the manual.

Individual or group test: 20–30 minutes. Two forms.

A Look at Literature   *Diagnostic: Specific Skills*
Addision-Wesley, 1969   *Grades: 4–6*

Measures the appreciation of literature, prose, and poetry. Students react to short selections from children's literature. Questions measure comprehension, perception of literary qualities, and extension of meaning. Fifty multiple-choice questions are divided into two sections: part 1, which is read by the teacher, and part 2, which is read silently by the student. Yields raw and converted score.

Group test: 60–70 minutes. Two forms.

McCarthy Individualized Diagnostic Reading Inventory   *Informal Reading Inventory*
Educators Publishing Service, 1976   *Grades: 2–12*

Contains reading passages from primer through twelfth, followed by questions itemized into specific skills and an optional survey of basic phonics skills. Yields inventory of student strengths and weaknesses.

Individual test: 60–90 minutes. One form.

McCullough Word Analysis Test   *Diagnostic: Specific Skills*
Personnel Press, 1963   *Grades: 4–5*

Assesses phonic and structural analysis skills through seven subtests of thirty items each. Subtests include initial blends and digraphs, phonetic discrimination (vowels), matching letters to vowel sounds, sounding whole words, interpreting phonetic symbols, dividing words into syllables and root words in affixed forms. Yields percentiles for each grade. Useful for diagnostic information.

Individual or group test: 60–70 minutes. One form.

Monroe Diagnostic Reading Test

Stoelting Company, 1928

Diagnostic Battery
Grades: Remedial students, any grade

Analytic tests include alphabet reading, word recognition, and oral reading as well as recognition of orientation, mirror reading, mirror writing, number reversals, word discrimination, sounding, and "b," "d," "p," "q," "u," "n" test. Yields profile of errors.

Individual test: untimed. One form.

Nelson Reading Skills Test
Nelson Silent Reading Test: Vocabulary and Paragraph

Riverside Publishing Company, 1977

Diagnostic Battery

Grades: 3–9

Assesses level of reading and reading strengths and weaknesses. Subtests include word meaning, reading comprehension, word parts (sound/symbol choices and identifying root words), reading rate, and an optional syllabication test. Yields grade equivalent and percentile rank for vocabulary, comprehension, and total. Rate given in words per minute. Item analysis provided.

Group test: 60 minutes. Two forms, three levels in each for grades 3–4a, 4b–6, and 7–9.

Peabody Individual Achievement Test (PIAT)

American Guidance Service, 1981

Survey
Grades: K–12

Tests five subtests in math, reading recognition, reading comprehension, spelling, and general information. Easel provided for easy administration. Yields grade equivalents and percentiles.

Individual test: 30–40 minutes. One form.

Performance Assessment in Reading (PAIR)

California Test Bureau, 1978

Literacy Test
Grades: 7–9

Measures minimal competency through printed materials encountered in school, home, and community. Seventy-two items, divided into two parts, include warning signs, street maps, card catalogues, encyclopedia entries, telephone directories, and bus schedules. Vocabulary, comprehension, and location/study skills emphasized. If junior high students master the PAIR skills, they should demonstrate proficiency on senior high competency tests required for graduation. Instructional prescriptions of individual needs and student grouping guidelines given. Criterion-referenced: passing/not passing.

Group test: untimed. One form.

Phonics Knowledge Survey

Teachers College, 1964

Diagnostic: Specific Skills
Grades: 1–6

Surveys content generally covered by basal readers including letter names; consonant sounds; long and short vowels; vowel generalizations; sounds of "c" and "g"; sounds of "y"; consonant blends; digraphs; vowel combinations; vowels followed by "r"; sounds of "qu," "oo," and "x"; beginning consonant combinations; and syllabication. No norms given. Provides diagnostic information.

Individual test: 10–30 minutes. One form.

Primary Reading Profiles (PRP)

Riverside Press, 1968

Diagnostic: Specific Skills
Grades: 1–2

Tests readiness and reading skills at the first and second grades by assessing reading maturity through the abilities of attention span, reasoning, general information, listening, following directions, phonic skills, word recognition skills, contextual skills, and comprehension. Test divided into three administrations. Yields raw scores, grade equivalents, quartiles (top 25 percent, mid 50 percent, and low 25 percent).

Group test: 90 minutes total time. Two forms.

Reading Diagnosis
Jamestown Press, 1981

Diagnostic Battery;
(with informal Reading Inventory)
Grades: 1–6

Battery includes oral reading and silent comprehension passages. Also includes tests of phonics, sight word recognition, vocabulary size, word meanings, letter and number recognition, spelling, handwriting, vision, hearing, interest inventory, and parent interview.

Individual or group test: untimed. One form.

Reading/Everyday Activities in Life (REAL)
Westwood Press, 1978

Literacy Test
Ages: 10 years and above

Assesses functional literacy for adults at basic education levels. Nine real-life reading selections are used in test (eg., signs, schedules). Directions and questions are on cassette tape, which is student controlled. Criterion-referenced: 80 percent correct indicates functional literacy.

Individual or group test: 50–90 minutes.

Reading Miscue Inventory
Macmillan, 1972

Oral Reading Miscue Inventory
Grades: Elementary, high school

Provides information on the strategies used by a student during oral reading. Student reads a four- to eight-page passage supplied by the teacher from any text or book. Passage should be difficult enough to generate miscues. Reading is taped and miscues are analyzed to determine use of language processes in reading. After reading, student retells story. Testing materials may be ordered in dittoed form rather than being supplied by the teacher. Yields analysis of miscues (graphic and sound clues, use of grammatical and semantic clues) and retelling scores.

Individual test: 15–20 minutes.

Rosewell-Chall Diagnostic Reading Test
of Word Analysis Skills
Essay Press, 1959

Diagnostic: Specific Skills
Grades: 2–6

Assesses skills in developmental order, including single consonants, consonant combinations, short vowels, rule of silent "e," vowel combinations, and syllabication. Yields ratings of competence/deficiency.

Individual test: 5–10 minutes. Useful for diagnostic patterns. Two forms.

Senior High Assessment
of Reading Performance (SHARP)
California Testing Bureau, 1978

Literacy Test
Grades: 10–12

Measures minimal competency in reading skills necessary for everyday life. Used as a post test measure of a competency-based education program for basic reading skills. Thirty displays represent forms and written materials encountered in daily living such as social security cards, telephone directory, charge account agreement, newspaper article, and so on. A new form published each year to minimize test security problems for schools using the test as a graduation requirement. Criterion-referenced (passing/not passing) and scaled scores.

Group test, untimed. One form.

Silent Reading Diagnostic Tests
Rand McNally, 1970

Diagnostic: Specific Skills
Grades: 2–6 and remedial

Assesses word recognition abilities including words in isolation (where student selects a word that describes a picture), words in context (selection of word completing sentence), visual structural analysis (separating affixed words), syllabication (dividing words into syllables using six rules), word synthesis (blending end-of-line hyphenated words), beginning sounds (selecting same sound as stimulus word), ending sounds, and vowel and consonant sounds (selecting letter that represents initial sound in oral word presented). Yields grade equivalents, percentiles, stanines.

Group test: 60–90 minutes. One form.

Sipay Word Analysis Test
Educators Publishing Service

Diagnostic: Specific Skills
Ages: 6–adult

Measures visual analysis, phonic analysis, and visual blending through seventeen subtests pinpointing specific strengths and weaknesses. Each subtest has four components: a "Mini-Manual," a set of test cards, an answer sheet, and an individual report. A manual covers topics not in Mini-Manual. Uses nonsense words and requires oral responses; no writing. Yields ratings of skill strengths and weaknesses.

Individual test: 10–15 minutes per subtest, 160–200 minutes entire test. One form.

Slosson Oral Reading Test (SORT)
Slosson Educational Publications, 1981

Survey
Grades: P–high school

This is a test of word recognition. Students are asked to read aloud twenty graded lists of words ranging from primer to high school. Yields reading grade level.

Individual test: 3–5 minutes.

Spire Individual Reading Evaulation
New Dimensions in Education, 1973

Informal Reading Inventory
Grades: I (1–6), II (4–10)

Contains a quick placement and a diagnostic reading evaluation in each set. Quick placement identifies instructional level through word recognition and silent reading comprehension; diagnostic evaluation includes word recognition and oral and silent passages. Comprehension questions following passages: main idea, detail, inference, vocabulary. Tests on ditto master. Yields independent, instructional (easy, medium, hard), and frustration reading levels.

Individual test: 30–35 minutes. One form.

SRA Reading Record, Grades 6–12
Science Research Associates, 1959

Diagnostic Battery
Grades: 6–12

Assesses strengths and weaknesses in ability to read school and everyday-life materials. Ten tests provide for a profile in rate of reading, reading comprehension, everyday reading skills, and reading vocabulary. Everyday skills include reading a telephone directory, advertisements, and an index. The vocabulary section includes technical vocabulary, sentence meaning, and general vocabulary. Yields raw scores, grade equivalents, and percentiles.

Group test: 3 minutes per test, 30 minutes total. One form.

Standard Reading Inventory
Klamath Printing Company, 1966

Informal Reading Inventory
Grades: 1–7

Contains word recognition test (PP–7) and oral and silent reading passages on grades preprimer through seven. Five comprehension questions following each reading passage: literal, inference, vocabulary. Yields independent, instructional (minimum and maximum), and frustration reading levels. Compares oral and silent reading rate and comprehension. Longest passage: 151 words.

Individual test: 15–20 minutes. Two forms.

Stanford Diagnostic Reading   *Diagnostic Battery*
The Psychological Corporation, 1966–1976   *Grades: 1–12*

Identifies strengths and weaknesses with an emphasis on low achievers. Subtests include auditory vocabulary, auditory discrimination, phonetic analysis, word reading, and comprehension. Yields percentile ranks, stanines, grade equivalents, and scaled scores.

Group test: approximately 2 hours. Two forms for each of four levels covering grades 1.6–3.5, 2.6–5.5, 4.6–9.5, and 9–12.

Sucher-Allred Reading Placement Inventory   *Informal Reading Inventory*
Economy Company, 1973   *Grades: 1–9*

Contains a word recognition test (PP–9) and reading selections from grades preprimer to nine. Each passage followed by five comprehension questions: literal, inference, critical, main idea, vocabulary. Yields independent, instructional, frustration reading levels, rate of reading, and oral reading error analysis. Longest passage: 191 words.

Individual test: 20 minutes. Two forms, each in separate booklet.

Test of Reading Comprehension (TORC)   *Diagnostic: Specific Skills*
Pro-Ed   *Grades: 2–12*

Tests silent reading comprehension through general vocabulary (words related to a common concept), syntactic similarities (understanding of similar but syntactically different sentences), paragraph reading (answering questions related to paragraphs), sentence sequencing, and vocabulary in math, science, social studies, and reading schoolwork directions. Yields scaled score for each subtest and basic comprehension quotient.

Group test.

Wide Range Achievement Test (WRAT)   *Survey*
McGraw-Hill, 1976   *Age: 5 years–adult*

A quick measurement of achievement in reading, spelling, and arithmetic. Contains two levels: level I, ages 5–11.5; level II, ages 12.0–adult. Reading section includes recognizing letters and orally reading graded word lists. Yields standard scores, percentiles, and grade ratings.

Individual test: 25–40 minutes.

Woodcock Reading Mastery Tests   *Survey and Diagnostic Battery*
American Guidance Service, 1973   *Grades: 1–9*

Screening and diagnostic battery including identification of script and italic letters, two levels of word identification, word attack of nonsense words, word comprehension through the completion of verbal analogies, and passage comprehension using the cloze procedure on sentences. Materials presented in stand-up easel kit for easy administration. Yields index of total reading based on performance on the five separate tests: easy reading, instructional, and frustration scores for each subtest and the total score; male and female and social norms percentiles; age equivalents; and standard scores.

Individual test: 30–40 minutes. Two forms.

Woodcock-Johnson Psychoeducational Battery   *Diagnostic Battery*
Teaching Resources   *Ages: Preschool to adult*

Four subtests of this 27 subtest battery test involve reading directly. They are: letter-word identification, word attack, passage comprehension, and reading interest. (See Test Inventories 3.1 and 4.1 for more information.)

Word Discrimination Test   *Diagnostic: Specific Skills*
Miami University Alumni Association, 1958   *Grades: 1–8*

Tests visual discrimination in reading confusable words. Each row contains one real word and four similar groups of letters. The student identifies the real word. Yields grade equivalents.

Group test: untimed but requires approximately 15 minutes. Two forms.

6

ASSESSING READING ACHIEVEMENT II
informal methods

This chapter continues the discussion of methods for assessing reading achievement. In the previous chapter, we discussed formal reading tests. In this chapter, we will describe informal means of testing, first concentrating on an overview of informal testing, then on several informal assessment measures and techniques. These latter include (1) observation of reading behaviors, (2) analysis of oral reading through informal reading inventories and miscue procedures, (3) methods of assessing reading comprehension through retelling techniques and the cloze procedure, (4) judging the students' perception of the reading activity, and (5) diagnostic teaching.

OVERVIEW OF INFORMAL
ASSESSMENT MEASURES

Informal, or clinical, measures differ from formal ones in several ways. Unlike formal tests, informal measures have not been normed on large sample populations. Therefore, a student's score cannot be compared with a normed sample. On the other hand, since standardized procedures need not be followed on informal tests, modifications in administration, scoring, and interpretation can be made more freely. For example, the teacher can give additional time for taking the test or feel free to encourage the student during the testing session. These types of modifications help to put students at ease, assure that they put forth their best effort, and assist in obtaining a more accurate picture of their reading abilities.

There are some important advantages to informal testing. Farr (1969), an authority in reading measurement, notes that research studies investigating the value of informal tests find that despite the lack of norms, informal tests can be reliable and valid measures of reading. Farr explains that several factors tend to make informal measures reliable. (1) More samples of reading behavior are likely to be taken with informal measures than with formal ones. (2) The samples in informal testing are often obtained over a period of time rather than at a single session. Unlike formal tests, informal measures can be readministered readily. (3) A wide variety of assessment techniques are used, including observation and diagnostic teaching techniques. Informal tests have other advantages. They are usually less expensive than standardized tests, and they can be designed to measure the effectiveness of specific instructional methods.

In Chapter 5, we discussed a two-level framework for assessing reading achievement. Informal testing can provide information for both levels of this framework. These two levels are: (1) the *general* level (this includes the level of reading achievement and the major areas of reading, such as word recognition and comprehension) and (2) the *diagnostic* level (this includes the in-depth investigation of specific areas of reading performance).

Although we have drawn a distinction between formal and informal tests, it is possible to gather informal information through formal tests. The discerning teacher constantly is alert to all clues, no matter how subtle, to clarify the diagnostic picture.

OBSERVATION OF READING

One of the most useful methods of assessing a student's reading behavior is through informal observation. Day-by-day observations by teachers who can respond immediately to the strengths and difficulties they observe are often as effective and even more practical than elaborate test batteries. Observation provides a way to assess many areas of reading not measured by tests, such as pupil interest, resistance to distractibility, and the ability to work independently to complete a task.

Strang (1968) recognized the crucial importance of observation when she encouraged teachers to be "child watchers." Teachers should learn to observe students, because through observation they can obtain valuable diagnostic information that can be put to immediate use. To observe successfully, teachers should have knowledge of behaviors and conditions associated with reading difficulties. They should also be familiar with techniques for gaining accurate insightful observations. Finally, it is important to understand and be able to interpret the behavior observed in students.

The student can be observed on many occasions during the day: during testing sessions, teaching lessons, free time and playground periods, group activities, and independent work periods. Although observations are not always recorded, it is helpful at times to have a systematic recording of significant student behaviors. Such a record can be useful to the teacher, the student, or the parent. Records may be kept through anecdotal observations that are dated, recorded, and filed. (See Chapter 3.) Another way of recording observations is through a checklist. A sample observational checklist is given in Table 6.1.

Observation also provides the opportunity to learn about how the student actually is using reading and language in the classroom. This type of observation is strongly recommended by Y. Goodman (1978), who refers to it as "kid watching." Two types of information can be gathered:

1. Does the student use reading in the classroom? Does the student read signs and directions in the classroom or depend on others? Does the student read for pleasure? Is the student reading in an increasing number of situations?
2. Does the student apply language skills to reading? A student who substitutes the word "car" for "vehicle" is making use of language in reading.

Teachers can also observe how students use writing and listening. For example, do students write independently? Do they like to write? "Kid watching" enables the teacher to observe the student's integrated use of language—including reading.

ANALYZING ORAL READING

A simple and straightforward way to learn much about a student's reading is to observe as the student reads orally. In this way, teachers can assess reading level (how difficult a book the student can read easily). They can also observe the kinds

Table 6.1 Observation Checklist

AREA	ADEQUATE	SOMEWHAT ADEQUATE	INADEQUATE	COMMENTS
Work Habits				
Quality of classwork _____				
Independent working habits _____				
Impulsivity _____				
Response to teacher questions _____				
Following directions _____				
Participation in class _____				
General health and nutrition _____				
Reading Habits				
Oral reading fluency _____				
Repetitions _____				
Stress during oral reading _____				
Relies on teacher aid _____				
Sight words: _____				
function (high-utility) words _____				
other words _____				
Phonics _____				
Consonants _____				
Consonant blends and digraphs _____				
Vowels _____				
Other _____				
Multisyllable words _____				
Blends sounds together _____				
Reversals (letters, words) _____				
Comprehension				
Factual _____				
Higher level _____				
Word meanings _____				
Loses place in reading _____				
Visual problems in reading _____				
Other _____				

of errors (or miscues) students make and how they proceed when a word is not known. In addition, teachers can determine whether the student understands the reading passage by asking questions about the selection.

Observation and informal analysis of oral reading provide answers to questions such as, Does the student use phonics skills to decode words? Does the student often repeat words? Is the pupil a word-by-word reader? Do word recognition errors make sense, thus indicating the use of language skills and context clues?

Three types of reading tests may be used to facilitate and systematize the analysis of oral reading: standardized oral reading tests, informal reading inventories, and the reading miscue inventory.

Standardized Oral Reading Tests

There are two kinds of standardized oral reading tests.

1. Some standardized oral reading tests are single-purpose tests that consist of graded passages for measuring oral reading level (the Gray Oral Reading Tests and the Gilmore Oral Reading Test).
2. Other standardized tests of oral reading are part of a diagnostic reading battery (the Gates-McKillop-Horowitz Reading Diagnostic Tests and the Durrell Analysis of Reading Difficulty.)

In both types of tests, oral reading scores are usually reported as grade-level equivalents (e.g., grade 2.5 or 5.7). The test manuals contain information for scoring, directions for administering, and statistical data on the validity, reliability, and standardization of the test. This type of test can be used according to the formal directions and then extended in use through clinical, informal interpretation. The test thus has optimal use, yielding the standardized statistical information as well as informal clinical information. The student's performance can be compared with others and also analyzed from an individual clinical perspective.

Informal Reading Inventories

Informal reading inventories contain sets of graded passages, generally ranging from the first to eighth grade level. Rather than giving a standardized single grade equivalent score, informal reading inventories indicate three different reading levels: the *independent*, the *instructional*, and the *frustration* reading levels.

Informal reading inventories include both commercially published inventories and teacher-made inventories. Commercial informal reading inventories are convenient to use because the graded passages and comprehension questions have been prepared for the teacher. Commercial inventories are discussed later in this chapter and described in Test Inventory 5.1 (in Chapter 5).

Teachers can construct an informal reading inventory from classroom materials. Basal reading series provide an excellent source. Procedures for constructing the informal reading inventory are presented later in this chapter.

Reading Miscue Inventory

Another instrument for analyzing oral reading is the *Reading Miscue Inventory* (RMI) (Goodman and Burke, 1972), a test developed by researchers with a "psycholinguistic" view of the reading process. In this test, the student reads one rather lengthy selection orally, and the strategies the student uses to figure out unknown words are analyzed. The RMI is more fully described later in this chapter.

INFORMAL READING INVENTORIES

Informal reading inventories (IRI) provide one of the best clinical procedures for observing and analyzing reading performance. As noted earlier, the IRI is an individual test that can be purchased or teacher-made, and it provides information on a wide range of reading behaviors.

The informal reading inventory was first suggested by Betts (1946) because of the inadequacies of existing reading tests. He found that the scores on the existing tests did not give enough information for a comprehensive reading diagnosis. Unlike the IRI, the existing tests did not permit the teacher to observe the pupil reading the types of reading materials used in the classroom.

A purpose of the IRI is to find a "fit" between the student's reading ability and the reading material selected for instruction. To accomplish this, the informal reading inventory provides information for identifying three levels of reading: independent, instructional, and frustration. The IRI also permits the teacher to analyze the student's oral reading and comprehension abilities.

Administering and Scoring the Informal Reading Inventory

The steps for conducting, scoring, and analyzing the informal reading inventory are illustrated in Figure 6.1.

The informal reading inventory consists of a series of graded reading selections. Briefly, the student reads orally from sequentially graded selections until the material becomes too difficult. Usually the test is constructed so that the student reads two passages at each grade level, one orally and one silently. After each passage is read, the student is asked comprehension questions. Starting with an easy selection and continuing on to increasingly difficult passages, the student finally reaches a frustration level. This is the level at which there are too many oral reading errors on words in the passage or the student can no longer answer the comprehension questions satisfactorily. Throughout the test, the teacher records (or codes) oral reading errors (sometimes referred to as miscues) and the student's responses to the comprehension questions.

There are many variations on the IRI. The type selected depends upon the depth of the diagnostic information desired and the theoretical framework of the examiner. Because the test is informal, the teacher can make adaptations to meet changing purposes and needs.

To give the IRI, select a period of about half an hour to work with an individual student. The student is seated across from the teacher and reads aloud from the "student copy" of a passage. The teacher records the students's performance on another copy. To keep the note taking unobtrusive, use a testing easel or

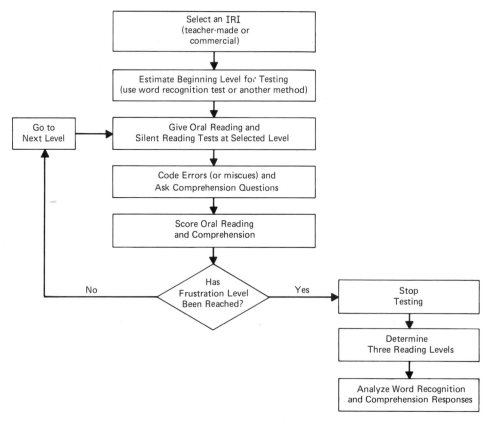

```
┌─────────────────────────────────┐
│         Select an IRI           │
│        (teacher-made or         │
│          commercial)            │
└─────────────────────────────────┘
                │
                ▼
┌─────────────────────────────────────────────┐
│     Estimate Beginning Level for Testing     │
│  (use word recognition test or another method)│
└─────────────────────────────────────────────┘
                │
┌───────────┐   ▼
│  Go to    │─▶┌─────────────────────────────────┐
│ Next Level│  │    Give Oral Reading and        │
└───────────┘  │  Silent Reading Tests at Selected Level│
               └─────────────────────────────────┘
                │
                ▼
┌─────────────────────────────────┐
│      Code Errors (or miscues) and│
│     Ask Comprehension Questions  │
└─────────────────────────────────┘
                │
                ▼
┌─────────────────────────────────┐
│       Score Oral Reading         │
│       and Comprehension          │
└─────────────────────────────────┘
                │
                ▼
          ◇ Has          ◇
    No   Frustration Level    Yes   ┌──────────────┐
 ◀───────  Been Reached?   ─────────▶│     Stop     │
          ◇              ◇           │   Testing    │
                                     └──────────────┘
                                            │
                                            ▼
                                     ┌──────────────┐
                                     │  Determine   │
                                     │ Three Reading Levels│
                                     └──────────────┘
                                            │
                                            ▼
                                     ┌──────────────┐
                                     │Analyze Word Recognition│
                                     │and Comprehension Responses│
                                     └──────────────┘
```

Figure 6.1. Flow Chart for Administering and Scoring the Informal Reading Inventory

place the scoring pad against or below the table. Since the reading inventory is different from other tests, prepare students by explaining that they will read selections both orally and silently, that they will be asked questions on the material, and that the selections will become more difficult as they go along.

WORD RECOGNITION TEST.   A word recognition test is often given prior to the reading of the IRI passages as a quick way to estimate the student's reading ability and to determine where to begin the testing of the reading passages. The student reads from word lists, which are graded lists of words. There is one word list for each level, from a preprimer level through grade six. (Directions for constructing word lists are given later in this chapter.)

Students read from these word lists, starting with the easiest list. Words can be exposed one at a time by covering the list with a blank sheet of paper and moving the paper down as the student reads. The teacher records the responses on the teacher's copy. The graded word lists are administered until the student scores below 60 percent on any list (for example, eight errors out of twenty words). However, the teacher uses the highest grade level at which the student performs at about 80 percent correct to indicate where to begin testing on the reading passages.

Performance on the word list can give the teacher much diagnostic information. Table 6.2 shows a sixth grade boy's performance on a second grade word recognition test. The complete recording of each response provides a basis for diagnostic information. An examination of the scored test (Table 6.2) shows that this student makes use of phonics but relies only on the beginnings of words as clues to identification. Some teachers find it very helpful to separate performance on the word recognition test into two columns: one column is used to record performance on instantly recognized words (sight words) and one column is used to record performance on words recognized after analysis.

READING PASSAGES.   A first task in administering the reading passages test is to estimate where to start testing, that is, the appropriate difficulty level of the beginning reading passage. This estimation can be accomplished in several ways: (1) give a word recognition test (as described); (2) use the information from previous achievement test scores; or (3) begin testing two levels below the student's present grade level. If the student performs very poorly at the estimated beginning level, testing should continue at an easier level.

Table 6.2   Scored Word Recognition Test

SECOND GRADE LEVEL	INSTANT RESPONSE	ANALYSIS RESPONSE
field	C	
banana	C	
mine	C	
awoke	away	c
sidewalk	C	
chocolate	C	
twenty	C	
week	C	
skin	C	
drop	drape	drew
cage	C	
bicycle	C	
yesterday	C	
splash	splat	splosh
till	C	
between	C	
coal	C	
what	C	
policeman	poleman	postman
frighten	C	
% Correct	80 % instant	85 % Total

At each reading grade level, the student reads a passage orally and then another passage silently. Before each reading, the student is given a brief introduction to the subject (e.g., "This is a story about a circus"). During the reading, the examiner makes notations on variations from the text (or errors) on a duplicate copy of the passage. Some reading specialists also time the reading with a stopwatch, a procedure appropriate for students of intermediate grade level or higher. If the student appears to be nervous about the timing, use a watch with a second hand or a digital watch. After reading each oral and silent passage, the student is asked comprehension questions. The test proceeds with increasingly difficult selections until the frustration level is reached.

CODING ORAL READING ERRORS.   A systematic method for coding errors (or miscues) is needed to record the student's oral reading accurately. It is important to record all variations from the text so that it will be possible to look back at the transcript at a later time and reconstruct the student's performance. Some teachers find it helpful to use a tape recorder so that they can later verify their coding. Even experienced examiners have been found to make inaccurate transcriptions of student's oral reading (Page and Carlson, 1975). Students can be put at ease when a tape recorder is used if they are asked to help the teacher operate the machine.

Commercial Informal Reading Inventories (IRI's) generally provide their own coding system. For teachers who construct their own IRIs, we suggest the following coding system.

1. *Omissions:* circle ~~on the table.~~

2. *Additions:* insert word added above a caret   on the ᴧ table   *little*

3. *Substitutions, mispronunciations:* write the word the student says above the word in the text: *on the table.*   *toast*

4. *Repetitions:* draw a wavy line below the words   *on the table.*

5. *Reversals:* same as substitutions.

6. *Examiner aid:* if the student hesitates for more than ten seconds and cannot continue, tell the student the word and write "P" above the word for "pronounced." (Note: pronouncing the word for the student might inflate the comprehension score. Therefore, many authorities suggest that the examiner should not supply the word during the administration of the IRI.)

For a more complete transcription, some teachers add the following coding symbols:

*   Words pronounced correctly, but with hesitations: *H*
*   Words that have been corrected spontaneously: *c*
*   Lack of punctuation: *I saw Mary. She was* . . . (This indicates the student ignored the period.)

An example of a coded IRI passage is shown in Table 6.3

Table 6.3   Sample IRI Passage

First grade level, oral passage
81 words
From:
MacMillan, *Lands of Pleasure*

Introduction: Did you ever go to the Food Fair at Carnival time?
We're going to read a story about two boys who will
be going to another kind of fair.

/ *To*

On the day of the fair, Ben got up as soon as it was light. After he had *sunny* ½   *has* ½

½

something to eat he ran to the barn. He had to get his calf ready for the fair. *fat* c

Tommy wanted to sleep, but he got up as soon as Ben did. He went with Ben *sun* ' ½   *walked* ½

to the barn.

inside ½

The boys looked in the barn. Ben's calf was not there! The two boys told their ½

The ½

father that Big Twin was not in the barn.

81 words

6 errors

93% oral reading score

Scoring System: ◯ for omission   for repetition ⌒⌒⌒
                    ⋀ for insertion   for examiner aid ℘
        write word for substitution   corrected C

''Ready for the Fair'' adapted from *The Little Twin* by Grace Paull. Copyright 1953 by Grace Paull. Reprinted by permission of Doubleday & Company, Inc.

COUNTING ERRORS AND SCORING ORAL READING.   Not all deviations from the text should actually be counted as errors. The error count depends upon the scoring system used, as well as the examiner's notion of what constitutes an error. The criteria for counting oral reading errors (or miscues) differs among reading authorities. Some reading authorities suggest counting all miscues equally (Johnson and Kress, 1965). Others differentiate between major and minor miscues, based upon whether there is a change in the meaning of the passage (Karlin, 1980; Alpert and Kravitz, 1970). Some authorities consider hesitations and repetitions as errors (Ekwall, 1976), while others do not. Because of the different ways of counting errors, the criteria for acceptable scores in word recognition accuracy also differ.

We believe that the method of counting errors should take into account the fact that the ultimate goal of reading is comprehension. Therefore, miscues that do not affect the meaning of the passage (or minor miscues) should count less heavily than those that do affect meaning (or major miscues). For example, in the sentence "Those boys will not be permitted to go," a minor miscue would be substituting "these" for "those." A major miscue would be substituting "permanent" for "permitted." The first does not affect comprehension as seriously as the second. We suggest that major miscues be counted as one full error and minor miscues be counted as one-half error. In addition, the repetition of an entire phrase should be counted as one-half error if the phrase is continuous, and a one-word repetition should not be counted as an error at all. Also, if the same mispronunciation is made over and over, it should only be counted once.

The following counting criteria are suggested:

	MAJOR MISCUE (AFFECTS COMPREHENSION)	MINOR MISCUE (DOES NOT AFFECT COMPREHENSION)
Substitutions	1 Error	$\frac{1}{2}$ Error
Omissions	1 Error	$\frac{1}{2}$ Error
Additions	1 Error	$\frac{1}{2}$ Error
Reversals	1 Error	$\frac{1}{2}$ Error
Repetitions	—	$\frac{1}{2}$ Error (2 or more words)
Aid by examiner	1 Error	—

Some deviations from the text are *not* counted as errors. They include spontaneous corrections and mispronunciations which are due to dialect or language difference. One word repetitions should not be counted as errors. Disregard of punctuation does not count as an error, although it should be noted for diagnostic analysis.

As the student reads, the teacher records each deviation from the printed text on a duplicate copy of the passage. After the reading selection is completed, the full errors and half errors are totaled. The percentage of correct words in the passage is computed to find the oral reading score. In the coded and scored passage in Table 6.3, there are 81 words, 6 errors, and 75 correct words. The percentage correct is therefore 93 percent.

$$\frac{75 \text{ (Words correct)}}{81 \text{ (Total words)}} \times 100 = 93\%$$

Table 6.4 presents a convenient way for finding the percentage of words correct in an oral reading passage. Simply find the intersection between the number of words in the passage and error count. For example, if the passage contains 150 words and the error count is 15, then the percentage correct is 90 percent.

SCORING COMPREHENSION.   After reading each passage, the student is asked questions to check comprehension. If the answer is incorrect, the examiner writes

Table 6.4 Table for Oral Reading Accuracy Score (each number indicates percentage correct)

NUMBER OF ERRORS

NUMBER OF WORDS IN PASSAGE	1	2	3	4	5	6	7	8	9	10	11	12	13	14	15	16	17	18	19	20	21	22	23	24	25	26
28–32	97	93	90	87	83	80	77	73	70	67	63	60	57	53	50	47	43	40	37	33	30	27	23	20	17	13
33–37	97	94	92	89	86	83	80	77	74	72	69	66	63	60	57	54	52	49	46	43	40	37	34	32	29	26
38–42	98	95	93	90	88	85	82	80	78	75	72	70	68	65	62	60	58	55	52	50	48	45	42	40	38	35
43–47	98	95	93	91	89	87	84	82	80	78	75	73	71	69	67	64	62	60	58	56	53	51	49	47	44	42
48–52	98	96	94	92	90	88	86	84	82	80	78	76	74	72	70	68	66	64	62	60	58	56	54	52	50	48
53–57	98	96	94	93	91	89	87	86	84	82	80	78	77	76	73	71	69	67	66	64	62	60	58	56	55	53
58–62	98	96	95	93	92	90	88	87	85	83	82	80	78	77	75	73	72	70	68	67	65	63	62	60	58	57
63–67	98	97	95	94	92	91	89	88	86	85	83	82	80	78	77	75	74	72	71	69	68	66	65	63	62	60
68–72	99	97	95	94	93	92	90	89	87	85	84	83	82	80	78	77	76	74	73	72	70	69	67	66	64	63
73–77	99	97	95	94	93	92	91	89	87	86	85	84	83	81	80	79	77	76	75	73	72	71	69	68	67	65
78–82	99	97	96	95	94	93	91	90	88	88	86	85	84	82	81	80	79	76	76	75	74	72	71	70	69	68
83–87	99	98	96	95	94	93	92	91	89	88	87	86	85	84	82	81	80	78	78	76	75	74	73	72	71	69
88–92	99	98	96	96	94	94	92	91	89	89	88	87	86	84	83	82	81	79	79	78	77	76	74	73	72	71
93–97	99	98	97	96	95	94	93	92	90	90	88	87	86	85	84	83	82	80	80	79	78	77	76	75	74	73
98–102	99	98	97	96	95	94	93	92	91	90	88	88	87	86	85	84	83	81	81	80	79	78	77	76	75	74
103–107	99	98	97	96	95	95	94	93	91	91	89	89	88	87	86	85	84	82	82	81	80	79	78	77	76	75
108–112	99	98	97	96	96	95	94	93	91	91	90	89	88	87	86	85	85	83	83	82	81	80	79	78	77	76
113–117	99	98	97	97	96	95	94	93	92	92	90	90	89	88	87	86	85	84	84	83	82	81	80	79	78	77
118–122	99	98	98	97	96	95	95	94	92	92	91	90	89	88	88	87	86	84	84	83	82	82	81	80	79	79
123–127	99	98	98	97	96	96	95	94	93	92	91	91	90	89	88	87	86	85	85	84	83	82	82	81	80	79
128–132	99	98	98	97	97	96	95	94	93	93	92	91	90	89	89	88	87	86	85	85	84	83	82	82	81	80
133–137	99	99	98	97	97	96	95	94	93	93	92	91	91	90	89	88	87	86	86	85	84	84	83	82	81	81
138–142	99	99	98	97	97	96	95	95	94	93	93	92	91	90	90	89	88	87	86	86	85	84	84	83	82	81
143–147	99	99	98	97	97	96	95	95	94	94	93	92	92	91	90	89	88	87	87	86	85	85	84	83	83	82
148–152	99	99	98	98	97	96	96	95	94	94	94	93	92	91	90	90	89	88	87	87	86	85	85	84	83	83
153–157	99	99	98	98	97	97	96	95	94	94	94	93	92	91	91	90	89	88	88	87	86	86	85	84	83	83
158–162	99	99	98	98	97	97	96	96	94	94	94	93	92	92	91	90	89	88	88	88	86	86	85	85	84	84
163–167	99	99	98	98	97	97	96	96	95	95	94	93	93	92	91	91	90	89	88	88	87	86	86	85	84	84
168–172	99	99	98	98	97	97	96	96	95	95	94	93	93	92	92	91	90	89	89	88	87	87	86	85	85	85
173–177	99	99	98	98	97	97	96	96	95	95	94	94	93	92	92	91	90	89	89	88	88	87	86	86	85	85
178–182	99	99	98	98	98	97	96	96	95	95	95	94	93	93	92	91	91	90	89	89	88	87	87	86	86	86
183–187	99	99	98	98	98	97	96	96	95	95	95	94	93	93	92	92	91	90	90	89	88	88	87	86	86	86
188–192	99	99	98	98	98	97	96	96	95	95	95	94	93	93	92	92	91	91	90	89	88	88	87	87	86	87
193–197	99	99	98	98	98	97	96	96	96	95	95	94	94	93	93	92	91	91	90	90	89	88	88	87	87	87
198–202	99	99	98	98	98	97	96	96	96	95	95	95	94	93	93	92	91	91	91	90	89	89	88	88	87	87
203–207	100	99	98	98	98	97	97	97	96	96	95	95	94	93	93	93	92	91	91	90	89	89	88	88	87	88
208–212	100	99	98	98	98	97	97	97	96	96	95	95	94	93	93	93	92	91	91	90	89	89	88	88	87	88
213–217	100	99	99	98	98	97	97	97	96	96	95	95	94	94	93	93	92	92	91	91	90	89	89	88	88	88
218–222	100	99	99	98	98	97	97	97	96	96	95	95	94	94	93	93	92	92	92	91	90	90	89	89	88	89
223–227	100	99	99	98	98	97	97	97	96	96	96	95	95	94	94	93	92	92	92	91	90	90	89	89	88	89
228–232	100	99	99	98	98	98	97	97	96	96	96	95	95	94	94	93	93	92	92	91	91	90	90	90	89	89
233–237	100	99	99	98	98	98	97	97	96	96	96	95	95	94	94	94	93	92	92	92	91	91	90	90	89	89
238–242	100	99	99	98	98	98	97	97	96	96	96	95	95	94	94	94	93	93	92	92	92	91	91	90	90	89

NUMBER OF WORDS IN PASSAGE

the exact student response. A percentage-correct score is obtained for both oral and silent reading. For example, if the student answers 3 of 4 comprehension questions correctly, the comprehension score would be 75 percent on that selection. The oral and silent comprehension scores may be averaged to compute the average comprehension score at each level. (Some reading authorities suggest that oral and silent reading should not be averaged together but should be kept separate.) The testing continues until the average comprehension score falls below 70 percent. Table 6.5 gives the percentage correct scores for different numbers of comprehension questions.

Reading Levels Obtained From the Informal Reading Inventory

The unique and valuable assessment feature of the informal reading inventory is that the scoring system is functional. By indicating three different "levels of reading"—independent, instructional, and frustration—the IRI guides the teacher in choosing appropriate materials. Each of these levels is expressed in terms of a grade level (from preprimer through eighth or ninth grade). By knowing the student's functional levels of reading, the teacher can judiciously select reading materials for various reading purposes.

Reading levels are based on performance on the reading passages and do not include scores from the word lists. Levels are based on the (1) oral reading score and (2) the average comprehension score (of oral and silent passages). Commercial IRIs sometimes use slightly different criteria. The following criteria are suggested:

Criteria for Three Reading Levels

READING LEVEL			
	Oral Reading		Comprehension
INDEPENDENT	95–100%	and	90–100%
INSTRUCTIONAL	90–95%	and	70–90%
FRUSTRATION	Less than 90%	or	Less than 70%

INDEPENDENT READING LEVEL.   This is the level of material that the reader can handle easily and independently, without assistance from the teacher. This is the level to be used for free or recreational reading.

Oral reading : 95–100 percent
and
Average comprehension : 90–100 percent

INSTRUCTIONAL READING LEVEL.   This is the level of material at which the reader makes some errors and requires instructional aid to benefit from the reading. The teacher anticipates the difficulties and plans appropriate instruction.

Table 6.5 Table For Comprehension Accuracy Score (each number indicates a percentage-correct score)

NUMBER OF CORRECT RESPONSES

NUMBER OF QUESTIONS		1	2	3	4	5	6	7	8	9	10	11	12
	1	100											
	2	50	100										
	3	33	67	100									
	4	25	50	75	100								
	5	20	40	60	80	100							
	6	17	33	50	67	83	100						
	7	14	26	43	57	71	86	100					
	8	12	25	38	50	62	75	88	100				
	9	11	22	33	44	56	67	78	89	100			
	10	10	20	30	40	50	60	70	80	90	100		
	11	9	18	27	36	45	55	64	73	82	91	100	
	12	8	17	25	33	42	50	58	67	75	83	92	100

Students should be placed in instructional level materials for most direct instruction.

> Oral reading : 90–95 percent
> and
> Average comprehension : 70–90 percent

FRUSTRATION READING LEVEL.   At this point, the material becomes too difficult for the reader, even with assistance. This level should be avoided because effective learning cannot occur. The reading teacher can provide a real service to classroom and subject area teachers by finding books at the student's instructional level.

> Oral reading : below 90 percent
> or
> Average comprehension : below 70 percent

When administering an IRI, it is sometimes difficult to determine when a stable frustration level has been reached. If a student falls only slightly below the frustration criteria, teachers should continue testing to make sure the frustration level has been reached.

LISTENING COMPREHENSION LEVEL.   In addition to the three reading levels, the IRI enables the teacher to obtain an assessment of the student's listening level. After the three reading levels have been determined, the teacher reads passages aloud to the student, starting at the frustration level, and asks comprehension questions on the passages. The highest level at which the student gets 70 percent or more of the answers correct is the listening level. This listening level provides a rough estimate of the student's level of understanding language (receptive language). It is used by some diagnosticians as one measure of the potential for reading. The listening level is discussed in Chapter 4, under Informal Assessment of Language.

OTHER CRITERIA FOR DETERMINING READING LEVELS.   The original criteria for determining reading levels suggested by Betts (1946) were

	ORAL READING	COMPREHENSION
Independent level	99%	90% — 100%
Instructional level	95%	75% — 90%
Frustration level	90%	50% or below

We suggest that the Betts criteria be modified for two reasons. (1) Using the Betts criteria, the students' reading level is unclear when comprehension falls between 50 percent and 75 percent. (2) The Betts criteria are quite stringent because he suggested that students read a passage silently before reading it orally, a practice that is not currently in use. Certain modifications for the criteria were suggested by Powell (1970). The criteria suggested in this text (given earlier) combine elements of Betts, Powell, and psycholinguistic theory.

Interpreting the Scores
of the Informal Reading Inventory

The summary page (shown in Figure 6.2) is useful for summarizing IRI scores on word recognition, oral reading accuracy, oral reading comprehension, silent reading comprehension, and listening level. (A blank form of the IRI summary page is given in appendix D.)

In addition to determining reading levels, many other types of interpretations can be made from IRI scores. For example, to learn whether a student recognizes words better in isolation or in context, the word list recognition score can be compared with the oral reading accuracy score from the oral reading passages. By comparing columns 1 and 2 of Figure 6.2, we see that this student reads somewhat better in context than in isolation.

ANALYZING TYPES OF ORAL READING ERRORS.   The types of errors being made can be determined by analyzing the student's performance on the IRI. In this type of analysis, the teacher tries to detect the reasons behind the errors or miscues.

1. *Substitutions, mispronunciations.* These are the most frequent types of miscues. Substitutions which contain the same letters or sounds as the target word show that the student is using phonics. Substitutions that maintain the meaning of the text show that the student is using context. In addition, substitutions may depend upon the method used to teach reading. Barr (1972) found that students taught by phonics methods tended to produce nonsense substitutions using phonics. Those taught by sight word methods produced real words.

2. *Omissions.* Some omissions, particularly those of word endings, may be due to language differences and should not be counted as errors. Students who do not read carefully may skip over some words; these are not serious errors if meaning is kept in-

| | Used to Compute Reading Level | | | | Used to Compute Reading Level | |

| Level | (1) Word Recognition Scores | | Passage Scores | | | | (6) Listening Level |
	(Instant)	Total	(2) Oral Reading Word Accuracy	(3) Oral Comprehension Score	(4) Silent Comprehension Score	(5) Average Comprehension Score	
PP	(100)	100					
P	(90)	90					
1	(85)	90					
2	(80)	85	98%	100%	100%	100%	
3	(60)	65	97%	90%	90%	90%	
4			92%	70%	80%	75%	
5			84%	50%	40%	45%	80%
6							70%
7							50%
8							

Estimated reading levels:

Independent level   3

Instructional level   4

Frustration level   5

Listening level   6

Figure 6.2 IRI Summary Page

tact. Some students who have trouble with longer words may simply pronounce the first syllable, indicating a need for instruction in word analysis skills. Students who tend to omit whole lines or sections should be referred for a visual examination.

3. *Additions.* Words added to the text often represent an attempt to smooth out the meaning of the passage. If students have misread one word, they will often add additional words so that the entire sentence will be grammatical.

4. *Reversals.* Most beginning readers (of any age level) tend to make reversals. In fact, reversals are a symptom of a primary reading level. However, if reversals seriously hamper reading progress, they may indicate a perceptual problem.

5. *Repetitions.* Repetitions may indicate that the student is attempting to work out words. If readers are having trouble with one word, they may repeat an entire phrase to check the meaning in context. Because this is a desirable process, repetitions are not considered a serious error. Sometimes repetitions are due to nervousness.

6. *Aid by examiner.* This is the most serious of the miscue types. A student who relies on aid has an inadequate sight vocabulary and possesses few other strategies for analyz-

ing unknown words. Sometimes, students who rely on aid actually possess word recognition skills (such as phonics or context) but they have not learned to use them during reading. Other students have simply become psychologically dependent on the teacher.

7. *Hesitations, spontaneous corrections, and disregard of punctuation.* Although these miscues are not counted as errors, they do indicate some difficulty with the reading process. Hesitations and corrections show that the reader does not recognize words instantly. Disregard of punctuation and expressionless reading often indicate severe discomfort with the passage or show that the student does not see reading as a meaning-gaining process.

Oral reading miscues may also be analyzed to determine the strategies that the student uses to figure out words. Two examples of this type of analysis are given below. In the first, the student is making use of context clues; in the second, the student is using phonics clues.

Example 1. *Use of Context Clues*

                    a   woke   sunny   good
(On) the day of the fair, Ben got up as soon as it was light. After he had something to eat,

            wanted   cow
he ran to the barn. He had to get his calf ready for the fair.

Example 2. *Use of Phonics Clues*

                    far   sun   somebody
On the day of the fair, Ben got up as soon as it was light. After he had something to eat,

runs   bank   cat   far
he ran to the barn. He had to get his calf ready for the fair.

"Ready for the Fair" adapted from *The Little Twin* by Grace Paull. Copyright 1953 by Grace Paull. Reprinted by permission of Doubleday & Company, Inc.

It should be noted that reading errors made at the frustration level should not be analyzed with those made on the independent and instructional levels. Kibby (1979) found that including frustration level miscues in an analysis can give a distorted view of the reader's skills and strategies.

ANALYZING COMPREHENSION.   The IRI is also useful for analyzing comprehension skills. In general, the types of comprehension questions used on an IRI are varied. Comprehension questions include main idea, fact, inference, sequence, and vocabulary. By keying each question by its type, a student's comprehension errors can be classified readily. In this way, it is easy to see the types of questions which are missed. Oral and silent reading comprehension scores can be compared.

A comparison of columns 3 and 4 in Figure 6.2 shows that this student appears to be about equal in oral and silent reading. Since silent reading assumes greater and greater importance as the student becomes older, it is important that students learn to comprehend while reading silently.

Commercial Reading Inventories

Many teachers prefer using commercial reading inventories rather than constructing their own informal reading inventory. Commercial reading inventories are convenient to use and tend to be well constructed. In addition, some publishers provide a reading inventory to accompany their basal reading series. An Informal Reading Inventory which can be used directly with students is provided in Appendix D of this text.

When choosing a commercial reading inventory, there are several features to consider. (1) Are the passages long enough to permit oral reading patterns to stabilize? (2) Is there a provision of more than one form to allow for retesting or testing of silent reading? (3) Does the test provide a breakdown of oral reading miscues and the coding of different types of comprehension questions? (4) Does the test permit photocopying of materials for classroom use? (5) Is the difficulty level of the reading passages verified through a readability formula?

Widely used commercial reading inventories include Analytical Reading Inventory (Charles E. Merrill); Basic Reading Inventory (Kendall/Hunt); Classroom Reading Inventory (William C. Brown); Contemporary Classroom Inventory (Gorsuch, Scarisbrick); Ekwall Reading Inventory (Allyn & Bacon); Informal Reading Assessment Tests (Houghton Mifflin); Reading Miscue Inventory (Macmillan); SPIRE Individual Reading Evaluation (New Dimensions in Education); Standard Reading Inventory (Klamath); and Sucher-Allred Reading Placement Inventory (Economy Company). These reading inventories are described in Test Inventory 5.1 (in Chapter 5).

Constructing an Informal Reading Inventory

Informal reading inventories can be constructed readily by using a basal reading series. The chief advantages of developing one's own IRI are that it can be based upon materials the student is using, and that it is relatively inexpensive. Disadvantages are that constructing an IRI takes a great deal of time and requires a fair amount of technical knowledge.

To construct the IRI, the teacher must first select a basal reading series. It will be necessary to (1) select words for the graded word lists, (2) select passages for oral reading and silent reading, and (3) develop comprehension questions for the oral and silent reading passages.

WORD LISTS. The word lists contain twenty words selected randomly from new words for each difficulty level through grade six. Proper nouns (names, places) are excluded. It is usually unnecessary to test sight recognition beyond level

Table 6.6   Sample Word List

PREPRIMER	PRIMER	GRADE ONE	GRADE TWO
little	tree	birthday	field
is	something	them	banana
and	she	many	mine
ball	brown	could	awoke
no	black	eight	sidewalk
play	then	over	chocolate
big	would	pretty	twenty
it	now	hand	week
mother	like	another	skin
cat	friends	duck	drop
funny	men	teacher	cage
come	said	miss	bicycle
a	home	crayon	yesterday
rabbit	away	hot	splash
I	please	stop	till
look	store	grow	between
blue	food	had	coal
up	give	lunch	what
red	very	water	police
go	farm	those	frighten

GRADE THREE	GRADE FOUR	GRADE FIVE	GRADE SIX
cousin	alphabet	heroic	gigantic
highway	uncertain	chemist	wardrobe
allow	sample	convention	friction
circle	meant	location	lament
wonderful	exchange	anxious	reverence
peach	baseball	stadium	valor
laughed	yank	therefore	horrify
sentence	ideal	nephew	expression
sunrise	buyer	migration	cherished
rather	seashore	testimony	haunt
sailor	zipper	ungrateful	ponderous
market	butcher	talkative	boulevard
through	merely	wharf	shrewd
promise	phone	caravan	violin
everything	forward	pavement	barbaric
became	caterpillar	twilight	abbreviation
glove	linger	composer	existence
happiest	mosquito	vertical	hospitality
breathe	gobble	bother	canopy
cabbage	kennel	fleece	obligation

Compiled from E. C. Kennedy, *Classroom Approaches to Remedial Reading* (Itasca, Ill.: F. E. Peacock, 1977); E. B. Coleman, *Collecting a Data Base for the Reading Technology*, mimeo (El Paso: University of Texas, 1967).

six. Selections can also be made from other available graded word lists. A sample word list is shown in Table 6.6.

READING PASSAGES.   Each selection should be preceded by a motivational statement designed to orient the student to the subject of the passage. Two reading passages are selected at each reading level, one for oral reading and one for silent reading. The selections should become gradually longer as they increase in difficulty. The following guidelines for length are suggested: preprimer, 25–35 words; primer, 35–60 words; grade one, 75–100 words; grades two and three, 75–150 words; grades four and five, 160–220 words; grades six through ten, 200–400 words. Each selection should be able to stand alone, apart from the story from which it was taken, and still make sense and convey meaning. The teacher may wish to vary the kinds of samples selected to include fiction and informational material.

The reading grade level for each selection on the IRI can be checked by using a readability formula. A readability formula is a method for checking the difficulty level of a passage. For reading materials at grade levels one through four, the Spache formula is often used (Spache, 1953). For reading materials at grade levels four or over, the Dale-Chall formula is useful (Dale & Chall, 1948). A convenient way to determine readability level is the Fry Chart, as shown in Figure 6.3 (Fry, 1968). To use the Fry Chart, the teacher finds the intersection of the number of syllables and the number of sentences in a 100-word passage.

COMPREHENSION QUESTIONS.   After reading each selection, the student is asked a series of comprehension questions. The questions should be of various types (facts, main idea, inference, vocabulary, sequence). As a guide, passages from grades preprimer and primer should contain four to five questions; passages from grades one to two should contain five to eight questions; passages from grades three and up should contain ten questions.

Questions with two-choice answers (such as yes/no, either/or) should be avoided since the student has a 50:50 chance of guessing correctly. Questions should be clear. For example, in a story in which a child awakens, dresses, eats breakfast, and leaves for school, the question, "Tell me what Bobby did when he got up," is not clear. The student could give a partial answer. A better question would be, "Name three things that Bobby did when he got up." The answer to the questions should depend upon reading the passage rather than upon prior knowledge.

A PSYCHOLINGUISTIC APPROACH
TO ASSESSING ORAL READING:
MISCUE ANALYSIS

The psycholinguistic perspective of reading shapes the diagnostic process by recognizing that the reader brings a vast store of knowledge and language competence to the reading act. This perspective has enriched our understanding of the

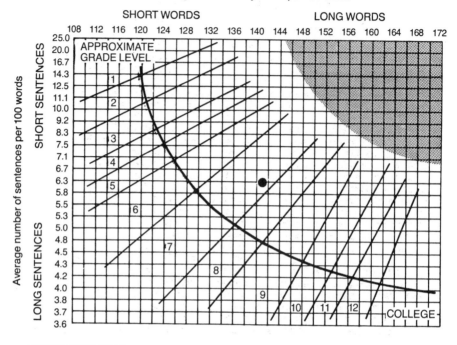

Average number of syllables per 100 words

Figure 6.3 Fry Readability Chart

Source: Edward Fry, reprinted from the *Journal of Reading*, April 1968, and *Reading Teacher*, March 1969. Reproduction permitted; no copyright.

DIRECTIONS: Randomly select 3 one hundred word passages from a book or an article. Plot average number of syllables and average number of sentences per 100 words on graph to determine the grade level of the material. Choose more passages per book if great variability is observed and conclude that the book has uneven readability. Few books will fall in gray area but when they do grade level scores are invalid.

EXAMPLE:

	Syllables	Sentences
1st Hundred Words	124	6.6
2nd Hundred Words	141	5.5
3rd Hundred Words	158	6.8
AVERAGE	141	6.3

READABILITY 7th GRADE (See Dot Plotted on Graph)

From Edward Fry, *Reading Instruction for Classroom and Clinic* (New York: McGraw-Hill, 1972), p. 231.

miscues that arise in oral reading. "Miscues" are the deviations from the printed text that the student makes while reading orally. Miscues should be viewed as diagnostic opportunities because through them readers reveal their underlying language and thinking processes.

The miscue analysis approach stresses that the student's underlying language patterns and structure give rise to the deviation. A reader's deviation from the printed text may be a positive effort to preserve comprehension (K. S. Goodman 1965, 1969; Goodman and Gollasch, 1980–1981; Y. Goodman, 1976).

Readers actually have two tasks to perform when reading. They must (1) decode the author's message and then (2) recode the message in a language that has meaning for them. Oral reading miscues may either reflect a "recoding" deviation or a "decoding" deviation. In a recoding deviation, students have understood the text but have translated it into their own words (which differ from the printed text). In a decoding deviation, the student has simply received the wrong message. Examples of both decoding and recoding miscues follow.

Example of a Decoding Miscue

Written Text: There was a star in the sky.
Student Reads: There was a trasts in the sky.

Example of a Recoding Miscue

Written Text: My mother goes to the store everyday.
Student Reads: My mother be going to the store everyday.

In the decoding example, the student did not understand the author's message. In the recoding example, the student understood the meaning of the written text but restated it in a familiar language pattern. If reading is viewed as the process of obtaining meaning from the printed word, then students should not be penalized for miscues that indicate a recoding of the text.

In summary, miscue analysis is a method of recording and analyzing oral reading in a systematic fashion to understand how the reader's underlying language patterns affect his or her reading strategies. Oral reading miscues provide valuable information about the student's reading by supplying clues about the reader's language, reasoning skills, and reading processes. From this perspective, reading has aptly been called a "psycholinguistic guessing game" (K.S. Goodman, 1967; Goodman and Burke, 1972).

The Miscue Analysis Procedure

The assessment procedure in miscue analysis is similar to the informal reading inventory in some ways, but different in other ways. The student is given one story of considerable length to read orally. To encourage production of miscues, the story should be at a level that is difficult enough to produce some reading deviations. As the student reads orally, the teacher marks all the miscues on a duplicate copy of the passage, using a coding system similar to that of the IRI.

Partial reproduction of text and reader's miscues:

And until someone said the magic name, the fruit would not fall
down from the tree, and no one could pick it~~o~~ no matter how
hard he pulled.
    So the people stood under the tree and looked up at the
beautiful, ripe fruit they could not eat.

Nine questions for reading miscues:

Reader	Text	Dialect 1	Intonation 2	Graphic Similarity 3 Y* P N	Sound Similarity 4 Y P N	Grammatical Function 5 Y P N	Correction 6	Grammatical Acceptability 7	Semantic Acceptability 8	Meaning Change 9
couldn't	*could*	*no*	*no*	✓	✓	✓	N	P	P	Y
it~~o~~ up	*it, ——*	*no*	*no*	——	——	——	N	P	P	Y
a	*the*	*no*	*no*	✓ ✓		✓	N	Y	Y	N

* Yes, partial, no.

Figure 6.4 Miscue Analysis *

*Coding Sheet from *Reading Miscue Inventory* by Yetta M. Goodman and Carolyn L. Burke (Copyright © 1972 by Carolyn L. Burke and Yetta M. Goodman). Reading passage excerpted from "Name of the Tree," from *City Sidewalks* (Bank Street Readers, Bank Street College of Education). Copyright © 1972, Macmillan Publishing Co., Inc.

After reading the selection, the student is asked to retell the story. The teacher scores the retelling for accuracy and completeness. A commercial instrument, the *Reading Miscue Inventory* (Goodman and Burke, 1972), contains passages and scoring sheets to help teachers put this procedure into practice (see Figure 6.4).

    After recording the oral reading performance, the miscues are analyzed. Goodman and Burke (1972) suggest that nine questions be asked about each miscue.

1. Does the miscue involve the child's dialect? (Dialect)
2. Does the miscue involve a shift in intonation? (Intonation)
3. Is there a similarity between the appearance of the word in the text and the miscue? (Graphic similarity)
4. Is there a similarity between the sound of the word in the text and the miscue? (Sound similarity)
5. Is there a similarity between the grammatical function of the text word and the miscue? (Grammatical or syntactic function)
6. Is there self-correction of the miscue? (Correction)
7. Is the structure in which the miscue occurs grammatically acceptable? (Grammatical or syntactic acceptability)

8. Is the structure in which the miscue occurs semantically acceptable? (Semantic acceptability)
9. Is there a change in meaning as a result of the miscue? (Meaning change)

These questions help the teacher to assess the student's reading strategies. For example, if questions 3 and 4 are answered yes, then the student is probably making use of phonics clues in reading. On the other hand, if questions 7 and 8 are positive, the student is making use of language context in reading. Sometimes students read too cautiously. For example, if the student self-corrects a miscue that had the appropriate grammatical function (question 5) and did not affect meaning of the text (question 9), then the correction was unnecessary, if reading is viewed as a meaning-getting process.

To illustrate miscue analysis more completely, a partial reading is given in Figure 6.4 and the student's miscues are presented along with an analysis.

Applying Miscue Analysis Concepts
to Informal Reading Inventories

The purposes for assessment are different in the miscue analysis diagnosis than they are in the traditional assessment of oral reading. In traditional diagnostic reading tests, word recognition deviations are usually noted without attention to changes in meaning or grammatical structure. For example, in the Gates-McKillop-Horowitz Reading Diagnostic Tests, the reading deviations from the text are regarded as errors and are classified as word omissions, word additions, repetitions, or mispronunciations. In the IRI, there is generally some consideration of the strategies that the student uses. However, in miscue analysis, the entire focus is upon the student's meaning-gaining processes.

The philosophy of a traditional informal reading inventory can be blended with the philosophy of miscue analysis. The following recommendations show ways to incorporate the psycholinguistic philosophy with the procedures for scoring an informal reading inventory.

1. Do not penalize the student for dialect miscues. These reflect the recoding process, not decoding.
2. Do not penalize the student for miscues that are corrected spontaneously.
3. Reduce penalties for repetitions to one-half point. These repetitions of words and phrases signal that a reader is looking back to more fully grasp the meaning of a passage.
4. Count only one-half point (not a full point) for miscues that do not change the meaning of the text.
5. Do not count repeated miscues (e.g., saying "Jane" for "John" several times) for more than one point.
6. When analyzing reading miscues, try to understand the process that the student is using. For example, extensive use of context clues indicates that the student is using meaningful language to figure out words. Overconcentration on saying the sounds of the words shows the student is only using a phonics strategy and is ignoring meaning.

ASSESSING READING COMPREHENSION

The psycholinguistic approach has developed two techniques for assessing reading comprehension. These are the retelling technique and the cloze procedure.

The Retelling Technique

Retelling a story is an excellent technique for assessing a student's comprehension. In effect, the student becomes an author. Unlike having the student answer comprehension questions, retelling encourages active participation in the assessment process (Hittleman, 1978; S. L. Smith, 1979). Through retelling, the teacher can assess many facets of remedial readers' abilities: the information from the text that they consider important, the schema (or concepts) they have brought to the text, their ability to integrate new information with old, and their ability to present information in an organized fashion.

To obtain the fullest value from the retelling technique, the student is asked to read the material silently, not orally. In this way the student will be telling the story to a teacher who (presumably) does not already know it (S. L. Smith, 1979). After reading the story, the student is asked to retell it. The teacher should not interrupt as the story is told. When the student has finished, however, the teacher may "probe" the retelling with questions for clarification of information. However, teacher questions should not be designed to add information the student has omitted. The teacher can organize the student's retelling in terms of

- Characters in the story
- Characteristics of the characters
- Events in the story
- Overall comprehension of the plot
- Theme of the story

Retelling techniques are explained more completely in the manual of the *Reading Miscue Inventory* (Goodman and Burke, 1972).

The Cloze Procedure

Another language-based method to analyze and diagnose reading performance is called the cloze procedure (Jongsma, 1980; Bormuth, 1968 a, b). In the cloze procedure, a passage is rewritten with words deleted. The student is to supply the missing words. The cloze technique has been used for a number of purposes in the field of reading: (1) as a test (how well an individual can read the material presented), (2) as a readability measure (what is the difficulty level of the reading material), and (3) as an instructional method (for teaching reading comprehension).

The cloze procedure requires students to make use of their language system, especially their syntactic and semantic cue systems, to comprehend written language. Based on the Gestalt idea of closure, the cloze procedure capitalizes on a person's impulse to complete a structure and make it whole by supplying a missing element. By omitting every "*n*th" word (that is, every fifth word, or seventh word, or tenth word) in a printed passage, the reader is invited to complete the passage and supply missing words. The advantage of this technique is that the reader must bridge gaps in both language and thought to supply the missing elements. A sample cloze selection is shown in Table 6.7.

Table 6.7 *Cloze Selection*

Often when people go _____ the movies, they find _____ a taller person is _____ in front of them. _____, they can't see over _____ person's head. If this _____ to a child, who _____ grown to full height, _____ or she may take _____ in the fact that _____ day they may be _____ tall adult. But for _____, who will grow no _____, the frustration of only _____ able to see half _____ screen is permanent.

(Answers: to, that, sitting, sometimes, the, happens, hasn't, he, comfort, one, a, adults, taller, being, the).

The procedure for designing a cloze test for assessment purposes is

1. Choose at random two or more samples from each selection of graded material to be included using the following criteria:
   a. Begin at the beginning of the paragraph.
   b. Use a continuous context.
   c. Select passages containing at least 250 words.
2. Delete every fifth word and replace the words with underlined blanks of uniform length.
3. Duplicate the paragraphs and present them to the students. Instruct them to write the word that they think is appropriate in each blank. If the test is administered individually, the student may simply say the word.
4. Score responses as correct when they exactly match the deleted words, disregarding minor spelling errors.

These are general procedures, not fast and firm rules. Opinions vary about how the cloze procedure is to be conducted. Among the suggested variations are the first sentence is left intact and the word deletions begin with the second sentence. The passage length may be shorter for younger students.

An estimate of the student's reading level can be obtained with the cloze test. First, the teacher must know the level of the selection being read. Use the designated grade level from the publisher, or to be more precise, use a readability formula to check difficulty level. A score of 44 percent correct on the cloze test is comparable to 75 percent on a conventional comprehension test and indicates an instructional level. A score of 57 percent of the cloze items correct is comparable to answering 90 percent of the items on a conventional comprehension test and represents the student's independent reading level.

CLOZE SCORE	READING LEVEL
44%	Instructional level
57%	Independent level

When using the cloze procedure to assess a student's reading level, the exact word that has been deleted should be the only acceptable correct response. This policy simplifies the scoring procedure, making it more objective. However, when the cloze procedure is used for instructional purposes, synonyms for the deleted words may be counted as correct. The use of cloze as an instructional procedure for teaching reading comprehension is discussed in Chapter 12.

ASSESSING THE STUDENT'S VIEWS OF READING

The student's view of the reading process, as well as the function it serves in living, profoundly affect the motivation to improve reading skills. In assessing the student's views about reading, the teacher can ask, "Why does this student read? What is the student's view of other people's reading?" Harste and Carey (1979) suggest that reading takes place within three life settings:

1. *A print setting*—the particular material the student is writing (e.g., book, flyer, label). Often, for example, students will react differently to labels that give directly useful information than to classroom materials.
2. *A situational context*—the type of situation the reader is in (classroom, home). This includes other people who are present, what has happened before reading, the purpose for reading.
3. *A cultural context*—the importance of reading in the student's culture or subculture, the function literacy serves for students and their peers. This includes the culture of the classroom.

The teacher should try to determine the student's perceptions of reading: Does the student understand that the purpose of reading is to obtain information and meaning? Often, students with reading problems become so frustrated that they lose sight of this goal. In fact, sometimes students think that the purpose of reading is to pronounce words correctly for the teacher! Goodman and Burke (1980, p. 46) suggest a series of questions that can be asked of students to determine their perceptions of reading.

1. What do you read outside of school? Why do you read those things? Do you ever reread them and why?
2. Why do you read anything?

3. Why do other people read? Do you know adults who read? What do they read and why do they read those things?

4. Why would you read this material (holding up specific material)?

If students do not know why others read, they can be assigned to investigate this question and report back.

In the *Burke Reading Interview* (Burke, 1976), students are asked to report on several issues related to reading, such as whether they consider themselves good readers, what makes a good reader, how a person having reading difficulties may be helped, and what students do when they come across words they do not know.

DIAGNOSTIC TEACHING

Diagnostic teaching is an extension of the assessment process. The perceptive teacher continues to collect diagnostic information while teaching the student. Typically, after giving both informal and formal tests, there is still much for the teacher to learn about the student. This can be accomplished by developing lessons that teach and test simultaneously and by noting the student's reactions to these lessons. Diagnostic teaching is also referred to as "trial lessons," "teaching probes," or "task analysis" (Roswell and Natchez, 1977; Gillespie and Johnson, 1974; Lerner, 1981).

Teachers obtain diagnostic information about the student's learning styles through short teaching lessons. For example, to see if the student learns well through a sight word method, the following procedure can be followed: First, teach some words visually by putting a few words on cards. Say the word while the student is looking at the word. A short time later, test the student on the word to see if it is remembered. Students who have fairly good visual memory abilities will have little difficulty remembering the word after a few repetitions. A similar procedure can be used in a diagnostic teaching session to assess a student's auditory and phonics learning abilities (Roswell and Natchez, 1977). A more detailed description of this procedure appears in Chapter 8.

In essence, a clinical teacher is always alert to the student's reactions in the teaching situation because these reactions provide invaluable diagnostic clues. Diagnostic teaching, however, goes one step farther. It is a teaching session deliberately designed for assessment rather than solely for teaching.

SUMMARY

Informal measures of reading achievement contribute valuable information to the reading diagnosis. Among informal measures and procedures used are informal observation, analysis of oral reading, informal reading inventories, miscue analysis, retelling techniques, cloze procedure, the reader's view of reading, and diagnostic teaching. Informal measures are clinical, and they differ from formal tests in several ways. Since such tests are not normed on large representative populations, they offer more leeway in administration. They also tend to sample a wider variety of reading behaviors.

Informal observation of reading provides one of the most valuable means of attaining diagnostic information. Teachers should learn to be "child watchers." A language-based approach to observation is called "kid watching."

One of the simplest and most obvious ways to learn about a disabled reader's reading is to observe the student reading orally. Standardized reading tests, informal reading inventories, and the reading miscue inventory may be used to assess oral reading.

The informal reading inventory is one of the most widely used assessment strategies. It is a systematized way to observe reading performance. The informal reading inventory consists of a series of graded reading selections. The student reads increasingly difficult material until a frustration level is reached. A system for coding errors is needed to accurately record the performance. Opinions differ in the field of reading about how to count errors in the informal reading inventory. Three reading levels are obtained from the IRI: an independent level, an instructional level, and a frustration level. Oral reading errors (or miscues) may be analyzed according to type (e.g., omissions, insertions, substitutions) or by the strategy the reader is using (phonics, context).

Commercial reading inventories are available, or teachers may construct their own. To construct an IRI, it is necessary to (1) develop word lists, (2) select passages for oral and silent reading, and (3) develop comprehension questions for both oral and silent reading.

Miscue analysis is a psycholinguistic approach to reading assessment. It regards oral reading deviations from the text as miscues (not as errors) and suggests that interpretations of the miscues take into account the student's processing of language. Recoding miscues must be distinguished from decoding miscues; the latter are less serious.

Two informal methods for assessing reading comprehension are the retelling technique and the cloze procedure. Retelling requires the student to tell a story after it is read. In the cloze procedure, a passage is rewritten with every fifth word deleted. The student must make use of both language and reading abilities to replace the deleted words. Scores are highly related to comprehension scores on standardized tests.

It is also important to understand the student's view of the reading process and its purpose.

Diagnostic teaching uses the teaching session to obtain assessment information. The purpose of the teaching is to collect diagnostic information through procedures similar to actual teaching situations.

PART III

remediation
of reading problems

The seven chapters of Part III present methods for teaching students with reading problems. The treatment of reading difficulties is referred to as "remediation," "clinical teaching," "educational therapy," or simply "good teaching." The term "remediation," as used in this book, is intended to encompass all these concepts.

Part III is organized as follows: Chapter 7 presents general principles of remediation. Chapter 8 covers characteristics of severely disabled readers. Special teaching strategies that are useful for severely disabled readers are given in Chapter 9. Chapters 10 and 11 deal with remedial methods for teaching word recognition: sight words and phonics (Chapter 10) and structural analysis, context, and language approaches to word recognition (Chapter 11). Improving comprehension through subskills and holistic approaches is the subject of Chapter 12. Finally, Chapter 13 deals with teaching vocabulary and the more advanced topics of study strategies and reading rate.

7
PRINCIPLES
OF
REMEDIATION

This chapter presents an overview of remediation. It contains (1) general principles of remedial teaching, (2) components of the remedial lesson, (3) techniques for building rapport, a strong teacher-pupil relationship, (4) ways teachers can make changes and modifications in the instructional setting to enhance successful learning, and (5) some special instructional considerations for teaching adolescents and adults.

PRINCIPLES OF REMEDIAL TEACHING

Some general principles are helpful in translating a diagnosis into an effective instructional program. These include beginning instruction at an appropriate level, using time effectively, proceeding from simple tasks to complex ones, using the student's strengths, and teaching reading rather than preaching about reading concepts. Each of these principles is described in this section.

Begin Instruction at an Appropriate Reading Level

One of the most important principles of remediation is to gear material to the student's instructional level of reading. For example, if Debra is capable of reading material at the fourth grade level, a seventh grade level book would be frustrating for her and would not facilitate learning. On the other hand, a second grade level book would be too easy and would waste valuable instructional time. Teaching should begin at Debra's instructional level—fourth grade. Berliner (1981) summarizes research findings that consistently show that students learn more when reading at a level at which they have a high rate of success.

Despite the good sense of this principle, a series of studies on actual teaching practices reveals that students—particularly low-achieving students—are often working in material that is too hard for them (Fisher et al., 1978 a, b).

Use Time Effectively

Since the time that can be devoted to remedial reading instruction is limited, it is important that this time be used judiciously. A number of studies have shown that a great deal of school time is not spent "on task" but, rather, on noninstructional activities (Fisher et al., 1978a, b). Time that has been allocated to reading instruction may actually be spent in activities such as taking students to and from class, passing out papers, and deciding which students will read. Berliner (1979) reports on second grade classrooms where students actually received less than one hundred hours of instruction in reading and math combined during an entire school year.

Many remedial readers exhibit behavioral difficulties, and their teachers must spend precious instructional time on discipline and other management procedures. McDermott (1978) found that students in a top reading group spent three times as much time on task as did students in the bottom group. Time is wasted on activities such as calling on students to read orally, which often becomes a complex negotiation for readers in low-achieving groups.

What can a remedial teacher do to utilize instructional time effectively? (1) Teachers can try to streamline noninstructional procedures by establishing firm routines for coming to class and settling down to work. (2) Teachers can call on specific students to increase their attention. (3) When students work or read independently, the teacher can observe them carefully to make sure that they are staying on task.

Proceed from Simple to Complex Tasks

Another principle of remediation is to begin teaching with simple materials so that concepts are easy for students to grasp. As learning progresses, however, tasks should become increasingly complex: (1) more difficult materials can be used; (2) the length of instructional materials can be increased (say, from a paragraph to a one-page story); (3) the rate of teaching can be speeded up; and (4) lessons can proceed from concrete to more abstract concepts. For example, abstract words may be used rather than concrete words. Stories about a student's own experiences are likely to be less abstract than stories about others.

Use the Student's Strengths

Students who need help in reading often have a long history of failure. Therefore, it is important for teachers to emphasize their strengths. To illustrate, when Peter began in the reading program, he had a large base of reading sight words but possessed few phonics skills. Deciding to capitalize on his strengths, his teacher first extended his sight word vocabulary. Only later, after Peter was comfortable in the reading program, was phonics instruction started.

In another case, a student's *interest* was viewed as her strength. Francine showed little progress in reading using standard materials, and she frequently missed classes. However, she was willing to talk about "monster" television shows. When the teacher brought "monster" books to class, she became interested and actively involved. Her attendance became regular, and she started to do independent reading.

Teach, Don't Preach

Often the teaching of reading becomes confused with other types of activities. A common error in instruction is the confusion of "preaching" with teaching. Simply because something has been told is no guarantee that it has been taught. To learn, students must actively apply principles in words, sentences, and paragraphs, not simply listen to the teacher. The following examples illustrate preaching and teaching.

CASE I: PREACHING

Teacher: "Look at what I have written on the board. What does it say?"

Sally: "Er."

Teacher: "Good. Now 'er' is a suffix and it means 'one who.' What does it mean, Jim?"

Jim: "One who."

Teacher: "Good. What suffix means 'one who,' Ann?"

Ann: "Er."

Teacher: "Excellent. Now open your workbooks to page 98. On this page are many words ending with the suffix 'er.' On the line next to each one, I want you to write the meaning of the word."

CASE II: TEACHING

Teacher: "Look at the words I have written on the board. Ann, will you read them aloud, please?"

Ann: "Teacher, painter, writer."

Teacher: "Good. Now, Jim, would you tell me what a teacher is?"

Jim: "A person who teaches."

Teacher: "Good (writes definition next to word). Now, Sally, would you tell me what a painter is?"

Sally: "A man who paints."

Teacher: "Is a painter only a man?"

Sally: "No, it can be a lady, too."

Teacher: "Can you define the word again?"

Sally: "Someone who paints."

Teacher: "Fine (writes definition next to word). Now, Ann, will you tell us the meaning of this last word?"

Ann: "A person who writes."

Teacher: "Very good (writes definition). All right, I want you to look very carefully at the three words. What do you see about them that is the same?"

Sally: "They all end with 'er'."

Teacher: "Good. Now look at the definitions. Do you see anything about them that is the same?"

Jim: "They all mean someone or a person who does something."

Teacher: "Excellent. Now think hard. If there is one thing about all the words that is the same and one thing about all the definitions that is the same, is there anything we can conclude?"

Sally: "That part of the word means a person who does something."

Teacher: "Right. But what part of the word?"

Ann: "Er."

Teacher: "Correct. Now can someone say the whole thing? What have we learned?"

Jim: "That 'er' means someone who does something."

Teacher: "Does it mean someone who does something in this word?" (Writes 'perfect' on the board.)

Ann:	"No."
Teacher:	"What's different?"
Sally:	"It's not at the end of the word."
Teacher:	"Then, can you reword Jim's statement? He said 'er' means someone who does something."
Sally:	" 'Er' at the end of a word means someone who does something."
Teacher:	"Good. Now let's think of some other words that have an 'er' at the end where 'er' means someone who does something, and then we'll see some words where 'er' at the end does not mean the same thing."

Although the second case is not finished, it is easy to see the difference between preaching and teaching. In teaching, the students are guided to make their own generalizations. Teaching takes more time initially than preaching. In the long run, however, teaching saves time since something taught well may not need to be retaught, whereas something preached usually must be preached again and again.

There are other types of activities that become confused with the teaching of reading. There may be "reciting" lessons, where a student is asked to recite rules formally. While knowing rules may be helpful, correct recitation does not mean that rules can be applied. Or there are "spelling" lessons, where students are asked to write teacher-dictated words. While teaching spelling is, of course, valuable, it is different from teaching reading.

COMPONENTS
OF THE REMEDIAL SESSION

Each remedial reading session should include at least three types of reading experiences. These are (1) focused instruction (skills instruction), (2) instructional reading, and (3) review of material (see Figure 7.1). In addition, recreational or independent reading can be either included in the reading lesson, or students can be encouraged to read on their own.

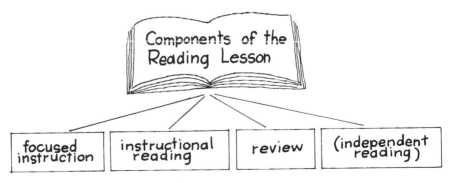

Figure 7.1   Components of the Reading Lesson

Focused Instruction

A block of time during each instructional session should be devoted to direct and careful teaching of the specific components of reading. Systematic teaching establishes the elements of reading firmly in students' minds. Focused instruction can be geared toward the teaching of reading skills, such as long and short "a" sounds, inferential comprehension, and meaning vocabulary. The teacher can use material from workbooks, instructional kits, and skills books for teaching.

However, the focused reading instruction does not have to be limited to skills. As an alternative, instruction can be geared to developing an integrated approach to reading. Activities might include written teacher-student conversations, reading to students, and experiences in predicting story endings. (These ideas are detailed further in Chapters 11 and 12).

Instructional Reading

Students should practice skills and strategies in the context of a reading situation. During instructional reading, students read a selection or story under the guidance of a teacher. This is followed by questions or a discussion of the material. The material chosen for instructional reading should be at the "instructional reading level" (refer to Chapter 6). At this level, students encounter some new words and concepts, but the students are under the guidance of the teacher, who anticipates difficulty and helps the students to master new material.

Review of Material

Remedial readers often have difficulty remembering material they have learned. Therefore, review is an important component of the lesson. The review may last only five or ten minutes, but it serves as a reminder that imprints previously mastered words and concepts. For example, many teachers begin the day by reviewing the sight words. Review is particularly important at the beginning stages of learning, for students who are just starting to acquire reading skills tend to forget them easily and need frequent practice.

Independent Reading

To establish permanent reading habits, students must find reading interesting, informative, and enjoyable. Independent reading is particularly important for students who have mastered beginning reading skills because it provides the wide reading they need to solidify gains. But even the most halting readers can enjoy certain books (for example, picture books) "all by themselves." For independent reading, students should be guided to choose books that are at an easier level than those used in instruction. These books are read on their own, without teacher help. Discussing independent reading with students encourages this activity, but discussions should not become testing sessions. Rather, they should focus on the student's enjoyment of the material.

If a student will not read books, the teacher can encourage the student to read other types of materials, such as television guides, newspapers, baseball and football programs, record jackets, popular magazines, and manuals. Students should be helped to realize the variety of reading material and purposes for reading that exist in the modern world.

Planning Balanced Lessons

Instructional and independent reading often receive too little emphasis in remedial lessons. Allington (1978) found that remedial readers, who are most in need of reading experiences, actually do the least amount of reading. During the reading session, the students in his study read, on the average, only forty-three words per session! Remedial sessions consisted largely of focused skill instruction (e.g., workbook pages, oral drills), neglecting sustained instructional and independent reading. Drawing an analogy from learning how to swim, would-be swimmers need focused instruction, given at the side of the pool, in activities such as breathing, leg strokes, arm strokes, and so on. However, unless they also receive practice in the actual act of swimming, they will never actually learn to swim. Similarly, students can only learn to read by practicing the actual act of reading. Therefore, remedial lessons must include a substantial amount of instructional and independent reading as well as focused instruction and exercises in specific skills.

BUILDING RAPPORT

The value of a successful teacher-pupil relationship cannot be overestimated; it may be far more important than the methods or materials that are used for instruction. Several principles serve as guidelines for building rapport.

Acceptance

Students should feel that teachers accept them as individuals. Often, poor readers are caught in a vicious cycle of reading failure and negative teacher reaction. By the time they have reached the need for special attention, behavioral problems tend to invite rejection by the teacher. Students may understand that they need help in reading, yet it is important to make them feel that, in total, they are likable people. Each remedial student should be accepted as a valuable and promising human being.

Success

Remedial students are in desperate need of experiencing success. Too often, their lives have been filled with unrelenting failure. If the tasks presented in the remedial lesson can be accomplished successfully, this goes a long way to establishing a solid relationship between the student and teacher.

Security

Remedial students also need to feel a sense of security in the instructional setting. One way to foster a sense of security is to start each instructional session with the same type of activity.

A student's sense of security can be easily shattered. For example, Ramon, a very shy pupil, had his sense of security shattered on the first day of his remedial reading work. When his teacher asked him what he wanted to do, he burst into tears. He wanted the security of being told what to do.

Eleven-year-old Teresa at first resisted coming to her special reading lesson. However, when the teacher made a "place" for her by covering the top of her desk with specially patterned paper, she felt she had a special location and became more willing to come to her lesson and settle down for instruction. If desks are shared with students who come at other times, movable name cards can be used.

Sharing Control

Human beings tend to learn better when they are involved and have invested in the learning. There are many ways in which students can share the responsibility for instruction with the teacher and thereby build a sense of ownership. They should be aware of the topics they are studying and the reasons for studying these topics. One teacher made five envelopes for her class: three for phonics principles (er, ar, or), one for new words, and one for words already mastered. The display of these envelopes made students aware of what they were studying, as well as their progress. Students can also share in the instructional process by finding materials for use in class. One teenager brought in words he had heard on television to begin a unit on meaning vocabulary.

Charting Progress

It is important to provide students with a sense of accomplishment. For example, evidence of progress can be charted easily by displaying a list of words that students have learned. When students enter a room in which several attractive sets of words are displayed on posters, they often try to read these posters, thus multiplying the learning effects. Displays of new words also serve as sight word practice for students at lower reading levels and as meaning vocabulary practice for those at upper levels.

In another example of charting, eight-year-old Samantha enjoyed her personal "bookworm" that the teacher displayed on the wall. Each segment of the worm represented a book she had read. For a group of teenagers who were working to improve reading rate, the teacher charted the progress of each student every day so that they could see how their rate of reading was improving.

When charting progress, however, it is important to remember that publicly displayed charts may embarrass the student who is making few or no gains. For some students, records of progress should be kept private. Chapter 10 provides many ideas for making charts.

Bibliotherapy

Bibliotherapy is a method of using books to help students work out personal problems. By identifying with the characters in the book and overcoming the problem along with the character, students are helped to deal with their own situations (Dreyer, 1977). For example, a student who is faced with the death of a member of the family could read a book about how another individual dealt with a similar problem. The reading experience helps the student to work out his or her own feelings and understand that others have faced and survived such hardships. The following steps are used in bibliotherapy: (1) determining the student's needs, (2) choosing the right book, and (3) discussing student's feelings. Teachers should recognize that bibliotherapy undertakes to deal with intensely personal feelings and should use this method cautiously.

THE SETTING

The teacher can change certain elements of the environmental setting, such as (1) the choice of individual or group instruction, (2) the distractions in the environment, (3) the variety of activities, and (4) the frequency and duration of instruction.

Group and Individual Instruction

Students may be taught individually, in a small group, or in a classroom setting. Some students require the personal attention of a one-to-one setting; others (particularly adolescents) resent being singled out. Students who lack self-motivation may not attend to work assigned to a group, whereas other students work diligently without the teacher's constant presence.

Students who have a long history of reading failure may have built up feelings of frustration, resentment, and despair (Roswell and Natchez, 1977). The group situation may help such students to see that their problems are not worse than those of others. Sometimes, however, students experience additional embarrassment by furthur exposure of their inadequacies and need individual instruction.

If the reading disability is severe, the situation may call for highly individualized special techniques. On the other hand, advanced reading skills are often taught more effectively in a group setting. For example, students who receive instruction in drawing conclusions or critical reading benefit from the stimulation of others. On a practical basis, group instruction is often selected because it is less expensive than individual instruction.

When group instruction is used, the optimum size of the group should be considered. Two studies suggest that reading groups up to six individuals are more effective than larger groups (Steirnagle, 1971; Cashdan, Pumfrey, and Luzner, 1971).

Another type of small-group work is called "peer tutoring." This refers to students teaching each other. Generally, one student is assigned to another as a teacher. Older students are often used to teach younger ones (cross-age tutoring), or the tutor and learner may be the same age. A noteworthy finding is that students who act as tutors often gain more in reading skills than do the students they are teaching (Sheenan, Feldman, and Allen, 1976). Careful teacher supervision is needed in a peer tutoring program. Peer tutoring has proven to be worthwhile for both the tutor and the learner.

Modifying the Environment

Often, students with severe reading difficulties are highly distractible and become overstimulated by an environment with too many temptations. Strauss and Lehtinen (1947) advocate providing a nondistracting setting for such students. They suggest reducing stimuli by modifications such as having students work in cubicles, covering windows, using a soft voice, and avoiding brightly colored clothing and jewelry.

Of course, not all students need such a restrictive environment; yet the concept of controlling stimuli can be applied to many instructional situations. For example, one teacher reduced the disruptive behavior of a very distractible group by facing their desks away from the door instead of toward it. Thus visitors entering and leaving the classroom were not in the sight line of the students. Another teacher built a three-sided cubicle out of a cutup cardboard box for an extremely distractible boy. The cubicle rested on his desk and gave him—and his neighbors—privacy (see Figure 7.2).

Figure 7.2

Varying the Activities

Another factor in the instructional setting is the planning of varied activities. Since students who need special instruction often have short attention spans, it is important to provide different instructional activities. For example, Ann, a restless and highly active nine-year-old, was just beginning to learn reading skills. Her teacher's objective for the lesson was to teach twenty-five sight words. To help Ann learn these words, her teacher used four different activities: playing a Bingo game with the words, fishing the words out of a fishbowl, choosing words from several alternatives, and reading words from a chart. By varying the activities, the teacher was successful in keeping Ann's attention during the remedial session.

Frequency and Duration
of Reading Instruction

One of the most important decisions that a teacher must make concerns the frequency of remedial instruction. Should a student receive instruction three times a week, or should the remedial sessions be limited to once per week? Spache (1981) suggests that frequent instructional sessions in reading facilitate learning for younger students, whereas longer, but fewer, sessions are appropriate for older students. Students with low-level reading skills typically need frequent teaching, since skills learned in beginning reading are easily forgotten from session to session. Further, since severely disabled readers can do little reading on their own, they need frequent sessions to practice newly acquired skills. Students who have acquired some proficiency, however, may need less frequent teaching. More advanced students require time to absorb material and to transfer skills to their class situation. A teaching session held on a weekly basis may suffice for encouraging the development of higher-level comprehension skills or refining meaning vocabulary.

The duration of the special reading program must also be considered. Should students be kept in a program only long enough to get a "start," or should they be kept in as long as possible? In general, research suggests that remedial readers will profit from instruction that is continued over a long period of time. Spache (1981) reviewed forty studies of reading programs of varying duration and concluded that students progress at the rate of about two months for each month of remedial instruction. On the other hand, short, intensive programs (5 to 15 weeks) appear to bring the greatest initial gains, (3.4 months' gain for every month of remedial instruction). These studies suggest that students continue to profit from long remedial programs but that short intensive programs produced the most rapid initial gains. Guthrie, Siefert and Kline (1978) found that students needed at least fifty hours of instruction to make permanent gains.

Although students continue to improve in reading proficiency while they are enrolled in remedial programs, some researchers have found that they tend to fall back to their former rates of reading gains after special instruction has terminated (Spache, 1981; Carroll, 1972). Unfortunately, this means that they fall farther and farther behind their average-achievement classmates. However, Guthrie, Siefert, and Kline (1978) found that students maintain learning-rate gains after remedial instruction has terminated. Measures can be taken to help students maintain remedial gains. Balow (1965) found that, when remedial reading teachers continued to have some contact with students after remedial instruction had stopped, the students continued to maintain high reading gains.

ISSUES IN TEACHING ADOLESCENTS

The numbers of adolescents and young adults receiving help in reading has increased in the past several years, as society has become more aware of the needs of older students. This section details some of the issues encountered when teaching reading to older students.

Emotional and behavioral problems tend to increase as pupils reach adolescence. Junior and senior high school students often have encountered failure on a daily basis for many years. The school provides little opportunity to escape from failure so the student may skip school or drop out to avoid facing the instructional situation. But while an adult may choose to change a job if conditions become intolerable, or may choose to remain on the job because of the monetary reward, the failing adolescent has no socially acceptable alternatives to school.

While adolescence has always been a trying time in the human growth process, it seems to have become even more difficult in today's society. Problems such as the rates of school nonattendance, academic disability, mental illness, school violence and vandalism, unemployment, sex-related problems, and drug abuse reach into the lives of adolescents throughout the nation (Cullinan and Epstein, 1979; Rossman, 1980). The ranks of the unemployed are swelled with adolescents who are illiterate or semiliterate. The problem of learning to read is intertwined with all these social, cultural, and personal problems. The ability to read, however, may provide the way out for a troubled teenager.

Adolescents vary widely in their receptivity to different methods of instruction. For example, two adolescent boys (Mark, 17, and Jeremy, 18) recently attended the reading clinic conducted by one of the authors. Both boys were reading at approximately the second grade level and had severe word recognition problems. Mark decided that, because of his severe problems, he would like to read easier material and was given second grade level materials. Although the books were geared toward the interests of younger children, Mark recognized that they helped him to learn the skills he needed for reading. Jeremy, however, wanted nothing to do with these materials. Instead, he wanted to pursue his interest in history. His reading materials were short newspaper articles and picture captions dealing with the life of former President John F. Kennedy. The needs of both adolescents were fulfilled in an acceptable way.

Disabled adolescent readers also have many similarities. In contrast to younger children, they tend to have a keen awareness of their reading problem. Teenagers may also be embarrassed about their inability to read, knowing that they face the possible ridicule of their peers. A limited amount of school time remains to help the reading-disabled adolescent. Finally, each adolescent faces the immediacy of soon entering the adult world.

There are several different kinds of instructional programs for adolescents. Some are designed to prepare teenagers for further schooling; others are intended to prepare them for the world of work. A survey of approaches being used with learning-disabled adolescents by Alley and Deshler (1979) revealed that five predominant program options are used:

1. *Basic skills remediation.* This approach attempts to improve basic academic skill deficits by providing remedial instruction. Students receive instruction at their current reading level. Stress is placed on improving deficit reading skills. A survey showed that 51 percent of the high school programs sampled use this approach.
2. *Tutorial curriculum approach.* This approach provides instruction in academic content areas. That is, the teacher helps students with problems they are having in content-area classes, such as English, social studies, or science. The approach tends to be used with readers who have mild to moderate problems. Roughly 24 percent of the programs surveyed used this approach.
3. *Functional curriculum approach.* This approach is designed to help students function in society. They are taught survival skills, that is, skills that will enable them to get along in the world outside of school. These skills include consumer education, completion of application forms, banking and money skills, and life-care skills. About 17 percent of the programs surveyed used this approach.
4. *Work-Study Model.* This approach teaches the adolescent job- and career-related skills by providing on-the-job experience. Students in the program typically spend half the day on the job and the remainder of the day in school. The survey showed that 5 percent of the respondents were using this approach.
5. *Other models.* This is a combination or variation of other approaches. Alley and Deshler (1979) suggest the use of a "learning strategies" model; the objective of this approach is to teach adolescents how to learn, rather than to teach specific content, in short, "learning how to learn." The remaining 3 percent of the adolescent programs in the survey consisted of other approaches.

ISSUES IN TEACHING ADULTS

Adults are reentering the learning situation in increasing numbers. Some are relatively young adults who have dropped out of school and now find themselves blocked from employment. Others, particularly women, have been out of the work force for many years and wish to reenter. Still others are currently employed but want to advance in their jobs or enhance their personal skills.

Many adults in reading programs were denied an opportunity for education in their youth. They may have lived in countries where free education was not provided, or perhaps they were forced to work in order to help support their families. Many adult learners are concerned with learning to speak and write the English language.

Characteristics of Adult Learners

Adult learners have many characteristics which set them apart from children and adolescents. The wise teacher takes these into account when planning a program.

1. *Adults need to view learning as useful.* Adults soon lose patience when they do not understand the usefulness of what they are learning. Unlike children and adolescents, adults have returned voluntarily to the learning situation. If learning does not serve their purposes, however, they will not continue. Adults of any learning level are goal oriented about their education. That is, they go to school for a specific purpose—learning to drive, learning skills for employment, or learning to read the newspaper. The teacher must ascertain what purpose the adult has for education, and then address it in instruction.

2. *Adults have a wealth of life experiences.* It is important to respect the fund of information and knowledge which all adults have accumulated. Adults may be remedial *readers*, but they are not remedial *people*. Each of the adults the authors has instructed has some area of expertise—be it knowledge of another country, politics, dancing, or playing a musical instrument. This knowledge needs to be respected. Often adult students can share expertise with each other and with the teacher, resulting in rich and varied classroom experiences.

3. *Adults have many life constraints.* Adult learners are often employed or have families. Thus, many constraints are placed upon their lives. These responsibilities may prevent even the well-intentioned person from attending some instructional sessions. Teachers need to be sympathetic and understanding of such situations. Often they can help them by enabling adults to bring small children to class.

4. *Adults may view their reading difficulties as permanent.* An adult who is out of the school situation may come to view a reading disability as a fixed, nonchanging condition. Thus, adults often place little hope in the instructional situation, and it is difficult to persuade them to enter remedial instruction, put forth effort, or attend regularly. Because of an adult's often lengthy history of failure, the emotional aspects of learning become very important. Adults may be unwilling to face the negative emotions associated with learning. For these reasons, it is important that the teacher of adults maintain a positive attitude and be hopeful about the future. Many adults improve their skills considerably through instruction.

There are many different types of programs for adults with reading needs. These include, of course, remedial reading instruction. In addition, there are other types of programs available.

1. *ABE and GED Programs* These two programs provide (1) Adult Basic Education—at elementary levels through eighth grade, and (2) high school level education. A person passing the GED examination is awarded a high school equivalence degree. Such programs are funded by the government and require group instruction. In Illinois, a minimum of twenty registrants is required for any program.

2. *Literacy Volunteers of America* This private organization trains volunteers to work with disabled adults in an individual setting and provides materials for tutoring. Programs are aimed toward the illiterate and semiliterate adult. A component for teaching English as a second language is also available.

3. *The Laubach Program* Frank Laubach, a missionary, developed a program for teaching literacy to millions of people worldwide. Materials include initial instruction in a pictorial alphabet. Laubach literacy materials are available through New Readers' Press (see the newspaper *News For You*, Appendix A).

SUMMARY

Several principles guide remedial programs. These include beginning instruction at an appropriate level of difficulty, using time effectively, proceeding from simple to complex tasks, using the student's strengths, and teaching reading rather than preaching about reading concepts.

A balanced reading lesson consists of the following elements: (1) focused instruction (where skills or separate parts of reading receive attention), (2) instructional reading (reading of passages and stories), and (3) review. Independent or recreational reading should also be encouraged.

Building rapport through a positive student-teacher relationship is an important part of a successful reading program. Guides for building rapport include acceptance, success, security, sharing control, and charting progress.

The instructional setting can be varied in several ways. Students can be taught in individual or group settings. Teachers can modify the environment and try to eliminate stimuli that distract from learning. Teachers should vary instructional activities to help students with short attention spans. Sessions for lower-level readers or young children should be short and frequent. Older, more advanced students should have longer, less frequent sessions. Remedial students experience greatest rate of gain in short, intensive instruction. However, fairly substantial gains also continue throughout longer programs. After remediation is terminated, students have difficulty maintaining gains.

Adolescents increasingly receive remedial instruction. These students present a special challenge to the teacher because they are very aware of their disability, may present many emotional problems, and will soon enter the adult world. Program options for adolescents include basic skills remediation, a tutorial curriculum approach, a functional curriculum approach, a work-study model, and a learning strategies approach.

Adults in remedial settings also must receive special consideration. Adults need to view reading as useful. Each adult has a wealth of life experiences. Teachers should recognize the many life constraints of adults. Finally, adults may view their reading difficulties as permanent. Program options for adults include ABE–GED programs, Literacy Volunteers of America, and the Laubach method.

8

SEVERELY DISABLED READERS I

characteristics

Most students who are referred for special reading instruction respond well and make considerable gains in a short period of time. But a small percentage seem to make few gains, even with well-taught and sensitive instruction. In spite of repeated attempts at reading instruction, these individuals remain, virtually, nonreaders. These students, who are considered "severely disabled readers," are the concern of this chapter and the next. The characteristics of severely disabled readers are examined in this chapter; strategies for teaching these students are presented in Chapter 9.

Experts from a variety of fields have come to believe that there is a "hard core" of reading disability cases who can only learn to read with extreme difficulty. For example, Critchley, a neurologist, states:

> Neurologists believe that within the community of poor readers there exists a hard core of cases where the origins of the learning defect are inborn and independent of any intellectual shortcomings which may happen to coexist. (Critchley, 1970, pp. 101–102)

Vernon, a reading specialist, asks:

> Is there, in addition to the normal variations in reading ability. . . an independent dyslexic syndrome lying outside of the normal range of variation? Are these innate disabilities aggravated perhaps but not caused by environmental circumstances? . . . The evidence . . . would seem adequate to establish the existence of a basic disability in at least some backward readers. (Vernon, 1971, p. 176)

These severely disabled readers are referred to as having a variety of conditions, including *word-blindness* (Hinshelwood, 1917), *primary reading disability* (Rabinovich, 1969), and *dyslexia* (Critchely, 1970). Perhaps the most widely-used term is dyslexia. This term is derived from the Greek roots *dys* ("not") and *lexia* ("read"). Because professionals in the field of reading are so often questioned about dyslexia, they should be familiar with the ways in which it is used. In fact, the term is used in a wide variety of ways. While all of the definitions center around poor reading, agreement stops there. Meanings of dyslexia include brain damage, central nervous system dysfunction, a general language disorder, and unspecified reading retardation (Lerner, 1981).

In an attempt to clarify the diverse uses of the term dyslexia, the Secretary of what was formerly the Department of Health, Education, and Welfare set up a committee to define the term. The committee found it impossible to reach agreement and concluded that the term dyslexia served no useful purpose (National Advisory Committee on Dyslexia and Related Reading Disorders, 1969). Despite this conclusion, use of the term dyslexia persists. It is frequently used by specialists in the medical professions, such as pediatricians, neurologists, and psychiatrists.

Whatever name is used for severely disabled readers, teachers of reading need to understand the learning characteristics of these students and be familiar with the special methods that are used to teach them. The instructional records and case histories of such students reveal certain characteristic traits. These characteristics include (1) a lack of prerequisite skills, (2) a failure to appreciate what reading is about (lack of cognitive clarity), (3) inadequate language development, and (4) learning styles that inhibit reading growth. Each is discussed in turn.

LACK OF PREREQUISITE SKILLS

Certain auditory and visual skills are prerequisites for learning to read. The role of these prerequisite skills in learning to read is discussed in this section. In addition, specific prerequisite skills are examined and some suggestions for their instruction are given. (Tests of these skills are described in Test Inventory 8.1 at the end of this chapter. Instructional programs for prerequisite skill development are described in Appendix A.)

The Role of Prerequisite Skills
in Reading

An ordered sequence of human learning occurs as the individual matures. As the child grows, a set of learning skills at one stage becomes the precursor for learning at a later stage. For example, before children learn to walk, they develop certain earlier abilities, such as holding on when walking, standing alone, and balancing their bodies without support. These abilities, among others, become prerequisites for walking.

Many educators and psychologists support the idea that the child needs certain prerequisite abilities and skills as the foundation for the successful learning of reading. In the field of reading, these prerequisites are often referred to as "reading readiness" skills and are deemed necessary for successful reading acquisition (Durkin, 1980).

The importance of prerequisite skills is also recognized in many fields allied to reading. In the field of developmental psychology, there is general recognition that human beings develop motor and perceptual skills early in life and that these become the basis for more advanced learning (Piaget, 1952; Gesell and Ilg, 1946). In the fields of special education and learning disabilities, a number of authorities have focused upon the development of "psychological processing" abilities (visual, auditory, and motor skills) and their role in reading (Kephart, 1971; Kirk and Kirk, 1971; Sawyer, 1980). Recently, scholars from several fields have investigated the role of "information processing" abilities as factors related to the successful acquisition of reading skills (LaBerge and Samuels, 1974; Torgeson, 1979).

The field of learning disabilities has been especially sensitive to the relationship between "psychological processing" abilities and academic learning. In fact, the phrase "disorders of psychological processing" is used as part of the definition of a learning disability (see Chapter 14). These psychological processing skills can be considered prerequisite skills for reading. They are often referred to as perceptual deficits.

Although there is general agreement that reading is built upon certain prerequisite abilities, be they called "readiness," "psychological processing skills," or "information processing," there is some disagreement about the precise role of these skills in teaching remedial reading. In particular, controversy exists about when these skills should be taught and whether training in them is useful.

For a number of years, teaching psychological processing skills (such as visual, auditory, and motor skills) was "fashionable," particularly in the learning disabilities field. The technique came to be misused and overused as a remedial strategy. In some cases, instruction in these skills was given to students who did not require such intense instruction, such as moderately disabled readers or even to normal children. In other cases, the teaching of processing skills was substituted for the teaching of reading rather than used as a prerequisite to the reading task.

Not surprisingly, the abuse of this kind of teaching has led to questions about the wisdom of teaching processing skills (Hammill and Larsen, 1974, 1975; Salvia and Ysseldyke, 1981; Velluntino et al., 1977; Balow, 1971; International Reading Association, 1976). Among the critical questions asked are the following:

- Is there value in analyzing a student's perceptual processing abilities?
- Do tests of perceptual processing abilities measure what they are supposed to?
- Is there evidence of improvement in reading following perceptual process training?

There is sharp disagreement about the answers to these questions. Some authorities conclude that psychological processing training is ineffective and that there is little value in obtaining this type of information about a severely disabled reader. Instead, they recommend that emphasis be placed on the teaching of academic skills, excluding the processing abilities that may underlie these skills (Hammill and Larsen, 1974; Salvia and Ysseldyke, 1981; Arter and Jenkins, 1979).

Other authorities, however, continue to support the value of a perceptual processing approach to teaching severely disabled readers (Lund, et al., 1978; Minskoff, 1975; Kavale, 1981, 1982). They point out that much of the research which is critical of processing skills training had tested these skills in situations where they were not likely to succeed. For example, research was conducted using students too old to benefit from perceptual training; experimental groups were not carefully controlled; and the time period for the research was not long enough to demonstrate positive effects.

Although researchers continue to debate the merits of the perceptual processing approach, teachers cannot afford to wait for the final answers. Meanwhile, they are faced with the problems of teaching severely disabled readers on a daily basis.

We believe that the teaching of perceptual processing and prerequisite skills remains a valid and valuable approach for severely disabled readers.

Teachers, however, should plan instruction of these skills in a judicious manner. Some guidelines are given below:

1. Instruction in prerequisite or psychological processing skills is more likely to be needed by severely disabled readers than by students with mild reading problems. Using the analogy of swimming instruction, why teach a student to jump into a pool if that student is already proficient in diving?

2. Not every severely disabled reader should be taught processing skills. Such instruction is needed only if a) there are specific processing deficits and b) if it appears that these deficits are interfering with reading acquisition.

3. Teachers should teach skills in relation to reading tasks. The closer the prerequisite instruction is to the actual reading situation, the more effective it will be. If the student cannot learn phonics because that student cannot blend component sounds, then the prerequisite skill of blending should be taught. Similarly, using reading-related materials, such as letters and words, to teach auditory and visual discrimination is more effective than using environmental sounds or geometric shapes (Barrett, 1965b).

4. Teaching processing skills is not a substitute for the teaching of reading. Psychological processing skills are prerequisites for learning to read, and training in these skills can help the severely disabled reader eventually to learn to read. However, training in perceptual processing skills is not, by itself, a method for teaching reading.

With these cautions in mind, processing skills can be an important and useful part of the remediation of severely disabled readers. Tests of processing or prerequisite skills are given in Test Inventory 8.1.

Combining Prerequisite Skills and Reading

Prerequisite skill instruction may be combined with reading stategies to formulate an effective program for severely disabled readers. Several strategies may be used to combine information about the student's strengths and weaknesses in processing abilities with strategies for reading improvement.

1. *Training ability weaknesses.* If the student has a severe lack of readiness in a specific ability area, the development of the prerequisite skill may enhance the total level of functioning and prepare the student for future learning. If the student lacks a specific prerequisite skill for learning to read by a particular method, that skill could be taught. For example, if students cannot visually discriminate one letter from another, practice in the recognition and discrimination of letters may enhance their ability to learn sight words.

2. *Teaching through ability strengths.* Another strategy is to select an area of prerequisite strength and match it with a reading method utilizing this strength. For example, if a student is strong in visual skills, the teacher could use a visual approach such as the sight word method. If the student shows auditory strength, the teacher could use a sound-symbol or phonics methods. Some research has ques-

tioned the effectiveness of this approach (Jones, 1972; Lilly and Kelleher, 1973; Robinson, 1972; Sabatino and Dorfman, 1974). However, for severe cases of reading disability, knowledge of the student's intact abilities provides useful clinical information for the diagnostic and remedial planning.

3. *Use a combined approach.* This method utilizes both approaches. It instructs the student with a method that uses the area of strength and at the same time trains the area of weakness.

Visual Prerequisites

Visual skills include a cluster of abilities in which information about the world is taken in through the eyes and interpreted. These skills include visual discrimination, visual sequencing, visual memory, and a related ability, naming alphabet letters.

VISUAL DISCRIMINATION. Visual discrimination is the ability to see likenesses and differences in visual stimuli. For example, can the student pick out two letters or words that look the same? Reading requires the reader to discriminate between visually similar letters and words (*on, no; dog, boy; b,d*). With practice and training, students can learn this skill. Visual discrimination can be taught using many types of objects such as geometric shapes. We recommend, however, that letters and words be used for visual discrimination exercises since these are most closely related to reading (Barrett, 1965a, b). Pupils having problems acquiring reading skills because they confuse letters and words can be helped with the following exercises:

1. The student matches words that are the same in a row. For example,

    today: dobay tobay today todab

2. The student is given a sheet of paper containing many words and is asked to circle all the examples of one word.
3. The student lists all the words that begin or end with a given letter. A clear example of the letter should be in front of the students.
4. The student copies a series of letters or words.

VISUAL SEQUENCING. Visual sequencing involves the ability to perceive objects and letters in an appropriate order. Words in the English language owe their unique identity to the order of their letters. Thus "on" is one word, and "no" is another. Therefore, sensitivity to sequence is an important prerequisite for reading. The following exercises can be used to help the student develop visual sequencing abilties:

1. Students can arrange alphabet letters to match words.
2. Students can look for words that contain a certain sequence of letters, such as "igh."

3. One visual sequencing problem common to many remedial readers is reversals of letters. For example, the student reads "was" for "saw." Ways of overcoming reversals are discussed in Chapter 11.

VISUAL MEMORY.   This refers to the ability to remember stimuli (letters and words) that are presented visually. Many students, particularly those who have trouble learning sight words, appear to have problems in this area. However, research does not provide evidence that visual memory itself can be substantially improved (Samuels, 1973). What students can learn, with training, is how to combine several types of clues to enhance their memory for words. Therefore, activities in this area should be related closely to reading tasks, utilizing words and letters.

1. The teacher holds up a word for five seconds and then puts it down. The student then tries to identify it from choices printed on a card.
2. The teacher holds up a word for five or ten seconds and then puts it face down. The student tries to write it from memory. Several exposures may be given. This method is also useful for learning sight words.

NAMING ALPHABET LETTERS.   The ability to name letters has been found to be an excellent predictor of reading achievement. Despite this finding, it should be noted that 1) letter-naming ability is not an essential prerequisite skill for learning to read and 2) that training students to name letters does not automatically increase reading abilities (Samuels, 1972; Venezky, 1975). Nevertheless, students often feel more comfortable if they can identify letters, which are the building blocks of reading.

Several cautions should be observed when teaching letter names. First, instruction in alphabet recognition should be done with the letters out of order. It should not be assumed that students who can recite the alphabet in order (i.e., "a, b, c, d, e, . . . ") can recognize letters when they are out of order. Second, many remedial readers need practice in matching uppercase letters to lowercase letters. Other remedial students recognize uppercase letters but are unsure of lowercase letters which are visually more confusing. The following activities are suggested for helping students to recognize and match letters:

1. Have students look for and collect letters from magazines, putting all the "a's" on one page, all the "b's" on another page, and so on.
2. Give students a page filled with letters and ask them to find all the examples they can in one minute.
3. Give students exercises with lowercase letters on one side of the page and uppercase letters on the other side and ask them to match them.
4. Use poems and children's books, based on the alphabet. These books and poems appeal to many ranges and interests (see Appendix A).

Many commercial programs contain activities for training visual prerequisite skills. In most of these programs, however, visual skills training is combined with motor skills training. Among the activities found in these programs are cutting, coloring, and tracing. The relationship of motor skills to reading is somewhat unclear. It does appear that these fine motor skills have a higher relationship to reading than large motor skills (deHirsch, 1966).

Auditory Prerequisites

Auditory skills include a cluster of abilities in which information taken is perceived through the sense of hearing. Many auditory processing skills have been identified as prerequisites for reading (Dykstra, 1962). Skills related to auditory perception include auditory discrimination, rhyming, blending, auditory memory, sound segmentation, and knowledge of letter sounds.

AUDITORY DISCRIMINATION.   Auditory discrimination refers to the ability to hear differences in sounds. In relation to reading, auditory discrimination is the ability to distinguish differences in phonic elements or phonemes. Can the student tell if two spoken words are the same or different? Teachers should make sure that what appears to be an auditory discrimination problem does not stem from another cause. Some problems appear to be auditory discrimination problems but are actually due to a loss of hearing acuity or to differences of the student's language from standard English (Knafle and Geissal, 1977). Such students need other therapies. Some exercises for those students who do need to improve auditory discrimination are given below:

1. Say a list of words and ask the students to raise their hands whenever a word beginning or ending with a certain syllable is said. It is helpful for the teacher to stand behind the student so that visual clues are avoided.
2. Use the procedure described in exercise 1 with single letter sounds.
3. Show two or three pictures with verbal representations that are close in sound (e.g., ride, red, rod). Then say a word representing one of the pictures. The student selects the correct picture.

RHYMING.   The ability to rhyme is essential to learning to read with the analytic phonics, or the linguistic, approach. This method for teaching reading requires that the student recognize words that are a part of a rhyming "word family." Teachers should realize that dialect-different and foreign-language-speaking students may have learned other rhyming systems. For example, both the French and Persian (Iranian) rhyming systems are different from that used in English.

It is sometimes difficult to accurately assess rhyming abilities. For example, the student may not be able to answer the question. "What word rhymes with 'at'?" Instead, the teacher might ask (especially with younger students), "What word does 'at' make you think of?" Or the teacher might start a sequence, such as: "at, bat, ... " If the teacher is flexible in the assessment of rhyming, students often demonstrate unexpected rhyming abilities.

Rhyming can be taught using a variety of interesting and motivating activities. Some suggestions for teaching this skill follow.

1. Say two words and ask the student if they rhyme.
2. Have students complete rhyming couplets, such as

    It is a nice day
    I would like to. . .
    At first provide two or three choices, only one of which rhymes. Then ask students to think of a rhyming word. Some students get so involved in this exercise that they begin to create their own rhyming couplets!
3. Songs and poems can be used to teach rhyming. The *Mother Goose* rhymes are a particularly good source. Pupils can fill in missing rhyming words or memorize these lovely poems.

BLENDING.   Blending refers to the ability to combine isolated letter sounds into words. This ability is very important if a student is to learn to read through a synthetic phonics method, where letter sounds are blended together to form words. Some students can produce individual letter sounds but can get no farther than helplessly repeating these isolated sounds, such as "p"-"e"-"t." To use phonics effectively, students must be able to form words from isolated sounds. It should be noted that blending is a somewhat artificial skill, since sounds produced in isolation are different from sounds in words.

Teachers can use a sequence of activities (from easy to hard) to help children learn this vital skill. A suggested sequence for teaching blending skills follows. Not all students will need to start at the very first stage.

1. Pronounce a two-syllable word with the syllables disconnected. Ask, "What word is this?" (for example, "bas-ket").
2. Next, select a one-syllable word with three sounds (e.g., "rat"). Say the word with the last sound separated: "ra-t." The student is asked to blend the sounds and identify the word.
3. Then say the word with the first sound separated from the middle and ending sounds: "r-at." The student blends the sounds and says the word.
4. Finally, the word is divided into three distinct sounds: "r-a-t." The student blends the sounds and says the word.

Words with four and five sounds may then be presented for the student to blend and identify. Words need not exceed five sounds.

AUDITORY MEMORY.   Human beings use their auditory channel to remember most types of information. For example, to remember phone numbers, people "rehearse" them orally. Auditory memory is important in learning phonics. When students are using a decoding process, they must store separate sounds in their memory long enough to blend them together into words. There is also evidence that auditory memory plays a part in learning sight words (Richek, 1977-8). To develop auditory memory while maximizing reading skill, exercises should concentrate upon words and sounds. Some suggestions follow:

1. Present sentences orally and have students repeat the sentences. The sentences should become longer as more mastery is attained.
2. Present groups of syllables or unrelated words for repetition.
3. Have students memorize songs and poems.

SOUND SEGMENTATION.   Sound segmentation refers to the ability to recognize that words spoken orally can be divided into smaller units or sounds. This concept is necessary for acquiring reading skills. It is particularly useful for students learning synthetic phonics (Liberman, 1973). Sound segmentation appears to be a learned skill rather than a natural one. Liberman (1977) finds that there are no natural acoustic divisions between the component sounds in words.

> The phonemes that comprise spoken sounds . . . cannot be clearly isolated, and they do not maintain their constancy in different syllables or words. Phonemes examined in terms of their acoustical properties are found to overlap in time rather than to follow neatly after one another in the sound stream, and are also found to vary acoustically in different speech contexts. (Wallach and Wallach, 1982, p. 157)

Because of these facts, students must often be specifically taught to segment sounds. Although exercises in auditory discrimination, blending, and letter sounds will reinforce the concept of sound segmentation, direct instruction may also be needed for this concept. Wallach and Wallach (1982) found that instruction in segmentation dramatically increased the reading abilities of remedial readers. They suggest that segmentation instruction may be easily given using two methods:

1. Separate the beginning phoneme of a word from the rest of the words by a pause. The teacher can say "*m—an*" and have students identify the first phoneme. Students can also pronounce these separated words.
2. Use a "stuttering" pronunciation such as *p-p-p-an*. The student first imitates the teacher and then proceeds alone.

Wallach and Wallach feel that the vowel sound attached to stopped consonants when they are pronounced alone (e.g., *puh, buh*) does not hamper students' learning. Teachers can feel free to use the above strategies even though they must pronounce isolated consonants.

Other effective programs of teaching segmentation include the "ABD's" of Reading (Williams, 1980) and a program known as phonematic hearing, or sound counting (Ollila, Johnson, and Downing, 1974). The following steps for teaching sound segmentation are based on the phonemic hearing program. Commercial materials are not needed to implement this program.

1. First, choose words that contain the same number of sounds as letters and that also can be pictured (i.e., "c-a-t," three sounds; "b-a-n-d," four sounds).
2. Show the word and its matching picture. Give the students "sound counters" (for example, tongue depressors). Ask the students to say the word slowly with the teacher and put a counter in place each time a sound is heard.

3. Present students with pictures of objects, but no words. The student says the word orally and places a marker for each sound that they hear. This stage is very difficult and requires considerable practice.

4. Combine the sound counting with spelling. The student places letters on the markers when the picture is shown and spells the word by placing the markers correctly. (This stage is optional for teaching the concept of sound segmentation.)

LETTER SOUNDS.   If students are to learn by a phonics method, they must know the sounds related to the letter symbols. Often, severely disabled readers confuse the concept of letter sound with the letter name. To avoid this confusion, some commercial programs teach only the letter sounds (for example, DISTAR). This practice can be followed by teachers if students exhibit such confusion.

Students must learn the sounds that are related to consonant letters as well as those sounds that are related to vowels. Because consonant letter sounds are more stable and easier to learn, they are generally taught first. (Vowel letter sounds are extremely variable, and therefore they are usually taught after the pupil has acquired some reading fluency.) Consonant sounds are classified into those where the breath flow continues (such as *s*, *v*, *th*) and those where the breath flow stops (such as *b*, *t*). In general, consonants that continue are easier to teach, with the "s" sound being the easiest of all. Students are often amused when taught that "s" is the sound that *Sammy Snake* makes. Several ways of teaching letter sounds are suggested:

1. Use mnemonics or memory devices (such as *s* for "snake" and *b* for "ball").
2. Present words and ask the student to produce the first or last sound.
3. A variation of the preceding suggestion is enjoyed by nonreaders. The teacher says a sentence, leaving out the last word. This word is then printed. The student produces the beginning sound and then tries to guess the entire word.

FAILURE TO APPRECIATE
WHAT READING IS ABOUT

Learning to read requires that the student first understand what reading is all about. Young readers and some severely disabled readers lack an understanding of the reading process. They are confused about such basic concepts as (1) why people read, (2) what people do when they read, and (3) what is meant by sounds, words, and sentences. They do not understand that reading is a meaningful process. In other words, they lack "cognitive clarity" about the reading process.

In investigating students' concepts about reading, Downing (1971–1972) found that primary school children were unclear about the reading process and unable to describe the purposes and actions of readers. In another study, Downing (1973–1974) found that most children did not understand the reading terms such as "words" and "sounds." This research suggests that these concepts are not automatically acquired and that teachers must provide instruction to some students so that they can develop adequate "cognitive clarity" about reading.

The concepts of "words" and "sentences" can be taught using the "language-experience" approach. In this method, students dictate stories and the teacher writes them. Because the language in the stories is familiar, this provides an excellent method for bridging the gap between oral language and unfamiliar reading concepts. To teach the concept of a sentence, language experience stories can be duplicated and cut into sentence strips. After the concept of sentences is mastered, the concept of a "word" can be taught by duplicating the story again and cutting it into separate words. Some students become very excited when they finally understand what a sentence or word is.

The concept of sounds and syllables can also be learned using language experience stories. Words from the stories can be broken into syllables and sounds, and the student can be asked to identify them.

A tape recorder can be combined with the language experience approach to clarify reading concepts. Experience stories may be taped, sentence by sentence, and then played back. Students identify the number of words they hear in each sentence. They can also listen for words that begin with a certain sound, such as "s."

In addition to the language experience method, word cards containing sight words can be used to teach the concepts of sentences and words. Students can combine the cards into sentences and copy them, carefully noting the number of words.

INADEQUATE LANGUAGE DEVELOPMENT

Language facility is a prerequisite for reading. Therefore, reading disability can be viewed as one aspect of a general language deficit. The role of language in reading and the various facets of language are discussed in Chapter 4. Mounting evidence suggests that many severely disabled readers have inadequately developed language skills. Often, students who experience difficulty in learning to read have also experienced diffculty in the development of speech and oral language.

Language abilities can be improved through direct instruction in both receptive (or received) language and expressive (or produced) language. Although several commercial programs designed for language development are available, teachers can make a considerable impact on the language growth of their pupils through informal methods and procedures. The following are specific suggestions for fostering language growth in severely disabled readers.

1. A simple way to improve receptive language skills is to read to students. Choose materials that contain richer language patterns than students ordinarily use or can read. Poetry, folktales, and children's books are good sources of rich language patterns. Students with some reading fluency should be encouraged to read materials containing exemplary language models. Bill Martin's *Sounds of*

Language (see appendix A) series, for example, contains creative and stimulating language, which is controlled for reading level.

2. Since pupils absorb the language patterns of their environment, teachers should use rich language patterns in their speech to foster language growth. Some teachers deliberately use "hard" words and encourage students to ask questions about them.

3. Language should be used as a reasoning process in the classroom. Often, remedial readers have not been exposed to the use of language *as thinking* in a school setting. Instead, they are bombarded with orders, directions to be quiet, and other authoritative commands. Teachers can help students to use language as a reasoning process in both receptive and expressive modes. Rather than simply giving directions, teachers should take the time to explain their reasons for doing things. The teacher's conversations should contain many sentences on the order of "I did this because . . . " or "I felt this because . . . ". Teachers can also encourage students to verbalize their own reasoning and to question actively the reasoning of others. Through such procedures, students will come to see that thinking can be described and refined using language skills.

4. Techniques known as *expansion* and *extension* may be used to enrich expressive language. Expansion and extension are two ways in which mothers have been observed to enrich the language of their young children (Cazden, 1972). In expansion, adults restate what the student has said in a fuller form. For example, if a student says "I feel okay," the teacher might say "You're feeling well today?" Extension involves going beyond what the student says. The teacher might respond to "I feel okay," by saying "I'm glad you're feeling happy today. Did anything special happen?"

5. There are many "wordless" picture books which contain stories told entirely in pictures, without words. These books can be used to foster language growth, since students can "read" the pictures and then retell the stories in their own words. Teachers should encourage the use of rich language patterns to tell these stories. Language may be enhanced if students go through the book as they are telling the stories. Descriptions of several wordless picture books are given in Appendix A.

6. Finally, teachers may create a classroom atmosphere conducive to language growth by simply encouraging students to express themselves freely. Students can be encouraged to relate their experiences. Class conversations can be held about favorite TV programs or sports events. An active, verbal classroom is the best environment for encouraging language growth. To encourage free expression, teachers should be careful not to criticize students' language patterns.

Additional informal strategies for language growth and improvement are given in Chapter 12 (in the section on Sentence Comprehension) and Chapter 13 (in the Meaning Vocabulary section). Commercial programs for language development are also available. (See Appendix A.)

LEARNING STYLES OF
SEVERELY DISABLED READERS

Each individual has a distinctive learning style. Children, as well as adults, have different styles of acquiring information and knowledge. Among the factors that affect learning style are: reflective and impulsive tempo, field-independent and field-dependent cognitive styles, and attentional deficit disorders.

Reflective and Impulsive Tempo

One way to analyze styles of learning is to look at whether a learner's behavior is reflective or impulsive. A reflective individual will proceed with careful deliberation, considering alternatives before choosing a response to a problem. The impulsive individual will respond quickly, without apparent thought. There is substantial evidence to suggest that impulsive behavior is detrimental to school performance (Messer, 1976). Epstein, Hallahan, and Kauffman (1975) believe that impulsivity rather than low intellectual functioning accounts for much of the poor academic performance of students with school problems.

Teachers of remedial readers are very familiar with impulsive students. Such students speak without first considering their thoughts and race through written assignments with little consideration of right and wrong answers. When given a task such as matching figures, the impulsive student will draw lines from one figure to another without first inspecting the page. Impulsive pupils come to decisions too quickly, with insufficient time between stimulus and response. Keogh (1971) has urged that the diagnostic procedure for exceptional students include a measure of cognitive tempo (time for thinking). A test labeled the Matching Familiar Figures Test (Kagan, 1966) is available for this purpose.

The following methods are suggested to help students decrease impulsive behavior.

1. Brown (1980) has treated impulsivity successfully with modeling. This involves displaying videotapes of students with reflective behavior solving problem situations.
2. Douglas (1972) advocates asking students to "stop, look, and listen."
3. A cognitive training approach is suggested by (Abikoff, 1979). In this approach, the teacher first outlines how to solve the task (i.e., focus attention, correct errors). Students then do the task with the instructor giving verbal directions. Next, students whisper directions to themselves. Finally, they perform the task silently.
4. Impulsive students may also improve their attentional skills by focusing upon important aspects of a stimulus.
5. In a problem-solving approach, emphasis is placed upon steps, such as (a) defining the problem, (b) thinking of alternate solutions, (c) considering consequences of solutions, and (d) verifying the solution that is chosen.

Students can be overly reflective, as well as being too impulsive. Highly reflective individuals have difficulty making decisions. They may, for example, be too hesitant, refusing to pronounce a word until the word is analyzed thoroughly and they are sure of the answer. In the process of learning to read, some degree of risk taking is needed. The psycholinguistic approach to reading urges that teachers encourage students to guess words based upon their language knowledge (K. S. Goodman, 1967). Perhaps both impulsive and reflective styles are needed for reading success.

Field-Independent and Field-Dependent Cognitive Styles

Another learning style that affects learning to read is referred to as field-independent and field-dependent cognitive styles. A field-independent person proceeds with a task regardless of outside distractions. In contrast, a field-dependent person may be unable to do tasks alone or may be distracted easily. Witkin (1962) established that certain persons were relatively impervious to perceptual distractions in the "field" around them, whereas others were not. Keogh and Donlon (1972) showed that school-aged children with learning disabilities were significantly more field-dependent than a group of normal boys. Davey (1976) related reading performance to cognitive styles. He felt that field-dependent students needed explicit directions and guidance in doing assigned tasks. These students were also highly distractible. On the other hand, field-independent students could think for themselves. Thus, in comprehension, they would be able to infer an organizational or inferential structure without teacher guidance.

Attention Deficit Disorders

Students also differ in their ability to attend to a learning task. Some students lack "selective attention," the ability to attend to relevant stimuli while screening out irrelevant stimuli (Ross, 1976). If the pupil is not attending while the lesson is being taught, learning cannot occur, since information is never received. Ross believes that the selective attention skill is the critical factor that differentiates normal students from those with learning problems.

Selective attention helps to limit the number of stimuli being processed at any one time. Students are bombarded constantly by many stimuli, both external and internal. While the teacher is trying to teach a word in reading, there are many distracting stimuli in the pupil's world. Among the distractions are sounds in the room, noises outside, movement about the room, the temperature, the lights, the pupil's digestive system, and thoughts in the pupil's mind. However, the student must concentrate only on the reading task. Without selective attention, the student is overwhelmed with other stimulation. Unable to receive the desired information, the student fails to learn reading skills.

Three attributes of attention have been identified by Keogh and Margolis (1976): (1) The "set," or coming to attention, (2) actually attending to the task, and (3) concentrating over a long period. The first attribute refers to the set for learning. This is a very important phase and the severely disabled reader may not know

Table 8.1 Characteristics of Attention Deficit Disorder (ADD)

Attention Deficit Disorder with Hyperactivity

A. Inattention: at least three of the following:
1. Often fails to finish things he or she starts
2. Often doesn't seem to listen
3. Easily distracted
4. Has difficulty concentrating on schoolwork or other tasks requiring sustained attention
5. Has difficulty sticking to a play activity

B. Impulsivity: at least three of the following
1. Often acts before thinking
2. Shifts excessively from one activity to another
3. Has difficulty organizing work (this not being due to cognitive impairment)
4. Needs a lot of supervision
5. Frequently calls out in class
6. Has difficulty awaiting turn in games or group situations

C. Hyperactivity: at least two of the following:
1. Runs about or climbs on things excessively
2. Has difficulty sitting still or fidgets excessively
3. Has difficulty staying seated
4. Moves about excessively during sleep
5. Is always "on the go" or acts is if "driven by a motor"

D. Onset before the age of seven

E. Duration of at least six months

F. Not due to schizophrenia, affective disorder, or severe or profound mental retardation

Attention Deficit Disorder without Hyperactivity is defined by the same features as those of attention deficit disorder with hyperactivity except for the absence of hyperactivity; also, the associated features and impairments are generally milder.

Source: American Psychiatric Association, *Diagnostic and Statistical Manual of Mental Disorders, Third Edition,* Washington, D.C., APA, 1980, pp. 43–44.

how to come to attention. The second attribute refers to the actual learning and solving of problems. The third attribute, maintaining attention, means that the student must concentrate for a long period of time. Severely disabled readers, however, may be distracted easily and lose their powers of concentration. The assessment of problems in attention may provide valuable clues to understanding a student's reading problem.

The medical profession is also very much aware of the relationship of attention deficits to learning problems. A recent recommendation of the medical profession was that the term *attention deficit disorder* (ADD) be used to identify students who medical specialists formerly diagnosed as having "minimal brain dysfunction" (MBD) (*Diagnostic and Statistical Manual*, 1980). Their recommendation is that ADD be divided into two categories: (1) with hyperactivity and (2) without hyperactivity. The characteristics of ADD are shown in Table 8.1.

SUMMARY

Severely disabled readers are students with extreme difficulties in learning to read. Only a small percentage of students with reading problems fall into this category. Their characteristics include (1) a lack of prerequisite skills, (2) failure to appreciate what reading is about, (3) inadequate language development, and (4) atypical learning styles.

An ordered sequence of learning occurs as the individual matures. Each type of learning requires underlying prerequisite skills. Some severely disabled students need to be taught prerequisite skills. However, these cannot substitute for reading instruction. The teaching of prerequisite skills can be combined with teaching reading strategies.

There are visual and auditory prerequisites needed for reading. Visual prerequisites include visual discrimination, visual sequencing, visual memory, and naming alphabet letters. Auditory prerequisites include auditory discrimination, rhyming, blending, sound segmentation, auditory memory, and letter sounds.

Severely disabled students need to appreciate what reading is about and to develop clear concepts of the reading process. They may lack knowledge of reading terms (letter, sound) or knowledge of the purposes for reading. The language experience approach may be used to develop these concepts.

Severely disabled readers often need to further develop their oral language abilities. Teachers may do this through reading to students, exposing students to rich language models, expanding and extending speech, using language as a reasoning process, using wordless picture books, and encouraging students to use language freely in the classroom.

Severely disabled readers often have dysfunctional learning styles. They may react impulsively rather than reflectively. Their cognitive style may be field-dependent rather than field-independent. They may be unable to pay attention during the reading lesson and exhibit attentional deficit disorders. ADD has been recommended by the medical profession to characterize students with hyperactive behavior that interferes with learning.

Test Inventory 8.1   ***Tests of Prerequisite Skills***

Bender Visual-Motor Gestalt Test
Western Psychological Services, 1973   *Ages: 4 years–adult*

Subject copies nine designs that are interpreted for perception and organization. One interpretation system for children was done by Koppitz (1964).
   Individual test: 10–15 minutes. May also be used for personality interpretation.

Detroit Tests of Learning Aptitude (DTLA)

Bobbs-Merrill, 1967   Ages: 3-19 years

Tests visual, auditory, and motor processing abilities through nineteen subtests including verbal absurdities, free association, number ability, and social adjustment. Yields MA and IQ and may be used diagnostically.

Individual test: 1 hour.

Developmental Test of Visual Motor Integration (VMI)

Follett, 1967   Ages: 2-15 years

Student required to copy twenty-four geometric forms arranged in increasing order of difficulty. No erasures or second trials allowed.

Individual or group test: about 20 minutes.

The Marianne Frostig Developmental Test of Visual Perception (DTVP)

Consulting Psychologists Press, 1966   Ages: 4-8 years

Consists of five visual perceptual subtests including, (1) eye-hand coordination, (2) figure-ground separation, (3) constancy of shape, (4) position in space, and (5) spatial relationships. Yields scaled score, age equivalent, and perceptual quotient.

Group or individual test: 45 minutes.

Goldman-Fristoe-Woodcock Auditory Skills Test Battery

American Guidance Services, 1976   Ages: 3 years–adult

Assesses auditory perception through twelve tests that include auditory discrimination, memory for content, sound recognition, sound blending, and spelling of sounds. Yields percentile ranks.

Individual test: 2–3 hours for total test.

Goldman-Fristoe-Woodcock Test of Auditory Discrimination

American Guidance Services, 1970   Ages: 4 years–adult

Assesses auditory discrimination under quiet conditions and against noisy backgrounds. Administration controlled through use of an audiotape. Training procedure familiarizes subject with word associations needed in tape. Yields percentile score, standard score, and error analysis matrix.

Individual test: 25 minutes.

Harris Tests of Lateral Dominance

The Psychological Corporation, 1958   Ages: 7 years–adult

Tests individual's hand, eye, and foot dominance through eleven subtests including knowledge of left and right, hand preferences, dealing cards, and kicking. Ratings of strong right, moderate right, mixed, strong left, or moderate left are obtained as well as percentages for age levels.

Individual test: 15–20 minutes.

Illinois Test of Psycholinguistic Abilities (ITPA)

University of Illinois Press, 1968   Ages: 2-4 to 10-3 years

Assesses abilities to process cognitive information. Tests are divided into auditory-visual, receptive-expressive, and association-integration behaviors. There are twelve subtests, two of which are supplementary. (1) Auditory Reception: vocabulary assessment through such questions as "Do boys play?"; (2) Visual Reception: memory assessment through remembering a stimulus and finding a related picture; (3) Visual Sequential Memory: duplicating a pattern of abstract design chips; (4) Auditory Association: making verbal analogies as, "Grass is green, sugar is _____"; (5) Auditory Sequential Memory: repeating a series of numbers in correct order; (6) Visual Association: making visual analogies by selecting a picture to go with three others; (7) Visual Closure: finding an object when only part of it is shown; (8) Verbal Expression: describing an item; (9) Grammatic Closure: completing a sentence with the correct grammatical form; (10) Manual Expression: showing an understanding of the use of various objects; (11) Auditory Closure (supplementary): completing a word with one or more parts or syllables missing such as "da / y" (daddy); and (12) Sound Blending (supplementary): blending the sounds of a word together such as, c/a/t, after hearing it pronounced with time intervals between the sounds.

Yields scaled scores and age scores for each of the subtests and an overall psycholinguistic age.

Individual test: 1 hour. Examiner should be trained in administration.

Monroe Reading Aptitude Tests
Riverside Press, 1963   *Grades: Elementary*

Identifies those needing remediation and those ready to read. Basic visual tests assess discrimination of reversals, eye movements, and visual memory. Motor tests assess speed of movement and ability to stay on the lines. Auditory tests measure discrimination and blending. Language tests measure vocabulary. Additional subtests measure auditory story retention, speech defects and facility, vocabulary command, sentence ability, and motor control-visual memory. Percentiles given.

Group test: 30–55 minutes.

Motor-Free Visual Perception Test (MVPT)
Academic Therapy Publications, 1972   *Ages: 5–7 years*

Assesses visual perception through pointing. Five categories involved: (1) spatial relationships, (2) visual discrimination, (3) figure-ground, (4) visual closure, and (5) visual memory. Yields a perceptual quotient and perceptual age.

Individual test: 10 minutes.

Purdue Perceptual-Motor Survey
Charles E. Merrill, 1966   *Ages: 6–10 years for norms*
                                                  All ages, no norms

Surveys perceptual-motor abilities in the five areas of (1) balance and posture, (2) body image and differentiation, (3) perceptual-motor match, (4) ocular control, and (5) form perception. Yields a rating of 1 to 4.

Individual test: 20–30 minutes.

Revised Visual Retention Test
The Psychological Corporation, 1974   *Ages: 8 years–adult*

Assesses visual abilities through the use of ten designs or groups of designs. Four modes of administration are possible: (1) ten-second exposures with immediate reproduction from memory, (2) five-second exposures with immediate reproduction from memory, (3) design copying, and (4) ten-second exposure with delayed reproduction from memory. Yields a rating of superior to very defective. Norm tables provided for administration 1, 2, and 3. Detailed error analysis provided. Three forms available.

Individual test: 5 minutes.

Roswell-Chall Auditory Blending Test (RCABT)

Essay Press, 1963   *Grades: 1–4*

Three subtests require students to blend individual sounds, pronounced by teacher, into words. Yields ratings of inferior or adequate blending ability. Two forms available.
Individual test: 15–20 minutes.

Slingerland Screening Tests
for Identifying Children
with Specific Language Disability

Educators Publishing Services, 1970   *Grades: 1–4*

Assesses visual, auditory, kinesthetic, and perceptual-motor areas. Nine tests include copying, matching, remembering, writing, dictation, sound discrimination, and story retelling. Test uses words and letters rather than forms. No standardized scores.
Group test, except for test 9: 40 minutes.

Southern California Sensory Integration Tests

Western Psychological Corporation, 1972   *Ages: 4–10 years*

Detects and determines the nature of sensory integrative dysfunction through seventeen tests including figure-ground perception, position in space, finger identification, crossing midline of body, and right-left discrimination. Yields standard scores.
Individual administration: $1\frac{1}{2}$ hours. Requires administration by individual with specialized training on the test.

Wepman Test of Auditory Discrimination

Language Research Associates, 1973   *Ages: 5–8 years*

Assesses student's ability to discriminate the fine differences between English phonemes. Word pairs (man-pan) are read aloud, and the student notes whether they are the same or different. The student faces away from the administrator. Two forms available.
Individual administration: 5 minutes.

9
SEVERELY DISABLED READERS II
teaching strategies

This chapter continues the topic of severely disabled readers with a discussion of special methods and techniques for teaching reading. To facilitate discussion, the instructional methods for teaching reading to severely disabled readers are divided as follows: (1) adaptations of standard methods for teaching reading, (2) special remedial techniques that are designed specifically for severely disabled readers, and (3) behavioral management strategies for use with severe problem readers.

ADAPTATIONS OF STANDARD
READING METHODS

Often a technique designed for teaching reading in the developmental (or regular) classroom can be modified for use with severely disabled readers. When using standard methods, some cautions should be observed. A student may be confused if several approaches are used simultaneously. Therefore, avoid exposing the student to one method in the classroom, another method in a special class, and yet a third in instruction after school. Severely disabled readers need to have a consistent method for acquiring reading skills. Thus, the teacher should select a method which is based on the student's aptitudes for learning and use it consistently for a period of time.

It is also important to anticipate the slow pace with which severely disabled readers may acquire reading skills. This is particularly true for the beginning phases of instruction. One boy in our reading clinic spent ten weeks acquiring eight sight words. Although this seems very slow, even by remedial standards, the acquisition of words was a remarkable achievement for him. They were the first words that he was able to learn and retain consistently. Because progress is often very slow, it is important to chart each step in the road toward reading acquisition and accentuate successes.

Standard reading methods can be readily adapted for use with severely disabled readers. This section describes useful adaptations in (1) the sight word approach, (2) the language experience approach, (3) the synthetic phonics approach, and (4) the analytic phonics or linguistic approach. Adaptations of standard methods are relatively easy to use; they require few specialized materials and allow much flexibility in teacher presentation. Since these methods often produce rapid reading gains, it is recommended that instruction for severely disabled readers begin with one of these methods. If, after a trial period, these approaches prove not to be effective, the teacher should consider using one of the special remedial methods described later in this chapter.

To decide which adaptation of classroom methods to use, the teacher should consider (1) the student's learning strengths, (2) the student's preferences, and (3) other instructional programs that the student is using.

LEARNING STRENGTHS.   If the student exhibits distinct strengths in learning through either the auditory or visual modalities, the teacher can try matching the initial instructional method to these strengths. Generally, the visual modality is capitalized in the sight word and the language experience methods. The auditory modality tends to be capitalized in the phonics methods. If a method utilizing the stronger learning area is chosen, the student may also be given activities to build the weaker one (see Chapter 8).

A diagnostic word learning task can be given to determine the student's comparative abilities in learning through a visual method (sight word or language experience) and an auditory method (phonics methods). The student is given the task of learning two sets of words: six words are presented as sight words and six words are presented as phonics words. By comparing performance on these two tasks, the teacher can make a judgment about the student's learning strengths. Detailed directions for a word learning task are presented in Table 9.1.

Table 9.1　Diagnostic Word Learning Task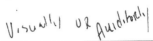

---

1. *Sight word task:* Words are "house," "children," "boy," "farm," "wagon."
   a. Print the words carefully on cards.
   b. Go through each word. Read it to the student, use it in a sentence, point out visual features of the word ("children" is long; "boy" is short, etc.).
   c. Mix up cards. Present five trials of the word, with the words mixed after each trial.
      (1) for the first three trials, pronounce incorrect words for the student and use them in a sentence.
      (2) For the last two trials, do not correct incorrect responses.
   d. Mark results of all trials on the form below.
2. *Phonics word task:* Words are "at," "bat," "cat," "rat," "fat."
   a. Print the words carefully on cards.
   b. Present the "at" card first; pronounce this word for the student. Present the other words by showing the "at" within the words and then blending the first letter ("at," "f-at," "fat"). Use each word in a sentence
   c. Mix up cards. Present five trials of the word, with words mixed after each trial.
      (1) For the first three trials, pronounce incorrect words by blending parts together.
      (2) For the last two trials, do not correct incorrect responses.
   d. Mark all results on the form below.
3. *Response form:* Mark correct or incorrect.

	Sight Word Task Trial						Phonics Task Trial				
	1	2	3	4	5		1	2	3	4	5
house						at					
children						bat					
boy						cat					
farm						rat					
wagon						fat					

Adapted from Barr, 1970.

Another method for determining learning strengths is suggested by Aaron (1978), who identified two groups of students with severe reading problems: (1) those students who have difficulty with word parts and phonics and (2) those students who have difficulty with whole words and sight words. Aaron distinguished between these two groups on the basis of a dictated spelling test. Students who had an aptitude for learning through a whole word or sight approach spelled words by remembering the whole word image. They did not consider the sound sequence. For example, they would spell "book" as "koo" or "father" as "faete." In contrast, those students who had an aptitude for learning phonics produced spellings that reflected word sounds. For example, they spelled "table" as "tabel" or "make" as "maek."

LEARNING PREFERENCES.   Another important factor in choosing a reading method is the student's personal preferences for learning. Some students prefer to "sound out" words, while others simply have an aversion to this activity. Sometimes disabled readers associate certain activities with "unpleasant," previous programs, and so they want to avoid that particular approach.

OTHER INSTRUCTIONAL PROGRAMS.   A third factor to consider in choosing a method for instruction is the student's other current instructional programs. The teacher should try to harmonize the remedial program with the student's existing classroom program or other reading programs. For example, if a student is using materials with a special alphabet (i.e., DISTAR) in the classroom, and books with a regular alphabet in the reading clinic, the student could well be confused, and learning would be impeded.

The Sight Word Method

The sight word method involves teaching students to recognize the visual form of words instantly, without further analysis. Although the teaching of sight words is explored fully in Chapter 10, special adaptations for very disabled readers are presented here.

The words to be taught should be selected very carefully. In general, long words are harder to learn than short words (Coleman, 1967), although an occasional long word serves to add interest. Concrete words are easier to learn than abstract words. For example, the student's name, parts of the body, the name of the school, and so on are far easier to learn than are *function* words such as "the," "when," or "to." The words selected for instruction should be also varied in configuration and number of letters to avoid visual confusion.

Words should be reviewed as often as possible so that they may be established firmly in memory. The teacher should be careful to use standard manuscript writing for all hand-made materials. Severely disabled readers tend to focus on very small differences and may be confused by a "d" with a tail attached.

COMBINING PREREQUISITE TEACHING WITH SIGHT WORDS.   Often, teaching some prerequisite skills to severely disabled readers helps to facilitate sight word learning. Two cases illustrate how prerequisite skills and sight word learning can be combined.

Elaine learned ten words rather easily, but then she began to confuse additional words. The teacher presented visual discrimination exercises using Elaine's new words. Three words were presented on a card, and Elaine had to circle the one that the teacher had read. After a week of practicing this exercise for ten minutes each day, Elaine had solved her confusion problems (see Figure 9.1).

For Robert, another student experiencing difficulties learning sight words, the teacher used a kinesthetic approach to learning. Robert's most difficult words were cut out of sandpaper, and he traced over the words with his finger while saying them.

If the sight word approach is used as an initial teaching method, the teacher may later incorporate some teaching of phonics relationships. For example, after Robert had acquired a sight word vocabulary of thirty words, his teacher started to use the "at" word family.

The Language Experience Method

Severely disabled readers often find the language experience method, in which students read stories they have created by themselves, to be highly motivating. Generally, students dictate stories to the teacher who writes them carefully in manuscript handwriting. Students then learn to read these stories and to recognize words from them. Disabled readers tend to feel a sense of ownership and excitement about having created stories. As detailed in Chapter 11, the language experience approach enables readers to become familiar with necessary concepts about reading, such as the concepts of word and sentence.

A disadvantage of using language experience stories with severely disabled readers is that experience stories are not controlled for reading difficulty. Since

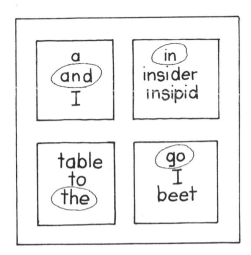

Figure 9.1   Elaine's Discrimination Exercise

they come from oral language, the sight word load may soon outstrip the student's reading ability. In this event, an occasional motivating language experience story may be interspersed with instruction in sight words. The language experience method is described more fully in Chapter 11.

Phonics Methods

The term "phonics" refers to teaching methods that concentrate on printed letters and their sound equivalents (sound/symbol relationships). Although there are several phonics approaches, they can be classified into two groups: the synthetic phonics approach and the analytic (or linguistic) phonics approach. Special adaptations for using these two methods with very severely disabled readers are given in this chapter. Phonics methods for use with other remedial readers are described fully in Chapter 10.

THE SYNTHETIC PHONICS APPROACH.   In the synthetic method, the student learns to blend letter sounds, or groups of letter sounds, into a whole word. For example, to read the word *rat*, the sounds for the letters *r*, *a*, and *t* are pronounced individually and then blended together. The synthetic approach often requires that the student learn certain phonics rules. A phonics rule, for example, would guide the reader to pronounce "rat" and "rate" differently.

If the synthetic phonics approach is chosen for severely disabled readers, teachers should make sure that they possess appropriate readiness skills. Skill in auditory blending and knowledge of letter sounds are important prerequisites for this method. Because some severely disabled students confuse letter names with letter sounds, we suggest referring to letters by using their sounds.

The synthetic phonics method is often very difficult for the disabled reader when it is first presented. Many readiness skills are needed and many task demands are made. However, once basic phonics concepts are mastered, the student often gains rapidly in reading performance.

Betty is an example of a student who learned through the synthetic phonics approach. As an intelligent thirteen-year old, with a long history of instructional failure, Betty was anxious to learn to read and was willing and able to memorize letter sounds and rules. Her teacher taught her the sounds of consonants and the long and short vowels. Although this was a tedious process consuming many months, Betty learned to sound out words rapidly once these initial steps had been mastered. In her second six months of instruction, Betty made over two years of progress and was able to read on her own.

THE ANALYTIC (OR LINGUISTIC) PHONICS APPROACH.   In the analytic method, the student looks at whole words that contain regular phonics patterns. Words are never broken apart, but, by presenting the words over and over again in patterns (or word families), such as "at," "bat," "cat" or "run," "sun," "fun," the student learns their sound regularities. Books using the linguistic approach are based upon patterns of word families, resulting in text such as

- Dan ran the fan
- Can Dan fan Nan?
- The pet is wet
- Is the pet wet?

The analytic phonics method often proves to be highly effective for teaching students who can recognize phonics correspondences but are not ready for a synthetic phonics approach. One important prerequisite skill for learning the analytic or linguistic phonics method is the skill of rhyming.

Ten-year-old Billy was a nonreader who was instructed by the analytic phonics approach for several months. His initial learning rate was about one word family per week. After four weeks of instruction, his rate of learning increased to about two word families per week. Billy's teacher controlled the word families carefully so that they would not be too similar. After each word family was learned, it was presented in a story. The words from the word family were at first color coded (with, for example, one family being yellow and another red). Billy's independent reading was done with books containing rhyming words such as Dr. Seuss's *Hop on Pop* and *Green Eggs and Ham* (see Appendix A).

Many older severely disabled readers prefer the analytic approach, as it allows them considerable independence. One thirteen-year-old boy learning by this approach decided to create his own book of word families. Under each word family ("ight," "ag"), he entered all the words he could find or think of.

SPECIAL REMEDIAL METHODS

When adaptations of standard or classroom reading methods are not successful with the severely disabled reader, special remedial methods can be used. These specialized methods are not normally used in the regular classroom since they may require special training, individual instruction, and more time than a classroom teacher can afford.

We have classified the special remedial methods into four categories: (1) methods that use the kinesthetic approach (or sense of movement), (2) methods that use phonics instruction, (3) methods that use oral reading, and (4) methods that use rebus (or stylized pictures). Materials for these methods are listed in Appendix A.

Kinesthetic Approaches

A variety of approaches, known as "kinesthetic" approaches, use the sense of touch to reinforce word learning. They include the VAK method, the VAKT method, the Fernald method, and the Cooper method.

THE VAK METHOD. The VAK method combines visual and auditory association with writing. The student sees and says the word while writing it from memory. Harris and Sipay (1980) outline the following procedure for the VAK method. The student (1) sees the word to be learned, (2) says the word, (3) tries to write it from memory, and (4) compares the results with the original word. This procedure is repeated until the word is reproduced correctly.

THE **VAKT** METHOD.   The VAKT method utilizes visual, auditory, kinesthetic, and tactile senses to reinforce learning. It is reserved, generally, for the most severe cases. The method emphasizes tracing and tactile stimulation to promote learning, and it is sometimes referred to as a "multisensory" approach. The student sees the word to be learned and listens to the teacher pronounce it. Then the word is traced as the student says it. For the tracing stage, words may be printed in crayon or another medium that raises the surface of the word from the paper. Finally, the student writes the word from memory.

There are many variations of the VAKT approach. Since some students learn best through physical movement, they require a more forceful kinesthetic and tactile stimulus than tracing and finger contact offer. For a stronger stimulus, students may trace over sandpaper letters or words or they may form the letters in sand or cornmeal poured into a tray to a depth of about one inch. Some students may benefit from tracing letters from different materials (raised letters of hardened starch, wire, pipe cleaners, or yarn), or from tracing letters in the air, or from tracing letters while blindfolded. These variations, however, are even more time consuming than the regular VAKT approaches and should be used only when needed.

THE FERNALD METHOD.   Grace M. Fernald and Helen B. Keller (Fernald, 1943) developed a method for use with severe reading disorders that combines the language-experience approach and the VAKT modes of learning. The approach is designed to be used on an individual basis. The Fernald method emphasizes the wholeness of words and does not expect the student to learn separate phonic elements. Because progress may be very slow, the method generally is used only when other methods have failed. Fernald outlines some very specific procedures. There are four stages in the Fernald approach. Each stage is a complete way of learning words. Students start learning words by stage 1; after this has been mastered they move to stage 2; and so on. The four stages of the approach are:

1.   Tracing and writing from memory individually presented words.
2.   Writing from memory individually presented words.
3.   Writing from memory words found in text.
4.   Learning by sight words presented in text.

Stage 1. At the beginning of stage 1, the student selects a word that he or she would like to learn to read. Then the following procedure is undertaken.

1.   The word is written on large cards or paper (in manuscript or cursive script) in chalkboard size using crayon. While writing, the teacher says the word.

2. Using one or two fingers, the student traces over the word while saying each part of the word as it is traced.
3. The tracing is repeated until the student feels that the word can be written (or printed) from memory.
4. The student tries to reproduce the word from memory without looking at the word. As the word is written, it is, again, pronounced in parts.
5. If the student cannot write the word correctly, the tracing procedure is repeated until the student is able to successfully write the word.
6. After the word is written correctly from memory, it is filed in an alphabetical word file box.

No errors are permitted during this procedure. If the student makes a mistake during the tracing process, or if the word is written incorrectly, the student is stopped and told to begin the process again. Any activities that break up word learning are discouraged.

After several words are learned, students begin to appreciate their powers to read and write words. At this time, students start to write their own stories. Words to be learned are now additional words that the student needs to write these stories. Again, new words are filed in the word file bank.

Stage 2. When the teacher feels that students no longer have to trace words for learning, they are ready for stage 2. In this stage, words may continue to be taken from the student's stories. The method for word learning differs from stage 1 in two ways: (1) the words may be presented on smaller cards (say, index-sized cards) and (2) the tracing stage is eliminated. In stage 2, the word is printed (or written) on a file card. The student looks at it, says it emphasizing its parts, and then attempts to write it while saying it without looking back at the original.

Stage 3. In this stage, students begin to read from actual texts, and the words to be learned are drawn from these texts. Index cards are no longer used for introducing words; rather, students learn words directly from text. Students are permitted to read whatever they desire to read. When new words are encountered, the student looks at the word on the printed page and tries to write it from memory. Words learned are again filed into the word bank.

Stage 4. In this stage, the student is able to read a word in text, say it, and remember it without the crutch of writing from memory. Students are encouraged to figure out unknown words by associating them with known words or by using context (or meaning) clues rather than by recognizing them by sight. Only words that the student cannot "figure out" are written down for further review. Identification of unknown words should precede reading. Fernald suggests that students survey material before they read it to locate unknown words and try to figure them out. If unknown words are subsequently encountered during reading, teachers are advised to supply them for students rather than to interrupt the meaning-gaining function of reading by letting students sound out words.

THE COOPER METHOD.   The Cooper method, a modification of the Fernald method, uses basal reading materials. The teacher first selects a basal reading series and determines the student's reading level, which is usually quite low. The teacher then has the student read the word list from which the book is constructed, and words that are not known are taught using the Fernald method. These words are practiced through reading the basal readers and also in isolation and context. In the meantime, students are instructed in visual and auditory prerequisite skills. Eventually, whole-word learning is to be replaced by learning words through phonics methods (Cooper, 1947).

Phonics Approaches

Some special remedial reading techniques emphasize the learning of phonics and phonics generalizations. These include the Gillingham method, the DISTAR Reading Program, the Hegge-Kirk-Kirk Remedial Reading Drills, and the Glass Analysis method.

THE GILLINGHAM METHOD.   The Gillingham method is a synthetic phonics approach employing a tracing technique for teaching single letters and their sound equivalents. The method is an outgrowth of the early work of Samuel T. Orton (1937), who studied the relationship of cerebral dominance to reading and language disorders. The Gillingham method requires specific instruction five times a week for a minimum of two years. Initial instruction may be divided into three parts: learning letter sounds, learning words, and using words in sentences (Gillingham and Stillman, 1970).

The Gillingham method emphasizes a multisensory approach. There are six sensory associations. These associations are particularly important at the initial stage, which is the teaching of letters. The six fundamental associations are:

- *V–A (Visual-Auditory).* Written words and letters are associated with their sounds. The student does not have to vocalize these sounds.
- *A–V (Auditory-Visual).* The sounds of letters and words are associated with the visual image. This is a spelling-like task.
- *A–K (Auditory-Kinesthetic).* The sounds of letters and words are associated with muscle action through speech and writing.
- *K–A (Kinesthetic-Auditory).* The student's hand is guided to trace or to write a letter form while associating it with the name or sound of the letter.
- *V–K (Visual-Kinesthetic).* Printed letters and words are associated with the muscular actions of speech and writing.
- *K–V (Kinesthetic-Visual).* The muscular act of speech or writing is associated with the visual appearance of the letters.

Learning letters and their sounds. This consists of three associations:

ASSOCIATION I

1. A visual and auditory (V–A) association with the letter name is established. The teacher shows a card with a letter on it and says the letter name, which the student repeats. In saying the letter, an A–K association is made. This step is the foundation for oral reading.

2. When mastery of the letter name has occurred, a visual and auditory association with the sound is developed. The teacher says the sound, while exposing the card, and the pupil repeats it. This also involves V–A and A–K associations.

ASSOCIATION II

The student develops the ability to relate the sound to the letter name. The teacher, without showing the card, makes the letter sound, and the pupil tells the name of the letter. This association is A–A. It is the basis for oral spelling.

ASSOCIATION III

1. The letter is printed by the teacher and its construction is explained. The student then traces over the original, copies it, and, finally, writes the letter from memory while averting his or her eyes from the paper. This association is V–K and K–V.
2. The teacher says the sound and the pupil must write the letter that has that sound, thereby developing the A–K association.

Reading Words. Learning to read words starts by blending letter sounds and spelling the words. The initial words taught contain two vowels, "a" and "i," and eight consonants, "b," "g," "h," "j," "k," "m," "p," and "t." The blended words follow a consonant-vowel-consonant pattern (CVC), and blending occurs by pronouncing the first consonant and vowel together ("ra") and then adding the final consonant ("rat"). At first, the words are limited to the vowels and consonants given above. Such words, commercially distributed on colored cards, are known as the student's "jewel case." Sample jewel case words are "hat," "hip," "bib," "jab." After these words are mastered, words containing other letters are added.

Combining words learned into simple sentences. After a basic set of words has been learned, the words are combined into sentences and stories, and the student learns to read these. Reading continues to be taught by a phonics method and combines spelling and dictation exercises.

The Gillingham method has been modified by Slingerland (1974), who has provided an extensive set of supplementary materials. Another set of materials based on the Gillingham approach has been developed by Traub and Bloom (1970). Their *Recipe for Reading* is accompanied by twenty-one supplementary readers.

THE **DISTAR** READING PROGRAM. The DISTAR Reading Program (Englemann and Bruner, 1978) is a highly structured decoding program that requires following a very specific step-by-step procedure. The emphasis is on programmed learning, drill, and repetition. It has proven to be successful for students with learning disabilities, mental retardation, and disadvantaged backgrounds (Guinet, 1971). In a review of research, Haring and Bateman (1977) found that DISTAR was successful with students who had experienced school failure previously. There are three types of DISTAR programs: one for language, one for arithmetic, and one for reading. Because we are concerned with remedial reading, only the reading program is discussed in this section.

In DISTAR, the teacher is given specific procedures and oral instructions to say throughout each step of the program. Pupil instruction is given in small groups for thirty-minute periods, five times per week. Skill mastery in the program is measured by criterion-referenced tests. If a student has not mastered skills, special additional lessons are provided.

The DISTAR program is based largely upon a synthetic phonics approach, with students being taught specifically the prerequisite skill of auditory blending, which is needed to form isolated sounds into words. Another distinctive feature of DISTAR is that, in beginning stages, the shape of some alphabet letters is modified so that they reflect letter sounds. Thus the letters "th" are written in a connected fashion so that it is apparent to the student that they are one sound. Or a silent "e" at the end of a word is written smaller than the rest of the letters. (See Figure 9.2.) While this alphabet gives students clues to sounding out words, the teacher must be cautioned that exposure to both the DISTAR alphabet and the ordinary alphabet may be confusing. The special alphabet of DISTAR is gradually phased out.

The DISTAR program is a complete reading program, containing both isolated drills and instructional reading. It uses a behavioral management approach, building in small progressive steps and using specified praise as reinforcement. Criterion-referenced tests are used to monitor progress. The teacher is guided in specific procedures and oral instructions through each step of the program.

The SRA Corrective Reading Program, Decoding A, B, and C (Englemann et al., 1978), is based upon the DISTAR concepts but is geared toward the older student (grades four through twelve). This program develops primary and intermediate reading skills using materials of interest to older students. As with the DISTAR program, instruction is constructed and guided very carefully. Materials include a teacher's management and skill manual, presentation books, and assessment materials. Students use stories, student contracts, and progress charts. There is also an SRA *Corrective Reading Program* which concentrates on comprehension.

HEGGE-KIRK-KIRK REMEDIAL DRILLS.   These exercises are designed to give students drill and practice in recognizing phonic elements and in blending letter

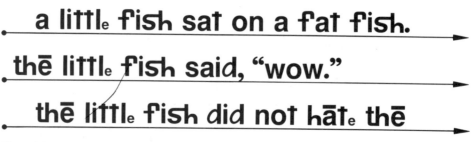

Figure 9.2 The DISTAR Reading Alphabet

From DISTAR® READING I by Siegfried Engelmann and Elaine C. Bruner. © 1974, 1969, Science Research Associates, Inc. Reprinted by permission of the publisher.

sounds (Hegge, Kirk, and Kirk, 1936). Each page of the workbook has lines of regularly-spelled words. Students practice by going across the page saying each word in a line. The method uses the principle of minimal change in component words; words such as "rat" and "ran" are presented side by side. Repetition and practice are also important. The method has proven successful with students who have failed to profit from conventional reading methods yet can be educated in phonics principles. The drills provide practice in isolated words, and they must be supplemented by reading contextual materials.

GLASS ANALYSIS. The Glass Analysis method (Glass, 1973) approaches words through clusters of word elements ("pl"-"ay") rather than individual sounds. It emphasizes "perceptual conditioning" to develop the ability to identify visual clusterings of letters in known words. The Glass Analysis system is designed to teach "decoding" rather than "reading." Reading is considered to be a response to meaning, whereas decoding, which precedes reading, involves knowing the sounds of a word and should be taught apart from reading. According to Glass, words are recognized first by viewing them as a whole and then by identifying structural sound elements and the letter clusters within them.

The Glass Analysis teaching procedure involves (1) presenting a whole word that is known to the student; (2) directing the student to note what clusters make specific sounds (e.g., for the word "track," the student notes which letters make the sound "tr" and which letters make the sound of "ack"); and (3) having the student look at letters and give the sounds that they make (e.g. the student is shown the whole word "track" and is asked to give the sounds of the letters "ack" and "tr"). It is recommended that the Glass analysis procedure be followed for about two ten-minute periods per day, five times a week.

The Glass Analysis materials are written on three levels. In addition to exercises using isolated words, paperback books are available that contain these words used in sentence contexts. These books provide some contextual reading.

Teachers can easily make their own word cards to teach this method. If they wish, Glass Analysis materials can be purchased commercially.

Oral Reading Approaches

These methods use oral reading to teach reading skills. Students listen to oral reading as well as reading orally themselves. Methods discussed include (1) the neurological impress method and (2) simultaneous listening/reading.

THE NEUROLOGICAL IMPRESS METHOD. This is a read-along technique that involves the teacher and student reading simultaneously (Heckelman, 1966). This method is particularly effective with reading disabled adolescents. The theory is that a new learning process, a neurological memory trace, is established when pupils see the words in print and hear both the teacher's and their own voices saying the words. Heckelman feels that students who are permitted to make mistakes without hearing the correct versions of text become imprinted with incorrect responses that are later difficult to eradicate. The neurological impress method exposes students to accurate, fluid oral reading while enabling them to contribute to the reading process.

In this technique, student and teacher try to read as much continuous material as possible. Students should begin reading with material that is approximately at their independent level and may have been read before successfully. Students are told to not be concerned about reading accuracy, but to try to read fluently, without looking back. Pictures are to be disregarded.

In the neurological impress method, the teacher and student both hold the material. The teacher is seated slightly behind the student, so that the teacher's reading goes directly into the student's right ear. Teacher and student read the material jointly. At first, the teacher reads slightly louder and faster, to imprint the correct responses in the student. As the student gains fluency and confidence, the teacher is instructed to read softer, and even to lag slightly behind the student. However, if difficulty is encountered, the teacher should rescue the student in a loud, firm manner.

When beginning this procedure, teachers should follow the text along with their finger at the pace of the reading. As the student gains confidence, he or she can begin to assume the responsibility for following the reading. Comprehension, and even the accuracy of the student's oral reading, are irrelevant to the aims of this procedure. Students should not be questioned on the content of the material or stopped for correction during reading. Use of this method may improve oral reading very quickly. If no improvement has resulted after four hours of instruction, the method should be discontinued.

SIMULTANEOUS LISTENING/READING.   Another read-along technique suggested for use with severely disabled readers is the simultaneous listening reading method (Harris, 1981). This has some similarities to the neurological impress method; however, the student reads silently while listening to the passage on audio tape. The student experiences the written word as naturally expressed oral language. In this way, he or she is provided with a firsthand experience in the act of fluent reading. Because severely disabled students have to work hard to decode words, they may have little experience with fluent, continuous reading. This method provides such experience. Several easy books accompanied by cassettes are useful for this approach.

The Rebus Method

In the rebus method, concrete symbols or pictures are substituted for words (see Figure 9.3). Students then learn to "read" these symbols and eventually transfer their skills to traditional print. Rebus, or symbol writing, was the first type of writing used by human beings, in Egyptian hieroglyphics. Some students find the rebus to be more concrete and easier to learn than a word. The rebus method is effective with students who lack basic concepts in reading. Banas and Wills (1979) found that the use of a small rebus or concrete symbol makes word cards easier to

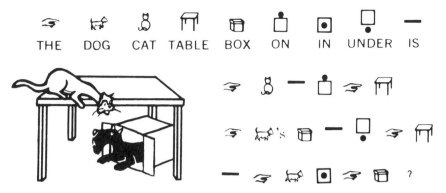

Figure 9.3 Peabody Rebus

Sample Rebus vocabulary and passage from *Peabody Rebus Reading Program* (Circle Pines, Minn.: American Guidance Services, Inc.). Reprinted with the permission of American Guidance Services, Inc.

master. The use of rebuses has been incorporated into the Peabody Rebus Reading Program. An example of text from this program is given above. In this program, the students learn forty pictures and symbols. As the program progresses, the symbols are gradually replaced with printed words. This program contains two readiness books and one reading book.

BEHAVIORAL MANAGEMENT STRATEGIES

The principles of behavioral modification have always been used by good teachers. Any time a teacher provides praise, gives gold stars, or charts progress, behavioral management strategies are being used informally. In this section, we provide more systematic approaches.

Behavioral management techniques concentrate upon improving the motivation and learning strategies of severely disabled readers rather than teaching reading by any specific method. Some reading programs, however, do incorporate behavior modification strategies (e.g., DISTAR).

Although there are several versions of the behavioral approach, all stem from a common theory of learning. The premise of "behavior theory" is that people are more likely to behave in a certain way when that behavior is reinforced or rewarded. Various applications of this theory are known as "behavior modification" (Skinner, 1963), "applied behavior analysis" (Lovitt, 1975a, b), and "behavior management" (Gardner, 1978).

Behavioral psychologists suggest that human activity can be modified by systematically arranging environmental events to produce a specific change in observable behavior. This approach requires the teacher to (1) observe and tabulate the behavior to be changed carefully and systematically, and (2) manipulate those conditions that affect a desired change in the student's behavior.

A "reinforcement" is used to encourage the student to behave in a desired manner. For example, the student may be given a positive reinforcement for saying a phonics sound correctly, reading a certain number of pages, or answering comprehension questions correctly. The desired behavior might also be nonacademic, such as staying in one's seat, paying attention for a certain period of time, or completing work. The reinforcements include stars, tokens, a smiling stamp face, the student's name on a chart, and approval from the teacher. Although general principles of behavior theory apply to all students, formal implementation of comprehensive behavioral management programs is complex and usually reserved only for very disabled or unmotivated students.

Implementing Behavioral Principles

To apply the behavioral approach to teaching reading, some basic decisions must be made (Lovitt, 1975b).

1. The teacher should identify the behavior to be modified and a reward (reinforcement) for reinforcing desired behavior.
2. The teacher should increase the reinforcement when performance is accurate and decrease reinforcement when nondesirable behavior is exhibited.
3. By eventually phasing out reinforcements, the student should come to engage in the desired behavior without the reward.

Two principles from behavioral theory are particularly useful in teaching reading, even if an entire behavior management system is not established. First, teachers should systematically pay attention to desirable behaviors rather than to undesirable ones. It is only human to point out (or try to correct) reading errors, lack of attention, and so on. However, often, more is gained by noting and encouraging the good things the student does. Human beings react well to attention, and behaviors that elicit responses from the teacher are likely to be repeated.

Second, teachers should plan instruction in small, easy steps. By presenting instructional tasks in this way, the student learns and the sense of accomplishment is increased.

Key Concepts in Behavior Management

REINFORCEMENT. There are two types of reinforcement: positive and negative. Positive reinforcement is a pleasurable event that follows the response. It increases the likelihood that the person will make a similar response in similar situations in the future; for example, if Judy is given a small token after finishing a reading workbook page, she is likely to finish the next page. Negative reinforcement is an unpleasurable event that follows an unwanted response and has the effect of increasing desirable behaviors; for example, if Joe does not read his book during the reading period, two tokens are taken away. Joe reads the book to keep the tokens. In general, positive reinforcement is preferred over negative reinforcement.

Contingency Management.   This involves the use of a desirable reinforcement to encourage the student to do something that he or she does not wish to do. If Sally completes her reading lesson, then she can work on the party preparations. This is also known as the *Premack principle* (1959).

Contingency Contracting.   This technique is used to make more formal arrangements between student and teacher. A written agreement is negotiated in which the student agrees to do something the teacher desires, and the teacher agrees to provide something the student wants in return. For example, the teacher and Tony sign an agreement that, if Tony learns twenty sight words, he will have an extra free period.

Token Reinforcement Systems.   In this system, reinforcers are accumulated to be exchanged at a later time for a more meaningful "backup" reinforcer. For example, the student can collect plastic chips that are exchanged later for candy, toys, gum, and so on.

Extrinsic and Intrinsic Reinforcement.   A goal of behavior management is to progress from extrinsic types of reinforcement to intrinsic reinforcement. Extrinsic reinforcers are items that the student finds pleasant initially and that serve to stimulate the desired behaviors. Intrinsic reinforcements are the feelings of pleasure generated by accomplishments. After a period of time, the extrinsic reinforcement should give way to intrinsic reinforcements; at this point, the extrinsic reinforcement should be withdrawn. Moving from extrinsic to intrinsic reinforcement is a crucial stage in behavior management, but often a difficult one to accomplish.

SUMMARY

In teaching severely disabled readers, teachers should first try an adaptation of a standard method of teaching beginning reading, for this permits the most rapid progress. The choice of this method should be based on student aptitude, student preference, and the other instructional programs that the student is receiving.

Four standard methods that may be modified for remedial use are (1) the sight word method (learning to recognize words instantly), (2) the language experience method (reading stories that students have written), (3) the synthetic phonics method (learning letter sounds and blending them together), and (4) the analytic phonics method (learning by the repetition of whole words in phonically regular patterns). The teaching of prerequisite skills may be combined with these methods.

If adaptations of standard methods do not succeed, special remedial methods may be used. These may be divided into four types: (1) kinesthetic approaches, (2) phonics approaches, (3) oral reading approaches, and (4) the rebus approach.

Kinesthetic approaches include the VAK, VAKT, Fernald method, and Cooper method. In VAK, the student attempts to learn a word by writing it from memory. In VAKT, the word is both written from memory and traced. The Fernald method involves four complete systems of learning, each done sequentially. First, students learn words that they choose by tracing and writing from memory. Second, words are merely written from memory and are used in student stories. Third, words are written from memory but are drawn from texts. Finally, words are learned from sight, phonics, and contextual analysis using text readings. The Cooper method is a modification of the Fernald technique in which words are taken from basal readers.

Phonics approaches include the Gillingham method, DISTAR, Hegge-Kirk-Kirk Remedial Drills, and the Glass Analysis method. Instruction in the Gillingham method is intensive and involves six multisensory associations. First, students learn associations to letter sounds and names; then, to read regular words; and, then, to combine these words in sentences. DISTAR is a synthetic phonics approach that teaches auditory blending and initially uses a controlled alphabet. In the Hegge-Kirk-Kirk drills, phonically regular words are presented in minimally contrasting patterns. In Glass Analysis, students learn to associate "sound clusters" with regular pronounciations.

Two oral reading approaches are the neurological impress method and simultaneous listening-reading. In the neurological impress method, correct word identification and a fluent model of reading are impressed upon the student by simultaneous reading with the teacher. In simultaneous listening-reading, the student listens to audiotapes while reading.

In the rebus approach (Peabody Rebus Program), the student learns to identify symbolic pictures and then moves to word identification.

Behavior management is the fostering of desirable behaviors by (1) breaking down behavior or learning into small steps and (2) reinforcing desired behaviors. Behavior management can be used to foster nonacademic learnings (paying attention, sitting in one's seat) or direct instructional behaviors (learning sight words). Intrinsic reinforcement should eventually replace extrinsic reinforcement.

10

IMPROVING WORD RECOGNITION I
sight words and phonics

The remedial student struggling to recognize words one by one in a forced, expressionless manner is a familiar experience for many teachers. Without comfortable word recognition abilities, the remedial student is trapped by the mechanics of reading and is unable to read for meaning. The ability to recognize words is basic to all other aspects of reading.

OVERVIEW OF WORD RECOGNITION

This chapter and the next are devoted to improving the ability to recognize words. This chapter presents (1) sight word clues and (2) phonics clues; Chapter 11 continues with (3) structural analysis clues and (4) context clues. Chapter 11 also contains information on language approaches (the language experience approach and the psycholinguistic view of word recognition), special problems in word recognition (such as reversals, finger pointing), and methods for helping with writing and spelling.

Types of Word Recognition

Word recognition clues are simply ways of learning words. It must be remembered, however, that learning words is only a means to an end—its purpose is to facilitate reading for meaning. Word recognition clues include

1. *Sight word clues.* The immediate or instant visual recognition of words (Chapter 10).
2. *Phonics clues.* The use of the predictable relationships between letters and sounds to recognize words (Chapter 10).
3. *Structural analysis clues.* The use of meaningful subunits of words for identification. Subunits include prefixes, suffixes, compound words, etc. (Chapter 11).
4. *Context clues.* The recognition of words through the meaning of the rest of the passage. Readers make primary use of their language knowledge and experience (Chapter 11).

These four clues, and methods of teaching each of them to remedial readers, will be discussed thoroughly in this chapter and the next.

Historical Perspective
of Word Recognition Instruction

Each of the word recognition clues—sight words, phonics, context, and structural analysis—is needed in learning to read. Throughout the history of teaching reading, instructional emphasis has shifted from one word recognition strategy to another.

Phonics was emphasized in the ancient Greek and Roman period when pupils were required to learn letters and the sounds they represented (Mathews, 1966). Later, the heroine of the eighteenth century children's book, *The History of Little Miss Goody Two Shoes* learned to read in this fashion. The phonics strategy was also emphasized with American Pilgrim children, who were required to recite the "ab," "eb," "ib," "ob," "ub," of the *New England Primer.*

By the 1920s, however, emphasis had shifted to the teaching of sight words. Educators of this period considered the learning of whole words more interesting for students than the learning of meaningless phonic elements. The sight word approach subsequently became the primary instructional strategy for teaching reading and was used for several years. Many adults remember learning to read by practicing sight words in the *Dick and Jane* series (*The Basic Readers*, Curriculum Foundation Series, Scott, Foresman, 1912–1962).

By the 1950s, there was a renewed emphasis on the teaching of phonics, probably a reaction to the overuse of the sight word method. A book that influenced the shift was *Why Johnny Can't Read* by Rudolph Flesch (1955), which charged that American children were falling behind because they were not being taught phonics.

In the 1960s and 1970s, the teaching of word recognition was influenced by new discoveries and insights in linguistics (the study of language). There are three linguistic influences on the teaching of word recognition in reading. One perspective emphasizes the teaching of context clues; another emphasizes structural analysis; the third emphasizes phonics.

The linguistic approach that emphasizes context clues is known as the *psycholinguistic perspective* of reading. This approach underscores the richness of the language and experience that students bring to the reading situation. Context clues are important because they enable students to make intelligent guesses of unknown words by utilizing the meaning of surrounding text and student's language and experiences to formulate intelligent "guesses" (Smith, 1973c).

A second linguistic perspective emphasizes the teaching of structural analysis. It is supported by research showing that English spelling is based on both sounds and on the meaningful parts of words. Therefore, students can use word parts to help them identify unknown words in reading. For example, the identification of the words "national" and "rational" depends upon knowing the base words of "nation" and "ration" and the "al" suffix. (N. Chomsky, 1970; Venezky, 1967 a, b; Chomsky and Halle, 1968).

The third linguistic perspective emphasizes the learning of phonics clues using a special linguistic (or analytic) strategy. This method is based upon the work of Bloomfield (1942), a structural linguist, who recommended that students learn to decode words through the careful repetition of word patterns in whole words (e.g., "cat," "bat," "rat"). Bloomfield believed that in teaching reading the words should not be broken apart into individual sounds. This approach is usually referred to as the "linguistic method" of teaching reading.

Although debates about the best approach to teaching word recognition continue, readers need to use all of these strategies. Therefore, teachers responsible for teaching remedial readers should be familiar with each word recognition method in order to help problem readers achieve independence and flexibility. Research shows that some teachers lack such familiarity. For example, one study showed that many teachers lack adequate knowledge about phonics and phonics rules (Lerner and List, 1970). The information needed to teach word recognition is given in this and the following chapter.

A FRAMEWORK
FOR TEACHING READING SKILLS

Disabled readers usually need a systematized way of learning reading skills. By using a system, students are led naturally from easier steps of learning to more difficult ones. A three-phase process is an effective way to teach many remedial reading skills. As pictured in Figure 10.1, the three phases are (1) introduction, (2) practice, and (3) transfer. This framework will be used in Chapters 10, 11, and 12 to guide the teaching of word recognition skills, comprehension skills, and vocabulary.

Figure 10.1 Three Phases for Teaching Reading Skills

1. *The introduction phase.* In this phase the student's attention is focused on the skill to be taught. There are many interesting ways to capture the student's attention.
2. *The practice phase.* Remedial readers need to experience many repetitions of a skill before they fully master it. During this period, the student practices the skill in a variety of ways.
3. *The transfer phase.* After a skill is practiced, it must be applied in instructional and independent reading. This phase is essential because it ensures transfer to the reading situation.

This three-step framework can be used to teach word recognition and comprehension skills in the remedial situation.

SIGHT WORD CLUES

Sight words are recognized instantly, without additional analysis. The aim of remedial word recognition instruction is to enable the disabled reader to recognize most words by sight, just as the fluent reader does. This frees the student to read for meaning.

Before formulating specific plans for sight word instruction, the teacher needs to know which words the student already knows and which still need to be taught. Detailed procedures for assessing sight word vocabulary are given in Chapter 6, under the section on the Informal Reading Inventory.

Readers who are just beginning to learn sight words often use pictures and configurations to aid them in word identification. Although these methods help severely disabled readers, they are not efficient ways of recognizing words.

Remedial readers at the beginning stages of reading frequently rely heavily on pictures. This reliance may actually deter word learning. Samuels (1970), reviewing an extensive series of studies, concluded that young students learn to read sight words better and faster when no pictures accompany the written test. For remedial students who overrely on pictures, the teacher can cover the pictures during reading. If a story is short, it can be rewritten on a separate sheet of paper and read without pictures.

There are times, however, when pictures are helpful in remedial instruction. For example, readers on beginning levels enjoy illustrating their sight words or the stories they have just read. Remedial students who have difficulty learning sight words often find that drawing pictures is a relaxing, yet relevant, activity to pursue on their own time.

Pictures are also helpful when students are practicing sight words on their own. For example, cards can be made with words on the front and pictures on the back, so that the accuracy of word recognition can be checked by the reader. Nouns and verbs, which can be illustrated easily, are the types of words that are most useful for picture sight cards. Pictures known as rebuses (see Chapter 9) can also be helpful in instruction. A rebus is pictorial writing, as shown in the example below. Students with extreme difficulty in learning sight words find that learning rebuses is motivating and easier.

Students who lack facility in sight words also depend upon configuration, the overall shape, form, and outline of a word. Using configuration clues, the words "red" and "rub" cannot be distinguished, but the words "birthday" and "rag" can. The configuration of words plays an important role in initial sight word learning (see the example below). Generally, when presented with several short words and one long word to learn, beginning students have little trouble with the long word because of the distinct difference in configuration. On the other hand, when presented with two long words, they often confuse them.

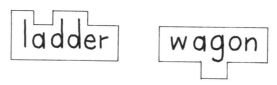

Configuration can sometimes aid in sight word learning. For example, one severely disabled reader found the word "wagon" easier to remember when reminded that "it goes down to the basement." In teaching very disabled readers, visually similar words should not be presented in the same lesson. For example, the words "boy," "bad," "dad," and "dot" are quite confusing if taught together.

Introducing Sight Words

The three-step framework of introduction, practice, and transfer will be used to discuss the teaching of sight words. In the first step—introducing sight words—teachers should know (1) the sources of sight words and (2) methods for introducing them.

SOURCES OF SIGHT WORDS.   Studies of English word frequency show that a few words are used repeatedly in reading material. For example, the one hundred most common English words account for more than 50 percent of all written material (Carroll, Davies, and Richmond, 1971). If the student does not know these common words, they should be a high priority for instruction.

Table 10.1 shows high-frequency words, which are referred to as "basic sight words." The list in Table 10.1 is based on the Dolch Basic Sight Vocabulary, updated by Johnson (1971). These words are most useful for remedial students reading on the preprimer through grade three levels. To separate easier words from harder words, teachers can make word cards that distinguish words by difficulty levels, putting the preprimer words on yellow cards, the primer words on blue cards, and so on. The words in the basic sight word list consist of both *concrete* words (nouns, verbs, adjectives) and *function* words (prepositions, conjunctions). Function words (such as "with," "the," "but") are abstract and are more difficult to learn.

Table 10.2 shows common picture words. These words are easier to learn since they are concrete. These words can also be put on word cards. Often, the word is placed on one side and a picture is put on the other.

Word cards for remedial teaching can also be purchased commercially. The Dolch word cards come in two packs: (1) the Dolch Basic Sight Vocabulary Cards, and (2) the Dolch Picture Word Cards.

In addition to words on basic word lists, students must learn to recognize many other words by sight. These can come from several sources. Students often enjoy bringing in words they want to learn to class. They may have found the words in "fun sources" such as magazines and comic books, or they may have heard them in conversation or on television. Although such words tend to be difficult (chocolate, foul-out) or emotionally laden (zap, pow), occasional use of these words provides interest and motivation. This technique is particularly successful with older remedial readers.

Sight words may also be selected from materials used in students' instructional reading. This method helps to integrate the sight word program with in-

Table 10.1 Basic Sight Vocabulary Words

PREPRIMER	PRIMER	FIRST	SECOND	THIRD
1. the	45. when	89. many	133. know	177. don't
2. of	46. who	90. before	134. while	178. does
3. and	47. will	91. must	135. last	179. got
4. to	48. more	92. through	136. might	180. united
5. a	49. no	93. back	137. us	181. left
6. in	50. if	94. years	138. great	182. number
7. that	51. out	95. where	139. old	183. course
8. is	52. so	96. much	140. year	184. war
9. was	53. said	97. your	141. off	185. until
10. he	54. what	98. may	142. come	186. always
11. for	55. up	99. well	143. since	187. away
12. it	56. its	100. down	144. against	188. something
13. with	57. about	101. should	145. go	189. fact
14. as	58. into	102. because	146. came	190. through
15. his	59. than	103. each	147. right	191. water
16. on	60. them	104. just	148. used	192. less
17. be	61. can	105. those	149. take	193. public
18. at	62. only	106. people	150. three	194. put
19. by	63. other	107. Mr.	151. states	195. thing
20. I	64. new	108. how	152. himself	196. almost
21. this	65. some	109. too	153. few	197. hand
22. had	66. could	110. little	154. house	198. enough
23. not	67. time	111. state	155. use	199. far
24. are	68. these	112. good	156. during	200. took
25. but	69. two	113. very	157. without	201. head
26. from	70. may	114. make	158. again	202. yet
27. or	71. then	115. would	159. place	203. government
28. have	72. do	116. still	160. American	204. system
29. an	73. first	117. own	161. around	205. better
30. they	74. any	118. see	162. however	206. set
31. which	75. my	119. men	163. home	207. told
32. one	76. now	120. work	164. small	208. nothing
33. you	77. such	121. long	165. found	209. night
34. were	78. like	122. get	166. Mrs.	210. end
35. her	79. our	123. here	167. thought	211. why
36. all	80. over	124. between	168. went	212. called
37. she	81. man	125. both	169. say	213. didn't
38. there	82. me	126. life	170. part	214. eyes
39. would	83. even	127. being	171. once	215. find
40. their	84. most	128. under	172. general	216. going
41. we	85. made	129. never	173. high	217. look
42. him	86. after	130. day	174. upon	218. asked
43. been	87. also	131. same	175. school	219. later
44. has	88. did	132. another	176. every	220. knew

From Dale D. Johnson, ''The Dolch List Reexamined,'' *The Reading Teacher*, 24 (February 1971), pp. 455–456. The 220 most frequent words in the Kucera-Francis corpus. Reprinted with permission of Dale D. Johnson and the International Reading Association.

Table 10.2 Eighty-five Picture Sight Words*

1. farm	23. telephone	45. mouth	67. ear
2. clothes	24. hat	46. nose	68. rollerskates
3. money	25. window	47. garden	69. sled
4. water	26. television	48. hand	70. radio
5. grass	27. car	49. snow	71. clown
6. fence	28. cookie	50. rain	72. bread
7. stoplight	29. apple	51. fire	73. tree
8. bus	30. school	52. dish	74. mirror
9. balloon	31. book	53. hair	75. bag
10. cake	32. chicken	54. children	76. pumpkin
11. duck	33. nurse	55. lion	77. flag
12. barn	34. store	56. world	78. candle
13. street	35. door	57. watch	79. castle
14. hill	36. doctor	58. picture	80. jewel
15. man	37. teacher	59. shoes	81. bicycle
16. house	38. egg	60. bed	82. baby
17. woman	39. rabbit	61. chair	83. sock
18. airplane	40. flower	62. table	84. horse
19. train	41. sun	63. spoon	85. ring
20. boat	42. cloud	64. fork	
21. dog	43. shadow	65. truck	
22. cat	44. eye	66. bird	

*Compiled from a survey of widely used basal readers.

structional reading because the student learns a word and then applies it immediately in a reading context.

Language experience stories (stories dictated by students) can also provide a source of sight words. (The language experience method is described in detail in Chapter 11).

METHODS OF INTRODUCING SIGHT WORDS. Sight words should be introduced slowly at first. As the instruction advances, the pace should quicken. To help the remedial student understand the meaning and use of new sight words, they can be introduced in a sentence. A sentence first serves to clarify the word and later to provide a useful prompt for recognizing the word.

Word cards are an effective way of introducing sight words. They contain words on one side and usually a picture or sentence on the other. Cards should be made of durable material, such as that used in index cards, and the writing on the back should not be visible from the front. For lower-level remedial readers, two additional cautions are in order: (1) the cards should be changed often, since poor readers tend to recognize words by smudges and bends on the card, and (2) all words should be presented in carefully done, standard manuscript writing to avoid confusion. For more advanced readers, cursive writing may be used, or the words can be written by the student to foster their sense of involvement.

If new sight words are taken from instructional reading, the teacher has two choices: either (1) introduce the word before a story is read or (2) allow the student to meet the word in a story without introduction. Both options have certain advantages. For readers struggling to acquire a sight vocabulary, it is advantageous to introduce the new sight words before the story is read. This alerts the student to new words and provides a sense of security during reading. More advanced readers, however, do not need to have new words introduced prior to reading. By encountering these words during reading, students are given the opportunity to identify unknown words independently. After reading, the student and teacher can jointly select words to add to the sight vocabulary list.

Practicing Sight Words

After sight words have been introduced, they should be practiced systematically. Practice provides review, enabling word recognition to become automatic. Severely disabled readers, who are often inconsistent in sight word learning, need to practice words at every instructional session, but only a small portion of any session should be used for this purpose. Intermediate or advanced readers may only need such practice on difficult or newly acquired words. When practicing sight words, it is often helpful to review their meaning and to use them in sentences.

Word cards that were used for introducing sight words can also be used for practicing them. Each reader can be given a set of personal cards. These can be filed in individual word banks, which are boxes (e.g., shoe boxes) with alphabetized slots for each letter. This procedure also helps to teach letter recognition and alphabetical order (Stauffer, 1970). A word bank is pictured below.

There are several interesting and motivating variations for practicing sight words with word cards. The teacher can simply ask students to read word cards, or students can select words such as "dog" or "animal" from word cards set before them. Many students enjoy forming sentences from their word cards. Older remedial readers can be asked to find the word card for a specific definition or for a missing word in a sentence. In another activity, the student classifies word cards into sensible groups, such as animals or people. For variety, many students also enjoy a "switch," in which the student asks the teacher to identify words. Finally, the student can be given a personal pack of sight word cards to practice at home with a parent or friend. The teacher, however, should retain a duplicate copy.

Games provide another way to practice sight words. Although such games are easily made, and thus can be designed for individual students, many games can also be purchased from teachers' stores or publishers. One type of game uses a "trailboard" such as that illustrated below.

The gameboard is made from a 2′ × 3′ piece of cardboard, laminated or coated with clear adhesive paper for durability. Illustrations can be obtained from magazines. (The example that is pictured above has a pirate theme.) Instead of writing words on the game path, the words to be used are supplied by word cards that are piled on the board, enabling the practice cards to be changed easily. The student rolls dice (or one die), picks up a word from the pile, and moves the number of spaces indicated, if the word can be read correctly. The card is then moved to the bottom of the pack. A spinner can be substituted for dice, and a few cards, such as "You have been lucky today and may move two spaces," add spice and suspense to the game. These games can be played with a teacher and a student or several students who may wish to practice words independently.

Another game for practicing sight words is Bingo. Cards are prepared containing the sight words, and each space is covered as the word is called. If a student (rather than the teacher) calls the words, the student must then say the word as well as recognize it. Bingo is a suitable activity for small- and large-group instruction.

In the game of Fish, words are written on cards with a small magnet attached to each and placed in a container such as a fishbowl or empty coffee can. The student is given a small "fishing pole" with a magnet "hook," which is used to fish out a word and say it. The student with the biggest "catch" is the winner.

Several other well-known games may be adapted for sight word drill. Checkers can be played with simplified rules on a board in which the squares contain sight words. Old Maid and Concentration card games can also be adapted for use with sight words. The teacher's imagination is the only limit to the creativity of the games that may be designed.

The "language master" is a type of recorder that is very useful for practicing sight words independently. Specially prepared cards have a sight word printed on the top of the card and an audiotape of the word on the bottom. The student reads the word from the card and then checks the reading by inserting the card through the language master, which plays back a recording of the word.

Transferring Sight Word Knowledge to Reading

After words are practiced in isolation, they must be used in a reading context. Remedial readers at beginning reading levels often have difficulty transferring the newly practiced words to actual reading.

STEPS IN TRANSFERRING SIGHT WORDS. In this section, a series of steps is outlined for students who have extreme difficulty in applying sight words to reading. Students with less difficulty will not need to follow each of these small steps.

1. For students having extreme difficulty, the first reading context can be limited to two or three words. Robert could not read sentences, so his teacher combined his sight words into skeletons such as "Robert is house, Robert is boy" and asked him to identify those that made sense and those that did not. (He found such sentences as "Paul is house" to be very funny.) Students can also be asked to combine their sight words in various ways and then to read them. These combinations can be copied onto a sheet of paper.
2. Next, students read full sentences. They can also compose sentences from their own sight words, and they can exchange sentences with others. If this procedure is used, be sure that students' printing is readable.
3. The next step is reading words in short stories. To make the transition gradual, one teacher cut out a "book" with each page in the shape of a cat. The book described the student's cat using one or two sentences on each page, as shown below. Teachers can

compose these books, or students can dictate them. In this case, they share many of the features of language experience stories. To focus attention on new words, students can underline them.

4. Finally, new sight words should be transferred to instructional and independent reading. When words for a sight word vocabulary are taken from instructional reading materials, the student will automatically apply new words in context.

INSTRUCTIONAL READING MATERIALS FOR APPLYING SIGHT WORDS.   Many reading materials are useful for practicing sight words in reading. These materials serve many other purposes, but they are especially appropriate for applying sight word skills. Types of reading materials include: (1) remedial reading series books, (2) easy reading books, (3) basal readers, and (4) real-life materials. General characteristics of these materials are described below; specific materials are listed in Appendix A.

1. *Remedial reading series books*. These are graded series of stories or articles. In addition to stories, these books often contain lists of new words, practice exercises for words, and comprehension questions. Usually, each story in a book is on a different topic. Examples of remedial reading series include *Reading for Concepts*, *Moving Along*, and *The New Cornerstone Readers*. Remedial reading series books are controlled for difficulty level; however, new words from one story tend *not* to be repeated in another. Thus, the teacher may prefer to use these books with students who have acquired some reading fluency.

2. *Easy reading books*. Often called "high-interest–low-vocabulary" books, these books concentrate on enjoyable reading experiences rather than on direct instruction. Thus, they do not include exercises for skill development. They contain several stories or one continuous story.

A useful feature of one type of easy reading books is their tightly controlled vocabulary. Some provide reading practice throughout 50 or 75 pages with a total vocabulary of 200 to 500 different words. This format enables a student to practice a sight word several times. The total vocabulary is usually listed at the end of the book. Examples of a series of easy reading books are the *Cowboy Sam Series* and the *Morgan Bay Mystery Series*. Because of their vocabulary control and interest, they are recommended highly for remedial readers at primary reading levels.

Other easy reading books are controlled for reading level, but they do not contain specified word lists or repeat a limited number of words. These may be used effectively to foster wide reading for students with some reading fluency. Examples are *Sports Profiles* and *Pacemates*. High-interest–low-vocabulary books are often geared cleverly to student interests (sports, superheroes, teenage problems) and are highly motivating.

3. *Basal readers*. These books are intended for developmental readers, but they can serve remedial purposes as well. At the beginning levels (preprimer, primer, first, second), sight words are introduced very slowly and are practiced over and over. Careful spacing and consistent practice make these materials useful for remedial readers who can only acquire sight words with difficulty. However, there are some disadvantages in using basal readers. They may remind students of past failures, or the style and content of the readers may be insultingly childlike for

some students. The success of basal readers depends largely upon the attitude of the student. With proper motivation, they can be effective with teenagers and even adult disabled readers. Although most basal readers use a sight word approach, some are organized to teach phonics. Thus, remedial teachers should be familiar with the philosophy underlying the series they select.

4. *Real-life materials.* This refers to the abundance of material that surrounds us, such as newspaper articles, captions of pictures, magazines, manuals, advertisements, and many other kinds of printed materials. These materials can be used to practice reading and sight words. The relevance of such real-life material makes vocabulary control a matter of secondary interest. Some instructional series, such as the *Basic Life Skills Series*, also concentrate upon students' ability to perform real-world tasks, for example, using a checkbook and reading job ads.

Charting Progress

Charting progress in sight word learning makes students aware of their accomplishments. Both progress charts and consistency charts can provide methods of keeping track of sight words.

THE PROGRESS CHART.   This chart records the new words a student has learned. The progress chart may take many different forms:

1. A remedial reader at a beginning level read Dr. Seuss's *The Cat in the Hat*. The teacher drew a large picture of the hero on top of the chart, and each new word was recorded in a different color (see picture below).

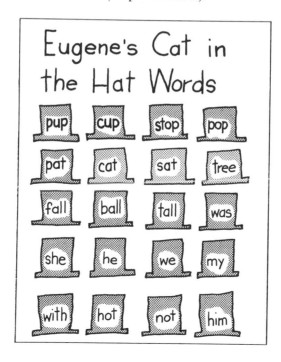

2. For recording interests in season, autumn words can be put in a witch's pot. Sports interests are also seasonal.

3. A catchy picture of a superhero, such as Popeye or Spiderman, surrounded by words can increase motivation markedly (see picture below).

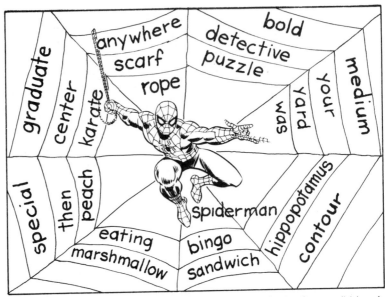

4. Special interests (or themes) of instruction may serve as the focal point of interest on a chart. Thirteen-year-old Mike's word chart was a jungle panorama containing several different animals, each labeled. A student studying the ancient Vikings had a Viking ship with the words written on the oars, the shields, and so on (see picture on top of page 211).

5. One teacher made a word mobile and suspended it from the ceiling.

THE CONSISTENCY CHART. A consistency chart records both sight words and their retention. An example is given below. New words are written from top to bottom, and the lesson dates are recorded from left to right. Each time that words are reviewed, a mark is placed next to the words read correctly. Some students prefer to draw a smiling face to indicate a correct word. Consistency charts encourage students to practice their words frequently. (See example, bottom of 211.)

Consistency charts can serve many purposes. They can be used to record correct applications of phonics principles or number of comprehension questions answered correctly, as well as progress in sight words. To help one remedial reader overcome shyness, the teacher outlined the students' name on a black sheet of paper. Then, for each sight word pronounced correctly, a silver star was put on the outline until the name was "spelled out in lights" (see example on page 212).

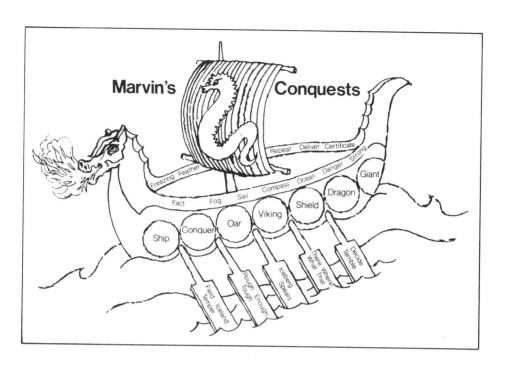

Marvin's Conquests

Robert's Word Web

	3/3	3/5	3/7	3/10	3/12
airplane	☆	★	☆	☆	★
bell	☆	☆	☆	★	☆
box			☆	★	
cap				★	★
doll		☆	☆	★	★
eye	★	☆	★	☆	★
fire	★	☆	★	★	★
hen			★	☆	★
money			☆	☆	★
mother		★	★	★	☆

Another teacher used a bank chart. After the student "deposited" the word (got it correct) three times, it was added to the "balance."

Function Words

Because the recognition of function words may be so troublesome for remedial students, they deserve special attention. Function words are the highly frequent but abstract words of English such as *if, but*, and *there*. They are distinguished from content words, which consist largely of nouns, adjectives, and verbs.

Function words are extremely frequent in text, but despite this frequency they are often difficult to master. These words tend to have irregular sound/spelling relationships and therefore must be mastered as sight words, since phonics rules often do not apply. In addition, function words can be confusing visually. Consider the words *there* and *them*. Because function words are so abstract in meaning, many students do not realize that words such as *the* and *what* are actually words (Cunningham, 1980). Such words cannot be easily pictured by remedial students.

Perfect mastery of all function words is not necessary for efficient reading (K. S. Goodman, 1967). Nevertheless, function words appear so frequently that, if they present difficulty, reading fluency will be hampered.

There are many ways to focus special attention upon these difficult words.

1. Because function words contain little meaning in themselves, they should be introduced in a meaningful context, such as a sentence. Association with context will help students to recall the word.
2. Lists of visually confusing words can be written and the pupil asked to circle the one that the teacher reads. In this way, students are helped to distinguish small visual differences.
3. Word wheels give much needed practice with visually confusing function words. Words are written around the circumference of a circular piece of paper that is mounted on cardboard. This paper is then covered with an equal-sized piece of paper that leaves space to expose only one word at a time. The student practices function words by turning the word wheel to reveal different words (see example on the top of page 213).

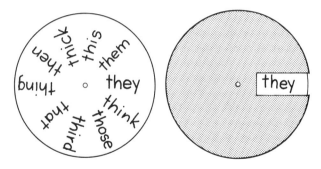

4. A story can be written, underlining the function words or printing them in red for the reader. This enables the student to apply these words in a reading context while calling attention to these "little words."

5. In the "star word" approach, one difficult word is printed on a large star containing some room for little silver stars. The word is then introduced as the "star word" of the day. During a teaching session, it is called to the student's attention at periodic intervals of between seven and ten minutes. Each time it is pronounced correctly, a little tinsel star is placed on the big star (see picture below). This procedure combines the highlighting of the word with the psychological principle of intermittent reinforcement.

6. Kibby (1981) has pointed out that only four of the "wh" function words begin with a silent "w" (*who*, *whose*, *whom*, and *whole*). If these are taught first, the other "wh" words (which, whether, when etc.) become easier to master.

Recognizing Words Instantly

Sight words should be recognized instantly. The remedial student who hesitates repeatedly or tries to sound out the word needs reinforcement in immediate recognition. Students can practice instant recognition with a tachistoscope, a device that flashes a word for a fraction of a second. Hand-held tachistoscopes can be made fairly easily. The one pictured on page 214 was made during the baseball season. Different sight words were exposed as the strip was pulled quickly through the hole. Commercial tachistoscopes are also available.

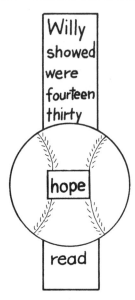

Another teacher made a chart with categories of both sight words and instant words. As the student learned to recognize words quickly, they were moved to the instant list. In the "one-minute game," students are timed to see how many words can be recognized in one minute. Words for this game can be written on tongue depressors so that students can handle them more easily.

PHONICS CLUES

A reader uses phonics clues to match the sound of a letter to a specific written symbol. Phonics gives the reader considerable independence by providing a valuable tool for decoding unknown words. In an extensive research summary of beginning reading methods, Chall (1967) showed that a phonics emphasis produced superior results for lower-achieving students. Weber (1972) also found that a decoding emphasis was associated with effective learning in inner-city schools.

Determining Specific Phonics Abilities

In planning a program, it is important to have knowledge of the student's phonics abilities. One method for assessing phonics abilities is to ask students to read a list of "nonsense words" that illustrate different phonics principles. Testing with nonsense words assures that the words cannot be read as sight words and requires students to use their phonics skills. (Although nonsense words are recommended for assessment, they should not be used for instruction.) Some common phonics rules are given in Table 10.3; a list of nonsense words for testing is given in

Table 10.3   Useful Phonics Generalizations

1. *Single Consonants*: Reading grade level 1
Generally, consonants are dependable in sound. They include *b, d, f, h, j, k, l, m, n, p, r, s, t, v, w, x, y,* and *z. C* and *g* have two common sounds (see item 7).

2. *Consonant Digraphs*: Reading grade level 1
These refer to two consonants that, when together, make one sound. Common digraphs are *sh, ch, ck, ph,* and *th* (as in *thy* and *thigh*). *Qu* is sometimes considered a digraph.

3. *Consonant Blends*: Reading grade level 2
These are two or three consonants blended together for pronunciation. Beginning blends include *st, gr, cl, sp, pl, tr, br, dr, bl, fr, fl, pr, cr, sl, sw, gl, str.* Ending blends include *nd, nk, nt, lk, ld, rt, nk, rm, rd, rn, mp, ft, lt, ct, pt, lm.*

4. *Single Vowels, Long and Short Vowels:* Reading grade levels 2–3.
Long vowels are sometimes called "free" or "glided" forms. Short vowels are called "checked" or "unglided." Examples are:

VOWEL	SHORT SOUND	LONG SOUND
a	apple	pane
e	egg	teeth
i	igloo	ice
o	pot	home
u	run	use, tuba

Long vowels occur (a) when a vowel is followed by a consonant and an *e,* the *e* is usually silent (e.g., *rate*), and (b) when a vowel ends a word or syllable (e.g., *be, begin*). Short vowels occur when a single vowel is followed by one or more consonants (e.g., *rat*). Words like *rate* are often constrasted to pairs such as *rat.*

5. *"R"-Controlled Vowels:* Reading grade levels 2–3
These include *ar* (car), *er* (her), *ir* (stir), *or* (for), *ur* (fur). Note that *er, ir,* and *ur* sound alike.

6. *Vowel Combinations:* Reading grade levels 2–3
Dependable combinations include *oa* (boat), *ai* (raise), *ee* (bee), *oi* (boil), *aw* (saw), *ay* (say), *ew* (blew), *ou* (loud). Less dependable combinations are *ea* (seat, bear), *ow* (cloud, low), *oo* (boot, look).

7. *Hard and Soft "C" and "G":* Reading grade level 3
Hard and soft sounds are

LETTER	SOFT SOUND	HARD SOUND
c	city	cut
g	general	gold

Generally, soft sounds are followed by *e, i,* and *y.* Hard sounds occur elsewhere. These principles are more dependable for *c* than for *g.*

8. *Silent Letters:* Reading grade levels 3–4
When consonant combinations cannot be pronounced together, the second is *usually* pronounced.

SECOND CONSONANT PRONOUNCED	FIRST CONSONANT PRONOUNCED
kn (know)	*rh* (rheumatism)
wr (wren)	*gh* (ghost)
pn (pneumonia)	
mn (mnemonic)	
gn (gnat)	
ld (would)	
lk (walk)	

Table 10.4. Studies on the usefulness of phonics rules were conducted by Clymer (1963), Bailey (1967), and Venezky (1967a,b).

Often younger remedial students and older severely disabled readers find the task of reading nonsense words too abstract. Thus, instead of reading nonsense syllables they simply pronounce real words. If teachers find that their students cannot pronounce nonsense syllables, a list of real words must be used for testing phonics skills.

For students at beginning levels, the teacher may simply show individual letters (such as *s,f*) and ask students to pronounce them. However, teachers should bear in mind that individual consonant sounds are sometimes distorted when said in isolation (note the sounds of *b, d*) and that vowels have many different sounds. Because of these problems, we do not recommend that teachers only present individual letters when other assessment techniques cannot be used.

Some remedial students know phonics principles and do well on phonics tests, but they cannot apply their phonics skills to the reading situation. These students need to be observed during oral reading, using procedures such as the informal reading inventory (see Chapter 6). The student who rarely uses phonics clues in reading needs help in the third (and final) phase of learning phonics, the transfer phase.

Some ways of assessing phonics skills are not recommended, since they give an inaccurate picture of students' abilities. 1. It is not recommended that students be asked to recite phonics rules and terminology. Ability to recite does not show if the student can apply these rules to words. Further, some students can apply rules without being able to state them (as can many adults). 2. It is not recommended that students be asked to spell words or to identify written words which match a word which the teacher pronounces (a task which also requires spelling). These procedures underestimate the student's phonics abilities, as most people can read more words than they can pronounce. Some commercial phonics tests require these types of tasks, and we recommend that such tests be avoided.

Introducing Phonics Skills

The three-step framework described earlier serves to structure the presentation of phonics skills. The three steps are: (1) introduction, (2) practice, and (3) transfer. Prior to introducing phonics skills, however, it is important to make sure that the student possesses the necessary auditory and visual prerequisite skills for learning phonics. It may be necessary to teach the prerequisite skills before teaching phonics (see Chapter 8).

Two basic approaches for introducing phonics are the *synthetic* approach and the *analytic* approach. In the synthetic approach to phonics, the student first learns individual phonic elements, for example, "s," "ee," "fl." The student then learns to form the word by putting these sounds together. Students need facility in the prerequisite skill of blending sound elements to use this approach successfully. The synthetic method, usually involves the use of phonics *rules*, a task that remedial readers often find very difficult. Phonics rules are easier to learn when

Table 10.4 Words for Testing Phonics Generalizations

These nonsense "words" can be used to test phonics mastery. They should be typed in a large typeface or printed neatly and presented in a list format or on individual cards. Students should be warned that they are not real words, when asked to pronounce them.

1. SINGLE CONSONANTS

bam
dup
sut
fep
jit
rez
dif
hak
jer

2. CONSONANT DIGRAPHS

shap
thip
nack
chep
quen

3. CONSONANT BLENDS

sput
crob
flug
dreb
streb
plut
grat
pind
gart
rupt

4. SINGLE VOWELS: LONG AND SHORT

mab
mabe
sot
sote
lib
libe
vo
vom

5. "R"-CONTROLLED VOWELS

dar
ser
tor
snir

6. VOWEL COMBINATIONS

toat
vay
zew
doil
roub
geet
rood

7. HARD AND SOFT "C" AND "G"

cit
cyle
cam
ges
gast

8. SILENT LETTERS

knas
gnip
wret
ghes

presented along with concrete word patterns. An example of combining a word pattern with the rule follows.

- *Rule:* When a vowel is followed by a consonant and a final *e*, the *e* is silent and the vowel is long.
- *Pattern: hat - hate*; *pan - pane.*

In the analytic (or linguistic) method of teaching phonics, words are presented as whole units and not broken apart into separate letters or sounds. Thus, the distortions created by saying isolated sounds, (such as *b* or *g*) are avoided. To illustrate how the linguistic approach might operate, all the words containing the sound unit *ay* might be presented together, followed by words containing another sound unit such a *ight*. By seeing these pattern words over and over, students become familiar with phonics generalizations. Rather than identifying individual component letters and phonics rules, students learn words by associating them with words already known. The word "pet," for example, might be associated with "let." A list of word families that can be used with the analytic approach follows:

ar	car	*ight*	right
at	cat	*ade*	shade
ap	cap	*eat*	meat
op	hop	*eet*	street
ot	hot	*ide*	side
et	pet	*ind*	find
ig	big	*ent*	rent
ip	rip	*ild*	wild
in	fin	*ake*	rake
ike	like	*ipe*	pipe

The two approaches to teaching phonics, synthetic and analytic, can often be used together. For example, word families may be used to illustrate principles in the synthetic approach. Or students may choose to "sound out" or synthesize words even when they are taught by the analytic approach.

Practicing Phonics Skills

Remedial readers need much practice before they are comfortable with phonics skills. Because the learning of phonics is very difficult for some students, remedial teachers should not become discouraged if progress is slow. Even students who are developing normally in reading require several years to master phonics. The following suggestions can help teachers to make the learning of phonics easier.

1. Allow students to pronounce words in their own speech patterns. For example, pupils with immature speech may pronounce *ride* as *wide*. If the student knows what the word means, however, there is no need to "correct" the pronunciation. This principle also holds for pronunciation variations due to dialect and language

differences. The aim of all instruction, including phonics instruction, is to get meaning from the printed page. If students can do this, "standard" pronunciation should not be required.

2.   Avoid teaching confusing elements together. For example, the five short vowels are very close in sound and students may get confused easily.

3.   Use concrete examples. Elements to be taught can be accompanied by cards containing example words and pictures. These will aid student memory. A picture of a boy, for example, will help students remember the sound of *b*.

4.   Use words that are meaningful to students. When introducing or practicing phonics, select words that the students understand. If they do not know the meaning of words, they will not be able to tell whether they have decoded them correctly.

Some suggestions for practicing eight different types of phonics elements are given below. The rules governing these elements appear in Table 10.3.

SINGLE CONSONANTS.   Consonants are the clues most often used by readers for identifying words (Shankweiler and Liberman, 1972; Williams, Blumberg, and Williams, 1970). To illustrate the importance of consonants, two messages are shown below; one contains only consonants, and one contains only vowels.

- C-ns-n-nts -r- -s-f-l
- -o--o-a--- a-e u-e-u-

The message (*consonants are useful*) is much easier to decode with only consonants present than with only vowels present.

The "Frank and Ernest" cartoon has been reprinted by permission. © 1980 NEA, Inc.

Since remedial readers rely so heavily on initial consonant clues, it is especially important to teach consonants in initial positions. Some consonants are easier to learn than others. Consonants with continuous sounds (s, m) are relatively easy to learn. Students can form associations to these continuous sounds. For example, associate the *s* with the sound of a snake and *m* with the sound for delicious food. Consonants with stopped sounds (*b, k*) are more difficult to learn. Teachers can make cards that serve as reminders of consonant sounds. These cards should contain the letter and a picture beginning with that letter sound. Several activities for practicing single consonants follow.

1. Students can look for magazine pictures that begin (or end) with consonant sounds. Labeling these pictures with the actual words they represent reinforces learning.

2. A picture dictionary may be constructed showing pictures beginning with the consonant sounds.

3. A board game can be constructed, which consists of squares or cards containing pictures. When a student lands on a square with a picture, the picture name and initial letter are given.

4. Charts can be made using pictures that either begin or end with a certain letter sound (say *l*). The letter should be printed at the top of the chart. Students can be asked to attach a clothes pin to the left of the picture if it begins with the target letter and to the right if it ends with the letter.

CONSONANT DIGRAPHS AND CONSONANT BLENDS. Consonant digraphs represent only one speech sound (examples are *ch*, *sh*). Consonant blends represent two or three speech sounds (examples are *fl*, *str*). Because consonant digraphs are easier to pronounce than are blends, they are easier to learn and should be taught first. Students need not learn how many sounds the digraph or blend represents, nor should they be required to pronounce them in Standard English. Instead, each element should be taught with an association; for example, they might be taught that *ch* makes a sound as in *chair*. Several activities for practicing digraphs and blends follow. The exercises given for single consonants can also be adapted for use with blends and digraphs.

1. A familiar object (such as a *ship*) can be cut out of paper with the word written on it. The word (*ship*) can be changed by pulling a paper strip which exposes new consonant digraphs and blends (*trip*, *flip*). The ship below is for practicing blends and digraphs; the mouse helps with single consonants.

2. Bingo may be adapted using words that contain consonant digraphs and blends.
3. Teenage remedial readers enjoy keeping notebooks of blends. Each blend is written on the top of a separate notebook page, and the students write as many words with blends as they can find.

LONG AND SHORT VOWELS.   The long sound of a vowel is equivalent to its letter name. Although long sounds appear to be single sounds to native English speakers, they are acoustically two sounds, the second being a glide. Speakers of other languages may have a difficult time recognizing that a long vowel sound is considered one sound in English. On the other hand, short vowel sounds may present difficulty because they are easily confused.

The short and long sounds of the five vowel letters are as follows:

LETTER	SHORT SOUND	LONG SOUND
a	apple	pane
e	egg	teeth
i	igloo	ice
o	pot	tote
u	run	tuba, use

Remedial readers find these vowel sounds easier to learn when the long and short sounds of each vowel are taught together (e.g., short and long "a"). This procedure avoids teaching the short vowels, which are very similar in sound to each other, together. In addition, by teaching the short and long sound of a single vowel at the same time, the teacher can demonstrate how they alternate in words. For example,

• rat, rate
• hat, hate
• man, mane
• pan, pane

The following activities for teaching long and short vowels help remedial students to learn these topics without having to verbalize complex rules.

1. A "silent *e* teapot" can be made, and words can be pulled through one side (see picture on page 222). The other side contains a paper tab. When the student pulls it, an *e* is exposed and a word containing a long vowel can be read. When the *e* is not exposed, a short vowel sound is used in the word.
2. A cardboard circle can be constructed that has both long and short vowel words around the circumference. A metal pointer can be attached. When the pointer is spun, the student reads the word to which it points (see example on page 222).
3. Cubes containing single vowel phonograms (with and without final *e*; for example, *ake*, *at*, *et*, *ape*) may be combined with consonants cubes to make words. These cubes can be bought commercially or adapted from Scrabble games. Students enjoy seeing how many words they can make in a two- or three-minute time span. Model word choices may be given by the teacher so that students do not have to spell words.

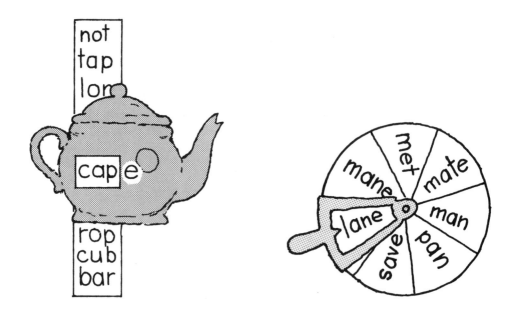

R-CONTROLLED VOWELS AND VOWEL COMBINATIONS.   Many remedial readers find that r-controlled vowels are easier to learn than vowel combinations. Generally, only five *r*-controlled vowels need to be taught, and three of these make the same sound (*er*, *ir*, and *ur*).

1.   *ar* (car)
2.   *er* (her)
3.   *ir* (fir)
4.   *or* (for)
5.   *ur* (fur)

There are also many combinations where two vowels occur together. Many such combinations have only one sound and are easily taught because the vowels make a dependable sound (*ay*, *ee*), but some combinations are less dependable (*ea*) (see Table 10.3). One often-used rule is "When two vowels go walking, the first one does the talking." That is, when two vowels appear together, the first one assumes its long sound (letter name) and the second is silent (e.g., *rain, coat*). However, this rule has many exceptions and holds true only about 45 percent of the time (Emans, 1967). As a result, many teachers prefer to teach each combination separately. Practice activities for *r*-controlled vowels and vowel combinations follow.

1.   A double flip chart, consisting of two sides, either of which can be flipped, may be constructed (see picture on 223). On one side, consonants are presented. On the other side, word endings using vowel combinations are given. The student can flip either side to see how many word combinations can be made. Meaningful words can be written down.

2. In a card game, each person is dealt five cards containing words. One player then picks a card from the remaining pile. If the player selects a word card containing the same vowel combinations as a word already held, both cards are placed on the table, providing that both words can be read. Each player tries to place a maximum number of cards out of his or her hand and onto the table. Packs of blank playing cards may be bought to construct this game, or regular playing cards may be adapted.

GENERALIZATIONS WITH *C* AND *G*.   The hard and soft sounds of *c* and *g* are shown below and in Table 10.4. Generally, the soft sounds are used when *c* and *g* are followed by *e*, *i*, or *y*. Hard sounds are used elsewhere. These principles are more reliable for *c* than for *g* (Venezky, 1967a), and some teachers prefer to only teach *c*.

LETTER	SOFT SOUND	HARD SOUND
"c"	city	cut
"g"	general	gold

A practice exercise for *c* and *g* follows.

1. A chart can record all the *c* or *g* words that the reader can think of. The columns can be labled *ca*, *ce*, *ci*, and so forth. Students may add more words as they find them.
2. Students can look for long words containing *c* and *g*. Words can be collected giving students one point for each word up to seven letters, and two points for each word of eight letters or more. Some teachers give an extra point for any word which is an exception to the *c* and *g* rules.

SILENT CONSONANTS.   When there is no sound for a letter in a consonant combination, it is referred to as a silent consonant (e.g., the *k* in *kn*). Generally, the second letter of a two consonant sequence is pronounced (*know*, *gnat*), but, when the second consonant is *h*, the first letter is pronounced (*ghost*, *rhumba*).

Practice exercises for silent consonants follow.

1. In check-a-match, a checkerboard is constructed with each square containing a silent letter word. The players move the checkers on the board according to rules. However, to stay on any square, they must pronounce the word written on it. Rules for checkers should be simplified.

2. A pad of paper can be given to students with words containing silent consonants written on each sheet. Each player, in turn, tears off a sheet and reads the one to five words on it.

Transferring Phonics Principles to Reading

Students need practice in contextual reading to become fluent with a phonics skill. Reading words on a list where all the words conform to the same pattern is relatively easy. When the words are embedded in sentences and paragraphs, however, the task is far more challenging.

STEPS IN TRANSFERRING PHONICS.   A structured sequence is suggested for transferring phonics to reading.

1. Words using the phonics element are practiced first in sentences, then in short stories. Attention is drawn to words by underlining or using colored markers. If teachers wish to deal with more than one phonics pattern, they should mark the two patterns separately (e.g., with red and yellow markers). The use of color coding should be phased out eventually.
2. Students can also look for phonics patterns in the independent or easy level reading that they do. For example, they may be asked to bring in some *short e* words.
3. The final step for transferring a phonics skill is to use it in instructional readings. For less advanced readers words containing certain phonics patterns may be pointed out before a passage is read. More advanced remedial students may simply read instructional material and afterwards find words that illustrate certain phonics principles. Or the teacher may locate words in the text for students to pronounce after reading.

The most important consideration in transferring phonics skills to reading is to urge students to sound out words that they do not know, rather than to rely on help from the teacher. Since remedial readers have often become discouraged about trying to sound out words, they must be encouraged systematically. For example, the student can be praised for attempting to figure out a word, even if the response is not correct. Or an informal reward system can be devised in which students are given a point, star, or other marker whenever an attempt is made to figure out an unknown word.

Some students in the remedial program know phonics but do not apply their skills in reading. For these students, instruction in phonics should concentrate on the transfer process. These students, in particular, need encouragement in the risk-taking needed to sound out words.

INSTRUCTIONAL MATERIALS FOR PHONICS.   If phonics instruction is intensive, the teacher may want to coordinate the instructional reading program with it. Several graded reading books concentrate upon introducing sounds systematically into reading.

The synthetic phonics approach can be coordinated with instructional reading. The published series that use this approach provide instructional reading rich in words that apply phonics principles. These series include *Phonetic Keys to*

Reading, the *Open Court Reading Series*, *DISTAR*, and the *SRA Corrective Reading Series*.

The analytic approach can also be coordinated with instructional reading. Suggested series include the *Merrill Linguistic Reading Program*, and the *Sullivan Reading Program*. The Dr. Seuss beginning-to-read books, such as *The Cat in the Hat* and *Green Eggs and Ham* are useful for the analytic phonics approach and they are well loved by students. All materials are listed in Appendix A.

An Example of a Complete Phonics Teaching Sequence

The stages of introduction, practice, and application can be combined into an effective teaching sequence for phonics. In Table 10.5, a complete sequence is given for teaching the consonant blend *str*. Note that the teacher checks prerequisite skills before proceeding. Since students may have different perceptual strengths and weaknesses, this lesson uses auditory and visual reinforcement to teach the phonics elements.

Decoding Multisyllable Words: Syllabication

As students progress in reading, they encounter longer words and must learn techniques to break them apart into syllables and decode them. Although syllabication rules are helpful, they are complex and sometimes undependable. Students must be taught to use flexibility, supplementing them with context clues (checking the meaning of the reading material).

A vowel sound called a "schwa" is found in many multisyllabic words. The schwa is simply an unaccented vowel, as in the words, *sofa, cotton*, and *about*.

Teachers and students should be aware that applying phonics principles for multisyllable words may only produce approximations to real words. The reader must match these approximations with words in their meaning vocabularies. For example, a student sounds out the two syllables *lit-tle* and recognizes that the word is *little*.

Despite these cautions, syllabication guidelines are very helpful for decoding multisyllabic words. Some rules are presented in Table 10.6. To test ability in syllabication, use the nonsense words in Table 10.7.

When teaching rules and principles for syllabication, the explanations should be accompanied by sample words that illustrate the rule. Even a few words can help to make abstract rules much more understandable.

The transfer phase is a crucial one for syllabication. When words are presented in a sentence, paragraph, or story context, the student is able to use the syllabication rules in a reading situation. Many remedial students have been taught principles for long words, but they have difficulty applying them. The teacher can identify target words in a reading passage by underlining or marking them. After reading the passage, the student is asked to pronounce the marked words orally.

As noted earlier, syllabication rules can be undependable. Thus they must

Table 10.5   Phonics Teaching Sequence

Checking Prerequisite Skills (for the "STR" sound)
A. Listen carefully to these two words. What do you hear in them that is the same? *strike, strict*
B. Listen and watch as I say and write each of the words.
C. Say the words after me as I point to them.

Introducing the Phonic Element
A. Look at this list of words. Pick out the word with the sound we are learning, read it aloud, then rewrite the word. *start, strap, past*
B. Listen to this list of words. Decide which word has the sound we are learning. Say it aloud and then write the letters which make up the sound. *tart, first, stroke*

Practicing the Phonic Element
A. Add the sound we are learning to each of the word endings written on this list. Write the entire word and say it. _____*ut,* _____*um*
B. Add the sound we are learning to each of the word endings that I say. Say the word aloud. Now write the words. _____*ing,* _____*and*

Transferring the Phonic Element
A. Read a sentence and fill in the blank with a word which begins with the new sound being learned. "John saw a _____ of lightning." *streak, strong, store*
B. In the final steps, the student practices reading *str* words in paragraphs and later instructional reading. The student can be asked to pick out *str* words after reading.

Table 10.6   Syllabication Rules

1. In a compound word, each small word is usually a syllable (e.g., cow-boy).
2. Structural word parts are usually syllables (e.g., re-wind; slow-ly).
3. Vowel combinations and "r"-controlled vowels usually retain their own sounds (e.g., taw-dry).
4. When a single vowel occurs in a multisyllable word:
   a. If it is followed by two consonants, it is generally given its short sound. This pattern may be referred to as VCC: "little," "apple," "rescue," "picnic". Teach this rule first with double consonants ("little," "apple"). Then teach different middle consonants ("rescue," "picnic").
   b. If it is followed by only one consonant, (1) the vowel may have its long sound (VCV, as in "lilac," "tuba," "solace"), or (2) the vowel may have its short sound (VCV as in "benefit," "several," "mimic"). Students should try the long sound first, then the short sound.
5. The letters "le" at the end of a word are pronounced as in rattle and nettle.

be supplemented with other word recognition clues. A four-step sequence to help achieve flexibility in decoding is suggested. This procedure combines syllabication with context clues, phonics, and structural analysis to help baffled remedial readers decode long words. In particular, many of our older remedial students have found this procedure to be helpful.

226

Table 10.7   Words for Testing Syllabication Abilities

Students may be asked both to divide these words into syllables using paper and pencil and to pronounce them.

1. COMPOUND WORDS	2. STRUCTURAL WORD PARTS
playdog	stipment
freeday	gaiter
	repainly

3. VOWEL COMBINATIONS	4a. VOWEL FOLLOWED BY ONE CONSONANT
tainest	waman
bayter	sowel
stirler	fomub
	setin

4b. VOWEL FOLLOWED BY TWO CONSONANTS	5. *LE* COMBINATIONS
mattel	rettle
fuddot	sontle
sandot	
dembin	

1. If you don't know a word, first reread the sentence and try to figure it out (context clues).
2. If that doesn't work, sound out the first syllable and then reread the sentence (phonics clues).
3. If you still don't know it, look for word endings and try to figure out the base word (structural analysis).
4. If you still haven't figured it out, sound out the whole word. Remember, you may have to change a few sounds to make the word make sense (phonics clues).

Teaching Exceptions to Phonics Rules

English contains many words that have irregular sound/spelling correspondences. Many of these exceptional words are the high-frequency function words (*of, the, was*). It is recommended that these words be taught thoroughly by sight so that the student does not need to sound them out.

There are, however, many other words that do not fit phonics principles. When students find that they cannot decode a word using phonics principles, they should be guided to use other strategies.

1. Try alternate pronunciations.
2. Use context clues.
3. Use structural analysis clues.

Because phonics rules are simply generalizations based on frequent word patterns, teachers should explain to remedial readers that some exceptions will be found in all reading material. Some remedial readers actually enjoy finding these exceptions and presenting them to the class or the teacher. Teachers can make lists of exceptional words along with those that have regular phonics patterns. Students should understand that, in spite of some exceptions, most words will conform to the phonics patterns they have been taught. Exceptions to rules should not be emphasized until students are quite familiar with the rules themselves.

SUMMARY

This chapter discussed two word recognition clues: sight words and phonics. (Two additional word recognition clues—structural analysis and context—are covered in Chapter 11.)

A three-step procedure for teaching a reading skill is (1) introducing the skill, (2) practicing the skill, and (3) transferring it to reading.

Remedial readers having difficulty learning sight words may use pictures or configurations (shapes) to identify words. These clues are inefficient and should not be encouraged.

A sight word is recognized instantly, without any analysis. In the introduction of sight words, words may be chosen from basic lists, student requests, language experience stories, or instructional reading material. After introduction, sight words should be practiced frequently. Finally, the transfer phase is important because remedial readers encounter difficulty applying sight word knowledge in reading. Steps for transfer for very remedial readers include using (1) a few words, (2) a sentence, (3) paragraphs, and (4) instructional reading.

Progress in sight words may be recorded in a progress chart of new words or a consistency chart, where words are reviewed at regular intervals. Function words (such as *in, the*) are difficult because they are abstract in meaning, phonically irregular, and often visually similar. Sight words may be presented quickly so that students learn to recognize them instantly.

Phonics refers to the recognition of words by the regular correspondences between their letters and their sounds. Having the student read nonsense syllables that illustrate phonics principles is a good assessment procedure. Procedures for teaching the following phonics elements were given: single consonants, consonant digraphs, consonant blends, long and short vowels, *r*-controlled vowels, vowel combinations, *c* and *g* rules, and silent consonants.

When teaching phonics, teachers should allow students to pronounce words according to their own speech patterns. Confusing elements should not be taught together. Words for practicing decoding skills should be within the students' speaking-listening vocabularies.

The approaches for introducing phonics skills are (1) the synthetic approach (sounds are blended together) and (2) the analytic or linguistic approach (whole words are presented according to sound patterns).

For mastery, phonics skills need to be practiced in a variety of ways. Instructional reading may be coordinated with teaching phonics. An example of a complete phonics teaching sequence was given, containing the procedure for checking prerequisite skills, as well as introduction, practice, and transfer.

Multisyllable words present problems because syllabication principles are complex and may be undependable. Syllabication rules were presented. Students should learn that strategies other than syllabication must sometimes be employed to decode multisyllable words. A four-step procedure for combining many types of clues is (1) rereading the sentence, (2) decoding the first syllable, (3) looking for word endings, and (4) sounding out the whole word.

Students must learn to deal with exceptions to phonics rules. For more advanced students, these exceptions may be pointed out. Students need to realize that most words, but not all, are regular in sound.

11
IMPROVING WORD RECOGNITION II
structural analysis, context, language approaches

This chapter continues the discussion of improving word recognition. First, we examine two additional word recognition clues: structural analysis and context clues. Then, we examine two language-based perspectives of word recognition: the language experience approach and the psycholinguistic perspective.

The strategies presented in this chapter help the reader read words by using meaning. Readers can learn to recognize the meaningful parts within words (as emphasized in the structural analysis strategy) or learn to use their oral language facility to recognize words (as emphasized in context, language experience, and psycholinguistic strategies).

In the final part of this chapter, remediation techniques are given for specific word recognition problems that are common in remedial readers. These problems include nonfluent oral reading, reversals, finger pointing, lip moving, and difficulty in reading silently.

STRUCTURAL ANALYSIS CLUES

Structural analysis refers to the process of recognizing words by identifying the meaningful parts within the words. For example, upon encountering the unknown word "playground," the reader might recognize that it is composed of two smaller words—"play" and "ground." By breaking the word into parts, the whole word is identified. To give an example at a higher level, when seeing the word "rewinding" in print, the reader can use structural analysis to recognize that it is composed of the elements "re," "wind," and "ing." The identification of a word's meaningful parts is particularly important for decoding multisyllabic words, which often contain several structural word parts (e.g., nation*ality*, mean*ings*).

Categories of Structural Analysis

Efficient readers use several different types of str

1. *Compound words.* Two root
   cowboy).
2. *Contractions.* Two word
3. *Suffixes.* These are attac
   actively).
4. *Prefixes.* These elements are
5. *Roots.* These form the main

Informal Assessment of Struc

Teachers can assess a stude
testing the student reading words in
(1) For words in isolation, show some
ask the student to identify compound
For silent reading, ask students to rea

several words containing structural word parts and have the students pronounce the words and identify the word parts. (3) For oral reading, analyze performance on an informal reading inventory. Students who consistently miss structural word parts (such as *ly* in *slowly* or *un* in *undo*) need directed instruction in structural analysis.

Introducing Structural Analysis

As with other word recognition skills, a three-step framework for teaching structural analysis will be used: (1) introduction, (2) practice, and (3) transfer.

When introducing structural analysis, the number of elements introduced at one time can be varied. For very disabled readers, one element should be introduced at a time (e.g., the contraction *can't*). More advanced students may be introduced to a group of elements (e.g., several contractions).

In addition to being able to identify structural elements, students must learn how prefixes, suffixes, and contractions change the function of a word in a sentence. To help students learn the function of structural analysis, words with the structural elements should be shown in sentences. For example, by presenting a contraction in a sentence, the student can readily see that other words could be used, for example, "The children don't (do not) want to play now."

Cards displayed for the student can help them to master structural analysis elements. The card should contain (1) an element, (2) a word using the element, and (3) the word used in a sentence. For example, the card might contain the suffix "ment," the word "employment," and the sentence, "The place of my employment is downtown." One teacher presented many suffixes (*ment, al, tion, ence*) to a rather advanced remedial student. To help the student master them, she displayed each of the elements on an $8\frac{1}{2}'' \times 11''$ piece of brightly colored paper. The motivating display looked almost like checkered wallpaper! As the student located words with different endings, she listed the words on the appropriate card.

Sometimes, instruction in structural analysis can be used to help prepare severely disabled readers for phonics. Some students do not understand that words consist of sound segments, and therefore they have difficulty learning phonics (Liberman, 1973). Structural analysis elements usually are composed of several letters and are therefore larger than the sound, or letter, segments used in phonics. These larger, more meaningful units are often easier for students to learn first. After learning that words can be divided into parts (e.g., *baseball*) students often can more readily understand the concept of sound segmentation (e.g., *-s-e-b-a-l-l*). Thus, teaching structural analysis serves as a bridge to teaching phonics. After students have mastered the concept that words can be divided into meaningful parts using structural analysis, they can more readily learn the concept of segmentation needed in phonics.

Practicing Structural Analysis Skills

Techniques to give practice in structural analysis are presented in the sections that follow.

COMPOUND WORDS. Compound words are formed from two words (e.g., *cowboy*, *steamboat*, and *railroad*). Compound words are an excellent introduction to structural analysis skills and may be taught starting at the first grade reading level.

The following exercises can be used to practice compound words.

1. In the game of word arithmetic, the student fills the pockets with words that make compound words and then reads the compound word, as illustrated in the picture below. If students have difficulties, words that go in the first slot may be put on pink cards, and words for the second slot on blue cards (e.g., *cow*, pink; *boy*, blue).

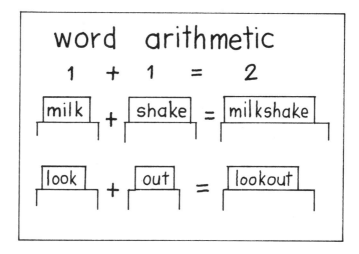

2. Pictures of words that form compound words are constructed and given to students. The students are then asked to put these in order to form compound words and to match them up with written words. This is illustrated in the picture below.

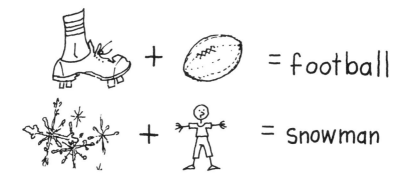

3. A card game can be played with two or more students, where each student is dealt five cards and then takes a turn picking cards from the pile. When a compound word can be formed, it is placed on the table. The object of the game is to make as many words as possible.

CONTRACTIONS. Contractions are two words that have been abbreviated into one by the use of an apostrophe. The student must learn to recognize that a contracted form has the same meaning as the full form. Since contractions are more common in speech than full forms, they generally are not difficult to teach and may be taught at early reading levels. Contractions that signal the future, such as *I'll* and *we'll*, and contractions with *would* (such as *he'd*) may be more difficult. Table 11.1 lists many common contractions. Practice exercises for teaching contractions follow.

1. "Contractors" are pieces of foldable paper, starting out as two words and then forming contractions. Students can guess what the contracted form of the two words will be and then check their guesses. An example appears in the picture below.

 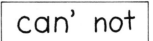

2. A story can be written out, with the full forms of many contractions used. The student is then asked to substitute contractions for the full forms.

SUFFIXES. Suffixes are elements that are added to the end of words. There are actually two types of suffixes:

1. inflectional suffixes, which change the plurality or tense of a word (*boys, jumped*) and
2. derivational suffixes, which change a word from one part of speech to another (*nation* to *national*; noun to adjective).

Table 11.1 Contractions

WITH "NOT"	WITH "WILL"	WITH "WOULD"	WITH "AM," "IS," "ARE"
aren't	he'll	anybody'd	I'm
can't	I'll	he'd	he's
couldn't	she'll	I'd	here's
didn't	there'll	she'd	it's
don't	we'll	they'd	she's
hadn't	who'll	we'd	that's
hasn't	you'll	who'd	there's
haven't			what's
weren't			where's
won't			who's
wouldn't			they're
			we're
			you're

WITH "US"	WITH "HAVE"
let's	they've
	we've
	you've

234

Inflectional suffixes (which include *s*, *ed*, *er*, *est*, *'s*) are quite common in spoken and written language and are taught generally at the primary-grade reading levels. However, they may present problems for speakers of nonstandard dialects or bilingual students. Since these students may not use inflections consistently in their speech, they may have trouble reading them. When working with such students, the teacher should point out the meaning signified by these inflections, but not be overly concerned about the student's pronunciation. If the student pronounces the word *Mary's* as *Mary* when reading orally, no correction should be made. Rather, the teacher should make sure that the student understands the meaning of the suffix (Labov, 1967). For example, the teacher might ask a student to identify the suffix and tell how it changes the word, *Mary*. Inflectional suffixes include

1. *The plural*. Examples: boys, parties.
2. *The past tense*. Examples: jumped, wanted.
3. *The possessive*. Examples: Mary's, dog's.
4. *The comparative*. Examples: fast, fastest
5. *The third-person singular*. Example: he sings.

Derivational suffixes change a word from one part of speech to another, and they are more difficult than inflectional suffixes. Examples are *identify-identification* (verb becomes a noun), *involve-involvement* (verb becomes noun). Because derivational elements are more common in writing than in speech (Ives, Bursuk, and Ives, 1979), students may lack conscious awareness of them.

Because of their frequency, knowledge of derivational suffixes helps students to recognize words. Linguistic research has shown that phonics generalizations often fail students who are trying to recognize multisyllabic words. However, the pronunciation of the word can be predicted if the reader has knowledge of the root word and the derivational suffix (N. Chomsky, 1970; Chomsky and Halle, 1968; Venezky, 1967a, b). For example, a student who recognizes that the word *extremity* is made from the word *extreme* plus a suffix *ity* can avoid having to use complex, undependable phonics rules to identify the word. Remedial readers, in particular, often find it easier to identify words using structural analysis rather than phonics.

Table 11.2 presents suffixes—both inflectional and derivational—divided into seven units, spanning from the first to the seventh grade reading level (Richek, 1969). Because they are easier, the inflectional suffixes are placed at the first grade reading level.

When teaching suffixes, students must practice with as many words as possible and use these words in sentence and paragraph contexts. Students should have experiences in using word changes (such as *relate-relation*, *warm-warmer*), in sentences so that the function of a suffix becomes vivid. On the other hand, students need not memorize the exact part of speech of a suffix (e.g., *tion* changes a noun to a verb). Although inflectional and derivational suffixes perform different functions, they are often practiced together in remedial instruction. Activities for practicing suffixes follow.

Table 11.2   Graded List of Suffixes

FIRST GRADE		SECOND GRADE	
er, est*	bigger, biggest	able	serviceable
s, es (plural)*	ponies	al	seasonal
s (possessive)*	Jane's	ing	singing
s (third person)*	she dances	ly	slowly
ed (past)*	waited	ness	bigness

THIRD GRADE		FOURTH GRADE		FIFTH GRADE	
y	cherry	ish	childish	ance	insurance
tion	relation	ive	impulsive	ity	serenity
ist	violinist	ful	beautiful	ent	excellent
ic	angelic	ency	presidency	age	postage
ize	idolize	ery	slavery	an	musician
ment	contentment	ous	famous		
		ate	activate		

*These are inflectional suffixes. Other suffixes are derivational.

1. A "time machine" may be constructed where past-tense forms can be used in changed sentences. The student fills in the blank word. An example is: "A hundred years ago, we (watched/watch) buggies in the street; right now we (watched/watch) cars." Illustrations from the past and present can be pasted on the chart. This may be called a "multiplication machine" for plural suffixes or a "comparer" for comparative suffixes.

2. Have students read a paragraph containing several underlined words that have structural analysis elements. Students can write the root word for each underlined word.

3. Students can make a "book of suffixes." On each page a suffix is printed (e.g., *ity*, *al*). Students look through old magazines, cut out words containing suffixes, and paste them on the page. The root and a sentence using the word may also be included.

4. A student is given a base word and is asked to form all words possible. One student made the following list from the base word "service."

    serving
    servant
    serviceable
    reserviceable
    nonservice
    server
    subservient

5. Give students root words and sentences requiring suffixes. They then fill the correct form into the sentence. Examples are
    a. *They sang the (nation) anthem.*
    b. *Is the woman a (relate) of yours?*
    c. *The Beatles were very (invent) composers.*

PREFIXES AND ROOTS. Many prefixes and roots used in English descend from Greek and Latin. Because both prefixes and roots contribute basic (or lexical) meaning to the words they form, they are often taught together. Examples of prefixes are *uni* (one) and *pre* (before). Examples of roots are *port* (to carry) and *script* (to write). A study of these word elements helps students to increase their knowledge of vocabulary meanings. Students who know the meaning of *script*, for example, can more easily learn the meanings of *postscript, prescription, scribe, inscription*. A list of useful roots and prefixes (Richek, 1969) is given in Table 11.3.

Table 11.3   Useful Prefixes and Roots

PREFIXES			ROOTS		
anti	antifreeze	against	astro	astrology	stars, heavens
aqua	aquarium	water	auto	automation	self
ante	antedate	before	micro	microscope	small
endo	endoderm	inner	aque	aqueduct	water
ex	exoderm	outer	bio	biosphere	life
ex	ex-president	former	dent	dentist	teeth
geo	geography	earth	dict	dictate	word
im	impossible	not	equi	equivalent	equal
non	nonparallel	not	itis	bronchitis	illness
post	posttest	after	graph	biography	write
pre	pretest	before	ling	linguistics	language
re	rewind	again	mid	amid	middle
semi	semisweet	sort of	ortho	orthodontist	straight
sub	subterranean	below	phobia	claustrophobia	fear
tele	television	far	phon	phonics	sound
trans	transistor	across	polit	political	politics
un	undo	not	script	scripture	writing
			sonic	resonant	sound
			spec	spectator	sight
			therm	thermometer	heat
			viv	vivid	life

NUMBERS	
mono, uni	1
di, bi	2
tri	3
quadr, tetr	4
quint, penta	5
hex, sex	6
hept, sept	7
oct	8
non	9
dec	10
cent	100
milli	1/1000
kilo	1000
hemi	1/2

Prefixes and roots are a somewhat more advanced topic than suffixes. Thus remedial students often have difficulty mastering these concepts. They may need several experiences of using the prefix or root in many different words and situations before they can see how its meaning can be generalized across many different words. Once this concept has been mastered, however, remedial students find these structural elements to be an enjoyable and efficient way of learning meaning vocabulary. The study of prefixes and roots often helps to give direction to a vocabulary program. Activities for teaching prefixes and roots follow.

1. The prefixes denoting number (*uni, bi, tri*, etc.) are relatively easy for students to master, and are often taught first. Students can make lists of words that contain each prefix (e.g., *uniform, unity, universe*). In a group setting, each student can be given one prefix and asked to find example words.
2. For more advanced students, a number of prefixes and roots are put on pieces of paper and posted on a bulletin board. When students encounter example words, they add them to the card.
3. Students can be asked to respond to sentences that use words in a contrasting fashion, such as
   a. *Would you read a biography or a biology?*
   b. *Do you listen to an autograph or a phonograph?*
4. Many product names and inventions are named using prefixes and suffixes. Students can find examples of these, using inventions (*microscope, telescope, binoculars, automobile*) and names (*Vitalis, biofeedback*, the *bionic* man, *Script* pens).

Transferring Structural Analysis to Reading

Because structural analysis elements are so frequent in text, most reading material will give substantial opportunity to apply this knowledge in the reading situation. After reading, students may be asked to pick out certain elements that they have met in their reading. For example, they may be asked to find ten suffixes or to give five root words that have endings attached. As mentioned previously, structural analysis is particularly useful in decoding multisyllable words. Students can be asked to identify multisyllable words after reading and to show how the roots, prefixes, and suffixes aid in decoding them.

CONTEXT CLUES

When readers use surrounding words in the text to figure out an unknown word, they are using context clues. This is an efficient and useful method for recognizing words. The use of context does not require the analysis and memory skills needed for phonics and structural analysis. More important, using context encourages the student to view reading as a meaningful language process. The function of context clues is illustrated in the following sentences, which contain nonsense words:

1. *The* zorp *was* wat *because nobody would play with him.*
2. *The* zorp *sat in the corner all alone and cried.*

Although the terms *wat* and *zorp* have never been encountered (because they are not words!), most readers could approximate their function and meaning using context clues.

Determining Use of Context Clues

In spite of the importance of using context clues, few measures have been constructed to assess proficiency in this area. Several informal procedures are suggested.

1. Students can be observed during oral reading. Students who make use of context clues will tend to stop and correct their mistakes when they realize that a sentence does not make sense. In addition, the miscues they do not correct are likely to make sense in the context.

2. The remedial student's performance on an informal reading inventory can be analyzed to determine if the miscues make sense in the passages. If at least fifty percent of the miscued words do make sense, context clues may be considered a reading strength (see Chapter 6).

3. The teacher can also determine whether reading words in a contextual situation is a help or hindrance by having the student read a passage orally. Then, write a list of some miscued words and a list of some correctly read words. Ask the student to read the words from the lists. If the student recognizes fewer words on the list than were recognized when reading the passage, the context serves an aid. Conversely, if the student performs better on the list, the context is a hindrance.

Introducing Context Clues

The three-phase instructional framework (introduction, practice, transfer) is again used for teaching context clues. When introducing context clues, it is important that teachers encourage students to "guess" at unknown words by using their knowledge of surrounding material. Students should learn that guessing words is a desirable way to figure them out.

Context clues can be introduced in several different ways. Students may be given a nonsense word in a passage and asked to guess the real word that it represents. For example, after reading the following sentences, students may guess what a "pizzle" is.

1. *Your* pizzles *are very important to you.*
2. Pizzles *help you to eat.*
3. *If you take good care of them, they will stay a nice white color.*

For some students who have difficulty dealing with nonsense words, a real word may simply be covered up in a sentence. For example,

I will XXXXX the cake.

Students are asked to supply the word. Blachowicz (1977) suggests covering the word with adhesive tape and then "zipping" the tape off. For more advanced students, context clues can simply be introduced by telling them that a word can be identified using the surrounding words. Then the teacher can help the student to apply this knowledge to reading situations.

Practicing Context Clues

More advanced remedial readers do not need a practice stage and may go directly to the transfer of context clues to reading. However, for those students who need practice, some activities are suggested.

1. "Silly sentences" are constructed. A sentence missing a word is presented along with a pack of word cards to fit into the missing space. Students must tell which words make sensible sentences and which make "silly sentences."
2. Riddles make students aware of language clues. A sample riddle using clues is
   a. *I am big and gray.*
   b. *I have a trunk.*
   c. *I come from India or Africa.*
   d. *I am an* XXXXXXX.
3. A teacher or student reads a passage aloud, stops in the middle of a sentence, and asks the other pupils to guess the next word. The reasoning behind the guesses should be discussed.

Transferring Context Clues to Reading

Context clues only become effective when they are applied in a reading situation. Once students have learned about context clues, they should be urged to use this knowledge to figure out words while reading. When unknown words are encountered, students should be reminded consistently to reread the sentence and try to figure out the word through context.

Since remedial students often are afraid to take the risks involved in "guessing" at words, they need encouragement. One teacher kept a special chart. Each time the student tried to figure out a word using context clues, a star (along with the word and sentence) was put on the chart. It is also important to praise students for making intelligent guesses, even when they are wrong. For example, if a student reads *She had black hair* for *She had blond hair*, the attempt should receive positive comment even though it was not accurate. If no meaning change is involved in an incorrect guess, many reading authorities advise that the oral reading not be interrupted to correct this miscue (K. S. Goodman, 1965).

Words that students have encountered in reading and have figured out using context can be written on word cards, along with the original sentence. When students review these words and cannot remember the word, they can refer to the sentence and try to figure it out using the context clues in the sentence.

LANGUAGE-BASED APPROACHES TO WORD RECOGNITION

Two approaches to word recognition based upon the student's oral language facility are (1) the language experience approach and (2) the psycholinguistic approach. Both approaches provide integrated experiences in reading rather than concentrate on separate word recognition clues or skills.

The language experience approach is an effective and highly motivating way to teach word recognition to remedial readers. Students compose personal stories that are then used for their reading instruction. Generally, students dictate their stories to the teacher, who records them in writing. Because students have actually produced these stories, they are anxious to read them. In addition, students can see the direct relationship between speech and reading, for language experience stories are "talk written down."

To be most effective, the stories should be about experiences that are exciting and of personal interest to the student. A recent first-hand experience such as a field trip, an exploratory trip around the school, an unusual event happening to the students or their friends, a good book that has been read to them, or an exciting television program provide the opportunity to develop a language experience story.

Language experience stories may be used for individual teaching, or they may be used for teaching groups. With groups, the entire group of students can dictate stories, or the students can dictate stories individually and exchange them.

One problem that arises in using this method for remedial instruction is that students with reading disabilities have problems composing a story. The student may have a language disability or may simply be unused to talking in a school situation. Students who encounter this difficulty may be started with a partially developed language experience story. Some ideas for story starters follow.

1.   "The Witch's Brew," a cloze (or deleted word) selection, was used in a remedial setting for several years. Students filled in the missing words, and an informal "contest" developed among several pupils to see who could create the funniest story.

THE WITCH'S BREW

The old witch decided to make a brew.
She put in some . . . and some . . .
Then she added some . . .
She stirred and stirred.
The brew looked like . . .
It smelled like . . .
The witch took a taste and turned into a . . .

2.   Comic strips may be brought in. Sometimes the talk in the comic strip "balloons" can be deleted, and students can dictate what the characters might have said. Or, for less advanced students, the words can be left on the comic strip, and the teacher can read them. After this, students can dictate a summary of the story to the teacher.

3.   Many picture books for children are now being written without words. Students can "read" these wordless picture books and then tell the teacher the story of the book. (Appendix A lists several wordless picture books.)

4.   A secret object can be brought in a paper bag. The student can try to guess what it is by shaking it, estimating the weight, guessing the first letter, or ask-

ing the color. (The teacher should answer all questions simply "yes" or "no.") Then the object can be shown. This is usually very effective in producing stories.

5. An interesting or unusual item can be brought in. One teacher brought in an apple with one bite taken out of it.

After using a few of these starter techniques, students are often able to produce entire language experience stories on their own.

Students who do not speak Standard English will probably dictate stories using their own language patterns. In fact, as students become more comfortable and involved with the language experience method, informal and nonstandard speech forms will probably increase. A dilemma develops as to whether to write the story as the student dictated it or to change it to Standard English. Many authorities recommend that teachers retain the student's own syntax (or grammatical forms) when writing a language experience story (Stauffer, 1970; Wilson, 1981).

While teachers can preserve pupil's grammar, language experience stories should be written in standard spelling. Thus, even if a pupil pronounces the plural of the word *ask* as *ax* or *axes*, it should be written down as *asks*. Teachers should also be careful to use standard manuscript printing.

The individuality of the language experience approach makes it ideal for teaching many reading skills in a personal manner. Students can pick out words from their own stories to add to sight vocabulary. Stories also can be used to point out phonics or structural analysis or how to guess an unknown word from context. Language experience stories can also teach such concepts as *word* and *sound* to very disabled students (see Chapter 8).

Many teachers make permanent records of language experience stories. For an individual student, the stories may be printed or typed and collected in a notebook. For groups, the stories may be duplicated so that all students in the group have a copy. Older students often prefer to print (or type) their own stories.

The flexibilty of the language experience approach enables it to serve many purposes for different types of students. In her book *Teacher* (1963), Sylvia Ashton-Warner described teaching culturally disadvantaged Maori children on the island of New Zealand. She had children bring in "key words" that they chose to learn. Often, the student selected words that were packed with emotional content, such as *kiss* and *knife*. The freedom that these students felt in bringing in such words pointed to their comfort with the instructional process.

Although the language experience approach is used most widely with younger children, it is also very effective with older students who are at lower reading levels. For example, in one high school special education room, ten teenage boys decided to create disaster stories. They dictated stories entitled *The Roach, The Big Flood, The Crash, The Day the World Ended,* and *The Tidal Wave*. After their teacher wrote the stories, the boys edited them as a group to make them even more frightening. Final copies, some several pages long, were then typed and duplicated. The typed copies were then used as scripts for tape-recorded stories, which were made complete with sound effects and musical backgrounds (Beethoven's Ninth Symphony was used). After composing and editing these stories for several months, the boys improved their reading skills considerably. A portion of one story follows.

The Tidal Wave

Tom saw a tidal wave in his mind. He saw it about four or five times a week. He didn't tell anyone. The last time he saw the tidal wave he also saw the date that the tidal wave would happen. He told his Mother and Father and they sent him up to his rom. The next day he told everyone about his vision. They all just laughed. He went back home and took his family away.

About three hours later, strange things began to happen. Things started to blow. On the news they said that the rain was coming from unknown sources. The wind will be going about one-hundred-seventy-five miles an hour. The tidal wave will hit in about one hour. The news told everyone to leave the area.

So it hit. The wind started to blow harder and harder . . .

Despite its motivational value, there are some students for whom the language experience approach is not effective. Since words for language experience come from oral vocabulary, these words may accumulate faster than they can be learned. For example, Al, one severely disabled reader, had to give up learning to read by this approach because his inability to read his own experience stories eventually frustrated him. Instead, Al had to learn by a sight word approach, with only an occasional language experience story.

The Psycholinguistic Approach

The psycholinguistic framework views word recognition in a somewhat nontraditional manner. Research studies have shown that readers do not read every word; instead, they "sample" certain words in the text to determine the meaning of the passage (K. S. Goodman, 1967; F. Smith, 1973b). The efficient reader makes use of experience, meaning, and the syntactic structure of the text to get the information needed. The psycholinguistic perspective has provided new insight into the teaching of remedial word recognition. Some of the implications of the psycholinguistic approach follow.

1. Perfect word recognition is neither necessary nor desirable since the efficient reader only samples material. In fact, too much concentration on the words in the text will disrupt the student from reading for meaning. Readers should concentrate on the general sense of the passage rather than on specific words.
2. Material for reading should be written in a natural language style so that students can use their language competency to figure out unknown words.
3. Phonics is not an important source of reading clues. Often, the reader loses the meaning of a passage while trying to sound out words (Sherman, 1979; Hittleman, 1978; F. Smith, 1973a). Because phonics rules are very complex, direct instruction is not advised. Students may learn phonics generalizations through wide reading experience.

4. Context clues are extremely important for they encourage the reader to interact with the text and to bring his or her knowledge of the world to the reading process.
5. Silent reading is strongly encouraged because it allows the reader to sample the text independently rather than to read every word.

The psycholinguistic perspective, then, emphasizes the total context of reading, the reader as a sampler of words, and the use of language and meaning in reading. Psycholinguists advocate instructional strategies that enable students to deal with unknown words without losing comprehension (Goodman and Burke, 1980). These include

1. *Dealing with unknown words.* When readers come across words they don't know, a variety of methods may be used:
   a. Encourage students to say "blank" to themselves when they are stopped by an unknown word. This avoids "getting stuck" on the word and encourages readers to use their language processes as they read. By continuing the reading, they may acquire enough clues to figure out the word.
   b. Substitute a short name for a long or unusual word, particularly a proper noun. For example, "Vespuccio" may be called "Ves."
   c. Use bookmarks to record places where difficulty is encountered in reading. After the reading is completed, some of these marked words can be discussed with the teacher.
2. *Assisted reading.* This method is useful for students who have difficulty recognizing words. The teacher begins by reading in unison with students. Gradually, students are allowed to take over more and more of the reading, but they are supported by the teacher when necessary. Assisted reading may be done by a teacher and student, by a group of students, or by a student with a tape recorder as well as in many other combinations.
3. *Repeated language refrains.* Books with predictable language, or repeated language refrains, are excellent for word recognition practice at primary levels. Predictable language repeats language patterns and may be found in the refrains of songs ("The farmer in the dell, Heigh-ho the diary-oh, The farmer in the dell"), in nursery rhymes ("London Bridge is falling down"), and in Easy-to-Read books, particularly those dealing with folktales. Reading these repetitive refrains, at first together with the teacher, gives the remedial student much needed confidence and experience in word recognition. (For a listing of predictable language books, see Appendix A, section on language development.)
4. *Selected deletions.* This procedure is similar to the cloze technique. Prepare a passage by deleting words that the student finds difficult. The student then determines the deleted words using context. This method is particularly useful for function words, which are predictable from context, yet often difficult to read. Using this technique, students learn that they need not identify these troublesome words through sight recognition if they can predict them from context.

As with any other approach, the psycholinguistic perspective is more useful for some remedial readers than for others. For many remedial readers, however, the fresh approach of the psycholinguistic perspective dramatically fosters reading growth. It is especially useful for remedial students who lack motivation for reading once they have acquired basic reading skills. Remedial readers have often become too passive in the reading process. The psycholinguistic approach counteracts passivity by stressing active questioning and independent reading.

One of the authors observed a group of eight-year-old disinterested remedial readers learn to read almost overnight using the assisted reading technique with the book *Curious George*. At first the teacher, Ms. Scott, simply read the book to the students aloud. Then, she encouraged the children to supply easier words (*Curious George, Africa*). The teacher and children kept rereading the book, with the children gradually supplying more and more of the text. After the children had mastered *Curious George*, they went on to sequels such as *Curious George Rides a Bicycle* and *Curious George Gets a Job*. The technique of assisted reading was combined with writing language experience stories to form a motivating, whole language approach. These children were transformed from passivity to taking an active interest in their reading growth.

However, psycholinguistic approaches are not equally useful for all students. Many remedial students need extremely focused instruction, including time on direct school tasks, drill, group activities directed by the teacher, and fairly routine classroom organization (Berliner, 1981). Severely disabled readers usually need focused drill on words to ensure that basic word recognition skills enable them to use their oral language and experience base in reading. Pflaum and Pascerella (1979–1980) found that learning-disabled children reading at a very low level (first grade level) were unable to profit from instruction in using context clues. Thus, while the psycholinguistic perspective makes many important contributions, teachers should consider the needs of each individual learner before using this approach.

SPECIAL PROBLEMS IN WORD RECOGNITION

Remedial readers often have special problems in word recognition that impede progress. These problems include (1) nonfluent oral reading, (2) reversals, (3) finger pointing and lip moving, and (4) difficulty in silent reading. Techniques for alleviating these problems are presented in this section.

Nonfluent Oral Reading

Halting, hesitant oral reading is a problem common to many remedial readers. A teacher who is concerned about hesitant reading should first determine whether the student is reading material that is too difficult. If the material is found to be of appropriate difficulty, then steps should be taken to ensure more fluent reading.

Research studies show that certain teacher practices, while well intentioned, may hamper fluency. Teachers interrupt remedial readers during oral reading far more often than they interrupt normal readers. When normal readers make a miscue during reading, teachers tend to allow them to continue reading. In contrast, teachers very frequently interrupt remedial readers to correct a high percentage of their miscues (McDermott, 1978; Allington, 1978). Allington found that percentages of interruption were 24 percent for normal readers, but 68 percent for remedial readers. Unfortunately, when readers are interrupted, they lose the chance to check meaning and correct miscues on their own. In addition, constant correction may be demoralizing to remedial students. How can teachers encourage disabled students to develop independent strategies for fluent oral reading?

We have found the following series of steps helpful in improving hesitant oral reading and developing independent strategies for fluent oral reading.

1. Select a reading passage and introduce the student to difficult words.
2. Have the student read the passage silently.
3. Then ask the student to read the passage orally, informing him or her that you will not interrupt and that unknown words should be figured out by rereading the sentence.
4. After uninterrupted oral reading, the student can check some words with the teacher.

Consistent use of this procedure improves reading fluency and lessens students' dependence on teacher aid.

For more advanced students the "repeated readings" method may be used (Harris, 1981; Samuels, 1979). The student is given a short reading passage of 50 to 200 words. The reading passage may be part of a story or a separate self-contained narrative. The student reads the selection to the teacher, and the teacher records the reading speed and the number of word recognition errors. The reading selection is practiced until the student feels capable of reading it fluently at a predetermined reading rate. The student then reads the selection orally for the teacher a second time, and both the reading rate and number of word recognition errors are again recorded. This process is repeated until the predetermined criterion rate has been achieved. Then the student moves on to another reading selection.

The student's improvement is charted in both the areas of oral reading rate and of oral reading accuracy (lack of errors). This graphic evidence of improvement provides positive reinforcement, and encouragement. According to Samuels (1979), as the student's speed is increased through repeated readings, word recognition errors tend to decrease and comprehension is improved. Through the process of repeated readings, the decoding (or word recognition aspects) of reading the passage become more automatic and require less attention. Consequently, students are able to focus attention on understanding the passage.

Remedial readers often read in a word-by-word fashion. There are several other procedures which help in eliminating word-by-word reading.

1. The teacher composes flashcards consisting of phrases rather than words and presents them rapidly for recognition. This will teach the student to perceive phrases rather than words. A tachistoscope may be used for this purpose.
2. Passages that involve reading with expression, such as those designed for choral reading or drama, can be used to help students read in a more connected fashion.
3. Students can be directed to read a passage with "a lot of" expression. A prize is given for the student who reads with the best (exaggerated) expression.
4. Sentences are taken from books and the student is asked to divide them into meaningful parts and then to read each part as one phrase.

Remedial students also have difficulty using punctuation effectively. Techniques to encourage the use of punctuation follow.

1. The teacher reads the sentences in a book with exaggerated expression to emphasize punctuation. Students then echo what the teacher has read. This works particularly well in group situations.
2. A single sentence is written with varying punctuation marks. For example, "Mother said, 'John went to the park.'" "Mother said, 'John went to the park!'" "Mother said, 'John went to the park?'" Students are asked to read these sentences with appropriate expression.
3. Commas and subordinate clauses also may cause difficulty. To help students, a simple sentence is first presented. Then subordinate clauses are added, one by one. Students must read these increasingly longer sentences with appropriate expression. After an initial presentation of this technique, students may do their own sentence building. An example is
   a. *John went to the store.*
   b. *John, who is my brother, went to the store.*
   c. *John, who is my brother, went to the store, which is on the corner.*
4. Many beginning remedial readers tend to stop at the end of a printed line, regardless of the punctuation. To teach students to continue reading, a sentence may be written several times by the teacher using different line endings.

Reversals

Many individuals with first, second, and third grade reading levels tend to reverse certain letters and words while reading. For example, they may substitute *b* for *d*, or *no* for *on*, or *saw* for *was*. In fact, it is not uncommon for poor readers at this level to produce backward "mirror writing." The tendency to reverse letters and words has sometimes been interpreted as a symptom of deep-seated problems in reading or brain dysfunction (Orton, 1937; Johnson and Myklebust, 1967). However, in most cases, reversals simply indicate a lack of experience with reading material. They are seen often in normally achieving children reading at primary-grade levels (Spache, 1981; Harris and Sipay, 1980). Reversals also may occur in teenagers and adults who are just learning to read. In fact, Krise (1949) found that reversals could be induced in postcollege graduate students if an artificial language were used.

One reason that students make reversals is that reading is the only process in which symbols change because of their directional orientation. Thus, the only difference between the letters *b* and *d* is that one faces right and the other left. On the other hand, a real-life object, such as a chair or a dog, maintains its identity regardless of its orientation in space. A student beginning to read may not yet realize that the orientation of letters and words makes a difference in reading.

There are four types of reversals: (1) a single letter (*b* for *d*), (2) a whole word (*saw* for *was*), (3) a partial word (*left* for *felt*), and (4) the reversal of the order of the words in a sentence. However, letter reversals, particularly the substitution of *b* and *d*, are most common.

When a remedial reader exhibits reversals, the teacher must decide whether to provide special instruction to eliminate them. If the reversal is only occasional, no special instruction is warranted. If, on the other hand, reversals are frequent and interfere with effective reading, then special instruction to overcome them is needed. There are several methods for eliminating reversals.

To correct reversals of single letters, concentrate on one letter at a time. For example, to correct a *b* to *d* reversal, first concentrate on *b*. Teachers can make a large *b* chart that contains the letter *b*, a memory word (e.g., *boy*), and pictures that start with *b*. Accompanying this, several words that begin with *b* can be learned by sight. One teacher cut out a $2' \times 3'$ felt *b* and pasted it on a board. The student reinforced the *b* concept by tracing over the letter (kinesthetic method). After the concept of *b* has been mastered thoroughly, the teacher should wait a while before introducing the letter *d*. This "divide and conquer" method is very effective for remedial readers. Other methods are the following:

1. Flashcards may be made containing confused words and students may practice with these cards.
2. The first letter of confusable words may be underlined or written in a color other than black.
3. The pupil can trace the confusable letter or word on a large card and then write it from memory.
4. The student can manipulate letters on a felt or magnetic board to form words that are reversed frequently.

Finger Pointing and Lip Moving

Finger pointing and lip moving inhibit fluent reading and should be discouraged. Both habits encourage the reader to read word-by-word and to vocalize or subvocalize (i.e., to repeat words either by saying them aloud or by making subaudible throat movements). However, finger pointing and lip moving also can act as a crutch that makes the student comfortable and facilitates word recognition. These behaviors are characteristic of, and normal for, primary-grade-level readers. In addition, if material is too difficult, individuals of any reading level may finger point or move their lips. Thus, these behaviors are one indication that reading material is frustrating.

Extensive finger pointing is one symptom of visual difficulties. Students who need to finger point in order to keep their place in reading should be referred for a visual examination. However, if the student simply lip reads or finger points from force of habit, these behaviors should be eliminated. First and most effective, the student should be made aware of the habits, told how they are inhibiting reading, and asked, respectfully, to eliminate them. This simple procedure, plus an occasional reminder, often rectifies the problem. Finger pointing can also be eliminated more slowly by providing a marker to replace the finger and the gradual elimination of use of the marker. For lip moving, students may be asked to consciously close their lips while reading.

Difficulty Reading Silently

The mature reader reads silently almost exclusively. Indeed, when called upon to read orally, most adults realize how extensively their oral reading skills have atrophied. To facilitate mature reading, silent reading should be used in remedial instruction as much as possible. Yet even the most cursory survey of instructional situations shows an extensive amount of oral reading. This is true for three sets of reasons.

1. Beginning readers form their first conceptions of reading from oral language. As a result, they are most comfortable when reading is related to language through oral reading. In fact, it is sometimes impossible for remedial readers at beginning stages to read silently. While we recognize the legitimacy of these needs, remedial students should be moved into silent reading as soon as they are at all comfortable with the reading process.
2. Many teachers are comfortable with oral reading because they feel that both students and teacher are "doing something" during the instructional time. Teachers often feel that oral reading provides continuous diagnosis and monitoring of unknown words. While this is true, teachers must weigh the advantages of diagnosis against the disadvantages of forming dependent reading habits in their students.
3. Many students have simply become used to reading orally. These students think that the aim of reading is to put on a performance rather than to learn new information and concepts. Such students must be convinced that silent reading is valuable and that it is "adult." One effective method is to ask them to go out and observe five adult readers to see whether they are reading silently or orally. This procedure generally convinces them that silent reading has merit.

Certain procedures help silent reading become meaningful for the reader. To stress the importance of silent reading, it should be done before oral reading. It is helpful if the oral reading that follows only serves a very specific purpose, such as finding information in a text, proving a point, or dramatizing a play. Often the student need not reread the entire passage orally. Finally, students should be given direct motivation for reading silently. The teacher should stress the information that the student will find in the text. If teachers follow silent reading with questions and discussions, students will be helped to see it as meaningful.

HELPING WITH WRITING
AND SPELLING

Throughout this book, we have stressed that all language processes—reading, writing, speaking, and listening—are related. Very often, a student with reading problems will have accompanying writing and spelling problems. Because students must face daily classroom demands for spelling and writing, it is helpful for reading teachers to know some techniques to help students address these problems.

In addition, activities that concentrate on one aspect of language tend to increase abilities in other areas. For example, improving a student's ability to spell may help increase awareness of phonic elements in reading. Helping students to write increases their awareness of the authorship process and the elements involved in reading. If students increase their abilities with written language, they become more comfortable and confident with all aspects of print, including the reading process.

Reading and writing may be combined effectively in instruction. The language experience approach, discussed earlier in this chapter, is one way of doing this. In Chapter 12, further suggestions are made for using "written conversations," journals, and several other methods (see section, "The Psycholinguistic Approach to Comprehension"). J. P. Smith (1982) reports teaching a remedial reading program through writing. The twelve-year-old student was taught strategies for writing about his personal experiences and editing his writing. In a one-semester period the boy increased his reading level markedly. In addition, the teacher noted that writing helped him to understand complex sentences and to apply the phonics skills he was also learning.

Students with remedial reading problems may also exhibit problems with their handwriting skills. These problems may involve use of space in writing (both between letters and words or descent and rise of letters), or nonstandard formation of letters. Many manuscript errors involve q, g, p, y, and j. These letters may be reversed, or not descended below the line. In cursive writing, the most common mistakes are with a, e, r, and t. The most common types of errors involve not closing letters (such as o) and making incorrect loops (as when e looks like i).

Teachers of reading can informally help students with handwriting through the following methods.

1. Make sure the paper and pencil are in the correct position. Often students hold the paper too far down.
2. Use lined paper for students with difficulties. Some paper has a separate line for letters that descend (such as p). If students have extreme difficulty with spacing, the spaces between letters and words can be penciled in lightly.
3. Have students trace their sight words. Students can trace over fully written out sight words, or the teacher can outline words using dashes.
4. Have students copy the teacher's writing. At first, students can write underneath the teacher's writing, permitting easy comparison. Because students with handwriting problems often have to write very slowly, tracing may be done outside of class.

Handwriting is a difficult skill and students should be praised for each step in acquiring facility.

Spelling is another area of difficulty for remedial readers, as well as for many good readers. The fact that English is not always regularly spelled according to sounds makes it difficult for readers. In addition, spelling demands many abilities such as sequencing, visual and auditory memory, and a knowledge of sound regularities.

There are two major approaches to teaching spelling (Lerner, 1981). In the first, students are taught the predictable relationships between letters and sounds. They learn, for example, that the sound /oy/ at the end of a word usually corresponds to the letters oy. This method can be integrated with a phonics approach to reading. A second approach is to teach spelling by simply having children memorize the spelling of frequent words. This method can be used with a sight word approach to teaching reading.

Like handwriting, spelling is a skill which is difficult to master. In fact, even very literate adults seldom master it perfectly, and many famous geniuses were notoriously bad spellers. Since spelling a word is more difficult than reading it, teachers should use caution when giving instruction in spelling. It is unwise to insist that students learn to spell every reading word. Students who are motivated to improve their spelling may pursue several activities.

1. Students may choose to learn the spelling of certain favorite sight words.
2. As phonics patterns are taught (for example, *ow*), students may choose to learn spelling words that represent that pattern (cow, how).
3. Students may learn to spell their personal "word demons," words that they often misspell in writing.
4. Students may practice a multisensory method for certain words. This includes tracing the word, writing it, and trying to visualize it.

Spelling errors provide a rich source of diagnostic information to the reading teacher. For example, if students often ignore certain sound patterns in spelling, the teacher may find that they also need reading instruction in these phonics elements. Aaron (1978) suggests that severely disabled readers may be given a dictated test to see if they use sound patterns in spelling at all. The use of patterns suggests some aptitude for reading phonics instruction; otherwise, sight word instruction may be more appropriate (see Chapter 9).

SUMMARY

Structural analysis clues refer to meaningful word parts, such as *ful* and *re*. Structural analysis is particularly useful in decoding long words. There are five types of structural analysis elements: (1) compound words, (2) contractions, (3) suffixes (both inflectional and derivational), (4) prefixes, and (5) roots. Because roots and prefixes provide lexical word meaning, they are often taught together. Structural analysis elements can be taught through introduction, practice, and application phases.

In context clues, the reader uses the sense of the surrounding passage to identify a word. When teaching context clues, it is important to encourage students to take risks in "guessing" words. While introduction, practice, and application phases may be used to teach context clues, some students may go directly from introduction to application.

Two language-based approaches to word recognition are (1) the language experience approach and (2) the psycholinguistic perspective.

In the language experience approach, students dictate stories that are written by the teacher and are used as reading material. Thus, students learn that reading relates to speech. It is important to provide an exciting stimulus for language experience, as remedial readers may have difficulties composing stories. Students working in groups can exchange stories. The language experience approach can be used with students of many ages. However, since language experience stories do not contain controlled vocabulary, severely disabled students may have difficulty reading them.

Since the psycholinguistic perspective views readers as "sampling" text rather than as reading every word, perfect word identification is not necessary. The reader's experience and oral language is of primary importance. Use of context clues is emphasized, and phonics is deemphasized. Material for reading should be written in a natural language style. Psycholinguistic techniques are most useful for remedial readers who lack motivation.

Special problems in word recognition include (1) nonfluent oral reading, (2) reversals, (3) finger pointing and lip moving, and (4) difficulty reading silently.

Fluent reading may be encouraged through minimizing teacher interruptions during oral readings and through the use of the repeated readings method. Reversals are normal in primary-grade-level remedial readers, regardless of age. They should only be corrected when they hamper reading seriously. A good procedure is to deal separately with two confusable elements (such as b and d). Finger pointing and lip moving hamper fluent reading, but remedial readers may need them as crutches. Silent reading fosters independence and reading for meaning. Teachers should systematically encourage silent reading.

Because all language processes are related, teachers of reading may choose to address the areas of writing and spelling. Such instruction can increase students' abilities, motivation, and comfort with reading.

12
IMPROVING
READING
COMPREHENSION

Comprehension is the essence of the reading act; indeed, it is the only purpose for reading. Yet thousands of remedial students in our schools are unable to understand what they are reading, even though they can recognize printed words. When asked to read orally, some of these students are capable of delivering a flawless performance. However, they are hopelessly perplexed when asked about what they have read. Thus, reading comprehension is particularly important for remedial readers.

The concept of reading comprehension is broad in scope, with many possible meanings. It has one meaning for Sandra, a first grade pupil reading her first story in a basal reader series. It has another meaning for Jerry, a teenager reading to understand the printed directions for assembling his newly purchased bicycle. It has yet another meaning for English Professor Jones, who is interpreting an intricate passage of a Shakespeare play. As an individual's ability to read develops, the multifaceted nature of comprehension expands. As shown in a classic study of mistakes made in comprehending paragraphs, reading comprehension involves several types of cognitive behavior (Thorndike, 1917).

This chapter deals with theories of reading comprehension and methods for helping remedial readers improve in their reading comprehension. The first part of the chapter discusses two ways of viewing reading comprehension in remedial readers: (1) as a set of separate skills and (2) as an integrated holistic process. The balance of the chapter deals with methods of teaching remedial reading comprehension. It includes methods for teaching comprehension as separate subskills and methods for teaching comprehension as a unified, or holistic, process.

© 1974 United Feature Syndicate, Inc.

COMPREHENSION: SUBSKILLS OR UNIFIED PROCESS?

The way in which comprehension is taught to remedial readers depends in large measure upon how comprehension is viewed. Two views of reading comprehension that shape remedial instruction are (1) the subskills view, which identifies comprehension as a cluster of separate identifiable subskills, and (2) the holistic view, which identifies comprehension as a unified, inseparable whole. Each view leads to different methods of teaching.

Traditionally, comprehension has been seen as a set of specific reading sub-skills (such as identifying the main idea, recognizing important facts, following directions, etc.). A purpose of the remedial reading diagnosis is to identify strengths and weaknesses in comprehension subskills. The remedial instruction which follows is designed to remediate deficit subskills through direct teaching of those subskills. For example, the subskill of "following directions" could be targeted for specific instruction.

Ordered sequences of comprehension subskills (called taxonomies) have been developed by several reading authorities, including Bloom et al. (1956), Barrett (1967), and Otto and Askov (1972). A theory called "mastery learning" (Bloom, 1968) is based upon the development of ordered sequences of subskills. According to this theory, all students can learn if they acquire each of the subskills through carefully sequenced instruction.

Do these subskills of reading comprehension actually exist, or are they an artifact created by reading authorities? This question has been the subject of much debate and research, and answers are conflicting. Research conducted by Davis (1968) showed that comprehension material could be factored into independent subskills. Farr (1969), however, found little evidence showing that reading tests measure specific subskills effectively. Guthrie's (1973) research shows that comprehension may appear to be a unitary process in good readers because these readers have integrated subskills into the reading act. On the other hand, it may be easier to show that subskills exist in poor readers, since such readers have not yet integrated their use of subskills. Teaching subskills seems to be effective for lower level or remedial readers. In a review of successful compensatory programs, Samuels (1981) found that most successful programs used a skills-centered curriculum with specific reading objectives. (Compensatory programs are designed to raise reading levels in low-achieving schools.)

An advantage of classifying reading comprehension into subskills is that it enables the teacher of remedial reading to divide effectively the very large concept of reading comprehension into smaller units that are manageable in instruction. Thus, the diagnosis of a specific subskill deficit can be matched easily to remedial instruction. The student's attention can be focused on reaching specific definable goals. Teaching subskills appears to be helpful in remedial reading.

Nevertheless, comprehension subskills must be integrated into the whole reading act if they are to be effective. As Guthrie (1973) has shown, good readers automatically combine subskills into the reading act. However, poorer readers, including remedial readers, may be struggling to acquire specific subskills and therefore using them in an unintegrated manner. Only by transferring and integrating subskills into general reading can remedial readers achieve effective reading (Jenkins and Pany, 1981). ". . . the purpose of learning a subskill is to transfer its use to natural reading contexts; and the goal of reading instruction is to transfer *all* subskills a reader has learned to reading texts in a fluent manner with adequate comprehension." Methods of integrating reading subskills are presented later in this chapter.

The Holistic Approach

The holistic approach to reading comprehension views reading as a unified act. The underlying premise is that all aspects of the reading process are related and that separate reading subskills can neither be identified nor taught effectively (Johnson and Pearson, 1975; Downing, 1982). The holistic view embraces and combines the many aspects of reading (including the reader, the reading material, and the reading environment). Of particular importance are (1) the knowledge the reader brings to the reading material and (2) the interaction between the reader and the reading material.

In many instructional approaches, the reader is viewed as a person who passively receives information from a text. In a critical analysis of this view of the reader, F. Smith (1971) contends that the reader's knowledge is more important to comprehension than is the text itself. "Schema theory," which is a research orientation to reading, emphasizes that each reader brings personal schemata, or sets of organized background knowledge, to the reading process. These schemata, in turn, shape reading comprehension as a reader's background knowledge interacts with the material in a text (Anderson et al., 1977; Rumelhart, 1981). Schema theory suggests that in order to truly read, the student must actively combine his or her existing schema with new information. Schema theory implies that the passive view that so many remedial readers take toward reading materials is caused by their relative lack of the background schema which would enable them to comprehend text effectively. Or, remedial students may not know how to effectively use their experiential background in the reading process.

The holistic view of reading comprehension has several important implications for remedial reading instruction. It stresses the importance of wide and varied reading. It also encourages students to use their language and thinking skills to participate fully in the reading process. Because reading is initially presented as an integrated act, the need to transfer acquired learnings from isolation into contextual application is avoided. Several instructional methods which are based on the holistic perspective are discussed in this chapter. They are the psycholinguistic approach, the directed reading-thinking activity, the cloze procedure, auding, and the theme approach.

The subskills and holistic views of reading present complementary perspectives and can be combined effectively. The subskills approach gives clear direction and focus to remedial instruction. The holistic perspective balances this by stressing the role of the reader's experiences, motivation, and participation in reading. Techniques derived from both perspectives can be integrated in ways suggested later in this chapter.

TEACHING COMPREHENSION SUBSKILLS

In this section, methods for teaching comprehension subskills are illustrated. Although there are several possible ways to classify comprehension subskills, the subskill categories described in this chapter are listed below in a hierarchical order, proceeding from easier to more difficult:

- Literal comprehension
    Understanding sentences
    Recognizing facts
    Following directions
- Organizational comprehension
    Finding the main idea
    Sequencing events
    Understanding a problem and solution
- Inferential comprehension
- Critical reading

The comprehension subskills are discussed as follows. First, informal methods for determining comprehension strengths and weaknesses are described. Then, the three-step framework for teaching each subskill is used: introduction, practice, and transfer.

Determining Comprehension Strengths and Weaknesses

In addition to the assessment techniques discussed in Chapters 5 and 6, there is often a need for supplementary information about students' comprehension abilities. By using appropriate questioning techniques, teachers can gain much knowledge about remedial students' comprehension processes. Teachers can ask different types of questions of the student to determine abilities in different comprehension areas. For example, one teacher varied the types of questions by asking one literal, one inference, and one critical reading question each time that the student read a passage. The student's answers showed that, although there was adequate literal comprehension skills, help was needed in both inferential and critical reading comprehension skills.

Teachers can also observe a student to learn about comprehension abilities. For example, by observing that a remedial reader was unable to retell simple stories in sequence, the teacher discovered that the student needed instruction in sequencing skills.

Introducing Comprehension Subskills

A deliberate and systematic way of introducing comprehension skills is needed for students with reading difficulties. Disabled readers should understand the characteristics of the skill being taught. For example, students should know the concepts of a "sequence" or a "main idea." One helpful technique is to establish the skill in an oral language context before it is introduced in reading. For example, a fourteen-year-old girl was introduced to the concept of main idea by being asked to classify the items in her purse. She gave a title to each group of objects (things for money, cosmetic items) and these became the main ideas. Another student was introduced to the concept of inference when the teacher assembled a group of pictures from which inferences could be drawn. The pictures included one of a man who was sleeping in a room with an air conditioner (inference: It was summer). Another picture had a group of frowning people (inference: They were unhappy).

Comprehension skills should be introduced in a concrete, personal manner. Since remedial readers often have a hard time relating to abstract concepts, they need examples that are within their range of experience. For example, ten-year-old Ursula could not understand the concept of main idea, so her teacher wrote a personal story of Ursula's shopping trip. Through this story, Ursula finally learned the concept of a main idea. To introduce the concept of sequence, the teacher asked eight-year-old Jonathan to list things he did in the morning. After his teacher mixed them up, he was able to put them back in correct order, thereby learning the concept of sequence.

Everyday materials can be used to make comprehension instruction more concrete. Instructions on packages, wrapping for food, signs, menus, schedules, and maps are all excellent materials for relating comprehension skills to the reader and showing how they are actually used.

Of course, not every remedial reader will need as much introduction as we have outlined in this section. In fact, some students can simply be introduced to a subskill in a reading context. However, teachers should ensure that students understand the basic concepts underlying a reading subskill.

Practicing Comprehension Subskills

Different methods for practice are suitable for different comprehension subskills. Strategies for practicing comprehension subskills are given for literal comprehension, organizational comprehension, inference, and critical reading.

LITERAL COMPREHENSION. Literal comprehension is the ability to understand the author's expressly stated ideas. Three types of comprehension are discussed here: sentence comprehension, comprehension of facts, and following directions. Strategies for practice proceed from easy activities to more difficult ones.

1. *Sentence comprehension.*   Remedial students sometimes have difficulty understanding sentences because of underlying language problems. Further, sentences in reading materials are usually more complex than are those used in oral language (Schallert et al., 1977). Since remedial students do not read widely, they lack experience with these difficult sentences types.

Sentences containing the following four features are likely to cause difficulty.

- Unexpected sentence order *(He sat AFTER he stood).*
- Deletion of information *(John saw Mary and HE said hello).*
- Difficult logical composition *(I won't do that UNLESS you do).*
- Sentences containing embedding *(Mary, WHO WAS IN THE ROOM, began talking).*

See Table 4.4, in Chapter 4, for further illustrations of difficult sentence types.

Sentence comprehension should be practiced using a rich variety of sentence types rather than concentrating on a few. This prepares remedial readers to understand the many types of sentences that they will meet in reading. Some of the activities listed below can be practiced in an oral language context as well as with print.

a.   Construct a board game with spaces that lead to a final destination. To move, the students must roll dice, pick a card, read it aloud, and then follow the directions. Directions consist of difficult sentences such as "Toss a coin after you have twirled a pencil" or "If you are not wearing the color red, blink your eyes."

b.   Sentence-building activities are often fun. The teacher starts with a simple sentence and students add on words or phrases. One teacher had a sentence that stretched a quarter of the way around the room.

c.   Older students may break sentences into their component parts. Use a red pen to mark the subject of a sentence, blue for the verb, and green for the object. Avoid technical linguistic terms.

d.   Long complex sentences may be broken into their simple parts, or kernels. An example of this follows:

Spiders, animals that many people dislike, are not actually insects, but are often mistaken for them.
Spiders are not actually insects.
Most people dislike spiders.
Many people mistake spiders for insects.

2. *Recognizing facts.*   Remedial students must learn to identify and remember important facts in a reading passage. Often, they indiscriminately pick out unimportant or trivial facts and do not recognize which facts are worth remembering. Instruction should guide the students to find the essential facts in the passage. Activities for understanding facts follow.

a. An object such as a hammer may be brought into a class and a sentence can be written such as "A hammer drives a nail into the wall." Then facts may be listed about the hammer that are both important and unimportant to the sentence. For example, important facts are "A hammer is heavy, a hammer has a flat surface to hit against a nail." An unimportant fact is the color of the hammer's handle.

b. Students can read stories and select the most important facts. The selections should contain both important and unimportant facts.

c. To present facts succinctly, newspaper writers use a system of answering the "Five W's and the one H." These are "who, what, where, when, why, and how." Have students read paragraphs or stories and then find the answers to these questions.

3. *Following directions.*   In school, as well as in other environments, students must follow exact directions, a procedure that requires precision and care in reading. Following directions is a particularly useful skill to teach remedial students who have very few comprehension skills. By learning to follow steps carefully, the student becomes more aware of the meaning-gaining function of reading and general comprehension is likely to improve. Activities for following directions follow.

a. Real-life and everyday materials may be used to teach following directions. These include labels from canned food, directions for opening packages, and recipes.

b. In treasure hunts, students have to follow directions. Each student can be given a different set of simple directions that enables him or her to reach a "treasure."

c. Origami, a paper-folding art that originated in Japan, may be used. Precise directions must be followed to make an object. Many books on this art can be found in the library and in bookstores.

d. Individual gamelike activities may be used to transform words if directions are followed carefully. For example,
    (1) *The word is HORSE.*
    (2) *Delete the first two letters.*
    (3) *Put the first letter of the alphabet after the R.*
    (4) *Put an I in the middle of the word.*
    (5) *What word do you have? (RAISE)*

ORGANIZATIONAL COMPREHENSION.   Organizational comprehension refers to ways of systematizing material to understand better and retain the content more easily. Three types of organizational comprehension skills are (1) main ideas, (2) sequence, and (3) problem-solution format.

According to classic studies in psychology, human memory is capable of remembering only about seven unorganized items at a time (Miller, 1956). To increase memory, it is necessary to organize things into meaningful categories. Since remedial readers often have basic memory problems, they should learn to process the information that they read in an organized form.

Different techniques are needed when organizing nonfiction and fiction material. For nonfiction material, which is often presented by topic, it is useful to find central or main ideas. Fiction material is frequently arranged in chronological order. For this reason, the two skills of detecting the sequence and locating the problem and solution in a story are useful.

1. *Finding the main idea.*   To find the main idea in a passage, the student must learn to organize the information around a central focus. Because students must abstract the main idea from the supporting facts, remedial readers often have difficulty with this skill. The activity of categorizing objects or words prepares students for the cognitive strategies needed for finding main ideas.

Main ideas should be taught along with the facts that support them (Pearson and Johnson, 1978). An example of a main idea with supporting details is

> Main Idea: *Dogs can be helpful.*
> Details: *Dogs can protect your house.*
> *Dogs can be trained to assist the blind.*
> *Dogs can help find criminals.*

Nonfiction material should be emphasized for practicing the main idea strategies, because stories or other types of fiction materials may not contain main ideas. When first practicing this strategy, the passages used should contain explicitly stated main ideas. Activities for finding the main idea follow.

a. Categorizing establishes organizational skills. Three stages of categorizing may be used for remedial readers. First, students categorize objects or pictures. Second, they practice these skills using cards containing words. Finally, they categorize statements or sentences into logical groups. In the second and third stages, cards containing the main idea can be mixed in with cards for details.

b. Have students distinguish between statements that support or do not support a main idea. One main idea may be given followed by a number of facts. Or the main idea may be put on a large card and the facts on smaller cards. In a more advanced variation of this game, the student is given two main ideas and several facts. The student must determine which facts support each of the two main ideas.

c. Have students find topic sentences (or sentences that state the main idea). Often, teachers start by using paragraphs where main ideas are at the beginning of the paragraph, then move to main ideas located at the end, and finally to those in the central portion. Selections used should have explicitly stated topic sentences.

d. Have students compose telegrams using only the essential information from paragraphs. The teacher states that, since telegrams are expensive, the students may only use twenty-five words. This is a particularly good activity for determining main ideas that are not stated explicitly in the text but must be inferred.

e. Have students choose or compose titles for selections. This activity is particularly good for paragraphs and selections where the main idea is not stated specifically.

f. In longer selections, students can outline main ideas and supporting facts. Instead of using traditional Roman numerals and letters, students can create visual outlines (Pearson and Johnson, 1978). See the example on page 262.

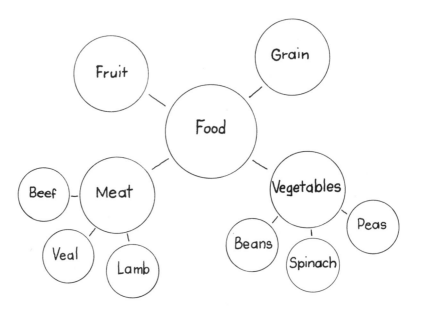

2. *Sequencing.* Since fictional material is organized in chronological order, sequencing skills are needed for understanding fiction. Students should be taught to recognize the sequential events that are most important; not every event in the story is worthy of attention.

To help students learn this comprehension skill, it is best to begin with events that must be given a certain order. For example, in playing a game of baseball, the action has a definite order (pick teams, play the game, cheer for the winner). After students are familiar with sequencing these types of activities, they may work with events whose order is not predetermined. Teachers should be aware that specific words or concepts in sequencing, such as "following," "then," "before," and "after," may present difficulty. Activities for sequencing follow.

a. Students can play the "suppose" game: Suppose you were eating a hard-boiled egg. Would you put salt on it or peel it first?

b. Comic strips can be used to teach sequencing. Three- or four-frame strips are best. Because some comic strips contain captions, this activity enables students to integrate thinking (by putting the frames in order) with reading (by reading the captions). Teachers may laminate these strips; each separate comic strip may be stored in its own envelope. Identifying numbers (1, 2, etc.) can be put on the back of the comic frames and on the envelopes.

c. A sequence "train" with pockets can be constructed. The events of stories the student has read may be written on cards and put in order on the train.

d. Students can be given paragraphs with sentences that are out of order and asked to put them in correct order. Selections containing paragraphs that have been mixed up may also be used.

3. *Problem-solution format.*   Here, stories are presented as having two elements: a problem and a solution. This strategy is useful because it enables remedial readers to summarize whole stories using two elements. It has been pointed out that stories have predictable structures or "grammars," just as sentences do (Stein and Glenn, 1979). However, these are too complex to teach to remedial readers. Problems and solutions provide a way to introduce the concept of story grammar in a form that is helpful to remedial readers. Mystery stories are particularly suitable for teaching problems and solutions. Activities for teaching problems and solutions follow.

a.   In the card game of Concentration, students match pairs of cards, one containing the problem, the other containing the solution. Five cards are dealt, and others are picked from the deck. Cards containing problems are printed in red, and solution cards are printed in blue. When students can find a matching problem and solution card, they lay them down on the table.

b.   Students are given three very short stories to read. After all are read, they are given three written problems and three solutions. The task is to state the story from which each has been taken.

DRAWING INFERENCES.   This is the ability to "read between the lines" and to determine the implied meanings of the author. When a student uses information to reason, conclude, or arrive at a new relationship, an inference has been made. Remedial readers often have particular difficulty with inference skills. Because their responses have so often been incorrect, they may be reluctant to take the risks of drawing conclusions that are not stated directly in the text.

To teach students inference skills, the teacher must learn to ask good inference questions. A good inference question has a right and wrong answer, and it requires the student to use some information within the passage. The following examples illustrate good and poor inference questions.

John looked at his watch. It was two o'clock and he was still waiting. He went back to reading his magazine. Finally a voice came over the loud speaker. "Ocean Airlines announces the arrival of flight 345 at gate 12." "It's about time," John muttered to himself as he walked to the gate.

• Good Inference Question: *Was the plane early or late? How do you know?*
• Poor Inference Question: *Whom do you think John was meeting?*

Inferences can be stressed with remedial students, even at the beginning levels of reading and can be drawn even from the most simple reading materials:

Look, look
Look at the snow

These two lines from a preprimer story lend themselves to inferential thinking. The teacher may ask, "What season of the year is it?" Drawing inferences from pictures and from stories that teachers read aloud are two additional ways remedial readers on beginning levels can practice this skill.

Inference has many components, such as predicting story endings, inferring traits of characters in a story, understanding the theme of a story, making comparisons, and inferring cause-and-effect relationships. All these subskills require that remedial students learn to think beyond the information presented in the text. Activities for drawing inferences follow.

1. Students can draw inferences from pictures. One teacher used a picture showing two children playing in a living room with raindrops on the window pane. Students were asked to tell why the children were not playing outside. A discussion of the answers stimulates further thinking.

2. Students read a story that has no ending and then supply a likely ending. An alternate procedure is to ask students to predict the outcome of stories. After prediction has taken place, they check with actual story endings. Predicted endings should be discussed.

3. To practice "cause and effect" relationships, students may match *if* sentence cards with *then* endings. For example, "If you drop a plastic glass filled with water," "then it will spill."

4. Students can "put words in people's mouths." First, a story containing several characters is read. As a follow-up, an event not in the story may be listed. Students state the words that the character would say if the event were to happen. This type of character study is a rather advanced form of inference.

5. After reading a story, the teacher may give a list of traits for one character, some descriptive, some not. Students check off the traits that they feel actually describe the character and defend answers in discussion.

CRITICAL READING.   Critical reading is the ability to evaluate and interpret the worth of reading materials. In a modern society, citizens are exposed to a wide variety of materials aimed at persuading them to buy products or to vote a certain way. Remedial students should learn how the printed word influences their attitudes, decisions, and lives. In particular, older readers, whose powers of judgment and reasoning may outstrip their reading abilities, enjoy developing critical reading skills, for these are "adult topics" that encourage self-motivation and independence.

As with inference, critical reading may be divided into separate subskills including distinguishing facts from fantasy, recognizing propaganda techniques, and evaluating the truth and worth of materials. Activities for critical reading follow.

1. Remedial readers can be asked to read sentences and determine if they are fact or fiction. "The ant had a birthday party" would be recognized as fiction; "The aunt had a birthday party" would be fact.

2. "Tall tales" or folktales about Paul Bunyan and other semimythical heroes can be searched for exaggerations. This technique can be used with popular "superheroes," such as Superman, who appear in the comics or movies.

3. Advertising material may be used effectively to help understand the use of propaganda. This is an excellent technique for group remedial instruction. Advertisements of automobiles or soft drinks can be collected, and students can look for the type of propaganda technique being used. Common propaganda techniques are:

- *Glittering Generalities:* Using words with positive associations such as "beautiful" or "just like Mom makes."
- *Name Calling:* Using negatively connoted words such as "cheat" or "less for your money."
- *Endorsements or Testimonials:* Association with respected people such as "Ninety-nine percent of all dentists use this product."
- *Plain Folks:* Suggesting that something is "down to earth" such as "A man of the people."
- *Snob Appeal:* Suggesting that a product will make a person popular or rich.
- *Bandwagon Approach:* Suggesting that a person should do something because everyone is doing it.

Transferring Comprehension Subskills to Reading

After a comprehension concept is established in the student's mind and has received some practice, it should be used in reading. In this way, students learn to use the skill in many different situations.

Because of the complex nature of comprehension skills, students should be exposed to an ordered sequence of difficulty. By beginning with shorter reading selections, the student can gradually work up to reading longer ones. For example, to teach the skill of finding the main idea, students can begin by finding the main idea in a single paragraph. Then they can move to a one-page story and then to finding the main idea in their instructional reading material. The difficulty of material should also be planned with care. In teaching sequencing, for example, a story in which events center around one person's actions may be easier than a story involving many people.

Several other methods can be used within an instructional reading period to foster the application of comprehension skills. These methods can be employed before, during, or after the instructional reading.

BEFORE READING.   It is very important that remedial readers be carefully prepared before they read material. Before reading, the student should (1) be given adequate background to read the material and (2) be engaged actively in the reading process.

Adequate background information is related to the concept of *schema*, which was explained earlier in this chapter. Students' schemata (the information they bring to the reading process) will affect their comprehension. To illustrate, two students might be reading about the topic of "knights." The schema of one student might include the knowledge that knights wore armor and fought on horses near castles. The schema of another student might include knowledge about chivalric traditions, the feudal system of the Middle Ages, and castle fortifications. The second student who brings richer schema to the reading process will therefore be able to draw more information from reading. It is important to investigate students' background knowledge (or schema) of the topic to be read. If the student lacks sufficient knowledge to read profitably, the teacher should supplement concepts (Crafton, 1981). Because knowledge is interrelated in conceptual schema, teachers should introduce new words and concepts in an interrelated fashion. For example, informal diagrams may be used to show relationships among concepts.

Background information is particularly important for remedial students and those with lower-level reading skills (Stevens, 1980). Because these students may have difficulty reading the material, it is very important that background knowledge and schema be as fully developed as possible before reading. Stevens (1982) found that increasing background knowledge of students before reading markedly improved the comprehension of lower-level readers.

Students' active participation in their reading is required for integrating new information with existing knowledge. Many remedial readers, however, are passive learners. To foster active involvement, students need a purpose for reading, such as reading to find an answer to a question. This purpose should be the basis for follow-up questions or discussions directly after reading.

DURING READING.   Silent reading fosters the development of comprehension skills because students absorb material at their own pace. Many students, accustomed to thinking of reading as an oral performance, resist silent reading. Suggestions for encouraging students to read silently appear in Chapter 11, in the section on special problems. The amount of material a remedial student can read silently is also important. Students should gradually increase the amount of text they read silently.

AFTER READING.   A follow-up of the reading can also help in the application of comprehension skills. Although questioning is the most common type of follow-up activity, teachers should vary their follow-up activities, enabling remedial readers to learn several strategies. Four types of follow-up activities for instructional reading include (1) comprehension questions asked by the teacher, (2) questions formulated by the student, (3) retelling, and (4) discussion.

1.   *Teacher-formulated questions.*   The teacher usually asks questions after the student has read a passage. These follow-up questions should be structured at a level that the student can handle with ease. Some remedial students can handle multiple-choice questions but not open-ended ones themselves. This procedure makes students aware of the different reasons given for reading the story. Teachers should continuously direct thinking by varying the types of questions asked and avoiding questions on trivial details. Questioning provides an opportunity for reviewing previously taught comprehension skills. For example, sequencing skills may be taught directly for one month and, thereafter, questions covering sequencing may be incorporated into instructional reading.

2. *Student-formulated questions.* More advanced remedial readers may be able to formulate questions by themselves. This helps them to be aware of the many different ways in which material can be comprehended and helps to develop independence. In the *request procedure* (Manzo, 1969), students and teachers alternate asking questions, and question formulation is based on answers to previous questions. Although student-formulated questions are effective in fostering thinking skills, many remedial students initially find it difficult to develop their own questions.

3. *Retelling.* Retelling stories is an alternative to questioning. The student is asked to tell the story after silent reading. Through retelling, the teacher can judge the student's ability to summarize and organize material. Retelling develops students' expressive language abilities. Retelling is discussed in Chapter 6.

4. *Discussion.* In some cases, discussion is the appropriate follow-up activity, especially for more advanced remedial students. Discussion fosters higher-level thinking and group involvement. Teachers may lead off discussions by suggesting one or two provocative issues. Since more outgoing students often tend to dominate discussions, teachers may choose to intersperse some indirect questions for quieter students, such as "Mary, do you agree with Tom and Jane?"

In each of these four techniques, teachers and other students may *model* a comprehension process for students who experience difficulty understanding the process. In the modeling procedure, students give the reasons behind their answers or statements. This reveals the thinking process that they have used to formulate responses. Students with comprehension difficulties can observe the processes that others use (Pearson and Johnson, 1978). Although modeling is most effective in group instruction, the teacher can serve as a model for the student receiving individual instruction.

TEACHING COMPREHENSION
AS A HOLISTIC PROCESS

In the previous section, methods were given for teaching comprehension subskills. This section reviews four approaches to teaching reading comprehension as a holistic process: (1) the psycholinguistic approach, (2) the directed reading-thinking approach, (3) the cloze procedure, (4) auding, and (5) the theme approach.

The Psycholinguistic Approach
to Comprehension

The psycholinguistic perspective of reading provides a framework for teaching word recognition (summarized in Chapter 11) as well as an approach for the remedial teaching of comprehension. As noted earlier, the psycholinguistic perspective is a somewhat nontraditional view of the reading process. In the traditional framework, one assumes that the recognition of words is followed by comprehension. In the psycholinguistic framework, however, readers use comprehension abilities to predict the words that occur next on the page. In this way, comprehension actually precedes word identification. The reader's knowledge of the subject, language base, comprehension, and word recognition are all in constant interaction. In fact, good readers do not "read" text; rather, they "sample" from it.

The psycholinguistic framework has several implications for teaching reading comprehension.

1. Prediction and hypothesis formulation about material are of paramount importance.
2. Students should use their total language and experience as a basis for reading.
3. All language processes (reading, writing, speaking, and listening) are interrelated. Strengthening one will improve all others.
4. Students should be exposed to a maximum amount of material to foster experiential and language growth.

Some nontraditional opinions about remedial reading have been expressed by psycholinguists. For example, F. Smith (1973b) believes that there is danger in the word "remedial" because the time devoted to instruction with remedial students will be spent on tests and drills rather than on reading. Psycholinguists urge that the primary emphasis of a remedial program be wide and extensive reading. They believe that the specific reading level of material is less important than its interest for the student.

The following comprehension strategies are suggested from the psycholinguistic perspective.

1. Reading to students is a highly recommended strategy for demonstrating that reading is a valued act from which information and enjoyment can be drawn.
2. Sustained silent reading helps remedial readers to improve comprehension. Sustained reading may be accomplished in a group as well as individually. It is important to have adults participate so that the process can be modeled. Reading should not be interrupted. If students encounter unknown words they should try to figure them out or mark the place with a bookmark.
3. Readers can learn to predict the content of a book without actually reading by surveying the jacket, the title, some pictures, the print size, and the size of the book. Readers can predict which book is likely to be fiction, which is likely to be difficult, etc.
4. The size and type of print also offers many hints about the message. This strategy is called *graphic variations* (Goodman and Burke, 1980). Students may also use the visual display (such as boldness of print, use of italics) to guess the author's intended message. Excellent sources of materials for this strategy include newspapers, magazines, and advertisements.
5. In reading an informational selection, students may be asked first what they would like to learn about the topic and what they already know. After reading, students review how their knowledge has been expanded. This strategy helps to build the remedial students' schema.

6. Writing is an important tool for teaching both reading and the importance of being literate. Since all writing is intended for later reading, the importance of reading receives automatic emphasis when writing is highlighted. Suggestions for using writing follow.

    a. Students can share "written conversations" with other students or with the teacher. This method requires students to write (instead of say) what they wish to communicate, and written replies are read. If students cannot write, they should pretend to write (that is, make some written marks) and then "read" what they have "written" (Goodman and Burke, 1980).

    b. Students may write journals, logs, or diaries of daily events.

    c. Teachers can write out questions and ask their students to answer in writing. Then further questions may be formed based on replies.

    d. Teachers and students may exchange notes or letters.

The psycholinguistic perspective offers a valuable orientation for teaching many remedial readers. This approach has proven to be highly motivating for students who view reading as a rote or meaningless task or who have developed emotional blocks to reading instruction.

The Directed Reading-Thinking Activity (DRTA)

The directed reading-thinking activity (DRTA) is an instructional method in which students first predict what they will read and then check their predictions through subsequent reading. Formulated by Stauffer (1975), DRTA has much in common with the psycholinguistic approach. In both, students are seen as actively seeking information from the material that they read. Stauffer believes that the essence of reading is thinking and that students must learn to apply the reasoning process to reading, starting early in their careers. The teacher plays a key role by constantly challenging readers to formulate, defend, and test hypotheses about their reading materials. Students come to realize that their predictions should be based on evidence.

We have found that DRTA is highly effective with many remedial readers. The novelty of the approach captures student attention and encourages them to take an active approach to reading. The approach is especially useful in guiding students toward higher-level comprehension. It may be used as a bridge to lead students toward inferential and critical thinking.

The steps for using DRTA follow.

1. Based on a small segment of material, the teacher guides students to predict what will happen next. Initial predictions may be based on the title, an illustration, or the first paragraph of a selection. During the prediction process, the teacher's role is to activate thought and to agitate it by asking students to defend their hypotheses.

2. Students are then asked to read further in the material to determine the validity of their hypotheses.

3. After students have read, they discuss which of their hypotheses were confirmed. The teacher asks for evidence to support the plausibility and correctness of the hypotheses.

4. After students have completed the three-step process using one segment of the material, they perform the process again on the next segment. The process continues until the entire text has been read. Throughout, the teacher serves as a mentor to refine and deepen the reading-thinking process.

DRTA is successful in both group and individual remedial settings. Reading material that is filled with suspense (such as mysteries) is especially useful for the DRTA technique.

The Cloze Procedure

The use of the cloze procedure as an assessment technique was discussed in Chapter 6. The cloze technique is also useful for teaching comprehension. In the cloze procedure, material is prepared so that words are deleted and replaced periodically by spaces of uniform length. Students are asked to fill in the blank spaces with the words they think are missing. For instruction, we recommend that every tenth word be deleted (rather than every fifth word as when the cloze procedure is used as a diagnostic test). An example is given below.

Mary saw Bob as he passed by the grocery _____. She waved to him and called out "Hello. _____ he came over to see her and he asked her _____ she was doing.

(Answers: store, then, how)

The cloze process serves several instructional purposes for remedial readers. First, it familiarizes students with complex grammatical structures and the words used to signal them. It also teaches the use of context clues. Finally, it encourages the use of inference skills to formulate guesses about missing words.

To foster these learnings, students should discuss their answers to cloze exercises. Discussion focuses attention upon the reasonableness of the words used as replacements. When the words that were used originally in the text are compared with those that students may have used, differences in syntax or subtle shades of word meaning are highlighted.

Remedial readers may encounter spelling difficulties in trying to fill in deleted words. If so, the teacher should provide spelling assistance or simply accept "approximate" spellings without correction. Cloze passages for remedial readers should be kept fairly short, limited to about twenty blanks. To aid students, the teacher may fully reproduce the text for the first portion and then begin deleting words toward the middle of the selection.

The cloze technique has many variations. Blachowicz (1977) recommends a synonym cloze in which students are given a word below the cloze blank and are asked to provide a synonym. Bortnick and Lopardo (1973) suggest techniques for older students. To increase awareness of syntax, certain parts of speech (nouns, prepositions) can be deleted. (However, not every noun or preposition should be deleted, as this makes the text unreadable.) To increase phonics or structural analysis awareness, certain letter combinations or letter endings may be deleted (such as *oi* or *tion*). Cloze passages may also be prepared with the first or last words of sentences deleted. Finally, cloze passages may be prepared from material in different content areas so that students become aware of different vocabulary and literary styles.

Auding

Auding is the activity of listening to oral text. This may be done through the use of a tape recorder or through listening to oral reading. Through auding, students can be exposed to harder material than they can read comfortably. Although auding is a simple technique, it may be extremely effective. Auding can serve two important purposes. First, if students' reading skills lag behind their language skills, auding gives them a way of building meaning vocabulary and absorbing information they can get in no other way. This activity often builds receptive language skills and schemata. Students can actually develop and practice many higher-level comprehension skills without reading simply by using their listening skills. Second, through listening to reading, students become motivated to learn to read because they become aware of the many interesting things that can be read. Aulls and Gelbart (1980) found that a group of seventh-grade remedial readers remarkably improved their comprehension when they listened to audio tapes while simultaneously following the text in a book.

Auding may be done in three ways.

1. Remedial students can listen to cassette tapes of books. They often like to follow along with the text as they listen. In this case, material must be easy enough to be *followed* through reading. Appendix A lists many books with accompanying cassettes.
2. Younger students often like to listen to the teacher read.
3. Students may listen to each other read. This gives remedial readers a chance to exhibit new successes, share books, and to become interested in other topics.

The auding activity has been used successfully in several programs. For example, C. Chomsky (1978) reports dramatic improvement in the reading levels of remedial readers who listened to tape recorded versions of books as they followed the text. The auding technique was particularly effective in increasing motivation for reading.

The Theme Approach

In the theme approach, students read and inquire into a topic that they find interesting. Since student interest is the central feature, remedial readers find this approach highly motivating. The theme approach is excellent for sparking enthusiasm and creativity. It also enriches the schema of students with limited backgrounds.

To illustrate the theme approach, several cases of students who have used this method successfully will be cited. Elizabeth, a seventeen-year-old, decided to concentrate on successful women who had, in her words "made it." Three women were chosen, one each from entertainment, sports, and business. Elizabeth read books about them and collected newspaper articles. She also watched sports events on television and listened to phonograph records and tape recordings. As each woman was studied, the teacher brought in technical vocabulary from the field that was represented. At the end of three months, Elizabeth had considerably improved her fifth grade reading level.

Edmund, a fifth-grader reading on a second grade level, became interested in Hawaii and volcanoes. He collected pictures on these subjects. The teacher gave Edmund an assignment of going to the supermarket to find the many ways in which pineapple could be purchased. This trip was written up into a language experience story. Travel brochures, annotated maps, and social studies textbooks were used for reading material. At the end of instruction, the teacher was given a fresh pineapple as a gift!

Twelve-year-old Eugene, reading on a third grade level, developed an interest in the escape artist, Houdini. After reading some easy books in the clinic, he read through all the other books in the school and local library. Before another hero replaced Houdini, he had made several trips to the central New York City Public Library.

The theme approach allows the reader to pursue an interest and thus motivates remedial readers to read widely and take an active orientation toward their reading. At the same time, the teacher may focus on selected comprehension skills that are relevant to the student's needs.

Remedial students may not be able immediately to think of a theme that they would like to study. The alert teacher can use information from the student's interest inventory (see Chapter 3), conversations, and responses to reading to suggest a motivating theme.

SUMMARY

The purpose of reading is to comprehend written material. Comprehension may be viewed as either a set of distinct subskills or a unified whole. Viewing comprehension as subskills permits the teacher and student to focus on the mastery of obtainable goals. The holistic view provides needed perspectives on the importance of (1) background knowledge and its organization (called schema) and (2) the reader's active participation in the reading process.

Background was presented on teaching comprehension through the use of subskills. A three-step framework was used: introduction, practice, and transfer. When introducing a comprehension subskill, the concept should be explained thoroughly. The use of nonreading activities and personalized activities often facilitates this.

In practicing comprehension, subskills were divided hierarchically:

1. *Literal comprehension:* Sentence comprehension, comprehension of facts, and following directions.
2. *Organizational comprehension:* Comprehension of main idea, sequence, and problem-solution format.
3. *Inferential comprehension.*
4. *Critical reading.*

In literal comprehension, sentence comprehension should be practiced with many types of sentences rather than just a few types. Remedial readers may have problems with sentences because of underlying language problems and inexperience in reading materials that contain complicated sentences. In the comprehension of facts, students must learn to distinguish important facts from unimportant facts. Often, students who show a low level of comprehension benefit from the close reading and concentration that results from following directions.

Organizational comprehension helps remedial students, who may have limited memory capacities, to remember material more easily. Main idea is a useful way of organizing nonfiction material. Sequence and problem-solution formats are often used for fictional materials. In teaching sequence, students should learn to identify important items to put into sequence. Organizing stories into problems and solutions effectively summarizes the "grammar" or form of a story in a way that is comprehensible for remedial readers.

Inference skills help readers to read beyond the text. They include prediction, inferring traits of characters, understanding story theme, making comparisons, and inferring cause-and-effect relationships. Remedial readers may have difficulty with the risk-taking behaviors required in making inferences.

In critical reading, the student evaluates material. Older remedial readers may enjoy using these skills. Subskills include distinguishing facts from fantasy, recognizing propaganda, and evaluating the truth and worth of materials.

Comprehension skills should be applied in context. Materials for application should go from short to long and from easy to difficult. Certain steps in instructional reading help to ensure comprehension. Before reading, the teacher should check (and, if necessary, augment) background knowledge (schema) and engage the reader's attention by giving a purpose for reading. During reading, silent, uninterrupted reading is preferred. Follow-up after reading includes comprehension questions, student-formulated questions (including the request procedure in which teacher and student questions alternate), retelling the story, and discussion.

The holistic perspective in reading comprehension includes (1) the psycholinguistic perspective (2) the directed reading-thinking activity, (3) the cloze procedure, and (4) the theme approach.

The psycholinguistic perspective views the reader as drawing samples from the text based on comprehension; thus comprehension precedes word identification. In this perspective, the use of total experience and language for reading, prediction in reading, the interrelationships of writing and reading, and the importance of wide reading receive emphasis.

In the directed reading-thinking activity, students predict what they will read and check these predictions through subsequent reading. A student predicts a small segment of material at each time until the story is finished. This fosters active reading and may serve as a bridge to inference skills.

In the cloze procedure, students supply words that have been deleted systematically from the passage. This fosters understanding of syntax, drawing inferences, and using context clues.

In auding, the student listens to material. Since students can listen to material more difficult than they can read, language growth is encouraged. In addition, auding motivates students to read.

In the theme approach, instruction is centered on a student's interest. This encourages building background knowledge and is very motivating for remedial readers.

13

IMPROVING MEANING VOCABULARY, STUDY STRATEGIES, AND RATE

This chapter deals with improving the skills of remedial readers in three areas: (1) meaning vocabulary, (2) study strategies, and (3) reading rate. Meaning vocabulary refers to the number of words a student understands. Study strategies enable students to learn in school and do assignments effectively. Instruction in reading rate helps the student to increase reading speed and to read at a rate appropriate to the task. Improvement of meaning vocabulary is needed by most remedial readers; more advanced remedial students may need to concentrate on study strategies and reading rate.

MEANING VOCABULARY

Meaning vocabulary refers to the number of words an individual can understand. Meaning vocabulary is different from word recognition, which refers to words that can be recognized on a printed page.

The development of an extensive meaning vocabulary is very important to reading. Poets and sages have emphasized the beauty and usefulness of words.

> Each new word . . . increases the scope of thought
> And adds its bit to humanity.
> *Bergan Evans*

> Good words are worth much
> And cost little.
> *George Herbert*

Informal Vocabulary Assessment

It is useful to compare students' meaning vocabularies with their abilities to recognize words in print. This helps the teacher to determine appropriate instructional strategies. If remedial students can recognize in print all the words that are in their meaning vocabulary, meaning vocabulary should be enlarged and improved. On the other hand, if students cannot read many of the words in their meaning vocabularies, they need further instruction in word recognition (see Chapters 10 and 11). The relationship of a student's meaning vocabulary to word recognition abilities can be determined by conducting an informal *vocabulary probe*, using a standardized achievement test, as follows:

1. Administer the vocabulary section of a standardized test according to test directions. Such tests require students to recognize words and to respond to their meanings. Score the test.
2. Administer the same test, this time with the teacher reading the words to the student. Here the student has only to respond to word meanings. Score the test.
3. If the score on the teacher-read test is higher, then the student needs instruction in word recognition. However, if the score on the teacher-read test is about the same, then the student needs to improve in meaning vocabulary.

For example, a sixth grader scoring 3.8 on the student-read test and 6.2 on the teacher-read test needs help in word recognition skills. A sixth grader scoring 5.0 on the student-read test and also 5.0 on the teacher-read test needs help in vocabulary. If the student has low scores on both administrations of the test, instruction in both word recognition and meaning vocabulary is needed.

Introducing Meaning Vocabulary

As in teaching other reading skills, a three-phase framework is used: introduction, practice, and transfer to reading. An essential ingredient of building meaning vocabulary is fostering an interest in words and their meanings. There are many effective ways to introduce new vocabulary to remedial readers.

SOURCES FOR VOCABULARY.   Where can a teacher look to find words that enrich a student's vocabulary? Since vocabulary is woven into every phase of our language and concepts, new words can be drawn from any aspect of student experience.

1. Remedial students can be asked to find words to bring to class—from television, newspapers, billboards, musical scores, or any other source. Sometimes students need encouragement. One teacher succeeded in encouraging students to find words by bringing in an empty cereal box and showing the students words such as *nutrition* and *riboflavin*. After this introduction, students were able to find new words in places that they had never thought of looking.

2. Another source for meaning vocabulary is the instructional reading materials used in school. For example, students want to learn words that are used in their science books.

3. The "theme" approach for remedial instruction discussed in Chapter 12 can also be used to find new words. For example, thirteen-year-old Ryan was interested in mysteries; he consequently learned such words as *sleuth*, *accessory*, *culpable*, and *blood type*. Because the words were interconnected, Ryan was able to build up sophisticated schema in this area. Thus, the teaching of vocabulary was integrated with extending concepts and experiential background.

4. The teacher is yet another source of vocabulary. Remedial students should be encouraged to stop teachers whenever they use unknown words. One remedial student called these "million-dollar words." Another teacher brought in one new word each day for her remedial classes. This was called the "word of the day." Soon some of the students also started to bring in words.

5. Word books and word lists may be used as sources for meaning vocabulary. For younger readers, we recommend the many word books that feature pictures. Scarry's *Best Word Book Ever* is one such book. Older remedial readers often like the sense of accomplishment that mastering word lists brings. Materials for these activities are listed in Appendix A.

METHODS FOR INTRODUCING VOCABULARY.   Teachers should emphasize both word pronunciation and meaning when introducing vocabulary to remedial readers. We like to divide introduction into three parts:

1. Pronouncing the word.
2. Giving a simple definition or picture.
3. Using the word in an illustrative sentence.

Teachers should record these three elements on vocabulary cards, or lists.

Direct experiences with words provides maximum impact in remedial instruction. For example, when teaching the meaning of concrete words, bring in real objects or provide pictures. The use of the senses (vision, touch, hearing) has been found to be very effective (Frasier, 1970). Field trips or other kinds of outings also provide a rich source of vocabulary growth. Afterward, students may talk about the new words they have encountered.

Practicing Meaning Vocabulary

Unless new words are practiced repeatedly, they are forgotten by remedial readers. Teachers who wish to foster long-term vocabulary growth can set aside a vocabulary practice period once or twice per week. Practicing words orally, and in groups, stimulates interest and excitement, which results in effective vocabulary learning.

Vocabulary growth takes place through (1) the expansion of vocabulary and (2) the enrichment of vocabulary. *Expansion* of vocabulary increases the number of words known, an area of particular importance for remedial students. In helping students to expand their vocabularies, word meanings should be carefully introduced and reinforced. The strategies for expanding vocabulary that are given in this section include keeping records, games for practicing vocabulary, dramatization, classification, learning vocabulary through context, and using the dictionary.

Enrichment of vocabulary deepens knowledge of words by fostering understanding of the many levels of word meaning and the interrelationships of words. Activities for enriching vocabulary include synonyms and antonyms, homonyms, multiple meanings, word history and figurative language.

KEEPING RECORDS OF WORDS.   By keeping records of words learned, students gain a sense of ownership and a convenient base for practice. The word file is one effective method of record keeping. Students can practice their words independently and add sentences to their word cards. Another method of record keeping is a class or personal dictionary. New words are entered under their first letter, with a definition and a sentence illustrating their use. Or words may be displayed on the bulletin board or wall, giving remedial students the opportunity to look at the words and to practice them throughout the day. Finally, students can be challenged to think of a creative way to keep records of their words. Student ideas in one remedial class included a laminated carpet and word placemats.

When working in groups, students can compare their lists or notecards, learning each other's words. Word lists can be expanded by using word derivatives.

For example, the word *suggest* can be expanded to *suggestion, suggests, suggestive,* and so on.

GAMES FOR PRACTICING VOCABULARY.   There are many group games for practicing vocabulary.

1.   Words can be placed in a fish bowl and students can be asked to "fish" for a word. Words "caught" are used in a sentence.
2.   Students choose a letter of the alphabet, and the teacher takes words that begin or end with that letter and asks students to use them in sentences.
3.   For larger remedial groups, students are divided into two teams. A word is chosen by a secretary. Members of the first team have to pronounce the word (1 point), use it in a sentence (1 point), and, for older students, define it (2 points). Since a class list is one that all students can look at, team members are encouraged to practice words with one another.

DRAMATIZATION OF VOCABULARY.   The technique of dramatization makes words more concrete for remedial readers, adding an experiential component to words (Duffelmeyer and Duffelmeyer, 1979). Skits may be written, acted out in an impromptu manner, or done in pantomime. For example, to demonstrate the word *snobbish*, fourth grade remedial readers presented a skit where several people said "Hello" to one of the actors and he didn't answer. Students were then asked to define the word *snobbish* and to check their definitions with the dictionary.

The commercial program "Word Theater" is extremely useful for dramatizing words that may be used at the third to sixth grade vocabulary level (see Appendix A). In this series, a preprinted skit is presented that students act out. One sentence, presented in italics, must be read aloud. Students who are not in the group of actors are asked to guess the meaning of the word.

VOCABULARY THROUGH CLASSIFICATION.   Another helpful way of learning unknown words is to attach them to known words. Much vocabulary learning takes place in this manner. McNeill (1970) describes a process of vertical and horizontal expansion in early vocabulary growth. This system can be used in teaching categorization.

Vertical vocabulary expansion involves the growth of categories that include other things. For example, a child may discover gradually that the concept *dog* can be broken down into several different categories (e.g., cocker spaniel, golden retriever, dalmation) and that *dog* itself is one classification of animal. Thus children learn that dog is one level in a vertical scheme.

Horizontal vocabulary growth refers to the enrichment and differentiation of words within the same category. Thus children may at first call many types of animals *dogs*. Later they learn to distinguish them into *horses, cows, mice,* and so on. At a higher level, students distinguish the concept *home* into *apartment, cottage,* and *house.* Teaching vocabulary through classification is recommended for remedial readers because it helps them to expand their experiential background and enrich their conceptual schema. Several activities may be used:

1. Give students sets of ordered words and ask them to fill in missing words (Johnson and Pearson, 1978), as seen in the example below.

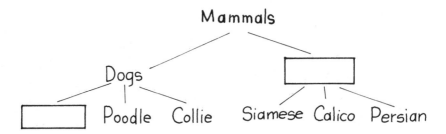

2. Ask students to describe as many kinds of workers as they can or all animals living in the sea. Groups of students can make joint lists of these words.
3. Using an interesting picture or word as a stimulus, ask students to think of as many words as they can. These words are then classified. For example, if the word *cold* is given as a stimulus, students may associate it with sickness (tissues, aspirin) or a cold temperature (ice, winter).

LEARNING VOCABULARY THROUGH CONTEXT.   An effective way to improve meaning vocabulary is to learn new words by inferring the meaning from conversations and reading. Gipe (1980) experimented with several methods of teaching third and fourth grade students new vocabulary words and found the context methods most effective. However, the process of gaining meaning from context is not easy for many remedial readers. To build vocabulary in this way, they must be encouraged to take risks and to make "intelligent hypotheses." (We often use these very words to encourage our students.)

Several methods may be used to encourage students to build meaning vocabulary through context. Students can write sentences in which they have encountered unknown words. For group instruction, these words are read aloud, and the class guesses the meaning of the words based on sentence context. Students' guesses are checked with dictionary definitions. For individual instruction, the student enters words on cards with the word on one side and the sentence in which it appeared on the other. The cards can then be reviewed periodically. If the student does not know the meaning of the word in isolation, the card is turned over and the context clues in the sentence are used to define the words.

A classification system for context clues often helps readers understand how to gain meaning from different types of context. Table 13.1 presents such a scheme. These ideas are adapted from Thomas and Robinson (1981) and Ames (1966). The first six strategies in Table 13.1 are useful for all remedial readers, even those with only beginning reading skills. Strategies 6 through 10 are better suited for more advanced students. The teacher should concentrate on one strategy at a

Table 13.1 Strategies for Learning Vocabulary Through Context

1. *Direct Explanation Clue.* The author defines the word directly.

   A *welder*, a person who puts pieces of metal together, is well paid.
   A *gerontologist*, who specializes in the problems of old age, gave a lecture at the nursing home.

2. *Words in a Class Clue.* Unknown words appear in a series that helps to define their meaning.

   Many colors were used, including yellow, blue, and *fuschia*.

3. *Inference Clue.* The word meaning can be inferred from the context. This type of clue is often combined with other types.

   Because of his quick temper and harsh words, he *offended* people.

4. *Synonym or Restatement Clue.* A similar word or idea is repeated.

   The boy had missed several baseball games, so the *lad* had to quit the team.

5. *Clues of Opposition.* Here words are defined by their opposites.

   Peggy was pleased, but Jane was *horrified*.

STRATEGIES 6–10: FOR MORE ADVANCED STUDENTS

---

6. *Mood or Tone Clue.* The tone of the sentence gives hints to word meaning.

   The *jovial* mood matched the good spirits and gay laughter of the people.

7. *Example Clue.* The author gives an example of word meaning.

   In every way, *literacy* was repressed during the Dark Ages. For example, far fewer people were able to read and write.

8. *Summary Clue.* The unknown word is a summary of several known circumstances.

   He had not eaten in two days. He had walked several miles and lost much weight. By the time he reached the town, he was *emaciated*.

9. *Experience Clue.* An experience common to people provides meaning.

   Because she had been so kind to him and helped him with his problems, he felt *affectionate* toward her.

10. *Familiar Expression Clue.* A common language pattern provides a clue to meaning.

    He shed some light on the situation before the meeting and during the meeting he *elucidated* it even further.

time, using several illustrative sentences. We have found this classification system a useful and well-organized way to instruct students.

USING THE DICTIONARY. The dictionary gives students independence in learning word meanings; however, it should not be overused as an instructional tool. Remedial students tend to find looking up word meanings tedious, and if they can learn words through other means, they should be encouraged to do so. Although dictionaries do supply definitions, they are not geared for instruction in correct usage. Sentences using words and discussions of words should accompany dictionary study.

The dictionary does have many uses, even though it does not provide a complete vocabulary program. The dictionary provides definitions, offers a means to distinguish among definitions, gives a key for pronunciation, and supplies the different forms of a base word. There are several levels of dictionary usage. Dictionary skills, organized from less advanced to more advanced are

1. *Alphabetizing words.* The use of the first letter in a word is taught first, followed by second letter, third letter, and so on.
2. *Locating words.* This includes opening the dictionary to the correct half or quarter to locate a word and learning to use key words to determine if a word is on a page.
3. Using the dictionary pronunciation key.
4. Determining the correct dictionary entry for different word forms. For example, the word *slowly* should be looked up under the word *slow*.
5. Determing which of several definitions should be used in a particular context.
6. Determining the historical origin of a word.

Some interesting games will help students to learn to use the dictionary effectively; these follow.

1. Making dictionary sentences. Students can open the dictionary to a given page and try to construct the longest sentence possible using words from that page (Moffett and Wagner, 1976). Words such as "the," "and", "is," "if," and "I" may have to be added.
2. Younger remedial readers can make pictures of dictionary words. They can record the page and the picture, and other pupils must then find the word in the dictionary.
3. Older remedial readers can see who can locate a word in the dictionary using the fewest opening "cuts." This exercise helps the students to locate words quickly.

SYNONYMS AND ANTONYMS. Synonyms (words that mean the same things) and antonyms (words with opposite meanings) may be used to enrich word meanings as well as to extend them. These can be taught to remedial readers to help them see the many different words in our language and how they relate.

One group of disabled fifth grade readers played a "synonym spot" game. They stuck round spots onto a paper leopard. Spots with words that meant the same thing (e.g., pretty, beautiful) were put together. Another teacher made pictures of a boy sitting, walking, and running. In order to encourage students to list as many synonyms as they could for these three activities, the pictures were kept up for several days. Another group of students played the "but" game for antonyms. For example,

> I am happy but he is sad.
> I am cold but he is hot.
> I am xxxxx but he is xxxxx.

Adolescent remedial readers like the "overused word" game. Since these students tend to use certain "in" expressions repeatedly (e.g., *cool*, *dude*, *right-on*), the game requires them to think of as many synonyms as they can. In a similar vein, students can think of synonyms for common words. One upper-level teacher asked remedial classes to read the sports page of the newspaper to determine how many synonyms could be found for *win* (e.g., *beat*, *top*, *clobber*) (Mozzi, 1980).

The connotations, or implied meanings, of words are an excellent way to use synonyms. Some words have similar meanings, but different implications. For example, to be a *moral person* is positive, but to be a *goody-goody* is negative. In the same way, it is desirable to be *slender* but not to be *skinny* or *scrawny*. Finding words such as these is an amusing way to add to meaning vocabulary.

A thesaurus is an excellent tool for teaching synonyms and antonyms. Students use the thesaurus to find words of similar meanings. Several excellent thesauruses are published for students at different levels. Many include exercises and guides for practice. The two-book series *In Other Words* is a useful junior thesaurus (see Appendix A).

HOMONYMS.   Homonyms are words that sound alike but are spelled differently and, of course, have different meanings. Examples are *to*, *too*, *two* or *way* and *weigh*. Homonyms can also be used to enrich vocabulary. Several excellent children's books dramatize the meanings of homonyms. These include *Amelia Bedelia*; *Come Back*, *Amelia Bedelia*; and *The King Who Rained* (see Appendix A).

MULTIPLE MEANINGS.   Words in English often have several meanings. The study of multiple meanings of words is another way to enrich vocabulary. Many students find unknown meanings of common words that they use to be fascinating. A high school remedial reading class found that the word *loaded* was used frequently in used car ads. Discussing the multiple meanings of this word, they determined that it could also be used to describe a rich person or an intoxicated one. One of our remedial readers was astonished to learn in a social studies class that a concession could be something other than a hot dog stand! One practice activity requires students to find several meanings of common words such as hot and cold. Or students may be asked to match a definition with a sentence.

It was cold outside   without a show of emotion
She treated him coldly   having a low temperature

HISTORY OF WORDS. A study of the historical development of words frequently stimulates interest. The words *sabotage, sandwich,* and *lynch* all represent names and events in history.

As noted in Chapter 4, English has two language roots: one similar to German and one similar to Spanish, French, and Italian. Pairs of words exist in English, stemming from both of these roots (e.g., *deer-vension, calf-veal, father-paternal*). This means that many English words have cognates in foreign languages. Students, particularly those with foreign-language backgrounds, may be interested in knowing about these cognates. Spanish and English have many similar words; for example, *furious, advice,* and *diary* are Spanish cognates.

Word history may also lead to the study of word parts (structural analysis). For example, the word part *uni* is descended from Greek, and the many words that incorporate *uni—unicycle, universe, unity, unicorn*—are all derived from Greek.

In addition, many remedial readers are fascinated with Greek and Roman mythology and the colorful stories of gods and goddesses. The words for many of the planets of the solar system are named after these deities (e.g., Venus, Mars, Pluto, Neptune). Asimov's book *Words from the Myths* (see Appendix A) helps more advanced remedial students become acquainted with these concepts.

Historical origins are also found in the names of many common objects, such as automobiles. *Chevrolet* was a famous car racer; *Cadillac* was a French explorer, *Seville* and *Granada* are names of cities; *Mustang* and *Pinto* are types of horses.

FIGURATIVE LANGUAGE. Figurative language acquaints remedial students with imaginative language use. Two types of figurative language that may be appropriate for use with remedial students are (1) similes (or comparisons) and (2) figures of speech.

In a simile, a trait is compared with an animal or object. Examples are:

    as quiet as a mouse
    as fierce as a tiger
    as white as snow
    as slow as a tortoise
    as sour as a lemon

Remedial readers can draw pictures to illustrate these and talk about the reasons behind the development of such phrases. Often, similes will fire student's creativity in art and other areas (List, 1982).

Figures of speech are somewhat more advanced. Examples are:

    He flew down the stairs
    She brought the house down
    I'm in a jam
    He was on his last leg
    I could eat a horse

Once again, these figures of speech lend themselves to excellent illustrations.

As with other reading skills, vocabulary must be applied to be learned effectively. To assure that students transfer new words to reading, teachers can compose stories containing these vocabulary words. In addition, the vocabulary words should be noted when they are encountered in print.

New vocabulary can also be applied in the context of oral language. Teachers should attempt to use student's new words in speech. A hallmark of success is when a remedial reader uses a word spontaneously. For example, Marvin's teacher knew he had learned two words when he heard Marvin call his classmates *rowdy* and his brother *belligerent*. Twelve-year-old Somali played a Words-in-Conversation game with his reading teacher. Any time he used a vocabulary word in a conversation, he was given a star. Soon, he began to think of a sentence the night before his lesson that he used upon walking into the room.

Students can also write sentences and paragraphs using their new words. Eleven-year-old Melva made a "flower" of the words she used in sentences. Each petal of the flower contained a sentence with a new word (see example below). Students can be encouraged to make up a longer sentence or to combine two words into one sentence.

Since poor readers may not demand meaning from text, they often subconsciously skip over unknown words. These students must learn to identify words as unknown when they are encountered in a reading context. In fact, some teachers prefer not to introduce difficult words before reading so that students will learn to pick them out. If this procedure is used, after reading a story or selection the teacher should ask if there were any troublesome words. If no difficult words are identified, then the teacher may try to find some unknown words that the student did not notice. Being able to identify that a word is unknown is the first step to learning the word.

STUDY STRATEGIES

Study strategies enable students to cope effectively with school tasks. Study strategies are particularly important for middle school and high school remedial readers who have mastered basic reading skills but still have difficulties in school. However, less advanced remedial students also need strategies to cope with homework assignments and tests. Instruction in study skills can be highly motivating because it is very relevant to classroom demands.

Assessing Study Stategies

Informal measures are useful in assessing a student's study strategies. Content-area teachers (mathematics, social studies teachers) can be asked about the student's ability to cope with demands in their areas. Some guiding questions are:

- Does the student complete reading assignments?
- Does the student complete written assignments?
- Does the student ask questions in class?
- Does the student answer the teacher's questions?
- Is the student alert and attentive during class?

The reading teacher can also assess study skills directly by using a content area textbook. For this purpose, the student should be asked to bring in a book he or she is currently using. The student first reads a portion of a chapter orally so the teacher can check reading fluency. If oral reading is fluent, the student then reads a portion of the chapter silently and summarizes it. The teacher assesses how well the summary is organized. Then the student skims through another chapter and tries to summarize it. Finally, the teacher turns to the back of that chapter and asks the student to locate the answers to study questions in the text. The teacher observes whether the student uses the chapter headings or leafs through pages. Students' behavior on these tasks gives a good indication of their study strategies.

Using Parts of Books

A student's textbooks are very useful for teaching study strategies. The student's text is familiar and students are usually anxious to learn the material for class. Using the textbook, remedial readers can begin to see how study material is organized. Among the parts of a text that are helpful in study are the title page, foreword, table of contents, chapter headings, index, and glossaries. Several activities are suggested in learning to use text books.

1. *Title pages.* Ask students to find the oldest and newest book (by copyright) they are using.

2. *Table of contents.* Students are given five or ten facts and asked in which chapter of a book they are located. The table of contents is used to give the answer.

3. *Chapter headings.* Students are asked to locate five facts using the headings within chapters.

4. *Making a book.* Joshua, a remedial reader on a third grade level, made a book of photography, filling it with pictures he had taken and captions. In addition to his textual material, he had a copyright page, a dedication, a table of contents, and a glossary.

Map Skills

Maps and globes are indispensible to the study of social studies and to an intelligent reading of current events. Many students with reading problems have particular trouble with these areas of "visual literacy." Teaching these concepts also serves to enlarge students' experiential background and schema. Students need to know several concepts, including geographical terms (city, state, lake, country) and direction terms (north, south). Map skill instruction for remedial readers may begin with maps of familiar territory such as maps of rooms, buildings, and the neighborhood.

Several activities may help students understand map concepts:

1. Students may make maps of their classrooms. This activity helps to clarify the concepts of direction and map scale.

2. Using road maps, students may plan a trip from one place to another, finding alternate routes.

3. Students may use the map of a country, or continent, to answer questions such as "If you were planning a trip from Mexico to Chile, what countries would you pass?"

Reading for Study

Students in the middle grades and in high school need to read material in order to study. Four components of studying discussed here are previewing, skimming and scanning, using a study system, and teacher-made summaries.

PREVIEWING.   By previewing their reading assignments prior to reading, students learn and retain the information better. It is particularly important for remedial readers to learn to preview effectively since they may have problems reading the actual text. Previewing is very helpful in studying social studies and science texts.

Steps in previewing a chapter are

1. Read the title.
2. Read first and last paragraphs.
3. Read the topic headings.

4. Look at figures, maps, charts, graphs.
5. Read the chapter questions.

Steps in previewing a book are

1. Look at the book title and jacket.
2. Read the first portion of the first chapter.
3. Look for illustrations, figures, and charts.
4. Look at the table of contents.

The so-called "five-minute summary" is a useful instructional technique. The student first surveys a chapter for five minutes and then summarizes the material in it. Because the procedure may be overwhelming to students at first, teachers should be supportive of students' responses. Teachers can also model the five-minute summary for students.

SKIMMING AND SCANNING. Skimming and scanning are two reading techniques that are useful for studying. *Skimming* refers to going through a selection quickly to determine if it is of interest and to get a general impression of the content. For example, a student may skim to find out if an article will be of help in writing a paper or if a fiction story will be enjoyable. Skimming strategies often are used in previewing.

Scanning refers to the ability to locate specific information such as phone numbers, names, and dates. A reader scans the text quickly until the relevant piece of information is located. Remedial readers should be taught a systematic approach to scanning. First, they should locate appropriate headings in chapters, or an index can be used if the material contains one. Then, the material should be scanned visually. Often, looking for a *key word* is useful. For example, if students want to locate the date of birth of former president John Kennedy, students might visually scan for the words *Kennedy*, *birth*, *born*, or a date. Students may first learn to scan for information using one page. The telephone book or another directory may be used for this. Textbook pages may also be used.

USING A STUDY SYSTEM. Often remedial students do not know how to go about studying assigned material. A systematic approach to studying will help older remedial readers to cope with demands of the school situation. One system for systematic study, outlined by Pauk (1974), is known as OK5R (Table 13.2). Pauk emphasizes that this system should be used flexibly. He warns that the student should not become like a knight who is overburdened with armor. The study system should be used only if it helps.

TEACHER-MADE SUMMARIES. Teachers can help students to read chapters that might otherwise be too difficult by giving them a teacher-made guide before

Table 13.2 OK5R Study Method

Before

O **OVERVIEW.** Sample the chapter to find out what it is all about. Glance at the headings and subheadings to determine what ideas are being explained, what problems raised, and what questions posed. Get the big picture. Don't burrow into paragraphs. Avoid "tunnel vision"! Headings and subheadings will be future categories (advance organizers). Overview to overcome inertia and gain momentum for studying.

During

K **KEY IDEAS.** All textbook writing is made up of just three literary elements: *main ideas, supporting material,* and *transitions.* Your main job is to separate the main idea from the mass of supporting material.

R1 **READ.** Read only a paragraph or short section; then stop to ask, What is the main idea? How do the supporting materials support it? Which transitional words point to the main idea, and organize the supporting material? Finally, What is it in this paragraph that I need to know to describe or tell others what I have read?

R2 **RECORD.** Record your comprehension! Make marginal notes and underline only key words and phrases. Better still, summarize main ideas and supporting materials in your notebook. Avoid summarizing sentence by sentence, for it's a sure sign you are missing the essential points. Chew on ideas, not words.

After

R3 **RECITE.** To counteract forgetting, *recite!* Cover your textbook or notebook page, exposing only the jottings in the margins. Then using your own words, recite aloud the ideas and supporting material. After reciting, check for accuracy. Read, record, recite in this way, paragraph by paragraph, until you complete the chapter.

R4 **REVIEW.** After reciting, take a fresh look at your notes to fit them into a complete picture. It is easier to remember one complete jigsaw picture than a multitude of separate, seemingly unrelated jigsaw pieces. So it is with individual ideas and the total picture they present. Also, notwithstanding reciting, some forgetting will occur, so intersperse an occasional review to keep retention at a high level.

R5 **REFLECT.** Now, mentally manipulate these ideas, turn them over, speculate on them, compare one with the other, notice where they agree and differ. Organize and reorganize them into larger categories, or compress them into smaller units. Finally, free these ideas from the chapter and the book by weaving them into your existing knowledge, blending the new with the old.

---

they read the chapter. The summary should be relatively short, easy to read, and have sufficient "white space." The summary topics might include:

1. *The topic.* State the title and the main topic of the chapter.
2. *New words.* Define difficult words. Include the page or sentence where the word is found.
3. *Ideas in the chapter.* Outline the main divisions or ideas and the topics they contain.
4. *Purpose for reading.* Give a specific purpose to help students focus their attention.

An alternative study aid is a teacher-made advance organizer (Ausubel, 1960). This is a paragraph or two that gives a very general overview of the framework for the chapter and helps students to relate their schema to the chapter content. For example, in a chapter about the American Pilgrims, students could be asked to think about how they might feel coming to a strange new country.

Students need to be taught how to use teacher-made summaries. Summaries will not be an effective study aid unless students are given a few practice lessons in using them.

Copyright © 1980 by Sidney Harris. Printed originally in *Phi Delta Kappan.*

READING RATE

Increasing reading rate is an instructional goal for advanced remedial readers. However, students should be fairly comfortable with word recognition, vocabulary, and comprehension before striving to improve rate. Instruction in reading rate is needed by those students who have mastered basic skills but are hindered by a slow or inflexible rate. However, many older remedial readers are motivated to improve their rate simply because of the publicity given this topic for adults in our society.

Assessing Reading Rate

Rate of reading may be assessed using informal measures. Students read a passage in a book silently. The teacher times the reading with a stopwatch. At the end of five minutes, the teacher says the word "mark" and students put a slash by the line they are reading. The words per minute (WPM) are determined by counting the total number of words read and dividing by five, for the number of minutes of reading.

Factors in Reading Rate

Although no one figure can be given as a "normal" reading rate, adult readers average about 250 words per minute. This rate is reached at about the ninth grade reading level. The norms given in Table 13.3 (adapted from Harris and Sipay, 1980) give estimates of reading rates for passages of average difficulty. Table 13.3 shows that reading rate continues to grow through the ninth grade reading level. Readers should have a variety of different rates. A relatively fast rate might be used for reading easy fiction material; a moderate rate for reading in school; and a slow rate for reading detailed directions. In short, reading rate should be flexible.

When reading material, the eye does not move at a smooth pace across the page. Instead, it uses *saccadic movements*, jumping from place to place. When the eye stops, it absorbs information, and this pause is called a *fixation*. A mature normal reader will make about three or four fixations in a line of print the size of this book. In general, the eyes move forward while reading print, but sometimes the reader feels obliged to retrace information. Eye movements that look back over previously read material are called *regressions*.

Table 13.3 Reading Rate for Passages of Average Difficulty

Grade Level	2	3	4	5	6	7	8	9	12
Range of average rates	70–100	95–130	120–170	160–210	180–230	180–240	195–240	215–260	225–260
Slow rate	—	—	120	160	180	180	195	215	225

From A. Harris and E. Sipay, *How to Increase Reading Ability, 7th ed.* (New York: Longman, 1980); Taylor, 1957; Hollander and Reisman, 1970.

In the past it was believed that training eye movements would increase rate. For example, students were asked to eliminate their regressions, or efforts were made to have fewer fixations. Educators have come to realize that this type of program is merely treating the symptoms of slow reading rather than its causes. If a student has frequent regressions, an attempt should be made to find out why the regressions are taking place rather than simply trying to eliminate them. Because eye movement patterns are dependent upon many reading habits and skills, eye movement training is not advised.

Specific Causes of Slow Reading Rate

Slow reading is often the result of inefficient reading habits. However, other specific factors may contribute to slow reading. These include (1) poor basic reading ability, (2) subvocalization or lip movement, and (3) a slow personal tempo.

1.   *Poor reading ability.* Students who are having trouble recognizing words or comprehending will do poorly on tests of reading rate. Such students should not receive instruction to improve reading rate until underlying skills have been improved. Often adolescents and adults voluntarily enroll in reading rate courses when they actually have more basic problems.

2.   *Vocalization and subvocalization.* Some readers "whisper" or *vocalize* during silent reading; others reproduce words inaudibly or *subvocalize.* Since vocalization and subvocalization are habits that limit reading rate, instructional strategies are an attempt to eliminate these inhibiting behaviors. Vocalization and subvocalization are a natural part of the developmental reading process. Therefore, a student with a low reading level may still require the support of vocalization and is not ready for rate training. On the other hand, if vocalization has become a crutch that is no longer needed, the teacher should try to eliminate it by presenting material rapidly so that students cannot vocalize. As described in the next section, tachistoscopic devices or controlled readers are useful for this purpose.

Although vocalization can be observed easily, teachers often are not sure whether students are subvocalizing. Cole (1938) suggests a procedure for determining subvocalization in students reading above the seventh grade level. An easy reading selection with several pages containing approximately the same number of words should be chosen. The student reads a page orally, while the teacher times the reading. Another page is read silently while the teacher times the student. If the rate is approximately equal for silent and oral reading, the student is probably subvocalizing.

3.   *Slow personal tempo.* People think and react at different rates. This difference, which may depend on metabolic rate or physical factors, affects the reading process. Buswell (1951) found that the rate of reading was related to the rate of thinking. However, research has also shown that even slow-tempoed individuals may profit by learning more efficient reading habits. For example, Braam (1963) was able to show reading rate gains for all high school seniors, including even the slowest readers.

Methods for increasing reading rate include (1) the general improvement of reading habits and (2) specific devices to improve rate.

IMPROVEMENT OF READING HABITS.   Much improvement in reading rate may be gained by simply making students aware of their problem and motivating them to improve. Some commercial programs promise wonders in rate improvement; however, reading rates of thousands of words per minute have yet to be substantiated by carefully conducted research.

Often, simply practicing a faster reading rate for an extended period of time improves rate markedly. The teacher selects a ten- to twenty-minute period for such practice. It is best to use one source of materials consistently, and this source should contain several fairly short selections (from one to three pages) that are at the student's independent level. Students should time their readings and keep a record of their progressive improvement. An example of a chart for doing this is given in Figure 13.1.

Even when students are working on improving rate they should be encouraged to maintain comprehension. Therefore, comprehension questions should accompany the rate exercises.

By emphasizing the importance of reading in meaningful phrases, students learn to read faster by absorbing material in meaningful language units. Fast readers tend to group their fixations in meaningful phrases such as

The boy / saw the dog / in the yard.

A slow reader will either read word by word,

The / boy / saw / the / dog / in / the / yard.

or group in meaningless phrases,

The / boy saw the / dog in / the yard.

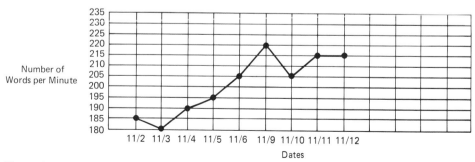

Figure 13.1   Sample Reading Rate Improvement Chart

To facilitate the perception of words in phrases, students may be given duplicated copies of text and asked to group words into phrases. The teacher should limit these selections to about one hundred words. After students mark these, they may compare their answers. To encourage phrase awareness, the student may be asked to read the text divided into such phrases orally.

SPECIFIC DEVICES FOR IMPROVING READING RATE.   Although machines may be used to improve reading rate, they are not a panacea. They should not be used to train eye movements but, rather, to help students to read in meaningful phrases and eliminate subvocalization. The tachistoscope, the controlled reader, and the reading pacer are devices to help improve reading rate.

The *tachistoscope* is a device that flashes words or phrases for a fraction of a second. If a teacher does not have the resources to purchase a tachistoscope, hand-held manual tachistoscopes may be made easily. A movable cover should expose and cover up the words. Teachers may estimate fast and slow exposure times effectively. Tachistoscopes may flash words on a screen or they may be hand-held devices.

Controlled readers may be used to help students improve their reading rate in whole passages. Reading passages, reproduced on a filmstrip, are flashed on a screen one line at a time. Rates of presentation may be controlled by the teacher so that the student can read progressively faster. Educational Development Laboratory's controlled reader (Appendix A) is one popular program.

A final device used to improve reading rate is the *reading pacer*. This machine can be placed over a book and is set at a given rate (say, 180 words per minute). It then covers the page from top to bottom at the preset pace. To read the page, the reader must stay ahead of the pacer. Pacers may be controlled manually; a popular one is the SRA reading accelerator (Appendix A).

SUMMARY

This chapter dealt with meaning vocabulary, study skills, and reading rate. While building a meaning vocabulary is a relevant activity for many remedial readers, the topics of study skills and reading rate are reserved for more advanced remedial readers.

Meaning vocabulary refers to the words that can be understood or used in speech or listening. Informal assessment procedures were given for determining whether a student's meaning vocabulary exceeds word recognition. If remedial students can recognize in print all the words in their meaning vocabularies, extension and expansion of word knowledge is needed.

A three-step framework was used for teaching meaning vocabulary: introduction, practice, and transfer. In introducing words, the teacher can pronounce the word, give a definition, and use it in a sentence. Sources for meaning vocabulary include student experiences, instructional reading, and word books.

Meaning vocabulary words must be practiced consistently. Methods were given for both expanding meaning vocabulary (adding new words to vocabulary) and enriching meaning vocabulary (exploring word relationships and deepening meanings). Extension activities include keeping records, dramatization, classification, learning vocabulary through context, and using a dictionary. Enrichment activities include finding synonyms and antonyms and using homonyms, multiple word meanings, word history, and figurative language.

Meaning vocabulary may be transferred in reading activities, speech usage (of students or teacher), and through writing activities. In applying vocabulary skills during reading, students learn to identify which words they do not know. This is an important first step in improvement of vocabulary.

Study strategies help students to cope effectively with school tasks. Teaching study strategies in remedial situations is motivating because students can apply these learnings to functioning in the classroom. Study strategies for remedial readers include using parts of textbooks effectively, using map skills, and reading for study. Reading for study includes previewing (gaining an orientation to material), skimming and scanning (quickly reviewing materials, looking for specific information in material), using a formal study system (the OK5R system was outlined), and using teacher-made summaries for study.

Improving reading rate is an activity that should be reserved for students who have mastered other reading skills. However, because of publicity on this topic, many types of remedial readers wish to improve their rate. Causes of slow reading include bad reading habits, difficulty with the material, vocalization and subvocalization, and slow personal tempo.

Reading rate cannot be improved by trying to improve eye habits. Rather, the reading competencies and strategies that underly these habits must be changed. Strategies for faster reading are: improving reading habits and using special devices. Habits can be improved by encouraging students to read faster through practicing and keeping systematic records and by showing students the importance of reading in phrases. Special devices to help students improve rate are the tachistoscope, the controlled reader, and the reading pacer.

PART IV

organizing for
reading instruction

14

READING AND THE LAW

reading and special education legislation

Educational services that are offered in our schools are shaped to some extent by federal and state laws. These laws regulate programs and provide funds for services. Educational services for students in remedial reading programs are supported by laws such as Chapter I (formerly Title I) in the Education Consolidation and Improvement Act of 1981. Educational services for students in special education programs are influenced by provisions of Public Law 94–142. Other relevant legislation, such as laws designed to protect student privacy, affect students in all school programs.

Federal and state laws play a vital role in many phases of the program. They help in determining the eligibility of students for service, in structuring the diagnostic and instructional plans, in training and certifying personnel, in guiding assessment and evaluation procedures, and in providing financial resources to support the program. It is important that classroom and reading teachers be familiar with these laws because they govern many decisions concerning students with reading problems. In addition, these laws designate certain responsibilities of the teachers and the schools.

READING LEGISLATION

Many remedial reading programs are created and supported, at least in part, by federal and state laws. These laws govern factors such as eligibility of the school for the funding, the purchase of instructional materials and equipment, and the training and certification of teachers. In addition, legislation protects the rights of students in remedial reading programs. The federal and state governments can exert influence on the nation's education through legislation that creates programs and governs funds. To qualify for funds, schools must meet the stated rules and regulations.

Reading programs are supported through sections of the Education Consolidation and Improvement Act of 1981 (*Reading Today*, 1981). The sections of this law that are of particular importance to remedial reading programs are called Chapter I and Chapter II. Chapter I (formerly Title I) is Financial Assistance to Meet Special Educational Needs of Disadvantaged Students. It is a block grant, distributed to the states on the basis of the former Title I. As one of the largest federal education programs, it supplies supplementary funds for compensatory education in reading and mathematics for underachieveing students in deprived areas. Chapter II is a block grant for several programs. Among those that affect reading are Basic Skills Development, which provides for the states to contract with other institutions to improve basic skills, including reading, and Reading Is Fundamental, a program that distributes free reading materials.

Since these programs have been placed into a block grant, each state has the responsibility to make decisions concerning distribution of the budget. If students with reading problems are to receive their fair share of these budget allocations, it is imperative that reading educators in each state make their state officials aware of the needs of students with reading problems. Reading teachers should know the process for obtaining funds to provide services for the disabled readers in their schools. If reading teachers are unaware of the political forces behind appropriations, they may unwittingly deprive their students of needed funds and programs.

Diagnosticians and teachers of students with reading problems should realize that the confidentiality of all reports and records of all students is protected under the law by the Buckley Amendment (1974). Students' records cannot be released without the consent of parents or legal guardian. Moreover, parents and students have the right of access to all records concerning their own case, or that of their child. This has important implications for how schools, teachers, and clinics go about collecting, recording, and storing information on students with reading disabilities. Privacy of audiotaped and videotaped, as well as written, records is guaranteed under the law.

SPECIAL EDUCATION LEGISLATION

Classroom and reading teachers play an increasingly active role in the evaluation and instruction of special education students. Teachers are often required to contribute to the diagnosis and instructional plan. Further, many handicapped students with reading problems are placed in the regular classroom for instruction, a policy known as *mainstreaming.* A survey of the placement of special education students showed that about 69 percent received instruction in the regular classroom (U.S. Department of Education, 1980).

The Field of Special Education

The field of special education evolved, historically, as a collection of categories of atypical children—children who deviated from the norm in some way: physically, developmentally, emotionally, or in the ability to learn. Categories of handicapped children included in the federal legislation of Public Law 94–142 are: deaf, deaf-blind, hard of hearing, mentally retarded, multi-handicapped, orthopedically impaired, other health impaired, seriously emotionally disturbed, specific learning disabled, speech impaired, and visually handicapped. In addition, the category of gifted and talented is usually included when considering exceptional students. (The federal definition of each category appears in Table 14.2, at the end of this chapter.)

Public Law 94–142

Landmark special education legislation was enacted with the passage of Public Law 94–142, entitled the Education for All Handicapped Children Act. Under this law all handicapped children and youth, ages three through twenty-one, have the right to a "free appropriate public education." Further, each state has a plan that is in compliance with the federal law. As a result, schools in every part of the nation are affected by this far-reaching legislation.

Public Law 94–142 is considered civil rights legislation, which guarantees education to the handicapped. This law has profoundly altered practices that had earlier led to neglect and substandard treatment of the handicapped. PL 94–142 is the result of what has been called the "quiet revolution," one hundred years of a slowly growing awareness and support of handicapped people (Abeson and Zettel, 1977). Several forces led to the passage of the law, including the dedicated and organized work of parents and special-interest groups that succeeded in getting lawmaking bodies to recognize the problem, a strong human rights movement with its demand for the protection of basic rights, and the support and backing of legislators.

As a result of the continued work of these forces, Congress maintained Public Law 94–142, as a separate categorical program in 1981, rather than placing it within a block grant with other social and educational programs (Council for Exceptional Children, 1981). In *categorical* programs, federal funds are allocated specifically to a program, and the program is regulated at the national level. In the *block* grant programs, the programs are clustered together and funds and decisions for budget allocations are placed in the hands of the individual states (Omnibus Budget Reconciliation Act of 1981). Public Law 94–142 retained its categorical status, with specific funds earmarked to support the special education program.

Important features of PL 94–142 are (1) nondiscriminatory testing, (2) the individualized education program (IEP), (3) the least restrictive environment, and (4) procedural safeguards. These features of the law are described briefly.

NONDISCRIMINATORY TESTING. Tests and procedures used for the evaluation and placement of handicapped students must be free of racial or cultural bias. Such materials or procedures are to be provided and administered in the student's native language, unless it is clearly not feasible to do so. Students cannot be evaluated or be placed on the basis of a single test.

THE INDIVIDUALIZED EDUCATION PROGRAM. The individualized education program (IEP) for each handicapped student is central to the implementation of PL 94–142. The IEP is actually a process involving several stages: (1) the referral of a student for evaluation, (2) the designation of an evaluation team, (3) the evaluation of the student by team members, (4) a meeting to analyze the evaluation information and make decisions about instruction and placement, (5) the development of a written plan, and (6) plans for review and reevaluation (Lerner, Dawson, and Horvath, 1980).

The written statement developed during the IEP process becomes the critical link between the handicapped student and the special education that the student requires. The student's teacher plays a critical role in both the development and the carrying out of the IEP plan. Further information on the content of the IEP and participants at the IEP meetings are presented in Chapter 15.

LEAST RESTRICTIVE ENVIRONMENT/MAINSTREAMING.   The "least restrictive environment" feature of the law requires that, to the maximum extent possible, handicapped children are to be educated with children who are not handicapped. The intent of this legislation is to give the handicapped student as much opportunity as possible to experience the mainstream of life with normal individuals. It is this part of the law that offers the basis for "mainstreaming" students in regular classrooms. Each IEP must contain plans for the time and ways of integrating the student into regular classroom activities. Of course, the nature and the severity of the handicapping condition will influence the kind and amount of integration that is appropriate.

In addition, schools must develop a "continuum of alternative placements," that is, an array of placement possibilities to meet the various needs of handicapped students.

Table 14.1 shows a continuum of alternative placements, ranked from the least restrictive to the most restrictive, in terms of being placed with nonhandicapped students. The least restrictive placement is the regular classroom. A more restrictive environment would be the resource room, in which the student would spend a portion of the day in the regular classroom. A still more restrictive environment would be a self-contained special education classroom, in which the student would have even less opportunity to be with nonhandicapped students. The most restrictive environment is homebound instruction.

The resource room where students come for educational services for a portion of the day on a regular basis and spend a portion of the day in the regular classroom is the suggested placement for many handicapped students who have reading problems. The resource room teacher should be a person who is trained in diagnosing and treating reading problems as well as in special education.

Table 14.1   Continuum of Alternative Placements

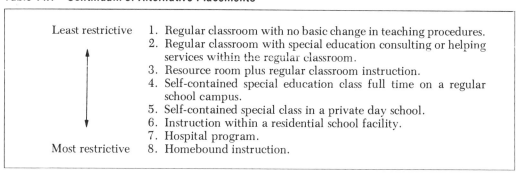

Least restrictive	1. Regular classroom with no basic change in teaching procedures.
	2. Regular classroom with special education consulting or helping services within the regular classroom.
	3. Resource room plus regular classroom instruction.
	4. Self-contained special education class full time on a regular school campus.
	5. Self-contained special class in a private day school.
	6. Instruction within a residential school facility.
	7. Hospital program.
Most restrictive	8. Homebound instruction.

PROCEDURAL SAFEGUARDS. PL 94–142 is designed to protect the rights of handicapped students and their parents in several ways.

1. Parents must consent in writing to having an evaluation for their child. The parents must also sign approval of the written IEP, the decisions and plans for instructing their child.
2. The assessment must be conducted in the student's native language and the findings reported to the parents in their native language.
3. The parents have the right of access to all educational information collected and used in decision making regarding their child.
4. Parents and students have the right to an impartial due process hearing if they are dissatisfied with the IEP decisions. The hearing is conducted by an impartial hearing officer appointed by the state. The parent can be accompanied and advised by an attorney or by individuals with special knowledge or training with respect to the problems of handicapped children. Further, the parent can appeal decisions made at this hearing to a higher hearing level. Action beyond this hearing would be a civil action lawsuit.
5. The confidentiality of all reports and records of all students is protected under the Buckley Amendment (1974). (See section on laws affecting reading.)

Mildly Handicapped Students and Reading Problems

Classroom and reading teachers are more likely to work with *mildly handicapped* students than with *severely handicapped* students. Mildly handicapped students are more prevelant, more likely to be placed in the regular classroom, and very likely to be in need of special reading help. The three categories of handicap that are sometimes clustered as mildly handicapped are (1) learning disabilities, (2) emotional disturbances, and (3) mild mental retardation. Students in these three categories often exhibit similar behaviors, and it is sometimes difficult to determine which is their primary problem (Hallahan and Kauffman, 1982). The term, *noncategorical* is also used to describe these students when they are grouped together. It should be noted that not all special educators advocate clustering students as mildly handicapped or noncategorical. Many schools see virtue in maintaining separate programs for each of the three categories.

Whether the students are classified as noncategorical or whether they retain their separate designation, it is these students who are most likely to have reading problems. Further, these students are likely to spend at least a portion of the day in the regular classroom. In fact, a recent survey indicated that 63 percent of the IEPs for such students showed that the academic area in which they needed most help was reading, along with oral or written language (U.S. Department of Education, 1980). The characteristics of students with these three exceptionalities are examined briefly in the next sections.

LEARNING DISABILITIES. About 3 percent of the school population is identified as learning disabled, as indicated by their IEPs. Learning-disabled students constitute a substantial portion of the handicapped population. Students with learning disabilities account for 32 percent of all handicapped students (U.S. Department of Education, 1980). As noted in Chapter 1, about 80 percent of the students receiving learning disabilities services have reading difficulties (Kirk and Elkins, 1975).

Defining learning disabilities has been difficult because of the heterogeneity, or the many types of problems, in the learning disabilities population. The federal definition of learning disabilities appears in Table 14.2. In addition, many states have developed their own definitions and criteria for identifying learning disabilities students. The major points in the federal definition are the following:

1. A severe discrepancy exists between the student's apparent potential ability for learning and the student's low level of achievement.
2. "Specific learning disabilities" means a disorder in one or more of the basic psychological processes. (Psychological processes generally refer to areas such as auditory processing, visual processing, language functions, and cognitive abilities.)
3. The problem is not primarily the result of visual, hearing, or motor handicaps; of mental retardation; of emotional disturbance; or of environmental, cultural, or economic disadvantage.
4. The learning disability exists in one or more of the following areas: oral expression, listening comprehension, written expression, basic reading skills, reading comprehension, mathematics calculation, or mathematics reasoning. (It is interesting to note that two of these areas pertain to reading.)

In addition, students with learning disabilities may exhibit other characteristics: symptoms of a central nervous system disorder, developmental imbalances (significant differences between strengths and weaknesses in abilities), hyperactivity and attention deficits disorders, poor motor development, and language delays and disorders (Lerner, 1981).

Another definition of learning disabilities has been proposed by the National Joint Committee on Learning Disabilities (an interdisciplinary group representing the organizations of the International Reading Association, Association for Children and Adults with Learning Disabilities, the Council for Learning Disabilities, the Division for Children with Communication Disorders, the Orton Dyslexia Society, and the American Speech and Hearing Association). The proposed definition is:

Learning disabilities is a generic term that refers to a heterogeneous group of disorders manifested by significant difficulties in the acquisition and use of listening, speaking, reading, writing, reasoning, or mathematical abilities. These disorders are intrinsic to the individual and presumed to be due to central nervous system dysfunction. Even though a learning disability may occur concomitantly with other handicapping conditions (e.g., sensory impairment, mental retardation, social and emotional disturbances) or environmental influences (e.g., cultural differences, insufficient or inappropriate instruction, psycholinguistic factors), it is not the direct result of those conditions influences. (National Joint Committee on Learning Disabilities, 1981).

A point that may be of interest to parents is that treatment for reading problems caused by a central nervous system dysfunction can be deducted as a medical expense on the parents' taxes. Tuition or tutoring fees paid on a physician's advice for a student who has severe learning or reading disabilities due to a physical problem is considered a medical expense (Internal Revenue Service, 1982).

EMOTIONAL DISTURBANCES.   As noted in Chapter 3, remedial readers often have accompanying emotional problems. However, when the emotional problem is so debilitating and severe that it is a primary problem and interferes with learning, it is viewed as a handicapping condition. It is easier to identify overt emotional problems, such as autism and schizophrenia, than the milder school-related handicaps.

In general, emotionally disturbed students are those who are troubled themselves and cause trouble for parents, brothers, sisters, teachers, and fellow students. They manifest behaviors that exceed the tolerance or understanding level of people with whom they are in contact, particularly in the school environment (Whelan, 1978). Some states, in their legislation, refer to the emotionally disturbed as *behavior disordered* or *socially maladjusted* students.

Kirk and Gallagher (1979) define a behavior disorder as a marked deviation from age-appropriate behavior that significantly interferes with the student's own development or the lives of others. The definition of emotionally disturbed students used in federal legislation includes one or more of the following characteristics evidenced to a marked extent over a long period of time (Bower, 1969):

1. An inability to learn that cannot be explained by intellectual, sensory, or health factors.
2. An inability to build or maintain satisfactory interpersonal relationships with peers and teachers.
3. Inappropriate types of behavior or feelings under normal conditions.
4. A general, pervasive mood of unhappiness or depression.
5. A tendency to develop physical symptoms, pains, or fears associated with personal or school problems.

A wide variety of deviant behaviors is exhibited by emotionally disturbed students. Their characteristics have been grouped by Quay (1972), who identified four clusters of behavior:

1. *Conduct disorders.* Disobedience, destructiveness, jealousy, and boisterousness.
2. *Personality disorders.* Feelings of inferiority, self-consciousness, social withdrawal, anxiety, depression, expressions of guilt and unhappiness.
3. *Immaturity.* Short attention span, clumsiness, passivity, daydreaming, preference for younger playmates, and other behavior characteristics of children lagging behind the agemates in social development.
4. *Socialized delinquency.* Being loyal to bad companions, being active in a delinquent group, stealing, and habitual truancy.

Because learning problems and emotional problems are so intertwined, it is often difficult to disentangle the emotional handicap from the learning disability. In practice, diagnosticians often disagree about which is the primary problem for an individual student. It is estimated that about 2 percent of the school population is emotionally disturbed; however, less than 1 percent was identified through the IEP evaluations (U.S. Department of Education, 1980). Probably many emotionally disturbed students are not recognized or they are identified as another category of special education.

EDUCABLE MENTAL RETARDATION.   There have been many attempts over the years to define mental retardation. As attitudes and needs of society and education have changed, so has the definition of mental retardation. The most recent definition of mental retardation is that proposed by the American Association on Mental Deficiency (AAMD).

> Mental retardation refers to significantly subaverage general intellectual functioning existing concurrently with deficits in adaptive behavior, and manifested during the developmental period. (Grossman, 1973, p. 11)

Kirk and Gallagher (1979, pp. 104–105) explain the three major parts of this definition of mental retardation as

> *Significantly subaverage intellectual functioning:* a score on a standard intelligence test that is lower than that obtained by 97–98 percent of the population.
> *Existing concurrently with deficits in adaptive behavior:* a lower level of independence and social responsibility than that expected of one's age and cultural group.
> *Manifested during the developmental period:* the problem is observable in childhood.

In the AAMD definition, there are four levels of mental retardation, in terms of the Wechsler Scales such as the *WISC-R* (Grossman, 1973):

TYPE OF MENTAL RETARDATION	INTELLIGENCE QUOTIENT RANGE
Mild mental retardation	55–69
Moderate mental retardation	40–54
Severe mental retardation	25–39
Profound mental retardation	24 and below

The level of mild mental retardation is often referred to as *educable mentally handicapped* (EMH). These students would be able to benefit from special reading instruction. In the earlier classification system of mental retardation (prior to 1973), the educable mentally retarded category included students with IQs from 70–80, or in some cases 84. Since this group is no longer designated as mentally retarded in the new classification system, these students are in the regular classroom, but are not identified as handicapped. Many of these students are in desperate need of special reading instruction.

Over 2 percent of the school population was identified as mentally retarded in their IEPs. This constitutes 22 percent of all handicapped children (U.S. Department of Education, 1980).

BILINGUAL LEGISLATION

Bilingual education is intended for students whose first language is not English. Legislation for bilingual education is a separate categorical program (Education Consolidation and Improvement Act, 1981). Thus, these monies are not distributed by block grants. There are a variety of different types of programs which have been supported under bilingual legislation, including separate classes with teachers who speak the native language of the students and resource room instruction where English is taught. Bilingual reading programs are described in more detail in Chapter 4.

MINIMAL COMPETENCY TESTING

A majority of states have passed legislation requiring schools to give minimum competency tests. Minimum competency refers to skills thought to be necessary for independent functioning in life, and usually those skills include reading skills. Students must pass the minimum competency tests to qualify for high school graduation. In some school systems, the tests are also used to promote students at certain grade levels. The minimum competency test movement has come about because of a demand for accountability by the state legislatures. The hope is that, by setting minimum standards, students will function at higher academic levels.

The minimum competency test movement brings up a number of serious questions for teachers of reading and very special concerns for the severely disabled reader. Among these questions are, Will teachers teach to the test, thereby invalidating the intent of the legislation? Will the test prevent poor readers from completing high school and receiving a diploma? Are there alternative ways in which to test the very poor reader and handicapped students? A final question concerns the legality of the minimum competency test. Will the courts find the test to be discriminatory and unconstitutional? The answers to the minimum competency issue are not in as yet, but it is a challenging subject for the reading teacher.

SUMMARY

Several federal and state laws affect the education of remedial and handicapped students.

Federal and state laws affect the remedial reading program. Under the Education Consolidation and Improvement Act of 1981, several sections support programs for reading. The Buckley Amendment regulates the privacy of student records.

There are also laws that affect children who receive special education services. Public Law 94–142, the Education of All Handicapped Children Act, requires that every handicapped child receive a free, appropriate public education, including special education and related services as needed. There are several important features of PL 94–142: nondiscriminatory testing, the least restrictive environment, the individualized education program, and procedural safeguards. (See Table 14.2 for the portion of PL 94–142 entitled "Definition of Handicapped Children.")

The term mildly handicapped is often used to cluster three categories of handicapped students: learning disabled, emotionally disturbed, and mentally retarded. When these problems are mild (as opposed to severe), common diagnostic methods and treatment methods are used. Students sometimes have several of these problems, and it is difficult to determine which of them is the primary one.

Bilingual legislation provides educational programs for students whose native language is not English.

Minimum competency testing is legislated by a majority of the states, and students must pass a minimum competency test before graduation from high school. These laws have many implications for the very poor reader.

Table 14.2   Definition of Handicapped Children, Public Law 94–142

Deaf.   Hearing impairment that is so severe that the child is impaired in processing linguistic information through hearing, without amplification, which adversely affects educational performance.

Deaf-blind.   Concomitant hearing and visual impairments, the combination of which causes such severe communication and other developmental and educational problems that they cannot be accommodated in special education programs solely for deaf or blind children.

Hard of Hearing.   A hearing impairment, whether permanent or fluctuating, that adversely affects a child's educational performance but is not included under the definition of "deaf."

Mentally Retarded.   Significantly subaverage general intellectual functioning existing concurrently with deficits in adaptive behavior and manifested during the developmental period, which adversely affects a child's educational performance.

Multihandicapped.   Concomitant impairments (such as mentally retarded-blind, mentally retarded-orthopedically impaired, etc.), the combination of which causes such severe educational problems that they cannot be accommodated in special education programs solely for one of the impairments. The term does not include "deaf-blind" children.

Orthopedically Impaired.   A severe orthopedic impairment that adversely affects a child's educational performance. The term includes impairments caused by a congenital anomaly (e.g., poliomyelitis, bone tuberculosis) and impairments from other causes (e.g., cerebral palsy, amputations, and fractures or burns that cause contractures).

Other Health Impaired. Limited strength, vitality, or alertness due to chronic or acute health problems such as heart condition, tuberculosis, rheumatic fever, nephritis, asthma, sickle cell anemia, hemophilia, epilepsy, lead poisoning, leukemia, or diabetes, which adversely affect a child's educational performance.

Seriously Emotionally Disturbed. A condition exhibiting one or more of the following characteristics over a long period of time and to a marked degree, which adversely affects educational performance: (1) an inability to learn that cannot be explained by intellectual, sensory, or health factors; (2) an inability to build or maintain satisfactory interpersonal relationships with peers and teachers; (3) inappropriate types of behavior or feelings under normal circumstances; (4) a general pervasive mood of unhappiness or depression; or (5) a tendency to develop physical symptoms or fears associated with personal or school problems.

The term includes children who are schizophrenic or autistic. The term does not include children who are socially maladjusted, unless it is determined that they are seriously emotionally disturbed.

Specific Learning Disability. A disorder in one or more of the basic psychological processes involved in understanding or in using language, spoken or written, that may manifest itself in an imperfect ability to listen, think, speak, read, write, spell, or do mathematical calculations.

The term includes such conditions as perceptual handicaps, brain injury, minimal brain dysfunction, dyslexia, and developmental aphasia. The term does not include learning problems that are primarily the result of visual, hearing, or motor handicaps; of mental retardation; or of environmental, cultural, or economic disadvantage.

A special set of regulations is set forth for learning disabilities in Public Law 94–142, including criteria for determining the existence of a specific learning disability. The evaluation may determine that a child has a specific learning disability if

    a. the child does not achieve commensurate with his or her age and ability levels in one or more of seven areas when provided with learning experiences appropriate for the child's age and ability levels;

    b. the team finds that a child has a severe discrepancy between achievement and intellectual ability in one or more of the following areas: oral expression, listening comprehension, written expression, basic reading skill, reading comprehension, mathematics calculation, mathematics reasoning.

Speech Impaired. A communication disorder, such as stuttering, impaired articulation, a language impairment, or a voice impairment, that adversely affects a child's educational performance.

Visually Handicapped. A visual impairment that, even with correction, adversely affects a child's educational performance. The term includes both partially seeing and blind children.

Gifted and Talented (part of PL 89–313, block grant of Title II, but not included in PL 94–142). Students who give evidence of high-performance capability in areas such as intellectual, creative, artistic, leadership capacity, or specific academic fields and who require services or activities not ordinarily provided by the school to develop such abilities fully.

15

REPORTS
AND RECORDS

Keeping records and preparing reports are essential ingredients of the remedial reading program. Although they may seem burdensome at times, accurate reports and records are vital to a good educational program. Regardless of the setting (regular classroom, special education resource room, or reading class or clinic), these reports and records assist teachers in establishing programs, in monitoring progress, and in communicating with others.

The topics described in this chapter are (1) the purposes of reports and records, (2) guidelines for writing reports, (3) diagnostic reports in remedial reading, (4) progress and final reports in remedial reading, (5) special education records and reports, including the IEP reports mandated under Public Law 94–142, and (6) record keeping.

PURPOSES FOR REPORTING AND RECORD KEEPING

Reports and records are needed to clarify information, to assist teachers, and to inform and help others working with the student. Specific purposes include the following.

1. *To measure progress.* When written records and reports are kept of the student's performance, they can be used to measure progress. A review of the record allows the teacher to specify (a) a baseline, or entry, level for the student's skills and (b) the progress that has been made during the time of instruction. In this way, instructional gains can be monitored easily.

2. *To record behavior and events.* Memory cannot supplant a written account. A specific incident and all its details may be clear in the mind of the teacher at the time of an episode, but without written notes, many of the important details are forgotten or overlooked a week or two later. Recording the information in a record book or report enables complex events to be recalled accurately.

3. *To communicate information.* When several professionals (reading teacher, social worker, classroom teacher) are working with the same student, it is necessary for all to have access to records and reports to share information. These written records help professionals to coordinate efforts in meeting instructional goals. Reports also serve to communicate information to parents or legal guardians.

4. *To assure continuous and consistent teaching.* Changes in the school staff and in their instructional responsibilities often occur without opportunities for personal communication. Accurate records can help to maintain a consistent instructional environment.

5. *To meet legal requirements.* Federal and state special education legislation, as discussed in Chapter 14, requires that certain records and reports be initiated and kept. Of special concern are the requirements mandated for the IEP, as specified in Public Law 94–142.

GUIDELINES FOR WRITING REPORTS

Several principles of report writing should be helpful as a guide for teachers.

1. *Use only material that is relevant to the case.* Sometimes information is gathered during the diagnostic process that is not appropriate for inclusion in formal reporting. Often a very thorough diagnosis will uncover a wealth of information, but some of that information is not pertinent to either the diagnosis or the treatment of the reading problem. For example, the clinician, noting Mary's obesity, may suspect that her overweight condition is caused by emotional frustration stemming from her academic failures. However, if this hunch cannot be substantiated with evidence, it should not be mentioned in the formal report.

2. *State information objectively.* Subjective and speculative evaluations, impressions, or guesses are out of place in a professional report. The report should be limited to substantiated, objective facts. For example, Lenore's tutor substantiated the fact that she was resistant to tutoring by reporting incidents where Lenore refused to read and two incidents where objects were thrown at the tutor.

3. *Avoid the first-person pronoun in formal reports.* Many professionals recommend that phrases such as *the diagnostician observed* or *the evaluator noted* be used rather than *I believe* or *my observation*. Words such as *I, my, mine,* and *me* should be avoided.

4. *Keep language simple and define technical terms.* Because a report is read by a variety of both professionals and nonprofessionals (including parents), the report should be written in a style that is easily understood. Technical terms should be defined carefully. Parents or paraprofessionals are often overwhelmed by such terms as "word recognition skills" or "6.2 grade reading level." These terms should be clarified. Either specify the meaning of a technical term or substitute nontechnical words that indicate the intended meaning. The report writer should try to identify with the parent who is asked to read the report.

DIAGNOSTIC REPORTING
IN REMEDIAL READING

In a diagnostic report, information from tests, the case history, cumulative records, observations, interviews and other sources are integrated into a coherent whole. The key function of the diagnostic report is to provide information to help plan the instructional program. The diagnostic report should suggest goals for the student's reading instruction and methods and materials for accomplishing these goals. In addition, the diagnostic report clarifies the patterns (such as correlated factors) associated with the student's problem. Finally, the report may recommend appropriate referrals outside of reading instruction (e.g., a physical examination).

The depth and thoroughness of the diagnostic report is related to the severity of the problem. As noted in Chapter 2, there are three levels of diagnosis: the survey level, the specific level, and the intensive level. Recommendations for report writing on each of these levels are the following.

The Survey Report

The survey report is used (1) to identify the needs of students with relatively minor reading problems and (2) to identify students who are in need of more intensive reading diagnosis. A survey diagnosis typically uses assessment instruments that can be administered in groups. As with the survey diagnosis, the survey report is relatively brief.

Very often the survey diagnosis is compiled in an informal manner by the classroom teacher and does not require a written report. When a written report is supplied, it can be read by the parent, remedial and special education teachers, or a member of the school administration, such as the school principal. Although there are, of course, variations in format, the survey report generally contains sections on

1. Data identifying the student (name, age, etc.)
2. Reading achievement—reading strengths and weaknesses
3. Further observations

The Specific Report

The diagnostic report at the specific level is generally written by the reading teacher. It is usually gathered in the reading clinic or in an individual diagnostic setting. Problems treated are likely to be somewhat more complex than are those at the survey level. This type of diagnosis gathers specific information about reading strengths and weaknesses and a determination of whether or not a reading disability exists. It also includes recommendations for instruction.

The diagnostic report at the specific level is somewhat longer than the survey report, reflecting a more in-depth diagnosis. It is written to be read by parents and educational professionals, in and outside the school setting. This report is geared toward planning for specific small-group instruction. The following information is usually included in the specific report:

1. Identifying data
2. Current reading capacity (or expected reading level)
3. Current reading achievement level
4. Reading strengths and weaknesses
5. Further observations
6. Instructional recommendations

The Intensive Report

The intensive-level diagnostic report is reserved for the most severe reading problems. It extends the specific diagnosis in several ways. First, it includes a relatively complete report of the student, taken from interviews with the parents and perhaps the student (see Chapter 3). This section details the physical history, family history, and characteristics of the ecological and emotional situations. Second, the intensive diagnosis extends the diagnostic procedure into tests of physical functioning, skills prerequisite to reading, and inquiry into the factors that may be correlated with the reading disability. As such, information collected by many professionals may be included in the report. Third, the intensive diagnosis is very detailed in the analysis of reading strengths and weaknesses.

To facilitate accurate record keeping, a diagnostic summary form is often used, as shown in Table 15.1. This summary is meant for the teacher's personal use and is used to gather information from different sources and placed in a central file. The summarized information can then be used to construct the report.

Table 15.1   Sample Diagnostic Summary

Diagnostician: _____   Date of Report: _____

Name: _____   Birthdate: _____   Age: _____

School: _____   Grade: _____   Sex: _____

Parents' Names: _____

Address: _____   Telephone Number: _____

Period of Testing: _____

   I.   Factors Associated with Disability
      A.   Ecological and emotional
          1.   Summary of parent interview and home factors: _____

                _____

                _____

          2.   School history and behavior: _____

                _____

          3.   Social and emotional history and behavior: _____

                _____

          4.   Interest inventory: _____

                _____

          5.   Sentence completion: _____

                _____

6. Test and observations

   Date: _____ Test/Observation: _____

   Result: _____

   _____

   _____

B. Physical Factors
   1. General health history: _____

   _____

   2. Visual acuity

      a. Wears glasses: ____ ____ _____ _____
                        yes   no   how long?   problem

      b. Last eye examination: _____
                                                              date

      c. Visual Screening test results _____

      _____

   3. Auditory acuity

      a. Last hearing test: _____ _____
                            date   results

      b. Audiometer results: _____

      _____

C. Language factors
   1. Language history: _____

   _____

   2. Tests and observations

      Date: _____ Test/Observation: _____ Result: _____

      _____

      _____

D. Previous diagnostic consultations

Name and title of professional: _____

Date: _____ Address: _____

Results: _____

_____

Name and title of professional: _____

Date: _____ Address: _____

Results: _____

_____

_____

II. Reading Achivement

A. Informal Reading Inventory

Name of inventory: _____ Date: _____

Independent level: _____

Instructional level: _____

Frustration level: _____

Listening level: _____

Comments and analysis of reading patterns: _____

_____

B. Reading achievement tests

Test	Level	Form	Date	Results

(Comments)

_____

_____

C. Diagnostic batteries and skills tests

Test	Level	Form	Date	Results

(Comments)

_____

_____

III. Learning Potential

A. IQ and other formal measures

Name of Test	Date	Results

B. Informal observations: _____

_____

C. Reading potential:

CA ____ MA ____ Reading expectancy age: _____

Reading achievement level: _____

Difference of expectancy and achievement: _____

Practical considerations: _____

_____

Is student a disabled reader? _____

_____

IV. Prerequisite skills

A. Visual and visual-motor

Test	Level	Form	Date	Results

Informal observations: _____

B. Auditory

Test	Level	Form	Date	Results

Informal observations: _____

C. Other

Test	Level	Form	Date	Results

Informal observations: _____

V. Observations of Behavior During Testing: _____

Although the intensive diagnostic report is prepared for the use of the parents and school, it is also likely to be used by noneducational professionals such as physicians and social workers. Therefore, accurate and professional presentation of data is extremely important.

The complete intensive diagnostic report usually contains several sections. However, depending on the case, not all sections need be included for all students. Sections include:

1. *Identifying data.* This includes the student's name, birthdate, parents' names, address and telephone number, grade placement, classroom, and teacher.
2. *Instruments used.* Because the diagnostic report may involve several tests, it is

useful to list these in one section. Test levels, forms, and dates of administration should be included. Often report writers include the scores attained in this section. For certain tests (such as intelligence tests), broad ranges rather than specific scores are generally reported.

3. *Current reading capacity (or expected reading level).*   The purpose of this section is to assess whether or not a student is reading below the level expected. When intelligence tests are used to determine current reading capacity or potential, results are given (usually reported in ranges), and the results of reading expectancy formulas are given. When practical considerations of reading expectancy are used, they are also included in this section. For example, a student's performance might be compared with the reading achievement of classmates. Chapter 4 details procedures for determining expectancy.

4. *Current reading achievement level.*   The student's reading achievement level is given in this section. Most achievement tests are divided into subtests that allow some comparison of reading ability. For example, performance on word recognition and comprehension subtests can be compared. Information given in this section may also include the results of the informal reading inventory and the grade placement of the classroom work that the student is doing.

5. *Analysis of reading strengths and weaknesses.*   In this section, the reading performance is described in detail. Test scores and an analysis of their meaning are included, as well as information gained through observation. Since several tests may be used to assess one type of skill, it is helpful to organize this section around different areas of reading.
   a. Oral reading skills
   b. Word recognition skills (sight words, phonics, context clues, structural analysis)
   c. Reading comprehension abilities
   d. Vocabulary level
   e. Study strategies
   f. Reading rate
   Only a few of the areas listed would be relevant to any reader.

6. *Analysis of prerequisite abilities underlying reading.*   The teacher may choose to assess prerequisite abilities, such as psychological processing (or readiness) skills, learning styles, or ability to pay attention. Interpretations of such tests should be included in this section.

7. *Factors associated with reading performance.*   In this section, factors that may have contributed to reading problems are summarized. These include ecological, emotional, physical, intellectual, and language factors as well as others. Evidence is collected from the interview, reports of classroom behavior, observation of the student, school records, and the reports of other professionals. Although the weight of evidence may suggest that one particular factor has caused a reading disability, the report writer should avoid absolute statements. Rather than saying "The visual problem is the cause of the reading disability," a more appropriate statement would be "The low score on the nearpoint visual acuity screening test suggests that visual problems may be a factor contributing to reading disability."

8. *Recommendations for referral.*   These should include all nonreading recommendations, such as referral to a pediatric neurologist, a social worker, or a speech-language pathologist.

9. *Recommendations for instruction.*   This section states whether, in the report writer's judgment, the student should receive further help in reading and suggests

the setting for the instruction. In addition, the examiner recommends initial instructional goals for the student and suggests methods and materials for accomplishing these goals.

10. *Recommendations for parents and classroom teachers.*   This section includes ways in which the student's instruction in the regular classroom can be adjusted. In addition, suggestions for the parents to help their child progress in reading are made.

Appendix C presents a sample diagnostic report.

PROGRESS AND FINAL REPORTING
IN REMEDIAL READING

Progress Reports

After a student is admitted to a remedial reading program, continuous progress records should be kept and progress should be reported to the student's classroom teachers, to the parents, and (depending on the age of the student) to the student. The report may be written or oral (as in the case of a parent conference).

The purpose of a progress report is to give information about the progress that has been made during a given instructional period. The format, content, and frequency of progress reports varies from one setting and situation to another. For example, a report for an individualized education program for students in special education placements must be developed on a regular basis, at least annually.

The progress report provides information on the growth that has taken place and also given the opportunity to reevaluate the initial diagnosis and teaching plan. If improvement has not taken place, then a change in teaching methods or materials may be considered.

Progress reports may be done in a narrative or a checklist form. A narrative progress report is most appropriate for a reading clinic and is usually written by a remedial reading teacher. The briefer checklist report is used often by a classroom teacher or a corrective reading teacher.

THE NARRATIVE PROGRESS REPORT.   A narrative progress report uses a prose format to relate the growth that has taken place. The sample clinical progress report illustrated in Table 15.2 contains basic informational data, the initial and present instructional levels, and seven areas of narrative description. It includes instructional goals, the methods and materials used for instruction, the progress that has been made, the student's attitude, goals for further instruction, recommendations for further instructional materials and methods, and overall prognosis for reading improvement.

THE CHECKLIST PROGRESS REPORT.   The briefer type of report contains information on the progress made in skill and achievement areas, special needs as revealed during the instructional process, comments on the student's attitudes and behaviors, and recommendations for further instruction. Since some teachers may

Table 15.2 Clinical Progress Report (narrative progress report)

Please Check:

1. Student's Name: _____ ____Semester Report

   Date: _____Grade: _____ ____Change of Instructor

   Clinician: _____ CA ____ MA ____ IQ ____

   Present Instructional Level: _____ Original Level: _____

2. Needs as of diagnosis or last report:

3. Materials and method used:

   Comments on use of materials and/or effectiveness of method:

4. Progress made: (including test scores)

5. Attitude toward instruction:

6. Special needs:

7. Recommendations:

8. Additional comments and prognosis:

Directions: Each of these four columns represents one working period. At the top, the student's current reading level should be recorded. Then, if a skill area has shown improvement, a check should be put in the area. Short comments may be made about each skill. This chart enables progress to be recorded over a longer period of time.

Remedial Reading Progress Report

Name: _____ Age: _____ Grade: _____ Teacher: _____

Code: _____ Skill Improved   Date Accepted in Program: _____ Initial Instructional Level: _____

Skill	Marking Periods			
	Date: _____ Reading Level: ___	Date: _____ Reading Level: ___	Date: _____ Reading Level: ___	Date: _____ Reading Level: ___
	Comments	Comments	Comments	Comments
I. Prerequisite Skills				
Auditory				
Visual/motor				
Language				
Other				
II. Word Recognition				
Sight vocabulary				
Phonics				
Consonants				
Consonant digraphs				
Consonant blends				
Long and short vowels				
Vowel controllers				
Silent letters				
C and G sounds				
Syllabication				
Structural Analysis				
Compound words				
Contractions				
Suffixes				
Roots/prefixes				
Use of context clues				
Other				
III. Comprehension				
Literal				
Organizational				
Inference				
Critical reading				
Other				
IV. Vocabulary Knowledge				
V. Study Skills				
VI. Reading Rate				
VII. Oral Reading Fluency				
VIII. Silent Reading Habits				
IX. Other				
Additional Comments				

(This student may be deficient in many other skills. Those checked are of prime importance and were worked on first.)

	1	2	3	4
Teacher				
Principal				

(Initial)

Figure 15.1 Checklist Progress Report

be instructing a large number of students, the writing of narrative reports for each student can become overly burdensome. Yet appraisals are necessary, particularly before a grading period. The checklist report assists in grading students and in making comments on report cards. Figure 15.1 illustrates a checklist progress report that is easy to complete yet contains required information.

Final Reports

A final report differs from a progress report in that it is issued at the termination of instruction. No further remedial work is required because the student is functioning adequately or because the student will no longer be attending remedial sessions. The report is usually sent to the parents and to other professionals who interacted with the student during the course of remedial treatment.

The format for the final report includes the following.

1. Identifying information, which in addition to other information, includes the dates of the first and last contacts and total number of sessions held.
2. The goals and methods of instruction, including (a) the student's needs upon entry to the program, (b) reading goals of the program and methods and materials used to accomplish them, and (c) nonreading goals and methods for accomplishing them (e.g., increasing confidence, increasing attention span).
3. Conclusions and recommendations, which include (a) present reading levels, usually based on posttests, (b) a listing of skills or areas still requiring attention, and (c) suggestions for corrective or developmental classroom methods and materials.

If the student has not been released from remediation but, for one reason or another, is terminating instruction, then the final section should detail present reading strengths and weaknesses and needs for further remediation.

SPECIAL EDUCATION RECORDS AND REPORTS

A very specific format of the diagnostic report is required for all handicapped children being served under Public Law 94–142. If a student is being evaluated for a possible handicapping condition (see Chapter 14), then under the law, a special education assessment is mandatory and the individualized education program requirements must be included. Teachers should also investigate the state and local regulations concerning the IEP procedures required for handicapped students as well as those rules and regulations in federal law.

The Individualized Education Program (IEP)

The individualized education program is a written statement for a handicapped student that is developed and implemented according to certain provisions of the law. It is a tool designed to assure that all handicapped children receive a free, appropriate public education, along with a variety of accompanying rights.

The IEP is developed at a meeting with a representative of the school, the teacher, the parent(s), and the student (when appropriate). The written statement on each student includes documentation of decisions reached about objectives, content, implementation, and evaluation of the student's educational program.

The term "individualized education program" itself is worthy of examination because it signifies certain essential intentions. "Individualized" means that the program is designed to meet the needs of a single student rather than a group or class. "Education" means that the program is limited to elements that are concerned specifically with education, special education, and related services in contrast to medical or other noneducational elements. "Program" means that there will be a statement of what will actually be provided for that individual student as distinct from a general curriculum plan that provides guidelines from which subsequently a program must be developed (Torres, 1977).

The purpose of the individualized education program is not to plan for the total instruction of the handicapped student. It merely sets forth in writing a commitment of resources to meet the student's needs. It is also a management tool to allow parents, teachers, and administrators to know what educational services have been allocated. Therefore, it is necessary for teachers to develop instructional plans (such as lesson plans) beyond what is included in the IEP (Hayes and Higgins, 1978).

Components of the IEP

The following components must be included in each individualized education program:

1. *A statement of the child's present levels of educational performance.* This component of the individualized education program refers to the student's level of functioning. In addition to reading, these levels might refer to other academic areas, vocational or prevocational skills, or self-help skills. The level of present performance could be expressed in norm-referenced terms (reading achievement of grade level 3.6) or in criterion-referenced terms (knows thirty-five sight words).

2. *A statement of annual goals, including short-term instructional goals.* This component provides for both an annual goal and measurable intermediate steps to meet this annual goal. The short-term objectives may be viewed as milestone steps between the student's present level and the anticipated annual goal.

3. *A statement of the specific education and related services to be provided to the child, and the extent to which the child will be able to participate in regular educational programs.* This component refers to the system of educational services and placement. The plan must designate how much time the student will spend with nonhandicapped students. It also indicates what related services are needed by the student (e.g., speech therapy, physical education). It is designed to assure that the "least restrictive environment" feature of the law is considered.

The team must decide how much integration into mainstream education is feasible and beneficial for the student. Some students will be able to receive services in the regular classroom; some will need services in a special education setting such as a resource room for part of the day; and still others who have more severe problems will require services in a self-contained special education setting for most of the day.

4. *The projected date for initiation of services and the anticipated duration of the services.*   The purpose of this component is to assure that treatment begins promptly. Therefore, the date for starting treatment must be included in the IEP. The length of time or duration of treatment also must be estimated.

5. *Appropriate objective criteria and evaluation procedures and schedules for determining, on at least an annual basis, whether the short-term instructional objectives are being achieved.*   This component of the law provides for follow-up and assures that the IEP and the student's progress will be reviewed at least annually. Thus, this component of the law mandates progress reports.

Participants at IEP Meetings

Public Law 94–142 is very clear in stating that there must be a team meeting to develop the individualized education program and in designating who should participate in that IEP meeting. The team should include

1. *A representative of the school* (someone other than the child's teacher, who is qualified to provide or supervise the provision of special education).   This representative could be the principal, the special education director, the director of the learning disabilities program, director of the reading program, or others with supervisory authority.
2. *The child's teacher.*   This could be the classroom teacher or the special education teacher of a self-contained room. It refers to the teacher of the child's current placement.
3. *One or both of the child's parents.*   Every effort must be made to have the parents in attendance. If the student has no parents, a surrogate parent must be appointed by the legal authority of the courts.
4. *The child, where appropriate.*   If the student is an adolescent, it might be appropriate to include the student in the planning meeting.
5. *Other individuals, at the discretion of the parent or the school.*   Other persons can be brought into the meeting by either the parent or the school. This could include individuals such as reading teachers, psychologists, speech-language pathologists, special education teachers, physical education teachers, nurses, physicians, child advocates, attorneys, private diagnosticians, and therapists. This is a long list of potential participants; however, care should be taken to keep the team small enough to be efficient and not overwhelm the parents.

There is no one specific form recommended for the IEP. Most states and school districts have developed their own IEP forms, although the contents must, of course, comply with the federal regulations. Teachers should be familiar with the forms used in their own schools. Table 15.3 illustrates a sample IEP form.

Table 15.3 Individualized Education Program (IEP)

IDENTIFICATION INFORMATION

Student Name: _____

Birthdate: _____/ _____/ _____   Age: _____   Sex: _____   Grade: _____

Parents(s) Names:_____

Address:_____   Telephone: _____

Language or Mode of Communication of the Home: _____   Of the child: _____

School District of Residence:_____

School Child Would Normally Attend:_____

Exceptional Characteristic(s) Determined: _____

Dates

Date of Referral: __/ __/ __

Date Case Study Evaluation Completed: __/ __/ __

Date of Multidisciplinary Conference: __/ __/ __

Date of Initial IEP Meeting: __/ __/ __

Anticipated Date of Annual Review: __/ __/ __   (at least annually)

Anticipated Date of Reevaluation: __/ __/ __   (every three years)

PARTICIPANTS IN THE IEP MEETING

Parent(s): _____   _____
            Print Name   Signature

           _____   _____
            Print Name   Signature

Representative of the Local
District of Residence: _____ _____ _____
                        Print Name   Signature   Position

Teacher(s): _____ _____ _____
             Print Name   Signature   Grade or Subject

            _____ _____ _____
             Print Name   Signature   Grade or Subject

Member of the
Evaulation Team: _____ _____ _____
                     Print Name   Signature   Position

Child (where appropriate): _____
                                Print Name

Other: _____ _____ _____
            Print Name   Signature   Position

       _____ _____ _____
            Print Name   Signature   Position

OBJECTIVE CRITERIA, EVALUATION PROCEDURES AND SCHEDULES FOR
DETERMINING WHETHER THE SHORT-TERM OBJECTIVES HAVE BEEN
ACHIEVED

Short-Term Objectives	*Criteria*	*Evaluation Procedures*	*Schedules* (if more frequent than annually)

PRESENT LEVELS OF EDUCATIONAL PERFORMANCE

ANNUAL GOALS

SPECIAL EDUCATION AND RELATED SERVICES

Special Education Instructional Program	*Date of Initiation* (beginning)	*Anticipated Duration* (ending)

Vocational Education (when appropriate)
      ____ regular   ____ specially designed

Physical Education ____ regular   ____ adapted
Related Services

Special Transportion

EXTENT OF PARTICIPATION IN REGULAR EDUCATION

Subjects and/or Activities   *Extent of Participation* (describe)

From *The Illinois Primer on Individualized Education Programs* (Springfield, Ill.: Illinois Office of Education, Department of Specialized Educational Services and Illinois Regional Resource Center, June 1979), pp. A1–A3.

RECORD KEEPING

In addition to writing reports, it is also important to keep records of student progress. Records assist the teacher in analyzing student problems accurately, planning ongoing instruction, making referrals, and writing reports. Types of records include attendance records, records of outside contacts, lesson plans, and anecdotal records.

Attendance Records

When formal records of attendance and tardiness are kept, the student is encouraged to come to class and the teacher has a valuable source of data to use in making decisions about continuing the instruction. Some teachers keep attendance charts that are displayed for students.

Records of Outside Contacts

It is valuable to keep a record of contacts that have been made with parents, other school personnel, or outside professionals. The recorded contacts may consist of phone calls, letters, conferences, or visits.

Lesson Plans

Perhaps the most detailed type of record is the plan that is developed for each lesson. Lesson plans generally consist of four parts:

1. *The objective.* This identifies the goals that the teacher is attempting to reach. These objectives are often stated in specific terms. An example might be, "To decode ten 'short a' words."
2. *The material.* The materials used might include the names and levels of readers, stories, workbooks, games, and teacher-made materials.
3. *The procedures.* The teaching steps used in the instruction are described in this section.
4. *Evaluation.* After the completion of the lesson, the student's performance and observational notes are recorded.

Less detailed instructional plans can also be used. Table 15.4 shows a lesson plan format abbreviated into a chart form. When keeping instructional records of this type, it is often helpful to record the overall goals of instruction for a semester on a separate sheet of paper.

Anecdotal Records

The anecdotal record provides evidence of behavior, reactions, and feelings. Such records document reactions to different people and instructional situations. Often, a situation arises in which a student reacts particularly positively, but the exact circumstances may be forgotten unless the incident is recorded. There are various ways in which to record anecdotal records. Some teachers prefer to write a

Table 15.4 Chart Lesson Plan Format

		INSTRUC- TIONAL		
	FOCUSED			
DATE	INSTRUCTION	READING	REVIEW	COMMENTS

Long-Term Objectives: 1. _____

2. _____

3. _____

4. _____

Topic 1 _____

Topic 2 _____

Topic 1 _____

Topic 2 _____

Topic 1 _____

Topic 2 _____

Topic 1 _____

Topic 2 _____

statement at each lesson. Others maintain a card file, with one card for each student. When something noteworthy happens, it is dated and recorded on that student's card.

SUMMARY

There are several purposes for keeping records and reports, including measuring progress, recording behavior and events, communicating information to others, assuring continuous and consistent teaching, and fulfilling legal requirements.

Guidelines for writing reports are (1) material should be relevant, (2) information should be objective, (3) first-person pronouns should be avoided, and (4) sentences and technical terms should be presented in an understandable way.

There are three levels of reports: the survey report, the specific report, and the intensive report. The survey report is used for relatively mild cases and for screening; the report is short. The specific report is used for more severe cases; it is detailed, somewhat longer, and designed for small-group instruction. The intensive report is for the most serious cases and provides in-depth information in many areas related to reading achievement.

Progress reports are written during the course of reading instruction. Either narrative progress reports or checklist reports can be used. Final reports are written when a student leaves the remedial program.

The individualized education program is a very specific type of diagnostic report, which is required for students who are being evaluated for special education. The components of the IEP include present levels of performance, annual goals and short-term objectives, educational services needed by the student, date for initiation of services, and criteria for review and evaluation.

Participants at the IEP meeting include a representative of the school, the teacher, the parents, the student (if appropriate), and other individuals at the discretion of the parent or school.

Types of records kept generally for remedial instruction include attendance records, records of outside contacts, lesson plans, and anecdotal records.

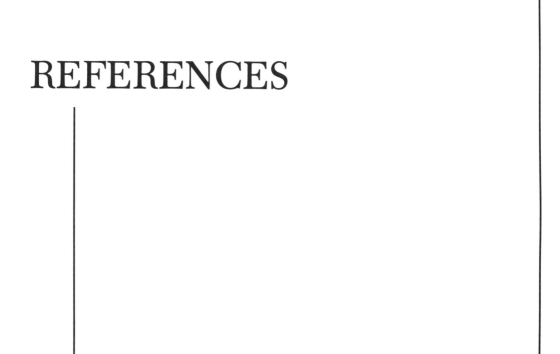

REFERENCES

AARON, P. G.   Dyslexia, an imbalance in cerebral information processing strategies. *Perceptual and Motor Skills*, 1978, *47*, 699–706.

ABESON, A, and ZETTEL, J.   The end of the quiet revolution: The education for all handicapped children act of 1975. *Exceptional Children*, 1977, *40*, 114–130.

ABIKOFF, H.   Cognitive training interventions in children: Review of a new approach. *Journal of Learning Disabilities*, 1979, *12*, 123–135.

ABRAMS, J. C., and KASLOW, F.   Family systems and the learning disabled child: Intervention and treatment. *Journal of Learning Disabilities*, 1977, *10*, 86–90.

ALBERT, M. L., YAMADORI, A., GARDNER, H., and HOWES, D.   Comprehension in alexia. *Brain*, 1973, *96*, 317–328.

ALPERT, H., and KRAVITZ, A.   *Individual reading evaluation.* Jericho, N.Y.: New Dimensions in Education, 1970.

ALLEY, G., and DESHLER, P.   *Teaching the learning disabled adolescent.* Denver: Love Publishing, 1979.

ALLINGTON, E. L.   Are good and poor readers taught differently? Is that why poor readers are poor readers? Paper presented at the annual meeting of the American Educational Research Association, Toronto, March 1978.

AMES, W. S.   The development of a classification scheme of contextual aids in reading. *Reading Research Quarterly*, 1966, *2*, 57–82.

ANASTASI, A.   *Psychological testing.* New York: Macmillan, 1976.

ANDERSON, R. C., REYNOLDS, R. E., SCHALLERT, D. C., and GOETZ, E. T. Frameworks for comprehending discourse. *American Educational Research Journal*, 1977, *14*, 361–381.

ANDERSON, R. C., and FREEBODY, P. Vocabulary Knowledge. In J. T. Guthrie (Ed.), *Comprehension and teaching: Research views*. Newark, Del. International Reading Association, 1981.

ARTER, J. A., and JENKINS, J. R. Differential diagnosis—prescriptive teaching: a critical appraisal. *Review of educational research*, 1979, *49*, 517–556.

ASHER, S. R. *Sex differences in reading achievement*. Reading Education Report No. 2. Champaign, Ill: Center for the Study of Reading, University of Illinois, October, 1977.

ASHTON WARNER, S. *Teacher*. New York: Simon and Schuster, 1963.

AULLS, M. W. *Developing readers in today's elementary school*. Boston: Allyn & Bacon, 1982.

AULLS, M. W., and GELBART, F. Effects of method of instruction and ability on literal comprehension of short stories. *Research in the teaching of English*, 1980, *14*, 51–59.

AUSUBEL, D. P. The use of advance organizers in the learning and retention of meaningful verbal material. *Journal of Educational Psychology*, 1960, *51*, 267–272.

BAILEY, M. H. The utility of phonics generalizations in grades 1 through 6. *The Reading Teacher*, 1967, *20*, 252–258.

BALOW, B. The long-term effect of remedial reading instruction. *The Reading Teacher*, 1965, *18*, 581–586.

——. Perceptual-motor activities in the treatment of severe reading disability. *The Reading Teacher*, 1971, *24*, 513–542.

BANAS, N. and WILLS, I. H. The vulnerable child: Prescriptive teaching from the DLTA. *Academic Therapy*, 1979, *14*, 363–368.

BARBE, W. B. Interest and the teaching of reading. *Education*, 1963, *83*, 486.

BARR, R. C. The influence of instructional conditions on word recognition errors. *Reading Research Quarterly*, 1972, *7*, 509–529.

——. The effect of instruction on pupil reading strategies. *Reading Research Quarterly*, 1974–1975, *10*, 555–583.

BARRETT. T. C. *The evaluation of children's reading achievement*. Perspectives in Reading No. 8. Newark, Del.: International Reading Association, 1967.

——. Visual discrimination tasks as predictors of first grade reading achievement. *The Reading Teacher*, 1965, *18*, 276–282. (a)

——. The relationship between measures of prereading visual discrimination and first grade achievement: A review of the literature. *Reading Research Quarterly*, 1965, *1* 51–76. (b)

The Basic Readers, Curriculum Foundation Series. W. S. Gray and H. M. Robinson (Eds.), Glenview, Ill.: Scott, Foresman, 1912–1962.

BERLINER, D. C. Tempus Educare. In P. L. Peterson and H. J. Walberg (Eds.), *Research on teaching: Concepts, findings, and implications*. Berkeley, Calif.: McCutchan Publications, 1979.

——. Academic learning time and reading achievement. In J. T. Guthrie (Ed.), *Comprehension and teaching: Research views*. Newark, Del.: International Reading Association, 1981.

BETTS, E. *Foundations of reading instruction*. New York: American Book, 1946.

BISSEL, J. The cognitive effects of preschool programs for disadvantaged children. In J. Bissel (Ed.), *Early childhood education readings*. New York: Holt, Rinehart and Winston, 1972.

BLACHOWICZ, C. Cloze activities for primary readers. *The Reading Teacher*, 1977, *31*, 300–302.

BLACKHURST, A. Noncategorical teaching preparation. *Exceptional Children*, 1981, *48*, 197–205.

BLOOM, B. S.   *Human characteristics and school learning.* New York: McGraw-Hill, 1976.
——.   *Stability and change in human characteristics.* New York: John Wiley, 1964.
——.   Learning for mastery. *Evaluation Comment*, 1968, *1.*
BLOOM, B. S. and others.   *Taxonomy of educational objectives: Handbook I, cognitive domain.* New York: David McKay, 1956.
BLOOMFIELD, L.   Linguistics and reading. *Elementary English Review*, 1942, *19,* 125–130; 183–186.
BOND, G. L., TINKER, M. A., and WASSON, B. B.   *Reading difficulties: Their diagnosis and correction* (4th ed.). Englewood Cliffs, N.J.: Prentice-Hall, 1979.
BORMUTH, J. R.   The cloze readability procedure. *Elementary English*, 1968, *45,* 236–249. (a)
——.   The cloze readability procedure. In J. R. Bormuth (Ed.), *Readability in 1968.* A research bulletin prepared by a committee of the National Conference on Research in English. Champaign, Ill.: National Council of Teachers of English, 1968. (b)
BORTNICK, R., and LOPARDO, G.   An instructional application of the cloze procedure. *Journal of Reading*, 1973, *16,* 296–300.
BOWER, E. M.   *Early identification of emotionally handicapped children in school.* Springfield, Ill.: Charles C. Thomas, 1969.
BOWLBY, J.   *Attachment.* New York: Basic Books, 1969.
BRAAM, I.   Developing and measuring flexibility in reading. *The Reading Teacher.* 1963, *16,* 247–254.
BRIGANCE, A. H. *Brigance diagnostic inventory of basic skills.* North Billerica, Maine: Curriculum Associates, 1977.
BRITTAIN, J.   Inflectional performance and early reading. *Reading Research Quarterly*, 1970–1971, *6,* 34–48.
BRITTON, G. E.   Danger: State adopted texts may be hazardous to our future. *The Reading Teacher*, 1975, *29,* 52–58.
BROWN, D. A. *Reading diagnosis and remediation.* Englewood Cliffs, N.J.: Prentice-Hall, 1982.
BROWN, R. T.   Impulsivity and psychoeducational intervention in hyperactive children, *Journal of Learning Disabilities*, 1980, *13,* 249–254.
BRUININKS, V. L.   Actual and perceived peer status of learning disabled students in mainstream programs. *Journal of Special Education*, 1978, *12,* 51–58.
BRYAN, T. H., and BRYAN, J.   *Understanding learning disabilities* (2nd ed.). Sherman Oaks, Calif.: Alfred Publishing, 1978.
BRYAN, T. H., and PERLMUTTER, B.   Immediate impressions of L D children by female adults. *Learning Disability Quarterly*, 1979, *2,* 80–88.
BRYAN, T. H., and SHERMAN, R.   Immediate impressions of nonverbal ingratiation attempts by learning disabled boys. *Learning Disability Quarterly*, 1980, *3,* 19–28.
BRYAN, T. H., WHEELER, R., FELCAN, J., and HENEK, T.   Come on dummy: An observational study of children's communications. *Journal of Learning Disabilities*, 1976, *9,* 661–669.
BUCKLEY AMENDMENT   [General Education Provisions Act, section 438 (title IV, PL 94–247)], 1974, amending the Elementary and Secondary Education Act of 1965.
BURKE, C.   The Burke reading interview. (Unpublished) Bloomington, Ind.: Indiana University, School of Education, Reading Department, 1976.
BUSWELL, G. T.   Relationship between rate of thinking and rate of reading. *School Review*, 1951, *49,* 339–346.
CARROLL, H. M. C.   The remedial teaching of reading: An evaluation. *Remedial Education*, 1972, *49,* 10–15.
CARROLL, J. B., DAVIES, P., and RICHMOND, B. *American heritage word frequency book.* Boston: Houghton Mifflin, 1971.
CASHDAN, A., PUMFREY, P. D., and LUNZER, E. A.   Children receiving remedial teaching in reading. *Educational Research*, 1971, *13,* 98–105.

CAZDEN, C.   The neglected situation in child language research and education. In F. Williams (Ed.), *Language and poverty*. Chicago: Markham, 1970.

————.   *Child language and education*. New York: Holt, Rinehart and Winston, 1972.

CHALL, J. S.   *Learning to read: The great debate*. New York: McGraw-Hill, 1965.

CHANDLER, M. J.   Social cognition: A selective review of current research. In W. F. Overton and J. C. Gallagher (Eds.), *Knowledge and development, Vol. 1, Advances in research and theory*. New York: Plenum, 1977.

Chicago Tribune, June 29, 1981.

CHING, D. C.   *Reading and the bilingual child*. Newark, Del.: International Reading Association, 1976.

CHOMSKY, C.   *The acquisition of syntax in children from 5 to 10*. Cambridge, Mass.: M.I.T. Press, 1969.

————.   Reading, writing, and phonology. *Harvard Educational Review*, 1970, *40*, 287–309.

————.   When you still can't read in third grade. After decoding, what? In S. J. Samuels (Ed.), *What research has to say about reading instruction*. Newark, Del.: International Reading Association, 1978.

CHOMSKY, N.   *Phonology and reading*. In H. Levin and J. P. Williams (Eds.), *Basic studies on reading*. New York: Basic Books, 1970.

CHOMSKY, N., and HALLE, M.   *The sound pattern of English*. New York: Harper & Row, 1968.

CLEMENTS, S.   *Minimal brain dysfunction in children*. NINDS monograph No. 3. Public Health Services Bulletin No. 1415. Washington, D.C.: U.S. Department of Health, Education and Welfare, 1966.

CLYMER, T. C.   The utility of phonic generalizations in the primary grades. *The Reading Teacher*, 1963, *16*, 252–258.

COHN, M.   Structured comprehension. *The Reading Teacher*, 1969, *22*, 440–444.

COLE, L.   *The improvement of reading*. New York: Holt, Rinehart and Winston, 1938.

COLEMAN, E. B.   Collecting a data base for a reading technology. Unpublished paper. University of Texas at El Paso, 1967.

COOPER, J. L.   A procedure for teaching non-readers. *Education*, 1947, *67*, 494–499.

COUNCIL FOR EXCEPTIONAL CHILDREN.   *Update*, 13, no. 2, October, 1981.

COUNCIL FOR LEARNING DISABILITIES.   Newsletter 7, Summer, 1981.

CRAFTON, L.   *The reading process as a transactional learning experience*. Unpublished doctoral dissertation. Bloomington, Ind.: University of Indiana, 1981.

CRITCHLEY, M.   *The dyslexic child*. Springfield, Ill.: Charles C. Thomas, 1970.

CROOK, W.   *Can your child read? Is he hyperactive?* Jacobson, Tenn.: Professional Books, 1977.

CULLINAN, D., and EPSTEIN, M.   *Special education for adolescents: Issues and perspectives*. Columbus, Ohio: Charles E. Merrill, 1979.

CUNNINGHAM, P. M.   Teaching were, with, what, and other "four letter" words. *The Reading Teacher*, 1980, *34*, 160–163.

DE HIRSCH, K. and others.   Predicting reading failure. New York: Harper & Row, 1966.

DALE, E., and CHALL, J. S.   A formula for predicting readability. *Educational Research Bulletin*, Ohio State University, 1948, *27*, 11–20, 28, 37–54.

DAVEY, B.   Cognitive styles and reading achievement. *Journal of Reading*, 1976, *20*, 113–120.

DAVIS, F. B.   Psychometric research on comprehension in reading. *Reading Research Quarterly*, 1968, *3*, 339–345.

DEUTSCH, M.   The role of social class in language development and cognition. *American Journal of Orthopsychiatry*, 1965, *35*, 78–88.

Diagnostic and statistical manual (DSM III). New York: American Psychiatric Association, 1980.

DOLCH, E.   A basic sight vocabulary. *Elementary School Journal*, 1936, *36*, 456–60; 1937, *37*, 268–272.

DORE-BOYCE, K., MISNER, M. S., and McGUIRE, L. D.   Comparing reading expectancy formulas. *The Reading Teacher*, 1975, *29*, 8–14.

DOUGLAS, V. I.   Stop, look, and listen: the problem of sustained attention and impulsive control in hyperactive and normal children. *Canadian Journal of Behavioral Science*, 1972, *4*, 259–281.

DOWNING, J.   Children's developing concept of spoken and written language. *Journal of Reading Behavior*, 1971–1972, *4*, 1–19.

———.   Reading—skill or skills? *The Reading Teacher*, 1982, *35*, 534–537.

DOWNING, J., and OLIVER, I.   The child's concept of a word. *Reading Research Quarterly*, 1973–1974, *4*, 468–482.

DREYER, S. S.   *The book finder: A guide to children's literature about the needs and problems of youth*. Circle Pines, Minn.: American Guidance Service, 1977.

DUFFELMEYER, F. A., and DUFFELMEYER, B. B.   Developing vocabulary through dramatization. *Journal of Reading*, 1979, *23*, 141–143.

DURKIN, D.   *Teaching young children to read* (3rd ed.). Boston: Allyn & Bacon, 1980.

———.   What is the value of the new interest in reading comprehension? *Language Arts*, 1981, *85*, 23–43.

DYKSTRA, R.   *The relationship between measures of auditory discrimination and reading achievement at the end of first grade*. Unpublished doctoral dissertation. University of Minnesota, 1962.

EKWALL, E. E.   *Diagnosis and remediation of the disabled reader*. Boston: Allyn & Bacon, 1976.

EMANS, R.   When two vowels go walking and other such things. *The Reading Teacher*, 1967, *21*, 262–269.

ENGLE, P.   Language medium in early school years for minority language groups. *Review of Educational Research*, 1975, *45*, 282–325.

ENGLEMANN, S., and BRUNER, E. C.   *DISTAR reading: An instructional system*. Chicago: Science Research Associates, 1978.

ENGLEMANN, S., BECKER, J., BECKER, W., CORINE, L., JOHNSON, G., and MEYERS, L. *Corrective reading program*. Chicago: Science Research Associates, 1978.

EPSTEIN, M., HALLAHAN, D., and KAUFFMAN, J.   Implications of the reflexivity-impulsivity dimension for special education. *Journal of Special Education*, 1975, *9*, 11–25.

ESTES, T., and VAUGHAN, J. L.   Reading interest and comprehension: Implications. *The Reading Teacher*, 1973, *27*, 149–153.

FARR, R.   *Reading: What can be measured?* Newark, Del.: International Reading Association, 1969.

FEINGOLD, B.   *Why your child is hyperactive*. New York: Random House, 1975.

FEITELSON, D. (Ed.).   *Mother tongue or second language*. Newark, Del.: International Reading Association, 1979.

FERNALD, G. M.   *Remedial techniques in basic school subjects*. New York: McGraw-Hill, 1943.

FEUERSTEIN, R.   *Instrumental enrichment*. Baltimore: University Park Press, 1979.

FISHER, C. W., FILBY, N. W., MARLIAVE, R., CAHEN, L. S., DISHAW, M. M., and MOORE, J. E., *Teaching and learning in the elementary school: A summary of the beginning teacher evaluation study* (BTES Rep. VII–I). San Francisco: Far West Laboratory for Educational Research and Development, 1978. (a)

FISHER, C. W., FILBY, N. W., MARLIAVE, R., CAHEN, L. S., DISHAW, M. M., MOORE, J. E., and BERLINER, D. C., *Teaching behaviors, academic learning time and student achievement*. (Final report of Phase III–B Beginning Teacher Evaluation Study.) San Francisco: Far West Laboratory for Educational Research and Development, 1978. (b)

FLESCH, R.   *Why Johnny can't read and what you can do about it*. New York: Harper and Brothers, 1955.

FRASIER, A.   Developing a vocabulary of the senses. *Elementary English*, 1970, *47*, 176–184.

FRY, E. A.   A readability formula that saves time. *Journal of Reading*, 1968, *11*, 513–516.

GAMEZ, G. I.   Reading in a second language: "native language approach" vs. "direct method." *The Reading Teacher*, 1979, *32*, 665–670.

GARDNER, G., and SPERRY, B.   Learning disabilities and school phobia. In A. Silvano (Ed.), *American handbook of psychiatry*. New York: Basic Books, 1974, Vol. II, 116–129.

GARDNER, W.   *Children with learning and behavior problems: A behavioral management approach*. Boston: Allyn & Bacon, 1978.

GESELL, A., and ILG, F. L. *The child from five to ten*. London: Hamish Hamilton, 1946.

GESHWIND, N.   Specialization of the human brain. *Scientific American*, September, 1979, *244*, 201–241.

GILLESPIE, P., and JOHNSON, L.   *Teaching reading to the mildly retarded child*. Columbus, Ohio: Charles E. Merrill, 1974.

GILLINGHAM, A., and STILLMAN, B. W.   *Remedial training for children with specific difficulty in reading, spelling, and penmanship* (7th ed.). Cambridge, Mass.: Educators Publishing Service, 1970.

GIPE, J. P.   Use of relevant context helps kids learn new word meanings. *The Reading Teacher*, 1980, *33*, 398–402.

GLASS, G. G.   *Teaching decoding as separate from reading*. Garden City, N.Y.: Adelphi University Press, 1973.

GOLDENBERG, I.   Reading in the first grade: An observational study of the hypothesis of self-fulfilling prophecy. In F. Kaplan and S. B. Sarason (Eds.), *The Yale psycho-educational clinic: Collected studies and papers*. Boston: Massachusetts State Department of Mental Health, 1969.

GOOD, T., and BROPHY, J.   Which pupils do teachers call on? *Elementary School Journal*, 1970, *70*, 190–198.

———. *Looking in classrooms*. New York: Harper & Row, 1973.

GOODMAN, K. S.   A linguistic study of cues and miscues in reading. *Elementary English*, 1965, *42*, 639–643.

———. Reading: A psycholinguistic guessing game. *Journal of the Reading Specialist*, 1967, *6*, 126–135.

———. Analysis of oral reading miscues. *Reading Research Quarterly*, 1969, *5*, 9–30.

GOODMAN, K. S., and GOLLASCH, F. V.   Word omissions: Deliberate and non-deliberate. *Reading Research Quarterly*, 1980–1981, *14*, 6–31.

GOODMAN, Y. M.   Miscues, errors and reading comprehension in J. Meritt (Ed.), *New Horizons in Reading*. Newark, Del.: International Reading Association, 1976.

———. Kid watching: An alternative to testing, *National Elementary Principal*, 1978, *57*, 41–45.

GOODMAN, Y. M., and BURKE, C.   *Reading miscue inventory*. New York: Macmillan, 1972.

———. *Reading strategies: Focus on comprehension*. New York: Holt, Rinehart and Winston, 1980.

GOULD, S. J.   *The mismeasure of man*. New York: W. W. Norton, & Co., Inc. 1981.

GOULDNER, H.   *Teachers' pets, troublemakers, and nobodies*. Westport, Conn.: Greenwood Press, 1978.

GROSS, A. D.   The relationship between sex differences and reading ability in an Israeli kibbutz system. In D. Feitelson (Ed.), *Crosscultural perspectives on reading and reading research*, Newark, Del.: International Reading Association, 1978.

GROSSMAN, H.   (Ed.). *Manual of terminology and classification of mental retardation*. Washington, D.C.: American Association on Mental Deficiency, 1973.

GUINET, L.   *Evaluation of Distar materials in three junior learning assistance programs* (Report RR 71–16). Vancouver, British Columbia: University of Vancouver, Board of Trustees, 1971.

GUSZAK, F.   Teacher questioning and reading. *The Reading Teacher*, 1967, *21*, 227–234.

GUTHRIE, J.   Models of reading and reading disability. *Journal of Educational Psychology*, 1973, *65*, 9–18.

GUTHRIE, J. T., SIEFERT, M., and KLINE, M.   Clues from research on programs for poor readers. In S. J. Samuels (Ed.), *What research has to say about reading instruction*. Newark, Del.: International Reading Association, 1978.

HALLAHAN, D., and CRUICKSHANK, W.   *Psychoeducational foundations of learning disabilities*. Englewood Cliffs, N.J.: Prentice-Hall, 1973.

HALLAHAN, D., and KAUFFMAN, J.   *Exceptional children: Introduction to special education* (2nd ed.). Englewood Cliffs, N.J.: Prentice-Hall, 1982.

HAMMILL, D., and LARSEN, S. C.   The relationship of selected auditory perception skills and reading. *Journal of Learning Disabilities*, 1974, *7*, 429–435.

———.   The relationship of selected visual perceptual abilities to school learning. *Journal of Special Education*, 1975, *9*, 281–291.

HARING, N., and BATEMAN, B.   *Teaching the learning disabled child*. Englewood Cliffs, N.J.: Prentice-Hall, 1977.

HARPER, R. J. II, and KILARR, G.   *Reading and the law*. Newark, Del.: International Reading Association, 1978.

HARRIS, A.   What is new in remedial reading? *The Reading Teacher*, 1981, *34*, 405–410.

HARRIS, A., and SIPAY, E.   *How to increase reading ability* (7th ed.). New York: Longman, 1980.

HARRIS, T. K.   Reading. In R. L. Ebel (Ed.). *Encyclopedia of educational research* (4th ed.). New York: Macmillan, 1969, 1094–1095.

HARSTE, J. C., and CAREY, R. F.   Comprehension as setting. In J. C. Harste and R. F. Carey, *New Perspectives in Comprehension*. Monographs in language and reading studies, *Monographs in teaching and learning*. Bloomington, Ind.: Indiana University, School of Education. Nov. 3, 1979.

HAYES, J., and HIGGINS, S.   Issues regarding the IEP: Teachers on the front line. *Exceptional Children*, 1978, *44*, 267–274.

HEBER, R. H., BARBER, S., HARRINGTON, C., HOFFMAN, C., and FALLANDER, C.   *Rehabilitation of families at RISK for mental retardation*. Rehabilitation Research Training Center in Mental Retardation Progress Report. Madison, Wis.: University of Wisconsin, 1972.

HECAEN, G. and KREMLIN, H.   Neurolinguistic research on reading disorders resulting from left hemisphere lesions: Aphasic and "pure" dyslexia. In H. Whitaker and H. A. Whitaker (Eds.), *Studies in neurolinguistics*, Vol. 2. New York: Academic Press, 1976.

HECKELMAN, R. G.   The neurological impress method of remedial reading instruction. *Academic Therapy*, 1969, *4*, 277–282.

HEGGE, T. G., KIRK, S., and KIRK, W.   *Remedial reading drills*. Ann Arbor, Mich.: George Wahr Publishing, 1936.

HINSHELWOOD, J.   *Congenital word-blindness*. London: H.K. Lewis, 1917.

HITTLEMAN, D. R.   *Developmental reading: A psycholinguistic perspective*. Boston: Houghton Mifflin (formerly Rand McNally), 1978.

HORNBY, P. A.   Achieving second language fluency through immersion education. *Foreign Language Annals*, 1980, *13*, 107–113.

HUNT, C.   The effect of self-selection, interest, and motivation on independent, instructional, and frustration levels. *The Reading Teacher*, 1970, *24*, 146–151.

HUUS, H.   Critical and creative thinking. In M. A. Dawson (Ed.), *Developing comprehension including critical thinking*. Newark, Del.: International Reading Association, 1968.

INTERNAL REVENUE SERVICE.   Publication 52. Medical and dental expenses. Washington, D.C.: U.S. Government, 1981.

INTERNATIONAL READING ASSOCIATION.   Resolution on learning disabilities. (Printed in *Journal of Learning Disabilities*, 1976, *9*, 8–9.)

————. Misuse of grade equivalents. (Printed in *Reading Research Quarterly*, 1981, *16*, follows p. 611.)

Ives, J., Bursuk, Z., and Ives, S. *Word recognition*. Boston: Houghton Mifflin (formerly Rand McNally), 1979.

Jenkins, J. R., and Pany, D. Instructional variables in reading comprehension. In J. T. Guthrie (Ed.), *Reading comprehension and teaching: Research views*. Newark, Del.: International Reading Association, 1981.

Jensen, A. How much can we boost IQ and scholastic achievement? *Harvard Educational Review*, 1969, *39*, 1–123.

————. *Bias in mental testing*. New York: Macmillan, 1979.

Johnson, D. and Myklebust, H. R. *Learning disabilities: Educational principles and practices*. New York: Grune & Stratton, 1967.

Johnson, D. D. The Dolch list reexamined. *The Reading Teacher*, 1971, *24*, 455–456.

Johnson, D. D., and Pearson, P. D. Skills management systems: A critique. *The Reading Teacher*, 1975, *28*, 757–764.

———— *Teaching reading vocabulary*. New York: Holt, Rinehart and Winston, 1978.

Johnson, M., and Kress, R. *Informal reading inventories*. Newark, Del.: International Reading Association, 1965.

Jones, J. *Intersensory transfer, perceptual shifting, modal preference and reading*. Newark, Del.: International Reading Association, ERIC–CRIER, 1972.

Jones M. B., and Pilulski, E. C. Cloze for the classroom. *The Reading Teacher*, 1974, *17*, 432–438.

Jongsma, E. A. *Cloze instruction research: A second look*. Newark, Del.: International Reading Association, 1980.

Kagan, J. Reflection-impulsivity. The general dynamics of conceptual tempo. *Journal of Abnormal Psychology*, 1966, *7*, 17–24.

Karlin, R. Teaching elementary reading (3rd ed.). New York: Harcourt Brace Jovanovich Inc., 1980.

Kaufman, A. S. The WISC and learning disabilities assessment: State of the art. *Journal of Learning Disabilities*, 1981, *14*, 520–526.

Kavale, K. Functions of the Illinois Test of Psycholinguistic Abilities (ITPA): Are they trainable? *Exceptional Children*, 1981, *47*, 496–513.

————. Meta-analysis of the relationship between visual perceptual skills and reading achievement. *Journal of Learning Disabilities*, 1982, *15*, 42–51.

Kennedy, E. C. *Classroom approaches to remedial reading*. Itasca, Ill.: F. E. Peacock, 1977.

Keogh, B. Problem solving strategies as psychological test data. Paper presented at the annual meeting of the American Psychological Association, Washington, D.C., 1971.

Keogh, B., and Donlon, G. Field dependence, impulsivity, and learning disabilities. *Journal of Learning Disabilities*, 1972, *5*, 331–336.

Keogh, B., and Margolis, J. Learning to labor and to wait: Attentional problems of children with learning disorders. *Journal of Learning Disabilities*, 1976, *9*, 276–286.

Keogh, B. K., Tchir, C. and Windeguth-Behn, A. Teachers' perceptions of educationally high risk children. *Journal of Learning Disabilities*, 1974, *7*, 367–374.

Kephart, N. *The slow learner in the classroom* (2nd ed.). Columbus, Ohio: Charles E. Merrill, 1971.

Kibby, M. Passage readability affects the oral reading strategies of disabled readers. *The Reading Teacher*, 1979, *32*, 390–396.

————. State University of New York at Buffalo, Personal communication, 1981.

Kirk, S. *Early education of the mentally retarded*. Urbana, Ill.: University of Illinois Press, 1958.

————. Behavioral diagnosis and remediation learning disabilities. In *Conference on exploration into the problems of the perceptually handicapped child*. Evanston, Ill.: Fund for the Perceptually Handicapped, 1966.

KIRK, S., and ELKINS, J.   Characteristics of children enrolled in child service demonstration centers. *Journal of Learning Disabilities*, 1975, *8*, 630–637.

KIRK, S., and GALLAGHER, J.   *Exceptional children* (3rd ed.). Boston: Houghton Mifflin, 1979.

KIRK, S. A., and KIRK, W.   *Psycholinguistic learning disabilities: Diagnosis and remediation*. Urbana, Ill.: University of Illinois Press, 1971.

KIRK, S., KLIEBHAN, J., and LERNER, J. W.   *Teaching reading to slow and disabled learners*. Boston: Houghton Mifflin, 1978.

KNAFLE, J. D., and GEISSAL, M. A.   Auditory discrimination tests: A linguistic approach. *The Reading Teacher*, 1977, *31*, 134–141.

KOLERS, P. A.   Three stages of reading in F. Smith (Ed.), *Psycholinguistics and reading*. New York: Holt, Rinehart and Winston, 1973.

KOPPITZ, E.   *Bender-Gestalt test for young children*. New York: Grune and Stratton, 1964.

KRISE, B. M.   Reversals in reading: A problem in space perception. *Elementary School Journal*, 1949, *49*, 278–284.

KRONICK, D.   An examination of psychosocial aspects of learning disabled adolescents. *Learning Disabilities Quarterly*, 1978, *1*, 84–86.

LaBERGE, D., and SAMUELS, S. M.   Toward a theory of automatic information processing in reading. *Cognitive Psychology*, 1974, *6*, 293–323.

LABOV, W.   Some sources of reading problems for Negro speakers of nonstandard English. In A. Frasier (Ed.), *New directions in elementary English*. Champaign, Ill.: National Council of Teachers of English, 1967.

LABOV, W., COHEN, P., ROBINS, C., and LEWIS, J.   A note on the relationship of reading failures to peer-group status in urban ghettoes. *The Florida F. L. Report*, 1969, *7*, 54–57, 167.

————. *A study of the nonstandard English of Negro and Purerto Rican speakers in New York City*. Final report, Cooperative Research Project 3288, Office of Education, Washington, D.C., 1968.

LAFFEY, J. L., and KELLY, D.   Test review: The Woodcock Reading Mastery Test. *The Reading Teacher*, 1979, *39*, 335–339.

LANDERS, A.   *Miami Herald*, October 9, 1979.

LAWSON, A. E., NORLAND, F. H., and KAHLE, J. B.   Levels of intellectual development and reading ability in disadvantaged students and the teaching of science. *Science Education*, 1975, *59*, 113–125.

LAZAR, I.   Does prevention pay off? *The Communicator*. Council of Exceptional Children, 1979.

LENKOWSKY, B., and LENKOWSKY, R.   Bibliotherapy of the learning disabled adolescent. *Academic Therapy*, 1978, *14*, 179–185.

LENNEBERG, E. H.   *Biological foundations of language*. New York: John Wiley, 1967.

LERNER, J. W.   *Learning disabilities: Theories, diagnosis and teaching strategies* (3rd ed.). Boston: Houghton Mifflin, 1981.

LERNER, J. W., DAWSON, D. and HORVATH, L.   *Cases in learning and behavior problems: A guide to individual education programs*. Boston: Houghton Mifflin, 1980.

LERNER, J. W. and LIST, L. K.   The phonics knowledge of prospective teachers; experienced teachers and elementary pupils. *Illinois School Research*, 1970, 39–42.

LIBERMAN, I.   Segmentation of the spoken word and reading acquisition. *Bulletin of the Orton Society*, 1973, *23* (Reprint No. 54).

LIBERMAN, I., and others.   Phonetic segmentation and recoding in the beginning reader. In A. S. Reber and D. Scarborough (Eds.), *Toward a psychological theory of reading*. Hillsdale, N.J.: Erlbaum, 1977.

LILLY, J., and KELLEHER, J.   Modality strengths and aptitude-treatment interaction. *Journal of Special Education*, 1973, 7, 5–14.

LIST, L. K.   *Music, art and drama experiences for the elementary curriculum.* New York: Teachers College Press, 1982.

LOVITT, T.   Applied behavioral analysis and learning disabilities, Part I. *Journal of Learning Disabilities*, 1975, 8, 432–443. (a)

———.   Applied behavioral analysis and learning disabilities, Part II. Specific research recommendations and suggestions for practitioners. *Journal of Learning Disabilities*, 1975, 8, 504–518. (b)

LUND, K. G., FOSTER, G., and McCALL-PEREZ, F.   The effectiveness of psycholinguistic training: A reevaluation. *Exceptional Children*, 1978, 44, 310–321.

MANZO, A. V.   The request procedure. *Journal of Reading*, 1969, 2, 123–126.

MARTIN, H.   Nutrition, injury, illness and minimal brain dysfunction. In H. Rie and E. Rie (Eds.), *Handbook of minimal brain dysfunction: A critical view.* New York: John Wiley, 1980.

MATHEWS, M.   *Teaching to read, historically considered.* Chicago: University of Chicago Press, 1966.

McCRACKEN, R.   Standardized reading tests and informal reading inventories. *Education*, 1962, 82, 366–369.

McDAVID, R. I.   Language and prestige: "Standard English." Revision of H. L. Mencken, *The American Language.* In N. A. Johnson (Ed.), *Current topics in language.* Cambridge, Mass.: Winthrop, 1976.

McDERMOTT, R. P.   Pirandello in the classroom: On the possibility of equal educational opportunity in American culture. In M. C. Reynolds (Ed.), *Futures of exceptional children: Emerging structures.* Reston, Va.: Council for Exceptional Children, 1978.

McNEILL, D.   *The acquisition of language: The study of developmental psycholinguistics.* New York: Harper and Row, 1970.

MEDRANO, P.   A psychiatric perspective of reading disability. In W. Otto, C. Peters, and N. Peters (Eds.). *Reading problems: a multidisciplinary perspective.* Boston: Addison-Wesley, 1977.

MESSER, S. B.   Reflection-impulsivity: A review. *Psychological Bulletin*, 1976, 73, 1026–1052.

Miami Herald, October 11, 1980.

MILLER, G. A.   The magical number seven, plus or minus two: Some limits on our capacity for processing information. *Psychological Review*, 1956, 63, 81–97.

MINSKOFF, E.   Research on psycholinguistic training: Critique and guidelines. *Exceptional Children*, 1975, 42, 136–144.

MOFFETT, J., and WAGNER, B. J.   *Student-centered language arts and reading, K–12* (2nd ed.). Boston: Houghton Mifflin, 1976.

MONDIANO, N.   The most effective language of instruction for beginning reading: A field study. In F. Pialorsi (Ed.). *Teaching the bilingual.* Tuscon: University of Arizona Press, 1974.

MONMEITH, M.   The reading teacher vs. children of divorce. *The Reading Teacher*, 1981, 35, 100–101 (ERIC-CRIER feature).

MOZZI, L.   Northeastern Illinois University, personal communication, 1980.

NATIONAL ADVISORY COMMITTEE ON DYSLEXIA AND RELATED DISORDERS.   Report to the Secretary of the Department of Health, Education and Welfare, August, 1969.

MOORE, D., and WIELAN, O.   WISC–R scatter indexes of children referred for reading diagnosis. *Journal of Learning Disabilities*, 1981, 14, 511–514.

MOORE, S.   Social cognition: About others. *Young Children*, 1979, 2, 54–61.

NATIONAL ASSESSMENT OF EDUCATIONAL PROGRESS. *Reading, writing, and thinking.* 1979–1980 Report. Washington, D.C.: U.S. Printing Office, 1981.

NATIONAL JOINT COMMITTEE ON LEARNING DISABILITIES. N.J.C.L.D. urges revised definition of learning disabilities. *The Reading Teacher*, 1981, 35, 134–135.

NELVILLE, D. The relationship between reading skills and intelligence test scores. *The Reading Teacher*, 1965, *18*, 257–261.

NEWBERRY, J., and GOLDSMITH, O. *The history of Little Goody Twoshoes.* London: John Newberry, 1766.

OLLILA, L., JOHNSON, T., and DOWNING, J. Adopting a Russian method for auditory discrimination training. *Elementary English*, 1974, *51*, 1138–1145.

OPTOMETRIC EXTENSION PROGRAM FOUNDATION, *Educator's guide to classroom vision problems.* Duncan, Okla., 1968.

ORTON, S. T. *Reading, writing and speech problems in children.* New York: W. W. Norton, 1937.

OTTO, W., and ASKOV, E. *Rationale and guidelines: The Wisconsin Design for Reading Skill Development.* Minneapolis: National Computer Systems, 1972.

OTTO, W., and SMITH, R. W. *Corrective and remedial teaching* (3rd Ed.). Boston: Houghton Mifflin, 1980.

PAGE, W. D., and CARLSON, K. L. The process of observing oral reading scores. *Reading Horizons*, 1975, *15*, 147–150.

PAUK, W. *How to study in college* (2nd Ed.). Boston: Houghton Mifflin, 1974.

PEARSON, P. D., and JOHNSON, D. D. *Teaching reading comprehension.* New York: Holt, Rinehart and Winston, 1978.

PEREZ, E. Oral language competence improves reading skills of Mexican American third graders. *The Reading Teacher*, 1981, *35*, 24–27.

PERFETTI, C. A. Reading comprehension depends on language comprehension. Paper presented at the Annual Convention, American Educational Research Association, San Francisco, 1976. (ERIC ED 120 688.)

PFLAUM, S., and PASCERELLA, E. Interactive effects of prior reading achievement and training in context on the reading of learning disabled children. *Reading Research Quarterly*, 1979–1980, *15*, 138–158.

PIAGET, J. *The language and thought of the child.* New York: Harcourt Brace, 1926.

——. *The origins of intelligence in children.* New York: W. W. Norton, 1952.

POWELL, W. R. Reappraising the criteria for interpreting informal inventories. In D. L. DeBoer (Ed.), *Reading diagnosis and evaluation.* Newark, Del.: International Reading Association, 1970.

PREMAK, D. Toward empirical behavior law I, positive reinforcement. *Psychological Review*, 1959, *66*, 219–233.

PRESTON, R. C. Reading achievement of German boys and girls related to sex of teacher. *The Reading Teacher*, 1979, *32*, 521–526.

PUBLIC LAW 94–142, Education for All Handicapped Children Act of 1975. U.S. Office of Education, Washington, D.C.

QUAY, H. C. Patterns of aggression, withdrawing and immaturity. In H. Quay and J. Werry (Eds.), *Psychopathological disorders of childhood.* New York: John Wiley, 1972.

RABINOVITCH, R. Dyslexia: Psychiatric considerations. In J. Money (Ed.), *Reading disability: Progress and research needs in dyslexia.* Baltimore: Johns Hopkins University Press, 1969.

RAPP, D. Food allergy treatment for hyperkinesis. *Journal of Learning Disabilities*, 1979, *12*, 608–616.

Reading Today, membership newsletter of the International Reading Association, August, 1981.

RICHEK, M. A. A study of the affix structure of English: Affix frequency, and teaching methods. Unpublished paper. Chicago: University of Chicago, 1969.

——. Effect of sentence complexity on the reading comprehension of syntactic structures. *Journal of Educational Psychology*, 1976, *68*, 800–806.

——. Reading comprehension of anaphoric forms in varying linguistic contexts. *Reading Research Quarterly*, 1976–1977, *12*, 145–165.

————. Readiness skills that predict initial word learning using two different methods of instruction. *Reading Research Quarterly*, 1977–1978, *13*, 200–222.

RIE, H., and RIE, E. (EDS.), *Handbook of minimal brain dysfunction: A critical view.* New York: John Wiley, 1980.

ROBINSON, H. *Why pupils fail in reading.* Chicago: University of Chicago Press, 1946.

————. Visual and auditory modalities related to methods for beginning reading. *Reading Research Quarterly*, 1972, *8*, 7–41.

ROSS, A. *Psychological aspects of learning disabilities and reading disorders.* New York: McGraw-Hill, 1976.

ROSNER, S., ABRAMS, J., DANIELS, P., and SCHIFFMAN, G. Dealing with reading needs of the learning disabled child. *Journal of Learning Disabilities*, 1981, *14*, 436–448.

ROSSMAN, L. The disabled adolescent reader. In D. Sawyer (Ed.), *Disabled readers.: Insight, assessment, instruction.* Newark, Del.: International Reading Association, 1980.

ROSWELL, F., and NATCHEZ, G. *Reading disability: A human approach to learning* (3rd ed.). New York: Basic Books, 1977.

RUMELHART, D. E. Schemata: The building blocks of cognition. In J. T. Guthrie (Ed.), *Comprehension and teaching: Research views.* Newark Del.: International Reading Association, 1981.

RUNION, H. J. Hypoglycemia—fact or fiction? In W. Cruickshank (Ed.), *Approaches to learning disabilities. Vol. 1. The best of ACLD.* Syracuse, N.Y.: Syracuse University Press, 1980.

SABATINO, D., and DORFMAN, N. Matching learning aptitude to two commercial reading programs. *Exceptional Children*, 1974, *4*, 85–90.

SALVIA, J., and YSSELDYKE, J. *Assessment in special and remedial education* (2nd ed.). Boston: Houghton Mifflin, 1981.

SAMUELS, S. J. Effects of pictures on learning to read. *Review of Educational Research*, 1970, *40*, 397–407.

————. Effects of letter name knowledge on learning to read. *American Educational Research Journal*, 1972, *9*, 65–74.

————. Success and failure in learning to read: A critique of the research. *Reading Research Quarterly*, 1973, *8*, 200–239.

————. The method of repeated readings. *The Reading Teacher* 1979, *32*, 403–408.

————. Characteristics of exemplary programs. In J. T. Guthrie (Ed.), *Comprehension and teaching: Research views.* Newark, Del.: International Reading Association, 1981.

SATTLER, Q. *Assessment of children's intelligence.* Philadelphia: W. B. Saunders, 1974.

SAVAGE, J. F., and MOONEY, J. F. *Teaching reading to children with special needs.* Boston: Allyn & Bacon, 1979.

SAWYER, D. Perceptual bases for reading difficulties. In D. Sawyer (Ed.), *Disabled readers: Insight, assessment, instruction.* Newark, Del.: International Reading Association, 1980.

SCHALLERT, D. L., KLEINMAN, G. M., and RUBIN, A. Analyses of differences between written and oral language. Technical Report 29. Urbana, Ill.: University of Illinois, Center for the Study of Reading, April, 1977.

SCHWEINHART, L. J., and WEIKART, D. P. Young children grow up. The effects of the Perry Preschool Program on youths through the age of 15. Ypsilanti, Mich.: Monographs of the High/Scope Educational Research Foundation, 1980, no. 7.

SHANKWEILER, D., and LIBERMAN, I. Y. Misreading: A search for causes. In J. Kavanaugh and I. G. Mattingly, (Eds.), *Language by eye and ear.* Cambridge, Mass.: M.I.T. Press, 1972.

SHEENAN, L. D., FELDMAN, R. S., and ALLEN, V. L. Research on children tutoring children: A critical review. *Review of Educational Research*, 1976, *16*, 355–385.

SHERMAN, B. W. Read for meaning: Don't let word study blind your students. *Learning Magazine*, (Nov., 1979), *8*, 41, 43–4.

SIPAY, E. R.   A comparison of standard reading scores and functional reading levels. *Reading Teacher*, 1964, *17*, 265–268.

SIPERSTEIN, G. N., BOPP, J. J., and BALE, J. J.   *Social status of learning disabled children.* Cambridge, Mass.: Research Institute for Educational Problems, 1977.

SKEELS, H.   A study of the effects of differential stimulation on mentally retarded children: A follow-up study. *American Journal of Mental Deficiency*, 1942, *46*, 340–350.

SKINNER, B. F.   Operant behavior. *American Psychologist*, 1963, *18*, 503–515.

SLINGERLAND, B.   A multisensory approach to language arts for specific learning disability children. Cambridge, Mass.: Educators Publishing Service, 1974.

SMITH, F.   *Understanding reading: Psycholinguistic analysis of reading and learning to read.* New York: Holt, Rinehart and Winston, 1971.

——.   The efficacy of phonics. In F. Smith (Ed.), *Psycholinguistics and reading*. New York: Holt, Rinehart and Winston, 1973. (a)

——.   Introduction. In F. Smith (Ed.), *Psycholinguistics and reading*. New York: Holt, Rinehart and Winston, 1973. (b)

——.   Twelve easy ways to make learning to read difficult. In F. Smith (Ed.), *Psycholinguistics and reading*. New York: Holt, Rinehart, and Winston, 1973. (c)

SMITH, J. P.   Writing in a remedial reading program: A case study. *Language Arts*, 1982, *59*, 245–253.

SMITH, N. B.   *American reading instruction* (rev. ed.). Newark, Del.: International Reading Association, 1965.

SMITH, S. L.   Retellings as measures of comprehension. In J. C. Harste and R. F. Carey (Eds.), *New perspectives in comprehension*, Monographs in reading and language studies, Monographs in Teaching and Learning. Bloomington, Ind.: Indiana University, School of Education, 1979.

SPACHE, G. D.   A new readability for primary-grade materials. *Elementary School Journal*, 1953, *53*, 410–413.

——.   *Investigating the issues of reading disabilities.* Boston: Allyn & Bacon, 1976.

——.   *Diagnosing and correcting reading disabilities.* Boston: Allyn & Bacon, 1981.

SPACHE, G. D., and SPACHE, E. B.   *Reading in the elementary school* (4th ed.). Boston: Allyn & Bacon, 1977.

STAUFFER, R. G.   *The language experience approach to the teaching of reading.* New York: Harper and Row, 1970.

——.   *Directing the reading-thinking process.* New York: Harper and Row, 1975.

STEIN, N. L., and GLENN, G. C.   An analysis of story comprehension in elementary school children. In R. R. Freedle (Ed.), *New directions in discourse processing* (vol. 2). Hillsdale, N.J.: Erlbaum, 1979.

STEIRNAGLE, E.   A five-year summary of a remedial reading program. *The Reading Teacher*, 1971, *24*, 537–43.

STERNBERG, L.   A component theory of intellectual giftedness. *Gifted Child Quarterly*, 1981, *25*, 86–93.

STEVENS, K. S.   The effects of background knowledge on the reading comprehension of ninth graders. *Journal of Reading Behavior*, 1980, *12*, 151–54.

——.   Can we improve reading by teaching background information? *Journal of Reading*, 1982, *25*, 326–29.

STRANG, R.   *Reading diagnosis and remediation.* Newark, Del.: International Reading Association. ERIC–CRIER, 1968.

STRAUSS, A., and LEHTINEN, L.   *Psychopathology and education of the brain-injured child.* New York: Grune & Stratton, 1947.

SWANSON, J., and KINSBOURNE, M.   Food dyes impair performance of hyperactive children in a laboratory learning test. *Science*, 1980, *207*, 1485–1486.

TABACHNICK, B.   Test scatter on the WISC-R. *Journal of Learning Disabilities*, 1979, *12*, 626–628.

TEMPLIN, M. *Certain language skills in children.* Minneapolis: University of Minnesota Press, 1957.

THOMAS, E. L., and ROBINSON, H. A. *Improving reading in every class* (3rd ed.). Boston: Allyn & Bacon, 1981.

THORNDIKE, E. L. Reading as reasoning: A study of mistakes in paragraph meaning. *Journal of Educational Psychology,* 1917, *8,* 323–332.

TORGESON, J. Factors related to poor performance on memory tasks in reading disabled children. *Learning Disabilities Quarterly,* 1979, *2,* 17–23.

TORRES, S. (Ed.). *A primer on individualized education programs for handicapped children.* Reston, Va.: Council for Exceptional Children, 1977.

TRAUB, N., and BLOOM, F. *Recipe for reading.* Cambridge, Mass.: Educators Publishing Service, 1970.

U.S. DEPARTMENT OF EDUCATION. *To assure the free appropriate public education of all children.* Second Annual Report to Congress on the Implementation of Public Law 94–142, The Education of All Handicapped Children Act. State Program Implementation Studies. Office of Special Education, 1980.

VELLUTINO, F., STEGER, B., MOYER, S., HARDING, C. and NILES, J. Has the perceptual deficit hypothesis led us astray? *Journal of Learning Disabilities,* 1977, *10,* 375–385.

VENEZKY, R. L. The basis of English orthography. *Acta Linguistica Hafniensia,* 1967, *10* (Copenhagen, Denmark). (a)

——. English orthography: Its graphical structure and its relation to sound. *Reading Research Quarterly,* 1967, *2,* 75–106. (b)

——. The curious role of letter names in reading instruction. *Visible Language,* 1975, *9,* 7–23.

VERNON, M. D. *Reading and its difficulties.* New York: Cambridge University Press, 1971.

VOGEL, S. A. Syntactic abilities in normal and dyslexic children. *Journal of Learning Disabilities,* 1974, *7,* 103–109.

——. *Syntactic disabilities in normal and dyslexic children.* Baltimore: University Park Press, 1975.

WALLACE, G., and LARSEN, S. C. *Educational assessment of learning problems: testing for teaching.* Boston: Allyn & Bacon, 1978.

WALLACH, L., and WALLACH, M. A. Phonemic analysis training in the teaching of reading. In W. M. Cruickshank and J. W. Lerner (Eds.), *Coming of age. (Vol. 3) The Best of ACLD,* Syracuse, N.Y.: Syacuse University Press, 1982.

WEBER, G. Inner-city can be taught to read: Four successful schools. Washington, D.C.: Council for Basic Education, 1972.

WECHSLER, D. *Wechsler intelligence scale for children—revised.* New York: Psychological Corp., 1974.

——. *The measurement and appraisal of adult intelligence* (4th ed.). Baltimore, Md.: Williams and Wilkins, 1975.

WELLMAN, B. Y., CASE, I. M., MENGERT, I. G., and BRADBURY, D. E. *Speech sounds of young children.* Iowa City: State University of Iowa, 1931.

WHELAN, R. The emotionally disturbed. In E. Meyen (Ed.), *Exceptional children and youth.* Denver: Love Publishing, 1978.

WHITE, B. *The first years of life.* Englewood Cliffs, N.J.: Prentice-Hall, 1975.

WIIG, E., and SEMEL, E. H. *Language disabilities in children and adolescents.* Columbus, Ohio: Charles E. Merrill, 1976.

WIIG, E. S., SEMEL, E. H., and CROUSE, M. A. The use of English morphology by high school and learning disabled children. *Journal of Learning Disabilities,* 1973, *6,* 457–465.

WILLIAMS, E. P. Behavioral techniques and behavior ecology. In A. Rogers-Warren, and S. Warren (Eds.), *Ecological perspectives in behavior analysis.* Baltimore: University Park Press, 1977.

WILLIAMS, J. P.   Teaching decoding with an emphasis on phoneme analysis and phoneme blending. *Journal of Educational Psychology*, 1980, *12*, 1–15.

WILLIAMS, J. P., BLUMBERG, E. L., and WILLIAMS, D. V.   Cues used in visual word recognition. *Journal of Educational Psychology*, 1970, *61*, 310–315.

WILSON, R. M.   *Diagnostic and remedial reading for classroom and clinic* (4th ed.). New York: Charles E. Merrill, 1981.

WITKIN, H. A.   *Psychological differentiation*. New York: John Wiley, 1962.

WOLFRAM, W.   *A sociolinguistic description of Detroit Negro speech*. Washington, D.C.: Center for Applied Linguistics, 1969.

WOODCOCK, R.   Personal communication, 1982.

WONG, B., and WONG, W.   Role-taking skills in normal achieving and learning disabled children. *Learning Disability Quarterly*, 1980, *3*, 11–18.

YARROW, D.   Emotional development. *American Psychologist.* 1979, *34*, 951–957.

YSSELDYKE, J.   Remediation of ability deficits: Some major questions. In L. Mann, L. Goodman, and J. Wiederholt (Eds.), *Teaching learning disabled adolescents*. Boston: Houghton Mifflin, 1978.

Appendix A

REMEDIAL INSTRUCTIONAL MATERIALS

I. REMEDIAL INSTRUCTIONAL SERIES

These sets of books build reading ability systematically through graded passages accompanied by comprehension development and words to add to reading/meaning vocabulary. (Reading level and interest level are measured in *grades* throughout, rather than *ages*. Interest Levels are given only when they differ from Reading Levels.)

Alike But Different

Goltry
Learning Trends, Globe

Reading Level: 1-2
Interest Level: 6-12

Paperback book contains twenty-four stories about teenagers followed by interesting comprehension and vocabulary exercises that are standard in format (word to remember, first things first, what makes sense, say that again please, etc.). Stories are two to four very short pages, with modern, visual drawings taking up much of the page. Four-page stories are divided into parts for reading.

Getting It Together

Goldberg and Greenberger
Science Research Associates

Reading Level: 2-6
Interest Level: 9-12

Three hard-cover readers, each written at a different level on life-problem themes such as divorce, pollution, elderly relatives in the home, being listened to, landlord problems, and violence in the schools. Each reader has the same stories, sequence, illustrations, and cover. Thus, they may be used to instruct readers at different levels at the same time. Comprehension exercises divided into four areas: literal meaning, analytical meaning, feelings, and ideas for research on special problems and ways in which to locate services related to the story problem.

> READING LEVELS
> Level 1:   2-3
> Level 2:   3-4
> Level 3:   5-6

High Action Reading Series

Newman Hansen, et al.
Modern Curriculum Press

Reading Level: 2-6

Vocabulary, comprehension, and study skills development. Three soft-cover workbooks at each of five levels. Each book develops skills in vocabulary, comprehension, and study. A typical lesson includes three reading pages followed by three to four pages of skill exercises. Subject areas include myths, magic, and mysteries.

Intrigue Series

Whitehead
Benefic Press

Reading Level: 2-4
Interest Level: 4-12

Absorbing tales of escapes, spies, and rescues with clever puzzles and maps encourage a high degree of involvement. Each of the six books in the series emphasizes vocabulary development and reading comprehension, map, chart, and study skills at the end of each chapter. Answers are provided at the end of each book for self-scoring.

READING LEVELS

Escape from Willing House	2.0	*The Jade Horse*	3.0
Pearls of Maslan	2.0	*Hidden Gold*	4.0
Danger in the Deep	3.0	*Cave of the Dead*	4.0

Key Text
Matteoni
Economy Company   *Reading Level: 1–8*

A basal series designed to meet the needs of students reading below level. Eighteen readers with full supplementary materials. Skills developed at a slower pace than in developmental readers.

McCall-Crabbs Standard Test Lessons in Reading
McCall and Crabbs
Teachers College Press   *Reading Level: 3–8*

Designed for improvement of reading comprehension. Each graded soft-cover book contains sixty three-minute reading selections followed by six multiple-choice comprehension questions. When scored, rough grade-level norms are obtained that can be used to chart student's individual progress.

READING LEVELS

Book A:	3–4	Book D 6–7
Book B:	4–5	Book E 7 +
Book C:	5–6	

Mini Units in Reading
Fox and Weiner   *Reading Level: 4–6*
Globe   *Interest Level: 7–12*

Paperback books containing one- to two-page short stories on contemporary (space computers), factual topics to interest teenagers. Several pages of skill development, including vocabulary introduction and literal and higher-level comprehension sections ("thinking it through," "reaching out"). Selections are grouped around themes such as "finding yourself" and "exploring the consumer world."

READING LEVELS
Book 1:   4–5
Book 2:   5–6

Moving Along Series
Brown, Truher, and Weise   *Reading Level: 1.5–4.5*
Benefic Press   *Interest Level: 4–12*

Three readers. Designed to meet the needs of seriously deficient junior and senior high school readers. Themes of sports, mystery, jobs, and social relationships presented in fiction, plays, and poetry. Phonics and vocabulary introduction and one question precede each controlled-length (1 1/2 pages) story. One critical question follows the selection. A placement test assists in determining placement in the program and an achievement test with each book validates growth in reading skills. Activity books appealing to a wide range of interests and abilities, and a teacher's guide with background information completes the series.

READING LEVELS

Get Going	1.5–2.5	*To the Top*	3.5–4.5
On the Way	2.5–3.5		

The New Cornerstone Readers

Bamman   *Reading Level: 1–4*
Addison-Wesley   *Interest Level: 1–6*

Remedial reading materials in a series of five paperback books designed to develop reading skills of students reading at or below grade level. Short stories are organized by interest units (e.g., careers, Vikings), and the questions and exercises following the stories teach word attack, vocabulary, comprehension, and study skills. There is an application of reading skills to other subjects (social studies, math, science) included in each book.

READING LEVELS

Alphabet Soup	1	*Drumbeats*	3
Baker's Dozen	2 (low)	*Elbowroom*	4
Crackerjacks	2 (high)		

The New Kaleidoscope Readers

Bamman et al.   *Reading Level: 2–7*
Addison-Wesley   *Interest Level: 7–12*

Eight soft-bound readers updated for today's remedial teenagers. Short articles (two to five pages) are organized into units and cover topics such as careers, sports, cars, and technology, progressing in difficulty from book to book. The books are well illustrated with line drawings, cartoons, and photographs. Accompanying questions and exercises provide practice in word attack, comprehension, vocabulary, and study skills.

READING LEVELS

One Thing at Once	2.4	*Five Words Long*	5.5
Two Blades of Grass	3.3	*Six Impossible Things*	6.2
Three O'Clock Courage	4.7	*Seven Is a Handy Figure*	6.7
Four Corners of the Sky	5.4	*The Eighth Day of the Week*	7.2

The New Open Highways Program

Aaron, Artley, Jenkins, et al.   *Reading Level: 1–8*
Scott, Foresman   *Interest Level: K–8*

A series of basal readers designed for reteaching and reinforcing basic reading skills. Hardbound books include stories, plays, and poems varying in length from one to several pages. Related workbooks (K–8) provide continuing skill reinforcement in decoding, comprehension, and studying. Readability at the beginning of each book is below grade level. Books intended for students at grade placement levels.

READING LEVELS

Get Set	1	*Speeding Away*	3
Ready to Roll	1	*Seeking Adventure*	4
Rolling Along	1	*Discovering Treasure*	5
More Power	2	*Exploring Afar*	6
Moving Ahead	2	*Blasting Off*	7
Splendid Journey	3	*Orbiting Earth*	8

New Practice Readers, 2nd Ed.

Anderson et al.   *Reading Level: 2–6*
McGraw-Hill, Webster Division   *Interest Level: 6–12*

An attractive series containing seven colorful soft-bound books with short nonfiction (e.g., nature, science) reading selections. Each two-page spread contains new vocabulary, a short reading selection, questions (each keyed to a specific skill), and vocabulary for the next selec-

tion. The teacher's manual includes an informal placement inventory. The first four books
have cassette programs to help students bring reading to the level of listening skills.

READING LEVELS

Book A:	2.0–2.5	Book E:	5.0–5.8
Book B:	2.5–3.5	Book F:	5.2–6.5
Book C:	3.7–4.8	Book G:	5.8–6.5
Book D:	4.4–5.5		

Reader's Digest New Reading Skill Builders, Silver Edition

Meyer, ed. *Reading Level: 1–6*
Reader's Digest Services *Interest Level: 4–12*

Compact, appealing paperbacks containing varied selections (six pages) taken from *Reader's Digest* issues. Four books at each of six reading levels. They may be used as remedial material, to supplement a basal reading program, or for individualization. Topics deal with adventure, animals, science, and some fiction. Each reading selection has key words at the beginning and short activities at the conclusion that check comprehension and vocabulary. In addition, duplicating masters (skill builders), cassettes, and records using music and sound effects are available for the advanced levels.

Levels 1–6 are on reading grades 1–6.

Reading For Concepts

Liddle
McGraw-Hill, Webster Division, 2nd ed. *Reading Level: 1.6–6.7*

Series of eight soft-cover books designed for the development of vocabulary and reading comprehension skills. Informative format contains readings about people, customs, science, and social studies. Each lesson is a one- or two-page story followed by seven or eight questions, each keyed consistently to a specific skill (such as main idea, locating facts), skimming, and vocabulary. New vocabulary words are included in back of each book. Cassette program available. Reading inventory test for pupil placement in teachers' guide.

READING LEVELS

Book A:	1.6–2.2	Book D:	3.6–4.2	Book G:	5.5–6.1
Book B:	2.2–2.8	Book E:	4.3–4.9	Book H:	6.1–6.7
Book C:	2.9–3.5	Book F:	4.9–5.5		

Spanish Reading Keys

Amato
The Economy Company *Reading Level: 1–3*

Basal reading series provides a complete program teaching reading in Spanish and then provides English as second-language activities for transition to English.

Sprint Reading Skills Program

 Reading Level: 2.0–4.0
Scholastic Book Services *Interest Level: 4–6*

Remedial reading program features stories and plays with a controlled vocabulary based on the revised Spache Readability Formula. Workbooks at each level combine prereading vocabulary, word attack exercises, a short reading passage, and postreading comprehension exercises. Independent reading books correlated to the vocabulary of the skills books in each unit are also included. Oral reading from a play provides teacher the chance to check student progress and hear miscues. Ditto masters are also available for reinforcement.

READING LEVELS
Level 1:   Grade 2
Level 2:   Grade 3

SRA Reading Laboratories

Parker and Scannell
Science Research Associates   *Reading Level: 1-9*

Set of individualized reading programs covering essential reading skills. Kits with color-coded cards allow students to work independently and progress at own rate. Primary level has folders with fiction and nonfiction selections and exercises following to build word analysis, vocabulary, and comprehension skills. Advanced levels include map, dictionary, and study skills. Kits provide self-correcting answer keys and progress charts. Also included are rate builders to develop speed of reading.

Triple Takes

Various authors   *Reading Level: 3-8*
Reader's Digest Services   *Interest Level: 3-12*

Series contains six levels (A–F) with two soft-cover books at each level. Exercises, which follow interesting one-page reading selections, cover areas of main idea, facts, inference, and vocabulary. Three types of content are included: academic, pleasure, and functional. Examples of functional reading are menus, cereal box advertising, filling out coupons, and following directions.

READING LEVELS

Level A:	3	Level D:	6
Level B:	4	Level E:	7
Level C:	5	Level F:	8

II. EASY READING BOOKS

These books are written specifically to provide poor readers with enjoyable reading materials. Although some contain skills exercises, the major focus is on continuous, motivational reading experiences. Some of these books contain controlled, repeated vocabulary where all words used are presented in a list at the end of the book. This feature helps teachers to coordinate sight word teaching.

Animal Adventure Series

Darby   *Reading Level: PP-1*
Benefic Press   *Interest Level: 1-4*

A supplementary series of animal stories based on factual information directed toward younger students. The set contains twelve hard-cover books with one continuous story in each book. There is an activity section and a vocabulary section in the back of each book. Cassettes and records are also available for disabled readers. Controlled vocabulary based on repetition, with a teacher word list.

READING LEVELS

Becky, the Rabbit	PP	*Skippy, the Skunk*	P
Squeaky, the Squirrel	PP	*Sandy, the Swallow*	P
Doc, the Dog	PP	*Sally, the Screech Owl*	P
Kate, the Cat	PP	*Pudgy, the Beaver*	1
Gomar, the Gosling	PP	*Hamilton, the Hamster*	1
		Horace, the Horse	1

Action, Double Action, Triple Action Kits

Scholastic Magazines

Reading Level: 2–6
Interest Level: 7–12

Each kit contains three to four original paperback titles with stories, plays, exercises, and cassettes featuring characters from various racial and ethnic backgrounds. Twenty copies of titles in each kit. Supplemental Action Books Library may be ordered. Library teaching guide contains suggestions for teaming the books with certain stories in the kit and provides comprehension/vocabulary skills material for ditto sheets.

READING LEVELS:

Action	2.0–6.0
Double Action	3.0–5.0
Triple Action	4.0–6.0

Beginner Books
Various Authors
Random House

In this well-known series of books for young readers, each volume contains a single story. Several have been written by a famous author of children's books. The reading level of each book is based on the Spache Readability Formula. Many of the titles use the analytic phonics (or linguistic or word family) approach—these are starred (*).

READING LEVELS:

Go Dog Go	1.5	*The Cat in the Hat Comes Back*	2.0
Put Me in the Zoo	1.5	*Sam & the Fire Fly*	2.0
*One Fish, Two Fish,		*Ann Can Fly*	2.0
Red Fish, Blue Fish*	1.7	*The King's Wish & Other Stories*	2.0
Are You My Mother?	1.7	*A Fly Went By*	2.1
Ten Apples up on Top	1.7	*The Cat in the Hat*	2.1
Robert the Rose Horse	1.7	*Bennett Cerf's Book of Laughs*	2.1
Hop in Pop	1.7	*Look out for Pirates*	2.1
*Little Black Goes to the		*I Was Kissed by a Seal at the Zoo*	2.1
Circus*	1.8	*Bennett Cerf's Book of Riddles*	2.2
A Fish Out of Water	1.8	*Summer*	2.2
Little Black, a Pony	1.8	*More Riddles*	2.3
You Will Go to the Moon	1.8	*The Big Jump & Other Stories*	2.4
Cowboy Andy	1.8	*Do You Know What I'm Going to	
The Whales Go By	1.8	Do Next Saturday?*	2.4
Stop That Ball	1.9	*The Bear's Christmas*	2.4
Green Eggs and Ham	1.9	*A Big Ball of String*	2.5
The Big Honey Hunt	1.9		

Breakthrough!
Sheldon and others
Allyn & Bacon

Reading Level: 1–8
Interest Level: 6–12

Mature reading in paperback series providing two or more books at each level. Each book contains one story. Sample titles are *The Time Is Now*, *Way Out*, *This Cool World*, and *Winner's Circle*. Concise teacher's guide pinpoints reading level, content, and point of view in each book. Skill masters for additional activities. Four of levels 1 and 2 also available in Spanish.

READING LEVELS

On the Level, Full Count....................	1	*This Cool World, How It is,*	
The Time Is Now, With It, Play It		*Coming Through*..........	5
Again, From the Top, Prime Time,		*The Big Ones, On the Spot,*	
Over and Out............................	2	*Making the Scene*..........	6
Winner's Circle, Way Out, Over the		*Point in Time, Busy Signal*	7
Edge......................................	3	*On the Move, Under the*	
Beyond the Block, Out of Sight,		*Wire*........................	8
Where It's At.............................	4		

Cowboy Sam Series

Chandler
Benefic Press

Reading Level: PP–3
Interest Level: 1–6

High-interest–low-difficulty supplemental reading series. Set of fifteen hard-cover, illustrated books with easy vocabulary. Stories relate to Western life with humorous situations and characters. Each book contains one continuous story. Workbooks and cassettes are available.

READING LEVELS

Cowboy Sam and Big Bill	PP	*Cowboy Sam and Shorty*	1
Cowboy Sam and Freckles	PP	*Cowboy Sam and Freddy*	1
Cowboy Sam and Dandy	PP	*Cowboy Sam and Sally*	2
Cowboy Sam and Miss Lily	P	*Cowboy Sam and the Fair*	2
Cowboy Sam and Porky	P	*Cowboy Sam and the Rodeo*	2
Cowboy Sam	P	*Cowboy Sam and the Airplane*	3
Cowboy Sam and Flop	1	*Cowboy Sam and the Indians*	3
		Cowboy Sam and the Rustlers	3

Cowboys of Many Races

Benefic Press

Reading Level: PP–5
Interest Level: 1–7

Stories about cowboys on the early Western frontier. Heroes come from minority groups (Black American, Spanish American, American Indian). Each book contains one complete story.

READING LEVELS

Cowboy Without a Horse	PP	*Cowboy on the Trail*	3
Cowboy on the Mountain	P	*Cowboy Soldier*	4
Cowboy Matt and Belleza	1	*Cowboy Marshall*	5
Adam Bradford, Cowboy	2		

Dan Frontier Series

Hurley
Benefic Press

Reading Level: PP–4
Interest Level: PP–6

High-interest–low-difficulty supplementary reading series. Ten hard-cover books on pioneer adventure. Each book contains one continuous story that depicts frontier life in the Middle West. Content emphasizes social and personal values. Each book includes a section on language, vocabulary development, and interpretive skills. Controlled vocabulary based on repetition; word list given. Cassettes available.

READING LEVELS

Dan Frontier	PP	*Dan Frontier and the Wagon*	
Dan Frontier and the New House ·	PP	*Train*	2
Dan Frontier and the Big Cat	P	*Dan Frontier: Scouts with*	
Dan Frontier Goes Hunting	P	*the Army*	2
Dan Frontier: Trapper	1	*Dan Frontier: Sheriff*	3
Dan Frontier with the Indians	1	*Dan Frontier Goes Exploring*	3
		Dan Frontier Goes to Con-	
		gress	4

The Deep Sea Adventure Series

Berres, Briscoe, Coleman, and Hewett   *Reading Level: 1.8–5*
Addison-Wesley   *Interest Level: 3–10*

Twelve science-related suspense stories for oceanography buffs. Controlled vocabulary based on word repetition; word list given. Teacher's manual provides specific plans for skill development and evaluation.

READING LEVELS

Storm Island	1.8	*Castaways*	2.6
The Sea Hunt	1.8	*The Pearl Divers*	2.8
Treasure Under the Sea	2.1	*Frogmen in Action*	3.1
Sea Gold	2.2	*Danger Below*	4.4
Submarine Rescue	2.4	*Whale Hunt*	4.7
Enemy Agents	2.5	*Rocket Hunters*	5.0

Dolch Independent Reading Books

Various Authors   *Reading Level: 1–4*
Garrard Publishing Co.   *Interest Level: 1–8*

Four series of books, each at a different reading level with thirteen to seventeen books in each series. Each book contains several short stories, including fairy tales, classics, circus life, and animal adventures. While interesting, books look like primary-level materials. The first two levels use the Dolch Basic Sight Words. The two higher levels use a controlled vocabulary.

First Reading Books, first grade reading level are

In the Woods	*Once There Was a Dog*
Monkey Friends	*Once There Was an Elephant*
On the Farm	*Once There Was a Monkey*
Tommy's Pets	*Once There Was a Rabbit*
Zoo Is Home	*Big, Bigger, Biggest*
Once There Was a Bear	*Dog Pals*
Once There Was a Cat	*Friendly Birds*
I Like Cats	*Some Are Small*
	Once There Was a Coyote

Basic Vocabulary Series, second grade reading level, uses Dolch Basic 220 words and 95 nouns. In addition, the books average one new word per page.

Animal Stories	*Lion and Tiger Stories*
Bear Stories	*Lodge Stories*
Circus Stories	*More Dog Stories*
Dog Stories	*Navaho Stories*
Elephant Stories	*Pueblo Stories*
Folk Stories	*Tepee Stories*
Horse Stories	*"Why" Stories*
True Cat Stories	*Wigwam Stories*

Folklore of the World Books. These are books of stories on the third grade level.

Animal Stories from Africa	*Stories from Italy*
Stories from Africa	*Stories from Japan*
Stories from Alaska	*Stories from Mexico*
Stories from Canada	*Stories from Old China*
Stories from France	*Stories from Old Egypt*
Stories from Hawaii	*Stories from Old Russia*
Stories from India	*Stories from Spain*

Pleasure Reading Books are "classics," adapted to the fourth grade level:

Fairy Stories	*Ivanhoe*	*Gospel Stories*
Anderson Stories	*Old World Stories*	*Bible Stories*
Aesop's Stories	*Far East Stories*	*Gulliver's Stories*
Famous Stories	*Greek Stories*	
Robinhood Stories		
Robinson Crusoe		

Face to Face
McCormick and Mathers　　　　　　　　　　　　　　　Reading Level: 4.0–4.9
The American Book Company　　　　　　　　　　　　Interest Level: 7–12

Stories are chosen for their readability and compelling interest for a teenage audience. Subjects ranging from friendship and honesty to adventure and comedy. Can be used with group or individual to provide practice in recognizing main idea, recalling facts, and categorizing and sequencing information. Kit includes four copies of each of ten books, activity program, student record ditto master, and teacher's guide.

Galaxy 5
Kelly　　　　　　　　　　　　　　　　　　　　　　Reading Level: 2
Children's Press　　　　　　　　　　　　　　　　Interest Level: 4–12

Follow Steve Estrada and Ellen Drake on the spaceship *Voyager* as they travel through the galaxies. Six adult space fantasy adventures in series. Sixty-four pages in each.

Impact on Reading
Lacampagne　　　　　　　　　　　　　　　　　　Reading Level: 3–6.9
Holt, Rinehart and Winston　　　　　　　　　　Interest Level: 7–9

Six paperback anthologies start students at lower level and lead them to higher level. Fine literature selections and two to three skill pages following each selection. For the student that is two to three years below level. Teacher's guide gives additional sample worksheets.

Incredible Series
Boning　　　　　　　　　　　　　　　　　　　　Reading Level: 5–9
Dexter and Westbrook　　　　　　　　　　　　　Interest Level: 5

Short books (45–50 pp.) with captivating visual format, containing many illustrations and few words per page. These story and adventure series are suspenseful and urge the reader to anticipate the end. Eleven titles.

King Classics Libraries
　　　　　　　　　　　　　　　　　　　　　　　　Reading Level: 5–0
King Features　　　　　　　　　　　　　　　　　Interest Level: 7–12

Twenty-four of the world's best loved stories skillfully adapted and presented in a graphic and colorful comic-strip format introduce the reluctant reader to the classics. Titles include *The Adventures of Huckleberry Finn, Robinson Crusoe, The Black Arrow,* and *A Christmas*

Carol. Each of the three libraries contains six copies of eight titles, thirty spirit masters, eight full-color posters, and a teaching guide. Also available are read-along cassettes for Libraries 1 and 2 and a new student workbook for each set with teacher's guide stressing facts, main idea, likenesses-differences, sequencing, and conclusions.

Know Your World Extra

Weekly Reader

Reading Level: 2–3
Interest Level: 7–12

Weekly classroom newspaper for remedial readers that gradually increases in difficulty as the year progresses. Contains news reports, movie reviews, personality profiles, articles on cars, fashions, sports, and television, followed by exercises that build language art and life skills. Teacher's edition provides background material, quizzes, and four reproducible skill masters.

Laura Brewster Mysteries

Eisenberg
Children's Press

Reading Level: 3
Interest Level: 4–12

A series of six "whodunits" keep the reluctant reader turning the pages from one cliffhanger to the next. Laura's escapades appeal to girls.

The Monster Series I and II

Blance and Cook
Bowmar/Noble

Reading Level: K–4

Supplementary reading series. Small soft-cover books, twelve books in each series. Each book contains a twelve- to fifteen-page story with gradual increase in vocabulary difficulty. Humorous stories dealing with everyday situations such as going to school or to the store. The main character in the book is a humorous, nonthreatening "monster" who acts like a person. Includes basic vocabulary. All books at the second grade level.

The Morgan Bay Mysteries

Rambeau and Rambeau
Addison-Wesley

Reading Level: 2–4
Interest Level: 4–11

Fast-paced, suspenseful, and often humorous mystery stories provide motivation for students reading below grade level. Each book contains a single story that is divided into chapters. Controlled vocabulary with word repetition; a word list is given.

READING LEVELS

Mystery of Morgan Castle	2.3	*Mystery of the Musical Ghost*	3.5
Mystery of the Marble Angel	2.6	*Mystery of Monks Island*	3.7
Mystery of the Midnight Visitor	3.2	*Mystery of the Marauder's Gold*	3.9
Mystery of the Missing Marlin	3.5	*Mystery of the Myrmidon's Journey*	4.0

Mystery Adventure Series

Bamman and Whitehead
Benefic Press

Reading Level: 2–6
Interest Level: 4–12

Young adult boy and girl test their deductive reasoning, courage, and determination as they solve mysteries. People of various ethnic groups are part of each story. Particularly appealing to girls, as a girl is one of the central characters. There is a glossary, map reading section, and factual material at the end of each book. Controlled vocabulary; all words above the grade level of the book are listed.

READING LEVELS

Mystery Adventure of the Talking Statues	2
Mystery Adventure of the Jeweled Bell	2
Mystery Adventure at Cave Four	3
Mystery Adventure of the Indian Burial Ground	4
Mystery Adventure at Longcliff Inn	5
Mystery Adventure of the Smuggled Treasure	6

Myth, Magic, and Superstition

Raintree Children's Books

Reading Level: 5
Interest Level: 4+

Even the most reluctant readers will be lured into these twenty short stories about the spooky world of ghosts and ghouls, haunted houses, and magic. Spine-tingling titles will stimulate student's imagination. Forty-eight pages per book; full-color and black-and-white illustrations.

Pacemaker True Adventures

Jerrome
Fearon

Reading Level: 2.0–2.5
Interest Level: 5–12

Dangerous, terrifying, true adventures of some of history's most fascinating figures. A few typical characters portrayed include Charles Lindbergh, Mata Hari, and Edmund Hillary. This eleven-book series features three complete stories in each book (32 pages each). Teacher's guide contains plot summaries, vocabulary, student exercises, and teaching suggestions.

Pacemaker Classics Previews

Fearon

Reading Level: 2–3
Interest Level: 5–12

Sound filmstrips and illustrated paperbound books (80–96 pages each) bring characters and events of classic novels to life. These classic works of literature have been shortened and adapted, but they retain the flavor and quality of the originals. Among the titles in the eight books are *Treasure Island* and *20,000 Leagues Under the Sea.* Teacher's guide contains suggestions, vocabulary, and comprehension questions.

Pace-Mates I, II, III

Children's Press

Reading Level: 1–4
Interest Level: 4–12

Use cassettes with narration and sound effects. Start students reading in accompanying books. Each Pace-Mate starts with a teaser blurb on the back of a book and then the cassette builds up suspense through the opening chapters. It asks tantalizing questions to enhance anticipation and then informs the students on what page to begin finishing the book on their own. Ten titles include *Flight to Fear*, *Dream of the Dead*, *Three Mile House*, *Village of Vampires*, and *Crash Dive*. Each set contains ten hard-bound books, ten cassettes, ten task cards, and a teacher's guide. Books available alone as Pacesetters I, II, III.

Pal Skill Kit

Xerox Education Publications

Reading Level: 1–5
Interest Level: 6–12

Small paperback books containing interesting short stories written to ensure successful reading experiences. There are four levels of difficulty (nine titles per level). The stories (11–15 pages) are built around themes including famous persons and events, boys' and girls' teenage problems, cars and cycles, and true-life adventures. Teacher's manual provides introduction, key concepts, discussion questions, and follow-up activities.

KIT A (3 of each title)		KIT B (3 of each title)	
9 Yellow Books	1.5–2.5	9 Blue Books	3.5–4.5
9 Red Books	2.5–3.5	9 Green Books	4.5–5.5

Prime Time-Mates

Children's Press

Reading Level: 2
Interest Level: 4–Adult

In this series, an introduction audio cassette accompanies each book. Mature format and multiracial heroes capture the imagination of adventure lovers. Sample titles are *Attack of the Cat, Cave-in, September Storm, Run from Danger*, and *The Pig Party*. In the cassette, expressive, word-for-word narrations with sound effects introduce the first part of these stories, and then the student is told the page to begin finishing the book independently. Each Prime Time-Mate contains one book, one cassette, and a task card with answers on the back. Books available separately as *Prime Time Adventures*.

Profiles: A Collection of Short Biographies

Clements and Burrell
Learning Trends, Globe

Reading Level: 3–4
Interest Level: 7–12

Twenty-four fascinating short selections (2–3 pages) of fact rather than fiction are contained in a soft-cover book. The subjects are outstanding men and women from many walks of life: sports, politics, education, show business, and medicine. Biographies include Enrico Caruso, Boris Karloff, Jim Thorpe. Teaching guide. Skill-building exercises follow each selection.

Racing Wheels Series

Dean
Benefic Press

Reading Level: 2–4
Interest Level: 4–12

Woody Woods and his friends take readers to the race track at Indy and the lore of auto racing. Although the characters are fictional, the training, equipment, and driving techniques are true and accurate. The end of each book contains a compendium of facts about people, cars, equipment, and races. Text and photographs combine to relate the theme of the story to the real world of racing. Controlled readability with repeated vocabulary and word list.

READING LEVELS

Hot Rod	2	*Stock Car Race*	3
Motorcycle Scramble	2	*Safari Rally*	3
Destruction Derby	2	*Road Race*	4
Motorcycle Racer	2	*Grand Prix Races*	4
Drag Race	3	*Indy 500*	4
Baja 500	3	*LeMans Race*	4

Reach: The Reading Extravaganza of America Cycling & Hydroplane Show

Hughes and Bond
The Economy Company

Reading Level: 3–5
Interest Level: 4–9

Exciting show business theme tape cassettes with lots of emphasis on student involvement and motivation to improve word perception and comprehension skills. Ideal for students with a negative basic attitude toward reading. Can be used individually for independent progress. Materials include tapes (audition, rehearsal, thirty-nine shows, and grand finale on twenty-one cassette tapes); consumable student's *Show Magazine* with exercises, stories, and tests; twelve supplementary readers; and teacher's annotated guide and record keeper.

Rock 'n Pop Stars

Children's Press

Reading Level: 4
Interest Level: 4–12

Unique series of fourteen biographies about the superstars of music showing how each star has attained success in the field of music. Each book contains thirty-two pages. Personalities include Aretha Franklin, the Beatles, Bob Dylan, Stevie Wonder, and Tony Orlando.

Secret Stories of the Sensational Super Heroes

Kraft and Stern
Children's Press

Reading Level: 4
Interest Level: 3–Adult

Captain America, the Fantastic Four, Spiderman, and the Incredible Hulk fascinate readers with their daring exploits. Comic-book format with solid pages of text interspersed. Comprehension questions accompany stories.

Space Science Fiction Series

Bamman, Whitehead, and Odell
Benefic Press

Reading Level: 2–6
Interest Level: 4–12

Men of the future face dangers in outer space on trips of exploration and negotiation. Involving reading with controlled vocabulary and extension sections for enrichment reading at the back of each book. Activity book and teacher's guide for series of six books.

READING LEVELS

Space Pirate	2	*Planet of the Whistlers*	4
Milky Way	2	*Invisco Man*	5
Bone People	3	*Ice Men of Rime*	6

Special Classics Library

Educational Teaching Aids

Reading Level: 2.1–2.8
Interest Level: 5–12

Abridged and adapted to retain their original excitement, these books are about forty pages long. Titles include *A Tale of Two Cities, 20,000 Leagues Under the Sea, The Jungle Book, The Last of the Mohicans, Robinson Crusoe, Treasure Island, Two Years Before the Mast,* and *The Moonstone.*

Spiral I and II Kits

Gunning
Continental Press

Reading Level: 2.0–4.5
Interest Level: 7–12

These kits contain sets of booklets that have informative, challenging reading selections appealing to a wide range of student interests. The major themes include teenage problems and choices, mystery, sports, and biography. Self-checking "Job Cards" for each book reinforce and improve reading skills. Placement inventory, teacher's guide.

READING LEVELS
Spiral   2.0–3.5
Spiral II   3.0–4.5

Sports for Everyone

Freeman and Church   *Reading Level: 3*
Children's Press   *Interest Level: 3–Adult*

Introductions for beginners that tell the how, what, when, and where of three nonteam popular sports: backpacking, surfing, and cross-country skiing. Forty-eight pages each book.

Sports-Mates

                                                                 Reading Level: 2
Children's Press   *Interest Level: 2–8*

Books are teamed with introductory cassettes. Expressive, word-for-word narrations with unique sound effects to introduce the first part of these *Sports Star* biographies. Sports personalities covered include Tracy Austin, Nancy Lopez, Reggie Jackson, Steve Garvey, and Walter Payton. Each motivational cassette contains expressive reading and sound effects. The cassette ends by asking questions to enhance the anticipation and then informs the students on what page to begin finishing the book on their own. Each *Sports-Mate* contains one hardbound book, cassette, task card, and vinyl jacket. Books available alone as *Sports Stars*. Each book is forty-eight pages.

Sporteller-Mates

                                                                 Reading Level: 3
Children's Press   *Interest Level: 4–Adult*

Books are teamed with introductory cassettes. Eight titles whose themes demonstrate the everyday conflicts the modern athlete meets in trying to win. Sample titles are *Catch the Sun*, *Foul Play*, *Race to Win*, *Strike Two*, and *Stroke of Luck*. Each story is presented dramatically on tape to a point where the reader is instructed to finish the story independently. Each *Sporteller-Mate* set includes 1 hard-bound book, 1 cassette, and a task card. Books available alone as *Sportellers*.

Sports Mystery Series

                                                                Reading Level: 2–4
Benefic Press   *Interest Level: 4–12*

Twelve stories of teen-aged boys and girls relate the problems they meet and overcome, the excitement they find in sports activity, and the ways in which they "find themselves" in the process. Boys and girls of different backgrounds and potentials seek and find their own success. Includes stories about track, football, gymnastics, skiing, golf, baseball, swimming, hockey, and tennis.

READING LEVELS			
Luck of the Runner	2	*Tip Off*	3
Ten Feet Tall	2	*Pitcher's Choice*	3
No Turning Back	2	*Scuba Diving Adventure*	4
Gymnast Girl	3	*Face Off*	4
Ski Mountain Mystery	3	*Swimmer's Mark*	4
Fairway Adventure	3	*Tennis Champ*	4

Sports Profiles

                                                                 Reading Level: 5
Raintree Children's Books   *Interest Level: 4–11*

Action-packed biographies that go beyond the glamor of the image and explore athletes as people, their beliefs, attitudes, and factors that make them the top in their field. The set includes sixteen titles, forty-eight pages each, and presents such sports heroes as Evonne Goolagong, Mohammed Ali, and Joe Namath.

Stories of Surprise and Wonder
Beyond Time and Space
Tales of Mystery and the Unknown

Potter *Reading Level: 3-6*
Globe *Interest Level: 4-12*

Three separate texts; each contains several stories that have been adapted without losing the impact of the originals. Selections are approximately six pages and are followed by study aids that stress comprehension, interpretation, and vocabulary skills. Discussion questions lead into the expression of original ideas. Illustrated text about 190 pages. Teacher's Guide.

> READING LEVELS
>
> *Stories of Surprise and Wonder (literature)*   3
> *Tales of Mystery and the Unknown*   6
> *Beyond Time and Space*   3-5

Turning Point: A Collection of Short Biographies

Kieszak *Reading Level: 3*
Learning Trends, Globe *Interest Level: 7-adult*

These stories consist of twenty-eight short (8–9 pages) biographies portraying famous people at "turning points" in their careers. Each selection is followed by skill-building exercises designed to help students master basic vocabulary and comprehension skills. Teacher's guide.

Turning Point I, II, III

McCormick and Mathers *Reading Level: 1.8-5.5*
Educational Challenges *Interest Level: 7-12*

Fifty stories of magic mystery, science fiction, sports, romance, and life situations designed to give students with marginal reading skills the success and pleasure of reading a complete book. Stories are grouped by skill focus at each of three levels. Each level contains four copies each of ten books, activities (sixty-two spirit masters), and teacher's guide. There are five levels, each containing ten books.

The World of Sports Series
The Challenge of Sports

Christ *Reading Level: 4-5*
Globe *Interest Level: 4-12*

World of Sports is two books (approximately 200 pages each) offering captivating short selections (3 pages) organized into different sports. Biographical sketches of great athletes appear in both books and are laced with illustrations, photographs, and diagrams. *The Challenge of Sports* includes sports such as skiing, volleyball, and swamp buggy racing. Each reading selection is followed by exercises providing practice with basic reading skills. Teacher's guide.

III. MATERIALS FOR SEVERELY DISABLED READERS

A. Prerequisite Skills.

1. VISUAL PERCEPTION-VISUAL MOTOR MATERIALS

- *Developmental Learning Materials.* Developmental Learning Materials. Many kinds of games and devices, including pegboards, sequential games, and parquety.
- *Dubnoff School Program 1 and Program 2.* Teaching Resources. Pattern cards, pegboards, orientation, and directionality exercises. Paper-and-pencil perceptual-motor exercises.

- *Eries Program—Perceptual Motor Teaching Materials.* Teaching Resources. Visual-perceptual devices and exercises.
- *Fairbands-Robinson Perceptual Motor Development.* Teaching Resources. Work-sheets and puzzles to develop hand-eye coordination, visual discrimination, form constancy, spatial relations, and so on.
- *Fitzhugh Plus.* Allied Education Council. Programmed workbooks in shape matching, figure completion, and shape identification.
- *Frostig Program for the Development of Visual Perception.* Follett Publishing. Paper-and-pencil activities to develop visual perception in five areas.
- *Pictures and Patterns.* Follett Publishing. Exercises for body awareness, visual-motor coordination, figure-ground, perceptual constancy, and position in space.

2. ALPHABET BOOKS

- *All in the Woodland Early,* Jane Wolen, William Collins, 1979. Features birds, animals, and insects of the North American woodland, described in verse for each letter.
- *Alligators All Around,* Maurice Sendak, Harper & Row, 1962. Miniature book (in *Nutshell Library*) uses alligators as main characters to develop the alphabet in a humorous format.
- *Ape in a Cape,* Fritz Eichenberg, Harcourt Brace, 1952. Book presents funny animals, and rhyming (fox in a box, goat in a boat) format appeals to young and older students.
- *Bruno Munari's ABC,* Bruno Munari, Collins & World, 1960. Everyday words are illustrated in bright colors with unique use of space and design. Each letter has one to five accompanying pictures and words.
- *John Burningham's ABC,* John Burningham, Bobbs-Merrill, 1964. Employs both upper-and lowercase letters. Illustrative words include iguana, wasp, and volcano.

3. AUDITORY PERCEPTION MATERIALS

- *Auditory Perception Training.* Developmental Learning Materials. A multimedia kit (cassette, spirit masters, etc.) for learning auditory perception.
- *Goldman-Lynch Sounds & Symbols Development Kit,* American Guidance Service, 1971.
- *The MWM Program for Developing Language Abilities.* Educational Performance Association. A kit of remedial materials based on language disabilities as diagnosed by the ITPA.
- *Semel Auditory Processing Program.* Follett Publishing. A program for remediating deficits in auditory comprehension skills.
- *Sound-Order-Sense.* Follett Publishing. A program to develop auditory perception abilities.

B. Language Development

1. KITS AND PROGRAMS

- *Distar Language I,* Engelmann, Osborn, Engelmann, SRA, 1972. Young children learn to make statements and respond to questions. Concepts taught focus on logical thinking, and schoollike language vocabulary development is included. Critics object to obligatory use of standard English forms and controlled, behavioral format. Kit contains teacher's guide, six presentation books (Books A–C, each having two parts), a storybook, a color book, and a set of 180 take-home materials.

- *Distar Language II*, Engelmann, Osborn, Engelmann, SRA, 1972. Reviews skills taught in Distar Language I; emphasizes language analysis and gives information about environment. Areas include synonyms and antonyms, classification, function, analogies, descriptions, and definitions. Kit contains teacher's guide, five presentation books (Books A–E), a storybook, and a set of 180 take-home materials.

- *GOAL Program Language Development Game*, Karnes, Milton Bradley, 1972. Based on the Illinois Test of Psycholinguistic Abilities. Helps children to acquire language skills basic to learning to read. Includes manipulative materials for group or individual use. There are 396 model lessons based on skill areas such as auditory and visual reception, auditory and visual association, verbal and manual expression, auditory and visual memory, and grammatic, auditory, and visual closure. Includes motivating pictures and games for children. The GOAL Program is available in several levels for varying age groups.

- *The MWM Program for Developing Language Abilities*, Minskoff, Wiseman, Minskoff, Educational Performance Associates. Based on twelve areas of the Illinois Test of Psycholinguistic Abilities. The program is designed for children ages three to seven; however, it may be used with remedial children to age ten. The kit includes noun, adjective, verb, and sorting cards (picture cards), five workbooks (for reception, association, closure, expression, and memory), and picture cards.

- *Sounds of Language Readers, Instant Readers, Owl Books*, Martin, Holt, Rinehart, and Winston. Builds language and reading skills through visual and sound stimulation. *Sounds of Language* contains a series of graded basal-type readers that concentrate on interesting and innovative visual formats and poetry, folktales, and visual word plays. Annotated teacher's guide and cassettes available. Three sets of *Instant Readers* (grades 1, 2, 3) contain ten titles, each of small books designed to interest readers (cassettes available). *Owl Books* come in three sets. Each contains several arithmetic, literature, science, and social studies books. *Little Owl*, K–2; *Young Owl*, 2–4; *Wise Owl*, 4–6.

- *Peabody Language Development Kits (Revised)*, Dunn, Smith, Dunn, Horton, and Smith, American Guidance Services. Program stimulates oral language skills in standard English and advances cognitive skills about one year per level. A multisensory approach is used, and divergent, convergent, and associative thinking is stressed. Four kits contain lesson plans and props (card decks, mascot, puppets, etc.); level P, ages 3–5; level 1, ages 5–6; level 2, ages 6–7; level 3, ages 7–8.

2. Word Books

- *Best Word Book Ever*, Scarry, Golden Press. Each two-page spread concentrates on a theme (e.g., vehicles at the farm). Illustrations of objects are accompanied by printed words.

- *The Cat in the Hat Beginner Dictionary*, Eastman, Beginners Books, Random House. Illustrated word meanings. Simple sentences demonstrate use of plural, past-tense, and "ing" endings.

- *My First Picture Dictionary*, Greet and Jenkins. Schiller, Lothrop. Color-coded words arranged in subject areas (people, animals, storybook characters, what we do, places) and alphabetized within each group. Words followed by plural forms, sentence, and illustration. Words in final section tell when, how, how much, where, which one, what color.

- *Little Monster's Word Book*, Mayer. Golden Book. Words and pictures with animal characters include seasons, feelings, weather, holidays and games, in upper- and lowercase letters. Number words and letters on inside covers.

- *Words, Words, Words, Words,* Corwin, Platt & Munk. Words and pictures identify parts of the body, things around the house, park, farm, grocery store, street, and zoo. The inside covers have words from A to Z, numbers, colors, and shapes, all with illustrations.
- *Push-Pull Empty-Full,* Hoban, Macmillan. Striking full-page black-and-white photographs for fifteen pairs of opposites (push-pull, in-out, wet-dry, etc.). Encourages interpretation and creativity.

3. WORDLESS PICTURE BOOKS

- *Alligator's Toothache,* de Groat, Crown Publishers. Tale of an alligator with a toothache who is afraid of the dentist.
- *Deep in the Forest,* Turkle, E. P. Dutton. Curious little bear enters the log cabin of a human family in early America; a clever inversion of the classic *Goldilocks* story.
- *Frog, Where Are You?* Mayer, Dial. Humorous story about a boy who looks for his lost frog; small-sized book.
- *Little Love Story,* Krahn, Lippincott. Describes the work involved in preparing a Valentine gift; cartoon-style illustrations.
- *Naughty Nancy,* Goodall, Atheneum. A small mouse is flower girl in her sister's wedding.

4. PREDICTABLE LANGUAGE BOOKS

- *The Three Billy Goats Gruff,* Marcia Brown, Harcourt Brace 1957. A charming retelling of this classic tale.
- *Goodnight Moon,* Margaret Wise Brown, Harper & Row, 1947. A child tells her feelings and thoughts to the moon.
- *The Very Hungry Caterpillar,* Eric Carle, Collins World, 1969. A caterpillar eats progressively bigger pieces of food.
- *The Mixed Up Chameleon,* Eric Carle, Thomas Y. Crowell, 1975. Another charming animal tale.
- *The Grouchy Ladybug,* Eric Carle, Thomas Y. Crowell, 1977. A continuation of the animal theme.
- *May I Bring a Friend?,* Beatrice Schnek de Regniers, Atheneum, 1972. A classic story of a young girl's feelings.
- *Millions of Cats,* Wanda Gag. A story of many cats told with magnificent woodcuts.
- *Henny Penny,* Paul Galdone, Scholastic, 1968. A classic retelling of the children's story.

C. Special Remedial Approaches

Corrective Reading: Decoding A, B, C

Engelmann and others   *Reading Level: PP–6*
Science Research Associates   *Interest Level: 4–Adult*

Daily thirty-five- to forty-five-minute lessons for adolescents and adults who need decoding skills. Teacher-directed work, independent applications, and tests of student performance. Level A: Word-Attack Basics, 60 lessons stress sounds, rhyming, sounding out, and word and sentence reading. Level B: Decoding Strategies, 140 lessons stress critical letter and word discriminations, letter combinations, story reading, and written answers to text questions. Level C: Skill Applications, 140 lessons stress word buildups, affixes, vocabulary, story reading with comprehension questions, and outside reading applications. Teacher scripts provide exact guides for teaching.

DISTAR Reading System
Engelmann and Osborn
Science Research Associates   *Reading Level: 1–3*

Highly structured, systematic reading program emphasizing synthetic phonics. Employs behavioral management strategies. Designed for use with small groups and teaches students to blend sound together using a modified alphabet. Requires teacher preparation for presenting sequences of programmed tasks taught by specific teaching techniques. Drill routine used.

Glass Analysis For Decoding Only
Glass and Glass
Easier to Learn   *Reading Level: 1–4*

Decoding skills using a letter-cluster method (rather than single letter or whole word). Immediate reinforcement is used to shape the decoding behavior of the student. Accompanying practice books provide sentence reading, questions, and answers. Four packets include starters, mediums, harders, completers.

Hegge-Kirk-Kirk Remedial Reading Drills
George   *Reading Level: 1–3*

Workbooks providing practice in phonics skills using regular pattern words in isolation. Words read across page in four parts: (1) consonants and short vowels, (2) combinations, (3) whole words, and (4) supplementary exercises.

Multisensory Approach to Language Arts for Specific Language Disability Children
Gillingham-Stillman
Educator's Publishing Service   *Reading Level: 1–3*

Contains complete program for teaching by a synthetic phonics approach. Materials include written exercises, manipulatives, and a "jewel box" of words.

Peabody Rebus Reading Program
Woodcock, Clark, and Davies
American Guidance Service   *Reading Level: K–1*

Uses pictographic symbols (or rebuses) to introduce reading and gradually phases to words. The program includes two levels: readiness and transition. In the first level, student acquires word endings, context and picture clues, answering questions, and left-right progression. In the second level, sounding out words, punctuation, and story reading are taught; rebus pictures are phased out.

IV. REAL-LIFE MATERIALS/FUNCTIONAL READING

These materials prepare adolescents and adults to face life tasks or vocational training.

Basic Life Skills
Cassidy   *Reading Level: 4–5*
Continental Press   *Interest Level: 9–Adult*

Practical experiences in business include job ads, using a checkbook, understanding credit, and reading and paying bills. Designed for secondary students and adults with limited reading ability. The lessons are printed on easy-to-use file folders, with accompanying activity worksheets. Teacher's guide.

Follett Coping Skills Series

Follett

Reading Level: Grades 3-5
Interest Level: Grades 9-adult

Sixteen workbooks teaching life-coping skills, organized around Adult Performance Objectives. Titles include *Finding Work, Getting Medical Assistance, Budgeting, Using Community Resources, Job Interviews, Banking, Child Care, The Law and You, Keeping a Job, Becoming a U.S. Citizen*, and others.

Follett Coping Skills Series

Turner
Follett

Reading Level: Grades 3-5
Interest Level: 1-adult

Series helps remedial readers to gain life-coping and success skills. Each of eighteen workbooks contains twenty-one lessons. Workbooks are divided into three series: (1) personal competence (*The Money You Spend, The Friends You Make*, etc.), (2) communications (*The Television You Watch, The Movies You See*, etc.), and (3) career guidance (*Looking for a Job, Changing a Job*). Written activities follow each lesson.

Life Skills Reading (See Section VI C)

News For You

Gridley, Editor
New Readers' Press, Laubach Literacy

Reading Level: Grades 1-3
Interest Level: Adult

Laubach publishes this four-to-six page newspaper each week (on Wednesday). It is adult in format but easy in reading levels. Levels A and B look the same but vary in reading level.

READING LEVELS
A 1-2
B 2-3

The Good Idea Books: Life Skills Reading

Enrich

Reading Level: 3-8
Interest Level: 4-12

Attractively colorful double pages that convert to reading center posters designed to help transfer classroom reading skills to practical, everyday world and to help them understand why they are learning to read. Lower-level titles are *Favorite Menus, Telephone Power, Chocolate Coated Reading, Using Cereal Boxes*, and *Sweepstakes*. Upper-level topics include *Baskin-Robbins Ice Cream, Yellow Pages, Great America*, and *Marine World/Africa*.

Level I: Reading, 3-6; interest, 4-12
Level II: Reading, 5-8; interest, 5-12

Pacemaker Vocational Readers

Glasner and Thypin
Fearon

Reading Level: 3
Interest Level: 7-12

Ten realistic career-oriented stories for students describing experience of a young adult deciding to get a job. Practical information is given about job getting and job keeping. Each job described is feasible for special-need students (auto mechanic, short-order cook, gardener, waitress, a day care center aide.)

Shop Talk: Vocational Reading Skills

Allyn & Bacon

Interest Level: 9-12

Six low-level English texts present the language and reading skills that students need on the job. Each booklet is devoted to a specific vocational area: agriculture, auto mechanics, carpentry, electricity, electronics, metal, and machines. Supplementary ditto masters accompanied by program.

Survival
Hall and others   *Reading Level: 7*
Holt, Rinehart and Winston   *Interest Level: 7–adult*

Single book presents skills including locating and renting a place to live, filling out applications for employment, registering to vote, and completing a W–4 form. Skillbooks can be ordered for each state's particular laws, bureaucracy, living conditions, and opportunities.

V. SYSTEMATIC PHONICS PROGRAMS

These may be divided into (A) synthetic and (B) analytic.

A. Synthetic Approaches

Breaking The Code
Lebo and Thomas
Open Court

Designed for problem readers. Uses a synthetic, highly structured approach, controlled by common phonics patterns. Includes special alphabet-sound cards that teach letter sounds rather than names, workbooks, response cards, cassettes, and games.

Keys To Reading
Matteoni, Lane, et al.
The Economy Company   *Reading Level: 1–6*

Presents controlled readability and repetition of common phonics patterns and features early introduction of comprehension strategies. Includes fiction, fantasy, essays, poetry, drama, and biographies. Each level includes text, activity book, supportive materials, and competency skills tests.

Speech To Print Phonics
Harcourt Brace   *Reading Level: 1–3*

Systematic approach to the teaching of synthetic phonics. A teacher-led program that helps students to develop phonics skills by saying letters and sounds and by identifying words with phonics patterns. Program contains 238 phonics practice cards, pupil response cards, and tests to be given at regular intervals. No application in reading context is given. Designed for use with large groups, although it can be adapted for small-group or individual use. Program presented in kit format.

B. Analytic (Linguistic) Approaches

Merrill Linguistic Reading Program
Wilson et al.   *Reading Level: 1–6*
Charles E. Merrill   *Interest Level: 1–8*

Highly structured analytic program concentrates on building a strong foundation in decoding skills. Program contains readers, skills books, reinforcement masters, mastery tests, and additional reading books for literature appreciation. Short, interesting stories are preceded by introduction of new vocabulary.

The Basic Reading Series
Rasmussen and Goldberg
Science Research Associates   *Reading Level: PP–6*

A basal series for remedial readers teaches decoding and comprehension skills in an analytic approach. Program includes Alphabet Book at readiness level and six additional levels, each containing a reader and a workbook. The program develops skills in a structured format and uses a carefully controlled vocabulary in stories, poems, and plays.

Sullivan Reading Program

McGraw-Hill
Reading Level: PP–4
Interest Level: PP–8

This series of softback workbooks uses an analytic phonics-linguistic approach to teach reading. The text uses a programmed format, where students fill in words into individual frames and then check their own answers. If students can be taught to use a programmed system independently, this program provides excellent material for individual work.

Programmed Reading
Sullivan and Buchanan
McGraw-Hill   *Reading Level: K–3*

Programmed, developmental format uses analytic approach. Series contains a prereading program followed by twenty-three individualized soft-cover pupil books, divided into levels 1–3. Student progresses individually through step-by-step instruction in word recognition and decoding skills. Continuous reinforcement is provided by allowing student to check own answers after completing each page. Fifteen storybooks for independent reading and ditto masters are available.

The Palo Alto Reading Program
Harcourt Brace   *Reading Level: 1–3*

Supplementary reading program. Twenty-one nonconsumable soft-cover books for levels 1–3. Each book contains two-page lessons with three parts (preparation, reading selection, follow-up). The prereading section includes introduction of vocabulary, compare and contrast, and grammar (i.e., syntax, homonyms). The reading selection (about one-half page) with illustration features high-interest material. Six follow-up questions include main idea, literal details, follow-up on vocabulary, and phonics. Also available are twenty-one reading workpads, readiness workpads, word cards, wall charts, ditto masters, and tests.

VI. MATERIAL FOR SKILLS DEVELOPMENT

This material fosters the systematic development of reading skills. First, materials that develop skills in several areas are listed, and then materials for word recognition, comprehension, meaning vocabulary, study skills, and rate development are listed separately. Although materials listed in these sections may contain some reading, primary emphasis is on focusing on different parts—or skills—that contribute to reading.

A. Multiskill Development   D. Vocabulary
B. Word Recognition   E. Study Skills
C. Comprehension   F. Rate

These materials develop reading skills in areas of word recognition, comprehension, and meaning vocabulary. Thus, they cannot be classified into any one reading area, but are useful for many areas.

A. Multiskill Development

Activity Concepts English

Reading Level: 5
Interest Level: 7–11

Scott, Foresman

These books integrate the teaching of reading, writing, listening, and spelling. They provide three years worth of curriculum, and are often used in English classes for those needing basic skills. Each book contains ten to twelve short stories and one novel. Book levels are 301, 302, 401, 402, 501, and 502.

Merrill Reading Skill Text Series

Johnson
Charles E. Merrill

Reading Level: K–6

A developmental reading skills program. Series of ten consumable workbooks. Two-page lessons include story, illustrations, and exercise page with a variety of questions about the passage covering such skills as main idea, details, implications, word recognition, and vocabulary. Some questions require student to write short-sentence answers. Includes audiovisual materials.

READING LEVELS

Going Places in Reading	1A	*Tracy*	3B
Bibs	1B	*Ben, the Traveler*	4
Mack	2A	*Tom, the Reporter*	5
Nicky	2A	*Pat, the Pilot*	6
Holly	2B		
Uncle Bunny	3A		

The Reading Practice Program

Harcourt Brace

Reading Level: 3–8

A set of 233 lesson cards, each card concentrating on a single skill. The kit is divided into the areas of decoding, vocabulary, comprehension, and language skills. Student works at own pace in areas of need. The kit includes pretests and posttests that are criterion-referenced and may be self-corrected by the student.

Skillbooster Series

Brown, Dramer, et al.
Modern Curriculum Press

Reading Level: 2–6

Specific skill development includes comprehension, vocabulary, and study skills. Series of small, soft-covered workbooks at five levels. Four to six skills covered at each level. Each book covers one skill area including following directions, building word power, increasing comprehension, facts and details, organizing information, and using references. High-interest subjects presented in widely varied format that includes puzzle pages, funny posters, and treasure maps.

Specific Skills Series
Boning
Dexter and Westbrook *Reading Level: 1–12*

Skill development in eight specific areas. Useful for focused instruction in remedial, corrective, and developmental settings. Eight specific skill booklets (nonconsumable) at each of twelve levels include (1) *Getting the Main Idea*, (2) *Getting the Facts*, (3) *Drawing Conclusions*, (4) *Following Directions*, (5) *Locating the Answer*, (6) *Detecting the Sequence*, (7) *Using the Context*, and (8) *Working with Sounds*. Each booklet focuses on the development of one reading skill on one reading level. Skills are usually placed in a short, reading context (sentences or paragraphs). Provides student with additional drill in area of need.

Picture Level
Preparatory Level
A = 1   E = 5   I = 9
B = 2   F = 6   J = 10
C = 3   G = 7   K = 11
D = 4   H = 8   L = 12

Study Cards
Scott Foresman *Reading Level: 4–6*

Card sets for independent review. Review cards to extend the following skills: main idea, context clues, critical thinking, vocabulary development. Includes the use of maps, graphs, and charts. Each card employs a different format, covering a wide variety of student responses, such as multiple-choice, fill-ins, and answering questions.

Set I   4   Set III   6
Set II   5

Supportive Reading Skills
Boning
Dexter and Westbrook *Reading Level: 1–12*

Supplements *Specific Skills Series*. Nonconsumable series of paperback booklets used for further development of reading skills. Each skill booklet focuses on the development of one reading skill on one reading level and contains multiple-choice exercises. Booklets are available individually or in boxes. Topics listed below are Bas = basic, 2–4; Int = intermediate, 5–6; Adv = advanced 7–9 (A = 1, B = 2, C = 3, D = 4, E = 5, F = 6):

Reading Schedules: A–F, Adv
Reading Ads: A–F, Adv
Interpreting Idioms: A–F, Adv
Mastering Multiple Meanings: A–B
Word-O-Rama: Int and Adv
Understanding Questions: A–F, Adv
Discovering Word Patterns: Bas, Int, Adv
Recognizing Word Relationships: Bas, Int, Adv

Rhyme Time: A–B
Learning to Alphabetize: A–C
Using Guide Words: D–F, Adv
Using a Table of Contents: A–F, Adv
Using an Index: C–F, Adv
Reading Homonyms: A–F, Adv
Reading Heteronyms: A–F, Adv
Reading Homographs: A–F, Adv
Phonic Analogies: A–C
Syllabication: B–F, Adv

Try This Series
Santeusanio and Batty
Harcourt Brace *Reading Level: 1–3*

This series of three kits is used for review and reinforcement of decoding, comprehension, language, and study skills. Each kit contains activity cards with erasable plastic overlays for student responses. Students may work independently charting progress on individual record forms.

Try This   1   *Now Try This*   3
Try This Too   2

Sights and Sounds

Kravitz and Dramer   *Reading Level: 2-5*
Learning Trends, Globe   *Interest Level: 4-12*

Two paperback books containing very short (150- to 300-word) stories of adventure, biography, history, and so on. Each story is followed by several pages of skill development in vocabulary and comprehension (understanding the story, what does it mean, finding the main idea, choose the best word, thinking about the story, fact finding).

READING LEVELS
Book 1:   2-3
Book 2:   3-4
Book 3:   4-5

B. Word Recognition

These materials may be used to practice word recognition skills.

BEST: Building Essential Skills Together

Harrison   *Reading Level: 1-3*
The Economy Company   *Interest Level: 1-Adult*

A tutorial program that deals with word analysis skills that may or may not be used with Keytext, a basal reading program for pupils experiencing problems in reading. Cassette tape explains the purpose and teaching procedure to teachers, parents, paraprofessionals, or peers. Complete set includes 200 3″ × 5″ picture and letter cards, 85 5″ × 8″ instructional cards, teacher handbook with cross-reference of skills to activity cards, cassette tape, and pad for recording.

Conquests in Reading

Kottmeyer and Ware
McGraw-Hill, Webster Division   *Reading Level: 2-6*

Building phonics and structural analysis skills in reading. Single remedial workbook covers a variety of phonics skills (synthetic approach) for word recognition. Also includes vocabulary development and some literal comprehension skills. Word lists for consonant and vowel practice and recognizing compound and multisyllable words.

READING LEVELS
Book A: 2.5-3.0   Book E: 4.5-5.0
Book B: 3.0-3.5   Book F: 5.0-5.5
Book C: 3.5-4.0   Book G: 5.6-6.0
Book D: 4.0-4.5

Discovering Phonics We Use Series

Meighten, Pratt, et al.
Riverside Publishing   *Reading Level: 1-6*

Series of seven illustrated workbooks teach and review phonics and some structural analysis skills. One-page lessons. Isolated skills with no context. Helps student to associate written symbols and speech sounds.

READING LEVELS

Book A:	1	Book D:	4
Book B:	2	Book E:	5
Book C:	3	Book F:	6

Dolch Word Cards

Dolch
Garrard Press   *Reading Level: 1–3*

Three sets of small word cards.

- *Dolch Basic Sight Vocabulary:* 220 words most frequently found in primary level readers.
- *Dolch Picture Word Cards:* 95 common nouns; word on front of card, picture on back.
- *Dolch Sight Phrase Cards:* Basic and picture words are combined in cards containing phrases.

Instructional Aid Kits

Barnell Loft   *Reading Level: 1–6*

Boxes of cards on five different topics to develop word recognition skills.

FOR PHONICS

Time for Sounds (pictured sound correspondences) 1–2
Riddle Raddle Rhyme Time (student constructs words from first letter and rhyming words) 1–2
Fun with Words (student constructs word from meaning and rhyming word) 1–6

FOR SIGHT WORDS

One Too Many (one too many words in a sentence) 1–2

FOR CONTEXT CLUES

We Read Sentences (students fill in word deleted from sentence; kits contain basic vocabulary) 1

Instructional Aid Packs

Barnell Loft   *Reading Level: 1–9*

These are packs of cards that emphasize word recognition skills. Each kit contains several topics. Each topic contains twenty-two to thirty-five cards to practice word recognition skills in isolated word format.

- *Decoding Set I:* K–1, matching letters, matching letters and words, matching initial consonants, matching final consonants, matching words, matching upper-and lowercase letters.
- *Decoding Set II:* Initial consonant levels (2), digraphs and final levels (2), vowels (2), word elements (six packs, grades 1–3).
- *Decoding Set III:* Compounds (six packs, 1–9), endings/suffixes (eight packs, 2–9), prefixes (six packs, 4–9), roots-stems (8 packs, 6–9).
- *Vocabulary Games:* Five word recognition/vocabulary games: Tack on (1–5), Swap (1–5), Turn About (1–5), and Strike Out.

Merrill Phonics Skilltext Series

Charles E. Merrill

Reading Level: 1.0–4.0
Interest Level: K–6

Supplementary reading series to teach phonics skills. Series contains readiness level and six additional levels of soft-cover books that concentrate on mastery of four major skills: auditory discrimination, sound-to-letter association, letter-to-sound association, and using context. Material is presented in one-page exercises.

READING LEVELS

The Costume Shop	1.0	*The Sign Makers*	2.5
The Costume Kids	1.5	*The Detective Club*	3.0
The Space Visitors	2.0	*The Whiz Kid*	4.0

Pacemaker Core Vocabularies 1 and 2

Hillerich
Fearon

Reading Level: 3–4
Interest Level: 7–8

These basic word lists accurately reflect the reading vocabularies of disabled readers as tested in representative schools in Arizona, California, Illinois, Ohio, and Oklahoma. The Pacemaker Core Vocabulary 1 consists of 1,021 words recognized in isolation by seventh-and eighth-graders reading 3.0 (95 percent accuracy). The Pacemaker Core Vocabulary 2 consists of 730 words recognized by seventh- through ninth-graders reading at 4.0 (95 percent accuracy).

Phonics Is Fun

Modern Curriculum Press

Reading Level: grades 1–3

Phonics and structural analysis skills. Series of three consumable workbooks teaching phonics skills. Books 2 and 3 introduce new skills and review skills taught in previous book. Emphasis on skills review; no contextual practice.

See, Also, Section IV: Instructional Material for Phonics.

C. Comprehension Skills

These materials concentrate on the systematic development of comprehension.

Basic Reading Units

Gunning
Continental Press

Reading Level: 2–5
Interest Level: 7–12

Four programs. Each program has four booklets covering six levels, A–F. Each booklet concentrates on one comprehension skill: (1) main ideas, (2) facts and details, (3) inferences, and (4) sequencing. Booklets provide high-interest, easy-to-read materials designed for older disabled readers. Topics include sports, true-life adventure, science, history, and biography. The booklets contain short reading passages, usually one page, followed by questions covering the skill to be stressed. Spirit masters of booklets also available as is a teacher's guide with answer key.

Catching On Series

Bereiter
Open Court

Reading Level: 2–6

Comprehension through cognitive skill development. Development of critical reading and thinking skills. Series consists of five soft-cover books, levels A–E. Level A may be begun in second or third grade and other levels follow in sequence. Unique format includes humor and absurdity to motivate thoughtful reading and reasoning. Excellent for students who need to focus on meaning.

Comprehension We Use
Mangrum
Rand McNally   *Reading Level: 1–6*

Soft-cover books contain one-page stories with comprehension questions following. Books teach students an actual strategy for such skills as finding the main idea and drawing inferences.

Corrective Reading: Comprehension A, B, C
Engelmann and others   *Reading Level: PP–Adult*
Science Research Associates   *Interest Level: 4–Adult*

Unique program that employs direct teaching to refine cognitive skills. Level A, *Thinking Basics*, contains 60 lessons stressing oral language, deductions, inductions, analogies, vocabulary building, and inferences. Level B, *Comprehension Skills*, contains 140 lessons stressing literal and inferential skills, reading for information, writing skills, following sequenced directions, analyzing contradictions, learning information. Level C, *Concept Applications*, contains 140 lessons stressing advanced comprehension applications: reading for information, analyzing arguments, reasoning. Student book available for each level; teacher book and student workbook available for level C.

Guidebook To Better Reading Series
Rambeau and Rambeau   *Reading Level: 2–6*
The Economy Company   *Interest Level: 5–Adult*

Teaches students reading below grade level critical comprehension skills and gives them an opportunity to practice on attractively packaged stories of adventure, mystery, survival, and intrigue. Supplementary readers, duplicating masters, lessons on sixteen cassette tapes, and teacher's handbook available.

Life Skills Reading
                                                          Reading Level: 3–5
Enrich Publishers, Division of Ohaus   *Interest Level: 5–8*

These colorful sets of programs develop interest in reading and critical reading abilities using sets of two-page laminated displays. Materials center around "real world" interests such as McDonalds and Baskin Robbins menus. They develop such skills as locating facts, interpreting facts, and extending facts. They can be used to create reading interest centers in the classroom. Ditto sheets are also available. Titles of sets include:

Favorite Menus	*Using Menus*
Telephone Power	*Yellow Pages*
Chocolate Coated Reading	*Frontierland*
Using Cereal Boxes	*Great America*
Sweepstakes	*Marine World/Africa U.S.A.*

Open-Ended Plays
Velder, Cohen, and Mazzarelli   *Reading Level: 3–4*
Learning Trends, Globe   *Interest Level: 6–12*

The twenty short, open-ended plays give students an opportunity to "put themselves into the story" and work out solutions to real-life situations. Students must supply endings for stories.

Some of the themes explored include developing personal values, choosing a life-style, and learning to live with a family. A list of characters and an introductory paragraph sets the scene. Ideas for writing and discussions are at the end of the text. Teacher's guide. Text is 160 pages.

Open-Ended Stories
Velder and Cohen
Learning Trends, Globe

Reading Level: 4-5
Interest Level: 7-12

None of the twenty short stories in this text has an ending. It is up to the student to supply a conclusion orally or in writing and defend his or her ideas. The stories are about realistic characters and cover drugs, cheating, prejudice, and loneliness. Question material for each story appears in the back of the book and is categorized as "Thinking About the Story" and "Thinking About the Ending." Teacher's guide. Text has 160 pages.

Multiple Skills Series
Boning
Barnell Loft

Reading Level: K-9

Half-page stories are followed by three to five comprehension questions: Each level follows a consistent question pattern. For example, on the introductory level, one main idea, one stated fact, and one picture clue; on levels 7-9, one main idea, two stated details, one inference, and one vocabulary question. Story and questions are two pages on first levels and one page on levels 3-9. Four books on each level.

> PICTURE LEVEL
> PREPARATORY LEVEL

Levels A–L are on reading grades 1–12.

Levels Picture, Preparatory, and 1–6 are available in Spanish.

Pronoun Parade (Instructional Aid Kits)
Barnell Loft

Reading Level: 1-5

Each packet contains several cards. On each card, three exercises require a pronoun in a sentence to be replaced by a noun. Three alternative nouns are given as choices. Five levels, A–E, grades one through five.

Reading Comprehension Series
Opportunities for Learning

Reading Level: 2-6

Set of ten boxes, each containing fifty cards. Each box covers a specific comprehension skill at five levels. The cards in each box are arranged in order of increasing difficulty. Reading selections are on one side, with questions covering the selection on the other side. Skills included are main idea, drawing conclusions, context clues, sequence, cause and effect, outcomes, inferences, reading phrases, noting detail, and understanding sentences.

Reading Comprehension Series
Resnick and Hyatt
Steck-Vaughan

Reading Level: 1-3
Interest Level: 1-5

Four levels of soft-cover consumable workbooks directed toward primary readers, but also effective as remedial material for older elementary students. One- or two-page illustrated stories about animals, children, pets, and everyday activities are followed by an interesting variety of exercises covering comprehension and vocabulary skills. To further reinforce skills, a review lesson is presented after each five lessons.

READING LEVELS

| Claws and Paws | 1 | Manes and Reins | 2 |
| Gills and Bills | 1 | Bones and Stones | 3 |

Reading For Comprehension
Walpole
Continental Press   *Reading Level: 2–9*

Stimulating reading and comprehension skills. Ditto masters at each level. Interesting reading selections (one-half page) followed by written exercises covering such areas as factual information, fact and opinion, analogies, inferences, and main idea. Workbooks also available at junior high level only.

Reading For Understanding
Thurstone
Science Research Associates   *Reading Level: 3–adult*

Each kit contains a series of four-hundred activity cards. Each card contains ten sentences or short passages with the last word missing. The student chooses the best of four suggested concluding words. These cloze selections help to develop sentence comprehension and inference skills. Selections cover areas such as education, politics, history, art, and philosophy.
    Placement test, student record book, and teacher's guide.

READING LEVELS

Kit I:	1–3
Kit II:	3–7
Kit III:	7–12

The Reading Power Tapes Program
Brown, Dann, and Herbst   *Reading Level: 4–5*
Learning Trends, Globe   *Interest Level: 6–12*

A multimedia program on twelve cassettes that presents good mysteries, true adventures, great moments in history, science fiction, and stories about famous people (twenty-four in all). Each story is divided into three parts. During the break, a reading skill is introduced and discussed. Plenty of examples are given before a student works independently in an accompanying workbook. Teacher's manual.

Reading, Thinking and Reasoning
Skills Program, Revised
Barnes, Burgdorf, and Wenck
Steck-Vaughn   *Reading Level: 1–6*

Set of consumable workbooks that contain one-page exercises to develop higher-order comprehension subskills through the grades. Skills addressed include developing conclusions, judging abstract or concrete, discriminating between definition and example. Books center on wide variety of skills rather than on systematic development. Teaches higher-level comprehension skills at primary levels.

READING LEVELS

Sunshine	1	*Beaming Sunshine*	1
Whispers	2	*Sharing Whispers*	2
Raindrops	3	*Falling Raindrops*	3
Footsteps	4	*Wandering Footsteps*	4
Snowflakes	5	*Drifting Snowflakes*	5
Clouds	6	*Gathering Clouds*	6
Landscape	7		
Seascope	8		

Reading-Thinking Skills
Maney and Kroehler
Continental Press   *Reading Level: 1-6*

Development of critical thinking skills. Sets of ditto masters or workbooks at each level. Readability level is one level below assigned level. Skill development includes units on organizing ideas, predicting outcomes, and inferences.

Signal/Tactics
Kneer, ed.   *Reading Level: 5-10*
Scott, Foresman   *Interest Level: 7-12*

Signal contains literature units interspersed with skills units. Accompanying tactics paperback books cover nine skill units including context, structure, sound dictionary, inferences, relationships, purpose, and main idea. Short articles included cover such topics as rock singers, FBI manhunt, and mobile construction.

GRADE LEVELS (Singles Books)

Sense	7	Nova	10
Image	8	Album	11
Gallery	9	Latitude	12

Strategies For Reading (Sentences, Paragraphs)
Robinson et al.
Allyn & Bacon   *Reading Level: 6-8*

Two workbooks; each presents ten strategies for comprehension. Sentence strategies include time signals and comparision signals. Paragraph strategies include contrasting ideas and the use of synonyms to follow ideas. Review lessons included.

Thinklab
Weber   *Reading Level: 3-9*
Science Research Associates   *Interest Level: Ages 11–late teens*

Thinklab is designed to develop problem-solving and thinking skills at various levels. It can be used with slow learners, either individually or in small groups. The materials are self-checking, nonconsumable cards, sequenced by difficulty. Teacher's guide includes answer key. There are 500 puzzle cards (four each of 125) and pupil progress sheets. Exercises in five areas deal with data, extrapolating beyond data, abstract relationships, analysis of patterns, and logical analysis.

The World of Entertainers
                                                      Reading Level: 4
Educational Insights   *Interest Level: 5-12*

Stars from the world of "celebrity land" fascinate the reader. Each star is presented on a one-page card in this kit. Six questions on the back of each star biography card are keyed to main idea, facts, vocabulary, sequence, cause and effect, and inferences. Each boxed kit contains forty-eight cards, nineteen spirit masters with follow-up activities, and teacher's guide.

The World of Sports
Shank, Miller, and Falstein   *Reading Level: 4*
Educational Insights   *Interest Level: 5-12*

High-interest profiles of athletes in a wide variety of sports fields presented on large, colorful cards. Each athlete is presented on a one-page card. Six questions on the back of each card are keyed to main idea, facts, vocabulary, sequence, cause and effect, and inferences. Each boxed kit contains forty-eight cards, nineteen spirit masters, one follow-up activity for each card, final activity, student progress sheet, and teacher's guide.

D. Vocabulary Skills

These materials develop vocabulary and language skills.

1. INSTRUCTIONAL MATERIALS

BASE: Basic Approach to the Structure of English
Ellis, Halley, Hauge, Allen
The Economy Company   *Interest Level: 4–Adult*

Music and sound effects highlight a vocabulary development program that emphasizes how words are structured by studying base words and affixes; thirty-three lessons on seventeen cassette tapes, self-scoring, consumable student book, and teacher's handbook.

Etymology (What's in a Name?)
Barnell Loft   *Reading Level: 5–9*

Six booklets concentrate on vocabulary development using names. Titles include *Your Surname, Sir* and *They Gave Their Names.* Includes spirit masters for duplication.

Interpreting Idioms (Supportive Reading Skills)
Boning   *Reading Level: 1–9*
Barnell Loft   *Interest Level: 1–Adult*

Clever, effective solutions to providing experience in understanding phrases and expressions that cannot be understood from ordinary literal meaning of individual words within them. An example is "Don't hold up the line." Units A–F (grades 1–6), one booklet; advanced (grades 7–9), one booklet.

Picto-Cabulary
Boning
Dexter and Westbrook   *Reading Level: 1–9*

Vocabulary development program in series of nonconsumable soft-cover exercise books. Books focus on themes and present pictures to help build interest in vocabulary. Basic word sets for primary readers (1–3); "Words Around the Neighborhood," "Words Around the House," "Words to Eat," "Words to Meet" for levels 4–6; and "Descriptive Words" for levels 5–9. One-page exercises use picture stimulus. Basic word set available in Spanish.

Strategies For Reading Words in Context
Robinson et al.
Allyn & Bacon   *Reading Level: 6–8*

Workbook format presents ten strategies for vocabulary words in context (e.g., using suggested meaning, using opposition) for figuring out words using contextual clues. Review lessons included.

Word-O-Rama (Supportive Reading Skills)
Boning   *Reading Level: 5–9*
Barnell Loft   *Interest Level: 7–Adult*

Excitingly illustrated exercises in booklets. One-page reading passages followed by fill-in sentences. Vocabulary development as well as a better understanding of many things stem from the clever format and presentation of the material. Example titles of the eight booklets: *Meet the Monsters, What's Your Phobia?, Oh Those Manias, Call the Doctor.* Teachers manual. Spirit masters for worksheets. Four units per level.

READING LEVELS

Intermediate Kit: 5–6
Advanced Kit: 7–9

Word Theater

Boning
Dexter and Westbrook   *Reading Level: 3-6*

Vocabulary development utilizing dramatization format. Each booklet contains 300 word skits. Students dramatize a word through a skit, and others guess the meaning of the word. *Word Theater* promotes use of visual images to improve comprehension. It incorporates all aspects of language: listening, reading, speaking, and writing.

READING LEVELS

Level C: 4 books (3)
Level D: 4 books (4)
Level E: 4 books (5)
Level F: 4 books (6)

2. VOCABULARY DEVELOPMENT SERIES

EDL Word Clues

Taylor et al.
Educational Development Laboratories   *Reading Level: 7-13*

Workbook series concentrating on "figuring out" words from approaches including context and word structure. Supplementary materials available.

Reading Around Words

Taylor and White
Instructional/Communications Technology   *Reading Level: 4-12*

In this workbook series, words are introduced in a paragraph and students must infer their meaning and then check meaning with definitions in back of workbook. Cassettes available to introduce words, or students can use workbook alone. Each lesson contains twelve words; twenty lessons in each book.

READING LEVELS

A: Grade 4 to
L: Grade 12

Wordly Wise

Hodkinson and Ornato
Educators Publishing Press   *Reading Level: 4-12*

Each unit contains four exercise sections and review crossword puzzles. Twelve words are introduced in each lesson. After each three lessons, a review is provided. Format includes quotes, poems, riddles. Levels 4–6 give lexical word parts; 7–9 give analogies, connotative meanings.

3. BOOKS ABOUT VOCABULARY

Amelia Bedelia

Fritz Siebel
Harper   *Reading Level: 1-3*

Amelia Bedelia is a maid who interprets instructions in the strict literal manner. Comical situations evolve from her interpetation of words. Also, *Come Back Amelia Bedelia.*

Homonyms
Joan Hanson
Lerner Publications   *Reading Level: 1–3*

This book, with delicate, attractive pen-and-ink drawings, illustrates homonyms on facing pages with words such as flower-flour, son-sun, peak-peek. Similar books by this author are *Synonyms* and *Antonyms.*

The King Who Rained
Fred Gwynne
Windmill/Wander   *Reading Level: 1–3*

A little girl pictures the things her parents talk about, such as "bear" feet, foot "prince" in the snow, "forks" in the road, and fairy "tails."

Words From the Myths
Issac Asimov
Houghton Mifflin   *Reading Level: 6–9*

Each page introduces the story of one word with an origin in classical mythology. Other books by this author include *Words of Science*, and *Words on the Map.*

4. DICTIONARIES, THESAURUSES

The American Heritage School Dictionary
Houghton Mifflin

Includes 35,000 words (main entries). Clear definitions, simple punctuation, and sample sentences. Illustrations, word histories, and grammar and usage notes.

In Other Words—A Beginning Thesaurus
Schiller and Jenkins
Lothrop, Lee & Shepard

Includes 102 entry words well known to first through fourth grade students. Provides synonyms and precise word meanings. Words explained in sentence form. Antonyms also included.

In Other Words II—Junior Thesaurus
Schiller and Jenkins
Lothrop, Lee & Shepard

Includes 300 entry words and 2,000 synonyms used in grades four through eight. Illustrative sentences, cross-references, and antonyms are also included. Index.

Macmillan Dictionary for Children
Macmillan

Includes 30,000 entries with realistic full-color illustrations, large type, and no diacritical markings. Sample sentence following each definition. Short articles give interesting language information.

The Super Dictionary
Holt, Rinehart and Winston

Using America's best-known comic-strip characters, the 4,000 entry words are defined clearly and concisely in story form with colorful illustrations. Plurals and past-tense words are included. Format is appealing to preschoolers and beginning and advancing readers.

Webster's New World Dictionary for Young Readers
Collins

Includes 44,000 words and terms. Contains the words that students are most likely to see and hear. Simplified pronunciation key. Includes common idioms.

E. Study Skills/Content Areas

Be A Better Reader (Basic Skills Edition)
Prentice-Hall, Inc. *Reading Level: 4-12*

Newly revised, offering a well-known program in an up-to-date new format. The books are designed primarily to provide reading skill development in various subject areas such as literature, current science, and social studies. In nonconsumable workbook format. Teacher's guide contains a diagnostic pretest and posttest, answer key, and suggestions. Level A (grade 4) to Level I (grade 12).

Content Readers
Harper & Row *Reading Level: 1-6*

Eight readers concentrating on reading in the content areas (social studies, science) accompany regular basal series. Each content area reader has an accompanying workbook.

READING LEVELS

From Dolphins to Dunes	1	*From Pyramids to Princes*	4
From Skyscraper to Squirrels	2	*From Falcons to Forests*	5
From Mysteries to Microbes	3	*From Lions to Legends*	6

Go: Reading in The Content Areas
Herber
Scholastic Press *Reading Level: 4-8*

Designed for teaching below-level readers and average readers skills in literature, social studies, math, and science. Each booklet begins below grade level and works up to grade-level skills. Paperback skill texts contain at least six lessons in each content area; optional ditto masters sets (fifty dittos) are supplementary.

Newslab
MacKenzie
Science Research Associates *Reading Levels: 4-9*

Newspaper reading skills in kit format. Kit with activity cards to promote newspaper reading skills in twelve areas including world news, local news, sports, advertisements, editorials, and cartoons. Individualized activities arranged in order of difficulty. Provides skill development in language arts, social studies, current events, and math. Gives practice in outlining, summarizing, and skimming. Student progress forms are included.

Reading in the Content Fields
Jamestown Press *Reading Level: 4-12*

At each grade level, the program contains separate paperback books in reading English, social studies, mathematics, science, and practical arts. Each booklet describes comprehension skills needed in that area, sample text reading, and twenty-five comprehension exercises. Cassettes also available to present book contents.

Middle level: grades 6–8; reading levels 4–8
Advanced level: grades 9–college; reading levels 8–12

Reading Power Exercises I, II
Koski and Burkhart
Allyn & Bacon

Reading Level: 4
Interest Level: 3–10

Spirit duplicator masters containing multiple choice cloze-type exercises modeled after state reading competency tests that emphasize content-area reading skills from science and social studies.

F. Rate Skills

Controlled Reader
Taylor and Frackenpohl
Educational Development Laboratories

Reading Level: 7–14

Program for improving rates accompanied by vocabulary and comprehension development. Set of passages contained in workbooks are duplicated on filmstrips, which are flashed, line by line, in a controlled reader machine. The rate of presentation of filmstrips may be controlled. Filmstrips contain motivating paragraph, introductory words, and passages. Workbooks add vocabulary check and comprehension questions keyed to specific skills.

READING LEVELS

GH–HG:	7,8	KL–LK:	11,12
IJ–JI:	9,10	MN:	13,14

Flash-X
Educational Development Laboratories

Tachistoscope may be hand-held and flashed by manual mechanism. Round shape (3" diameter) permits handling. Flash may be adjusted. Accompanying word and phrase cards.

Reading Accelerator
Science Research Associates

A lightweight, manually controlled machine which may be placed over book page. The book is read through the clear plastic covering of the accelerator while the opaque "pacer" covers the page at the preset rate. Speeds for the pacer are variable and are set by the reader.

APPENDIX B

ADDRESSES
OF PUBLISHERS
AND RESOURCES

ABBOTT LABORATORIES, Abbott Park, North Chicago, Ill. 60063.

ACADEMIC THERAPY PUBLICATIONS, 20 Commercial Boulevard, Novato, Calif. 94947.

ADDISON-WESLEY PUBLISHING CO., INC., Jacob Way, Reading, Mass. 01867.

ALLIED EDUCATIONAL COUNCIL, P.O. Box 78, Galien, Mich. 49113.

ALLYN & BACON, INC., 470 Atlantic Ave., Boston, Mass. 02210.

AMERICAN ASSOCIATION ON MENTAL DEFICIENCY, 5201 Connecticut Ave., N.W., Washington, D.C. 20015.

AMERICAN BOOK COMPANY., 135 W. 50th St., New York, N.Y. 10020.

AMERICAN GUIDANCE SERVICE, INC., Publishers Bldg., Circle Pines, Minn. 55014.

AMERICAN OPTICAL CO., Box 1, Southbridge, Mass. 01550.

ATHENEUM PUBLISHERS, 597 Fifth Ave., New York, N.Y. 10017.

BARNELL LOFT, LTD., 958 Church St., Baldwin, N.Y. 11510.

BAUSCH AND LOMB OPTICAL CO., Rochester, N.Y. 14602.

BENEFIC PRESS, 1900 N. Naragansett, Chicago, Ill. 60639.

BOBBS-MERRILL CO., INC., 4300 W. 62 St., Indianapolis, Ind. 46206.

BOWMAR/NOBLE PUBLISHERS, INC., 4563 Colorado Blvd., Los Angeles, Calif. 90039.

MILTON BRADLEY CO., Springfield, Mass. 01101.

WILLIAM C. BROWN CO., 2460 Kerper Blvd., Dubuque, Iowa 52001.

CALIFORNIA TESTING BUREAU (CTB)/McGRAW HILL, Del Monte Research Park, Monterey, Calif. 93940.

CHILDREN'S PRESS, 1224 W. Van Buren St., Chicago, Ill. 60607.

THE COLLEGE BOARD, 888 Seventh Avenue, New York, N.Y. 10019.

WILLIAM COLLINS & WORLD PUBLISHING CO., INC.,   2080 W. 117th St., Cleveland, Ohio
    44111.
CONSULTING PSYCHOLOGISTS PRESS,   577 College Ave., Palo Alto, Calif. 94306.
COMMUNICATION RESEARCH ASSOCIATES,   P.O. Box 11012, Salt Lake City, Utah 84111.
CONTINENTAL PRESS, INC.,   520 E. Bainbridge St., Elizabethtown, Pa. 17022.
COUNSELOR RECORDINGS AND TESTING,   Box 6184, Aklan Station, Nashville, Tenn. 37212.
CROWN PUBLISHERS, INC.,   1 Park Ave., New York, N.Y. 10016.
CURRICULUM ASSOCIATES,   5 Esquire Road, North Billerica, Mass. 01862.
DEVELOPMENTAL LEARNING MATERIALS,   7440 Natchex Ave., Niles, Ill. 60648.
DEVEREUX FOUNDATION,   Devon, Pa. 19333.
DEXTER & WESTBROOK LTD.   958 Church St., Baldwin N.Y. 11510.
DIAL PRESS,   245 E. 47th St., New York, N.Y. 10017.
DRIER EDUCATIONAL SYSTEMS   (see Jamestown)
E. P. DUTTON & CO., INC.,   2 Park Ave., New York, N.Y. 10016.
EASIER TO LEARN MATERIALS,   Box 329, Garden City, N.Y. 11530.
THE ECONOMY COMPANY,   Box 25308, 1901 N. Walnut St., Oklahoma City, Okla. 73125.
EDUCATIONAL CHALLENGES,   see Webster Division, McGraw-Hill.
EDUCATIONAL DEVELOPMENTAL LABORATORIES, INC.,   1221 Avenue of the Americas, New
    York, N.Y. 10020 (division of McGraw-Hill).
EDUCATIONAL INSIGHTS,   150 W. Carob, Compton, Calif. 90220.
EDUCATIONAL PERFORMANCE ASSOCIATES, INC.,   563 Westview Ave., Ridgefield, N.J. 07657.
EDUCATORS PUBLISHING SERVICE,   75 Moulton St., Cambridge, Mass. 02138.
EDUCATIONAL TEACHING AIDS,   159 Kinzie St., Chicago, Ill. 60610.
EMPIRIC PRESS   (see Pro-Ed)
ENRICH PUBLISHERS (DIVISION OF OHAUS),   2325 Paragon Dr., San Jose, Calif. 95131.
ESSAY PRESS,   P.O. Box 2323, La Jolla, Calif. 92037.
FEARON PITMAN PUBLISHERS,   6 Davis Dr., Belmont, Calif. 94002.
FOLLETT PUBLISHING CO.,   1010 W. Washington Blvd., Chicago, Ill. 60607.
GARRARD PUBLISHING CO.,   107 Cherry St., New Canaan, Conn. 06840.
GLOBE BOOK CO., INC.,   50 W. 23rd St., New York N.Y. 10010.
GOLDEN PRESS,   150 Parish Dr., Wayne, N.J. 07470.
GORSUCH SCARISBRICK PUBLISHERS,   576 Central Ave., Dubuque, Iowa 52001.
GRUNE & STRATTON, INC.,   111 Fifth Ave., New York, N.Y. 10003.
HARVARD UNIVERSITY PRESS,   79 Garden St., Cambridge, Mass. 02138.
HARPER & ROW, PUBLISHERS, INC.,   10 E. 53rd St., New York, N.Y. 10022.
HARCOURT BRACE JOVANOVICH, INC.,   757 Third Ave., New York, N.Y. 10017.
HISKEY PUBLICATIONS,   5640 Baldwin, Lincoln, Neb. 68508.
HOLT, RINEHART AND WINSTON,   383 Madison Ave., New York, N.Y. 10017.
HOUGHTON MIFFLIN COMPANY,   One Beacon St., Boston, Mass. 02107.
INSTRUCTIONAL COMMUNICATIONS TECHNOLOGY, INC.,   10 Stephar Pl., Huntington Station,
    N.Y. 11746.
JAMESTOWN PUBLISHERS,   Box 5643, Providence, R.I. 02904.
KENDALL/HUNT PUBLISHING CO.,   2460 Kerper Blvd., Dubuque, Iowa 52001.
KEYSTONE VIEW CO.,   2212 E. 12th St., Davenport, Iowa 52803.
KING FEATURES, EDUCATION DIVISION,   235 E. 45th St., New York, N.Y. 10017.
KLAMUTH PRINTING CO.,   320 Lowell St., Klamath Falls, Ore. 97601.
LANGUAGE RESEARCH ASSOCIATES,   P.O. Box 2085, Palm Springs, Calif. 92262.
LEARNING CONCEPTS,   2501 N. Lamar, Austin, Tex. 78705.
LEARNING TRENDS   (see GLOBE)
H. K. LEWIS LTD.,   P.O. Box 66, 136 Gower St., London, WC1E6BS, England.
J. B. LIPPINCOTT COMPANY,   521 Fifth Ave., New York, N.Y. 10017.
LAUBAUCH LITERACY   (see NEW READERS' PRESS).
LOTHROP, LEE AND SHEPARD CO., INC.,   105 Madison Ave., New York N.Y. 10016.

MAICO HEARING INSTRUMENTS,   7375 Bush Lake Rd., Minneapolis, Minn. 55435.

MACMILLAN PUBLISHING CO., INC.,   866 Third Ave., New York, N.Y. 10022.

McGRAW-HILL BOOK COMPANY,   1221 Avenue of the Americas, New York, N.Y. 10020.

CHARLES E. MERRILL PUBLISHING COMPANY,   1300 Alum Creek Dr., Columbus, Ohio 43216.

MIAMI UNIVERSITY ALUMNI ASSOCIATION,   Murstein Alumni Center, Miami University, Oxford, Ohio 45056.

MODERN CURRICULUM PRESS,   13900 Prospect Rd., Cleveland, Ohio 44136.

NEW DIMENSIONS OF EDUCATION,   925 Westchester Ave., White Plains, N.Y. 10604.

NEW READERS' PRESS   (LAUBACH LITERACY), Box 131, Syracuse, N.Y. 13210.

NORTHWESTERN UNIVERSITY PRESS,   1735 Benson Ave., Evanston, Ill. 60201.

OPEN COURT PUBLISHING CO.,   Box 599, La Salle, Ill. 61301.

OPPORTUNITIES FOR LEARNING, INC.,   8950 Lurline Ave., Chatsworth, Calif. 91311.

PERSONNEL PRESS,   191 Spring St., Lexington, Mass. 02173.

PLATT AND MONK (DIVISION OF GROSSET & DUNLAP, INC.)   51 Madison Ave., New York, N.Y. 10010.

PRO-ED,   333 Perry Brook Bld., Austin, Tex. 78751.

PSYCHOLOGICAL CORPORATION,   757 Third Ave., New York, N.Y. 10017.

PSYCHOTECHNICS, INC.,   1900 Pickwick Ave., Glenview, Ill. 60025.

RAINTREE PUBLISHERS LTD.,   205 W. Highland Ave., Milwaukee, Wisc. 53203.

RAND McNALLY & COMPANY,   Box 7600, Chicago, Ill. 60680.

RANDOM HOUSE, INC.,   201 E. 50th St., New York, N.Y. 10022.

READER'S DIGEST, EDUCATIONAL DIVISION,   Pleasantville, N.Y. 10570.

RIVERSIDE PUBLISHING CO.,   1919 S. Highland Ave., Lombard, Ill. 60148.

SCIENCE RESEARCH ASSOCIATION,   155 North Wacker Ave., Chicago, Ill. 60606.

SCOTT, FORESMAN AND COMPANY,   1900 E. Lake Ave., Glenview, Ill. 60025.

SCHOLASTIC BOOK SERVICES   (see SCHOLASTIC MAGAZINE).

SCHOLASTIC MAGAZINE, INC.,   50 W. 44th St., New York, N.Y. 10036.

SCHOLASTIC TESTING SERVICE,   480 Meyer Road, Bensenville, Ill. 60106.

SLOSSON EDUCATIONAL PUBLICATIONS,   140 Pine St., East Aurora, N.Y. 14052.

SRA   (see SCIENCE RESEARCH ASSOCIATES).

STECK-VAUGHN CO.,   P.O. Box 2028, Austin, Tex. 78768.

STOELTING CO.,   1350 S. Kostner Ave., Chicago, Ill. 60623.

TEACHERS COLLEGE PRESS,   1234 Amsterdam Ave., New York, N.Y. 10027.

TEACHING RESOURCES CORP.,   50 Pond Park Road, Hingham, Mass. 02043.

UNIVERSITY OF ILLINOIS PRESS,   54 E. Gregory Dr., P.O. Box 5081, Sta. A, Champaign, Ill. 61820.

WANDERER BOOKS (DIVISION OF SIMON & SCHUSTER, INC.),   1230 Avenue of the Americas, New York, N.Y. 10020.

GEORGE WARE PUBLISHING CO.,   316 South Street, Ann Arbor, Mich. 41808.

WEEKLY READER,   245 Longhill Rd., Middletown, Conn. 06457.

WESTERN PSYCHOLOGICAL SERVICES,   12031 Wilshire Blvd., Los Angeles, Calif. 90025.

XEROX EDUCATION PUBLICATIONS,   245 Long Hill Road, Middletown, Conn. 06457.

APPENDIX C

SAMPLE DIAGNOSTIC READING REPORT

This report is intended to serve as a sample for diagnosticians preparing intensive diagnostic examinations. Space is given at several points in the report to fill in relevant information. In addition, continuous text should be filled in at many points. Diagnosticians should realize that no standardized report form will completely suit the very individual needs of a remedial student and that this form must be adapted to the needs of every case. In addition, certain portions may be deleted, since the report covers a wider range of abilities than would be presented by any individual student. Portions may, of course, also be added. While this report attempts to take a broad view of reading diagnosis, it will probably not be suitable for every theoretical framework of the reading process. The report is intended only as a model that may be adapted freely, in whole or in part.*

* Notes on interpretation: Parentheses enclosing slashes indicate alternatives; that is, (we/they) indicates "we" or "they".

I. DIAGNOSTIC READING REPORT

Name of student	Date of report
Birthdate of student	Diagnostician
Sex of student	Name of school/institution
Present age	Address of school/institution
School (or setting) and grade	Phone of school/institution
Parents' names	Dates of diagnosis
Home address	
Home phone	

This is a diagnostic reading report of (student), who is currently _____ years of age. (Student) was referred to the reading clinic by _____. The reason for referral was _____.

II. ASSESSMENT INSTRUMENTS USED

Name of Test	*Level*	*Form*	*Score/Range*	*Administered by*

III. CURRENT EXPECTED READING LEVEL*

DISCREPANCY.   The level at which a student might be expected to read is important in determining whether or not that student has a reading disability. To determine (student's) current reading expectancy, the (test of intelligence) was administered. The score indicated that (student's) intellectual potential is currently in the (below-average/average/above-average) range.

It should be remembered that intellectual potential is influenced by many factors and is changeable under certain conditions. Previous estimates of potential level by (previous referrals) (agreed/did not agree) with the estimates of the current diagnosis.

Using a reading expectancy formula, it was estimated that (student) currently has the potential to read at the _____ grade level. Since (student's) reading achievement level† is at the _____ grade level,

---

* Both discrepancy criteria and practical criteria are given in this section. Diagnosticians may choose one or use both. Discrepancy criteria are given first.

† This score is usually the *total* score on the standardized survey test that was given to the student.

there is a discrepancy between current achievement and current potential of _____. At (student's) grade level, this indicates (student) (does/does not) have a reading disability.

PRACTICAL. The student's current instructional and life situation (pragmatic considerations) are important in determining if there is a reading disability. At present, (student) functions (considerably below/somewhat below/about as well as) the other students in (his/her) instructional situation. In addition, (student) (shows/does not show) a consistent pattern of reading failure.

In summary, (student's) reading disability can be classified as (mild/moderate/severe/not apparent).

IV. PRESENT READING ACHIEVEMENT LEVEL

To determine (student's) current reading level, the (survey test) was given. Currently (student's) achievement level is

at the _____ grade level. This means that (student) reads about as well as the average student at the _____ grade level who took this test,

at the _____ percentile when compared with others of (his/her) grade. This means that about _____% of the other students perform less well than (student).

In addition, the results of the (informal reading inventory/oral reading inventory) show that (student) is reading at the _____ grade level.

Classroom observations and reports of (student), (his/her) teachers, and parents show that (student) is working at the _____ grade level in (his/her) class.

The results of these and other tests and observations reveal that the area(s) of (word recognition/comprehension/meaning vocabulary/study skills/rate of reading) are currently most in need of remediation.

V. ANALYSIS OF READING STRENGTHS AND WEAKNESSES

Several diagnostic tests and procedures revealed patterns of reading strengths and weaknesses in (student's) performance.

V.A. Oral Reading Skills

As mentioned previously, the (informal reading inventory/oral reading inventory) was given. This test permits close observation of many facets of the student's reading.

Results are given as an independent level (where the student can read without assistance), an instructional level (where the student can read with assistance), and a frustration level (where the student can no longer read). These levels were determined from (oral reading/both oral and silent reading).

READING LEVEL   GRADE

Independent   _____

Instructional   _____

Frustration   _____

Some of the more difficult passages were read orally to (student). (His/her) oral comprehension indicated that the listening level (does not exceed the reading level/exceeds the reading level by _____ years).

(ADDITIONAL OBSERVATIONS OF (1) ORAL VERSUS SILENT READING, (2) PERFORMANCE ON WORD RECOGNITION PLACEMENT TEST, AND (3) ORAL READING PERFORMANCE VERSUS COMPREHENSION MAY BE ADDED HERE.)

The strategies a student uses during the oral reading of passages reveals many things about reading. (Student's) strategies revealed that_____.

(HERE, THE STUDENT'S (1) PATTERNS OF OMISSIONS, REPETITIONS, SUBSTITUTIONS, INSERTIONS, AID, AND SO ON CAN BE DESCRIBED AND/OR (2) THE PATTERNS OF MISCUES, SUCH AS USE OF PHONICS CLUES, CONTEXT, AND SO ON CAN BE NOTED.* ACTUAL EXAMPLES OF MISCUES ARE HELPFUL.)

(Student's) oral reading was (fluent/not fluent). (He/she) (recognized/did not recognize) words without hesitation and (did not depend/depended) upon teacher aid. In addition _____.

(Student's) comprehension patterns on this test revealed that (summarize strengths, weaknesses).

(SECTIONS Vв,Vc, Vd, Ve, and Vf INCLUDED ONLY IF RELEVANT.)

V.B. Word Recognition

The ability to recognize words is basic to good reading. To investigate further competencies in word recognition, tests, observations, and informal teaching procedures were given in the areas of (sight word recognition/phonics/structural analysis/context clues).

(USE THE FOLLOWING INTRODUCTIONS, IF RELEVANT.)

SIGHT WORDS. The term sight words refers to the words a student can read instantly without hesitation. (KNOWLEDGE OF BASIC SIGHT WORDS MAY BE SEPARATED FROM MORE ADVANCED SIGHT WORDS.)

---

* If the reading miscue inventory framework is used, these terms may be described as graphophonic, syntactic, semantic, etc.

PHONICS. This refers to the student's abilities to use the relationships between letters and sounds to "sound out" or decode words. (THIS SECTION CONTAINS STATEMENTS OF SKILLS THAT THE STUDENT HAS OR HAS NOT MASTERED.)

CONTEXT CLUES/USE OF LANGUAGE CLUES IN READING. A student's knowledge of language structure and information about the world are powerful tools for recognizing words. (DESCRIBE STRATEGIES.)

STRUCTURAL ANALYSIS. Students may recognize words by their component parts, such as recognizing the word "walked" by the components "walk" and "ed". (DESCRIBE STRATEGIES.)

V.C. Comprehension

Comprehension is central to the ability to read; without comprehension, no reading actually takes place. (DESCRIBE COMPREHENSION STRATEGIES, SUBSKILL STRENGTHS AND WEAKNESSES, ABILITY TO DEAL WITH LONGER MATERIAL, SILENT AND ORAL COMPREHENSION, INFORMAL OBSERVATIONS.)

V.D. Meaning Vocabulary

The number of words a student understands is an important factor in reading achievement. (DESCRIBE VOCABULARY TESTS, VOCABULARY LISTENING LEVEL ON READING TESTS, AND INFORMAL OBSERVATIONS.)

V.E. Study Strategies

It is important that students learn to apply their reading skills to the school study situation. (DESCRIBE TEACHER REPORTS, OBSERVATIONS, TESTS.)

V.F. Reading Rate

The ability to read at an appropriate speed is an important factor in upper-level reading skills. (DESCRIBE TEACHER REPORTS, OBSERVATIONS, TESTS.)

VI. ANALYSIS OF PREREQUISITE ABILITIES UNDERLYING READING

(SECTION *VI* USUALLY FOR VERY DISABLED, YOUNG, OR BEHAVIOR PROBLEMS ONLY.)

Students must possess certain underlying abilities before they can learn to read. These include (visual-motor and auditory skills/a knowledge of reading concepts/appropriate learning styles). These skills are often lacking in (severely disabled readers/younger students).

(INCLUDE *VI.A*, *VI.B*, AND *VI.C* ONLY IF RELEVANT.)

VI.A. *Visual-Motor Skills and Auditory Skills*

These skills form a basis for further learning. Tests, informal teaching tasks, and observations were done to assess these skills. (DESCRIBE. AN INFORMAL WORD LEARNING TASK MAY BE DESCRIBED HERE; SEE CHAPTER 9.)

VI.B. *Knowledge of Reading Concepts*

Students need knowledge of several fundamental concepts (letter, word) to be able to read effectively. Informal observations revealed that (student) lacked some of these concepts. (DESCRIBE.)

VI.C. *Appropriate Learning Style*

Often, disabled readers are hampered by personal styles that distract them from learning. Informal observation of (student) revealed that there were difficulties with (impulsive behavior/behavior being too dependent on the surroundings or "field"/attending to the instructor and the instructional task). (DESCRIBE TESTS AND SPECIFIC INCIDENTS, IF POSSIBLE.)

VII.   FACTORS ASSOCIATED WITH READING PERFORMANCE

Often, difficulty with the reading situation is associated with several factors such as the environment of the home and school, emotional factors, physical factors, intellectual factors, and language factors. Although these factors do not necessarily cause a reading disability, they may be important in treating the disability. The factors most important in (student's) case seem to be (home environment/school environment/emotional factors/intellectual factors/physical factors/language factors).

(INCLUDE *VII.A*, *VII.B*, *VII.C*, *VII.D*, *VII.E* AND *VIII.F* ONLY IF RELEVANT.)

VII.A. *Home Environment*

(Student's) home environment (appears to be supportive/may be a factor in the reading disability). (DESCRIBE RELEVANT INFORMATION.)

VII.B. *School Environment*

Teacher reports, observations, and interviews indicate that (student) (functions well/has some difficulties) in the school environment. (DESCRIBE

FACTORS INCLUDING COMFORT IN SCHOOL, ABILITY TO RELATE TO
TEACHERS AND PEERS, ABILITY TO COMPLETE WORK.)

Some factors in (student's) school history may have affected reading performance. These include (frequent absences/frequent transfers/starting reading instruction at a young age/difficulties in previous classrooms). (DESCRIBE FUR-
THER.)

VII.C. *Emotional Factors, Interest, and Motivation*

Emotional and motivational factors (seem to be/do not seem to be)
hampering reading performance.

(Student's) behavior during the testing situation was (appropriate and
friendly/somewhat inappropriate). (DESCRIBE.) In addition, reported life adjustment with peers, parents, and other adults seems to be (normal/not entirely
normal). (DESCRIBE.)

An informal instrument where (student) was asked to complete sentences
such as "I like . . ." revealed _____.
(DESCRIBE FURTHER TESTS OF EMOTIONAL FACTORS, IF RELEVANT.)

Attitude toward reading and interest in reading are other ways in which
emotions affect reading performance. (Student's) attitude toward reading is
(positive/neutral/negative). (He/she) (shows/does not show) a desire to learn to
read better. (OBSERVATIONS ABOUT VIEWING READING AS A MEAN-
INGFUL ACT AND INFORMATION-GAINING PROCESS MAY BE IN-
CLUDED HERE; SEE CHAPTER 6.)

(Student's) interests include _____.
These will help to plan an effective reading program.

VII.D. *Physical Factors*

(Student's) general health and health history is (good/fair/poor), indicating that health considerations (have not/may have) affected the present level
of reading performance. Health problems that may have affected reading are
_____. (GENERAL   LEVEL   OF
MATURATION MAY ALSO BE DESCRIBED AS A PROBLEM.)

The (vision test) was administered as a screening test to determine whether
visual factors could be interfering with reading. Results showed that (student's) vision (appears to be adequate for reading/may be interfering with reading). The
areas of _____ showed some problems.
(He/she) should be seen by an optometrist or opthamologist for further examination. Additional signs of visual strain were _____
_____).

The (hearing test) was administered as a screening test to determine
whether (student's) auditory acuity, or hearing, was adequate for reading. (Student's) hearing (appears to be adequate/may be interfering with reading). (He/she)
should be referred to an audiologist, otologist, or otolaryngologist. Additional signs
of hearing problems were _____).

VII.E. *Intellectual Factors*

The (test of intelligence) was administered to (student). As reported previously, (he/she) scored in the (above-average/average/below-average) range. Patterns of intellectual strengths and weaknesses revealed that _____ _____. In addition, informal observations revealed that _____.

VII.F. *Language Factors*

Since reading is based on language, a student's oral language development is an important determinant of reading abilities. (Student's) history indicates (normal speech and language development/problems in speech and language development). (DESCRIBE SPEECH OR LANGUAGE PROBLEMS.) Informal observations of (student's) language revealed that language and verbal interactions are (well developed/adequate/a potential source of difficulty). (DESCRIBE TESTS OF LANGUAGE IF RELEVANT.)

(INCLUDE *VIII* IF RELEVANT.)

VIII. RECOMMENDATIONS FOR REFERRAL

It is recommended that (student) be referred to a (type of specialist) for further investigation of _____.

IX. RECOMMENDATIONS FOR INSTRUCTION

(Student) (is recommended for/is not recommended for) remedial instruction at this time. This instruction should take place in (describe setting), approximately _____ times per week.

The most important goals for (student's) instruction are presently _____ _____. (DESCRIBE METHODS AND MATERIALS FOR ACCOMPLISHING THESE GOALS.)

X. RECOMMENDATIONS FOR PARENTS AND CLASSROOM TEACHER

Parents can be an important help in the reading situation. It is recommended that (student's) parents (maintain a positive attitude toward remediation, complimenting each success/provide enriching activities such as reading to (student) and take (him/her) on field trips/maintain an attitude of objectivity and some distance from the reading remediation). (EXPLAIN FURTHER.)

Classroom adjustments will help (student) overcome reading difficulties and feel more comfortable in the reading situation. It is recommended that (student's) classroom teacher make the following adjustments in the instructional situation: _____.

APPENDIX D

AN INFORMAL
READING
INVENTORY

This informal reading inventory was developed at the College of the Virgin Islands. It contains selections taken from the Macmillan basal reading series, and it is used with the approval of Macmillan publishers.

The IRI was extensively fieldtested at the College of the Virgin Islands and was recently refined and revalidated using a sample of remedial readers. In addition, the level of each reading sample has been checked using two readability formulas.*

Questions are keyed as follows:

I = Inference	WR = Word Recognition
F = Fact	COMP = Comprehension
S = Sequence	IND = Independent Reading Level
V = Vocabulary	INSTR = Instructional Reading Level
M = Main Idea	FRUST = Frustration Reading Level

*This Informal Reading Inventory was developed by graduate students at the College of the Virgin Islands under the direction of Dr. Lynne K. List.

Level	(1) Word Recognition Scores (Instant)	Total	(2) Oral Reading Word Accuracy	(3) Oral Comprehension Score	(4) Silent Comprehension Score	(5) Average Comprehension Score	(6) Listening Level
			Used to Compute Reading Level			Used to Compute Reading Level	
			Passage Scores				
PP							
P							
1							
2							
3							
4							
5							
6							
7							
8							

Estimated reading levels:
Independent level _____
Instructional level _____
Frustration level _____
Listening level _____

Figure A-1 IRI Summary Page

Table A-1 Graded Word Lists (Teacher's Worksheets)

(PP)		(P)		(1)	
1. little	____	1. tree	____	1. birthday	____
2. is	____	2. something	____	2. them	____
3. and	____	3. she	____	3. many	____
4. ball	____	4. brown	____	4. could	____
5. no	____	5. black	____	5. ate	____
6. play	____	6. then	____	6. over	____
7. big	____	7. would	____	7. pretty	____
8. it	____	8. now	____	8. hand	____
9. mother	____	9. like	____	9. another	____
10. cat	____	10. friends	____	10. duck	____
11. funny	____	11. men	____	11. teacher	____
12. come	____	12. said	____	12. miss	____
13. a	____	13. home	____	13. crayon	____
14. rabbit	____	14. away	____	14. hot	____
15. I	____	15. please	____	15. stop	____

16. look ____	16. store ____	16. grow ____
17. blue ____	17. food ____	17. had ____
18. up ____	18. give ____	18. lunch ____
19. red ____	19. very ____	19. water ____
20. go ____	20. farm ____	20. those ____

(2)	(3)	(4)
1. field ____	1. cousin ____	1. alphabet ____
2. banana ____	2. highway ____	2. uncertain ____
3. mine ____	3. allow ____	3. sample ____
4. awoke ____	4. circle ____	4. meant ____
5. sidewalk ____	5. wonderful ____	5. exchange ____
6. chocolate ____	6. peach ____	6. baseball ____
7. twenty ____	7. laughed ____	7. yank ____
8. week ____	8. sentence ____	8. ideal ____
9. skin ____	9. sunrise ____	9. fire ____
10. drop ____	10. rather ____	10. seashore ____
11. page ____	11. sailor ____	11. zipper ____
12. bicycle ____	12. market ____	12. butcher ____
13. yesterday ____	13. through ____	13. merely ____
14. splash ____	14. promise ____	14. phone ____
15. till ____	15. everything ____	15. forward ____
16. between ____	16. became ____	16. caterpillar ____
17. coal ____	17. glove ____	17. linger ____
18. what ____	18. happiest ____	18. mosquito ____
19. police ____	19. breathe ____	19. gobble ____
20. frighten ____	20. cabbage ____	20. kennel ____

(5)	(6)
1. heroic ____	1. gigantic ____
2. chemist ____	2. wardrobe ____
3. convention ____	3. friction ____
4. location ____	4. lament ____
5. anxious ____	5. reverence ____
6. stadium ____	6. valor ____
7. therefore ____	7. horrify ____
8. nephew ____	8. expression ____
9. migration ____	9. cherished ____
10. testimony ____	10. haunt ____
11. ungrateful ____	11. ponderous ____
12. talkative ____	12. boulevard ____
13. wharf ____	13. shrewd ____
14. caravan ____	14. violin ____
15. pavement ____	15. barbaric ____
16. twilight ____	16. abbreviation ____
17. composer ____	17. existence ____
18. vertical ____	18. hospitality ____
19. bother ____	19. canopy ____
20. fleece ____	20. obligation ____

ORAL FORM—Level PP (27 words)*

MOTIVATION: If you climbed a tree, how do you think you might get down if you needed help? Let's read a story about a boy named Mike to find out what he did.

Jeff said, "Here comes Daddy.

Here he comes with a ladder.

You can come down the ladder."

Mother said, "Mike can.

He can come down the ladder."†

COMPREHENSION CHECK

(F) 1. _____ Who is coming? (Daddy)

(F) 2. _____ What is Daddy bringing? (a ladder)

(I) 3. _____ What does Mother want Mike to do? (get down; come down the ladder)

(M) 4. _____ How is Mike going to get down? (using a ladder; climb down—1/2 credit)

SCORING GUIDE: PRE-PRIMER

WR ERRORS		COMP ERRORS	
IND	0–1	IND	0
INSTR	1½–2½	INSTR	½–1
FRUST	3+	FRUST	2+

* These and the following 19 samples can be used as models for teacher's worksheets.
†Adapted from "Can Mike Get Down?," in A MAGIC BOX, Level 4, Preprimer 2, *The Macmillan Reading Program*—Albert J. Harris and Mae Knight Clark, Senior Authors, p. 50 Copyright © 1970 Macmillan Publishing Co., Inc.

SILENT FORM—Level PP (29 words)

MOTIVATION: Do you have a bicycle? Let's read about Mike and Jeff who want to make a bike.

Mike said, "I want a big boy's bike.

Make it a big boy's bike, Jeff."

Jeff said, "Can you ride it, Mike?

Can you ride a big boy's bike?"*

COMPREHENSION CHECK

(F) 1. _____ What does Mike want? (a big boy's bike)

(F) 2. _____ Who is going to make the bike? (Jeff)

(I) 3. _____ What is a big boy's bike? (one that is bigger, taller, two-wheeler, etc.)

(M) 4. _____ What is the story about? (a boy who wants a big boy's bike)

SCORING GUIDE

COMP ERRORS

IND   0
INSTR 1
FRUST 2 +

---

* Excerpted from "The Little Wheels," in THINGS YOU SEE, Level 5, Preprimer 3, *The Macmillan Reading Program*—Albert J. Harris and Mae Knight Clark, Senior Authors, p. 35. Copyright © 1974, 1965 Macmillan Publishing Co., Inc.

ORAL FORM—Level P (54 words)

MOTIVATION: Do you think your mother ever worries about you? This is about a very worried mother. Let's find out why she's worried.

Billy is a little goat on a farm. He likes to eat and play.

He likes to run and jump. One day Billy didn't eat.

He didn't run or jump. He didn't play.

"Oh!" said his mother.

"My little goat won't eat." Mother Goat ran to Daddy Goat.

Mother Goat said, "Billy won't eat."*

COMPREHENSION CHECK

(M) 1. _____ Why is Billy's mother worried about him? (He isn't doing all the things he normally does–such as run, jump, play and eat)

(F) 2. _____ Name three things Billy likes to do on the farm. (Any combination of: eat, play, run, jump)

(F) 3. _____ Who did Mother Goat go to for help? (Daddy Goat)

(I) 4. _____ How do we know that Mother Goat went quickly to Daddy Goat? (It said that she "ran")

SCORING GUIDE: PRIMER

WR ERRORS		COMP ERRORS	
IND	0–2½	IND	0
INSTR	3–5	INSTR	1
FRUST	5½ +	FRUST	2 +

* Adapted from "The Goat Story," in WORLDS OF WONDER, Level 6, Primer, *The Macmillan Reading Program*—Albert J. Harris and Mae Knight Clark, Senior Authors, pp. 109–110. Copyright © 1974 Macmillan Publishing Co., Inc.

SILENT FORM—Level P (53 words)

MOTIVATION: Have you ever seen a dog riding on a bus? Let's read to find out how a little boy is going to take his dog, Bolo, for a bus ride.

"Bolo has to go to the dog show," said Jeff.

"How can I take him?"

"You can put him in something," said the busman.

"Then we will let him ride on the bus."

"That's good," said Jeff.

"I will get something to put him in. Then we can ride to the show."*

COMPREHENSION CHECK

(F) 1. _____ Where does Jeff want to take Bolo? (to the dog show—or—on the bus)

(F) 2. _____ Who tells Jeff how to put Bolo on the bus? (the busman)

(I) 3. _____ What might the "something" be that Jeff will get? (a box, etc.)

(M) 4. _____ Why does Jeff have to put Bolo in something? (so that he can ride on the bus, and be able to go to the dog show; so he doesn't bother other riders; etc.)

SCORING GUIDE: PRIMER

COMP ERRORS

IND   0
INSTR   1
FRUST   2+

---

* Adapted from "No Ride for Bolo," in WORLDS OF WONDER, Level 6, Primer, *The Macmillan Reading Program*—Albert J. Harris and Mae Knight Clark, Senior Authors, p. 63. Copyright © 1974 Macmillan Publishing Co., Inc.

ORAL FORM—Level 1 (73 words)

MOTIVATION: Have you ever tried to make something on your own? Let's read a story to see how a little boy felt about what he made.

One time at school Larry had to paint a flower.
Larry painted a blue and yellow one.
He thought it looked good.
Then Larry saw the flower that one of the other boys had painted. It was big and red. It had a bird on it. "My flower is not bad," thought Larry. "But that one is great. Why couldn't I paint a great flower?" Larry thought he would never do anything great.[*]

COMPREHENSION CHECK

(F)   1. _____ What did Larry do at school? (He painted a flower)

(F)   2. _____ What colors was the flower he painted? (Blue and yellow—give $\frac{1}{2}$ credit if only one is given)

(F)   3. _____ What did Larry think of his flower? (It looked good—or—it's not bad)

(S)   4. _____ What did Larry do after he looked at his own flower? (He saw a flower another boy painted)

(F)   5. _____ What did the other boy's flower look like? (It was big and red and had a bird on it)

[*] Excerpted from "Never Great," in Elizabeth Levy, BEING ME, Grade 1, Level 10, *Series r: The New Macmillan Reading Program*—Carl B. Smith and Ronald Wardhaugh, Senior Authors, p. 127. Copyright © 1980 Macmillan Publishing Co., Inc.

(I) 6. _____ What does Larry wish he could do? (Paint a great flower—or—do something great)

(I) 7. _____ Why might Larry think he'll never do anything great? (Because he thought the other boy could outdo him, etc.)

SCORING GUIDE: LEVEL 1

WR ERRORS		COMP ERRORS	
IND	0–3½	IND	0–1
INSTR	4–7	INSTR	1½–3
FRUST	7½ +	FRUST	3½ +

SILENT FORM—Level 1 (104 words)

MOTIVATION: Have you ever had people tell you that you weren't old enough or big enough to do something? How did you feel? Let's read about a little boy who wanted to show that he was old enough to take care of a little girl calf.

One day Tommy had something for the little calf to eat. She ran at it so hard that Tommy fell over. It hurt, but Tommy didn't cry. Ben laughed when Tommy fell over. "I told you so!" he said. "You can't take care of a calf. You are not old enough. You have to be big like me to take care of a calf." Tommy was mad. He yelled, "I can too take care of my twin!"*

*Excerpt adapted from THE LITTLE TWIN by Grace Paull. Copyright 1953 by Grace Paull. Reprinted by permission of Doubleday & Company, Inc.

COMPREHENSION CHECK

(F) 1. _____ What did Tommy have that made the calf run over to him? (something to eat)

(F) 2. _____ What made Tommy mad? (Ben told him that he was too little to take care of the calf—or—Ben laughed at him—½ credit for Ben said he wasn't as big as him)

(F) 3. _____ What did Ben do when Tommy fell over? (He laughed)

(I) 4. _____ What did Tommy do to show that he was mad? (He yelled)

(M) 5. _____ What does Tommy want to show to Ben? (He is big enough to take care of the calf)

(I) 6. _____ Why do you think the calf ran at the food so hard? (She was hungry, or might have been glad to see Tommy)

(I) 7. _____ Who was older, Ben or Tommy? (Ben) How do you know? (He said Tommy was little—or—he was big)

SCORING GUIDE: LEVEL 1

> *COMP ERRORS*
>
> IND   0
> INSTR 1–2
> FRUST 2½ +

ORAL FORM—Level 2 (109 words)

MOTIVATION: Can you swim, or would you like to learn to swim? Let's read a story about a boy who wants to learn how to swim.

Tommy and his mother and father went to the country each summer. This summer they took a house right beside a lake. "I'm so glad we're here," said Tommy. "I didn't learn how to swim last year, but *this* year I will. You wait and see."

"Good," said his father. "I'm glad
you want to learn now. Many of
the boys and girls here don't know
how to swim. We're getting a life-
guard to teach you. His name is Big
Jim, and I'm sure you'll like him."
Tommy did like Big Jim. Just the
same he couldn't do the things Big
Jim asked him to do.*

COMPREHENSION CHECK

(F) 1. _____ What was the name of the boy who couldn't swim? (Tommy)

(F) 2. _____ Where did Tommy's family go every summer? (the country—or—the lake)

(I) 3. _____ Where would Tommy and the other children go to swim? (the lake)

(F) 4. _____ What did Tommy want to do this summer? (learn how to swim)

(F) 5. _____ How did Tommy feel about Big Jim? (he liked him)

(V) 6. _____ What does it mean when the story says, "they took a house right beside a lake"? (they rented, stayed in, or lived in a house by the lake)

(I) 7. _____ Was it easy for Tommy to learn to swim? (No) How do you know? (He couldn't do the things Big Jim asked him to do)

SCORING GUIDE: LEVEL 2

WR ERRORS		COMP ERRORS	
IND	0–5	IND	0
INSTR	5½–10½	INSTR	1–2
FRUST	11 +	FRUST	3 +

*Adapted from "The Boy Who Couldn't Swim," in SHINING BRIDGES, Grade 2, Level 2, *The Macmillan Reading Program*—Albert J. Harris and Mae Knight Clark, Senior Authors, p. 94. Copyright © 1974 Macmillan Publishing Co., Inc.

SILENT FORM—Level 2 (112 words)

MOTIVATION: Do you like to go to the beach? Let's read a story about a girl whose home was right on the beach.

Jane Turner lived in a small hotel right on the beach. Her mother and father owned the hotel, and Jane was glad they did. People came there with children, and the children became Jane's friends. They went swimming almost every day. One of Jane's friends was a boy named Billy. One day Jane and Billy were playing with a beach ball, and Billy got hurt. The beach ball hit him on the mouth. For a second Billy was angry. He threw the ball so hard that it went way out over the water. Then a strange thing happened. As Jane and Billy watched, a big, dark animal jumped out of the water.[*]

[*] Adapted from "Jane and the Dolphin," in SHINING BRIDGES, Grade 2, Level 2, *The Macmillan Reading Program*—Albert J. Harris and Mae Knight Clark, Senior Authors, pp. 63–64. Copyright © 1974 Macmillan Publishing Co., Inc.

COMPREHENSION CHECK

(F) 1. _____ Where did Jane Turner live? (in a hotel—or—by the beach)

(F) 2. _____ Who owned the hotel that Jane lived in? (her mother and father)

(F) 3. _____ How often did the children go swimming? (almost every day)

(F) 4. _____ How did Billy get hurt? (the ball hit him in the mouth)

(I) 5. _____ How can you tell that Billy wasn't the only friend Jane had? (It said that he was *one* of her friends and the children who came to the hotel became her *friends*)

(F) 6. _____ What did the big, dark animal do? (jumped out of the water)

(M) 7. _____ Choose the best title for this story: a) "How Billy got Hit on the Mouth," b) "Jane's Friends," c) "The Hotel on the Beach," d) "A Surprise Visitor" (answer: a or c will be completely acceptable)

SCORING GUIDE: LEVEL 2

COMP ERRORS

IND	0
INSTR	1–2
FRUST	2½ +

ORAL FORM—Level 3 (151 words)

MOTIVATION: Have you ever been in a parade? Let's read a story about Sarah and the parade contest she was in.

Now to add to the fun, the buggy had stopped before the judges' stand. The burro was refusing to move. People, clapping and shouting, began telling Sarah what to do. Sarah knew what to do. Reaching down, she picked up the long switch from the floor of the buggy. Carefully she lifted it up. She moved the switch toward the burro until the hay on the string dangled just beyond Jinny's nose. Jinny moved toward it, but the switch moved, too. Jinny took one step and then another, but the hay was still beyond her. The trick had worked. Jinny was moving! The sound of people laughing and clapping rose on all sides. Jinny was the funniest entry, the judges decided. They gave Sarah a prize of twenty-five dollars. That evening Sarah and Linda fed Jinny in the back yard. "I guess Jinny's famous now, all right," Linda said. *

COMPREHENSION CHECK

(F)   1. _____ What happened to Sarah's buggy in front of the judges' stand? (it stopped)

(F)   2. _____ What was the name of Sarah's burro? (Jinny)

(F)   3. _____ What was on the end of the switch that got Jinny to move? (hay on a string)

(F)   4. _____ What did the judges decide was the funniest entry? (Jinny)

(F)   5. _____ What was the prize that Sarah won? (twenty-five dollars)

(V)   6. _____ In the phrase, "the string dangled just beyond Jinny's nose," what word does "dangled" mean? (hung)

(I)   7. _____ Why did Jinny move when she saw the hay at the end of the switch? (because she was hungry)

(I)   8. _____ What was the prize for first place in the category of funny entries? ($25.00. The judges thought Jinny was the *funniest*)

(I)   9. _____ Why does Linda think that Jinny is famous after the parade? (because everyone knows/remembers her; because she won)

(M)   10. _____ What lesson have you learned from Sarah by reading this story? (to be prepared for anything that might happen, etc.)

SCORING GUIDE: LEVEL 3

WR ERRORS		*COMP ERRORS*	
IND	0–7½	IND	0–1
INSTR	8–15	INSTR	2–3
FRUST	15½ +	FRUST	4 +

* Adapted from SARAH'S IDEA by Doris Gates, Illustrated by Marjorie Torrey (New York: The Viking Press Inc., 1938), pp. 243–44. Copyright 1938 by Doris Gates and Marjorie Torrey. Copyright renewed 1966 by Doris Gates and Tom Torre Bevans. Reprinted by permission of Viking Penguin Inc.

SILENT FORM—Level 3 (147 words)

MOTIVATION: Have you ever read or heard the story of Cinderella? It's the story of a young girl who marries a prince. Let's read another story about a prince who is looking for a wife.

Not far from the town was a castle where a young prince lived. The young prince was soon to be king and wanted to find a princess to marry. He heard of a beautiful princess who lived in Denmark. The princess loved pretty clothes. So the prince went to the town and bought a huge pile of their most beautiful cloth to take to the princess.

The prince was a kind and handsome young man, and the princess fell in love with him. She also loved all the gold cloth he brought with him. The prince promised the princess a new gown every day if she married him and went to live with him in his castle in England.

After many parties and balls, the prince and princess were married. They went to live in his castle near the town where the people made the beautiful cloth.*

COMPREHENSION CHECK

(F) 1. _____ Why did the young prince want to find a beautiful princess? (so he could marry her)

(F) 2. _____ What did the princess love? (pretty clothes)

(F) 3. _____ Where did the princess live? (Denmark)

(F) 4. _____ What did the prince buy for the beautiful princess? (a huge pile of beautiful cloth)

(I) 5. _____ Why did the princess fall in love with the prince? (because he was kind and handsome)

(F) 6. _____ What did the prince promise the princess if she married him? (a new gown every day)

---

* Excerpted from "A New Party in an Old Castle," in BETTER THAN GOLD, Grade 3, Level 10, *The Macmillan Reading Program*—Albert J. Harris and Mae Knight Clark, Senior Authors, p. 196. Copyright © 1974, 1965 Macmillan Publishing Co., Inc.

(S)   7. _____ What happened after there were many parties and balls? (The prince and princess got married.)

(F)   8. _____ Where is the prince's castle? (near the town where the people make the beautiful cloth or in England)

(F)   9. _____ How was the prince described in the story? (kind, handsome, and young. Full credit—2 or more; ½ credit—1)

(M)   10. _____ Explain why the prince and princess are probably both happy at the end of this story. (accept any reasonable explanation of how they both got what they wanted—the prince was able to marry the princess and she gets to have pretty clothes all the time)

SCORING GUIDE: LEVEL 3

COMP ERRORS

IND	0–1
INSTR	1½–3
FRUST	3½ +

ORAL FORM—Level 4 (173 words)

MOTIVATION: Have you ever tried to get rid of something you didn't want and found it very difficult to do? Read this story and see what happened when two men tried to get rid of something they didn't want.

Three weeks later, Steve and I were standing on the river bank at Dawson. A small boat was just arriving. There in the boat, with ears pricked up, sat Spot.

There was no getting rid of him any more. There were too many people in Dawson who had bought him on the Chilkoot River, and the story got around. Half a dozen times we put him on a steamboat going down the Yukon. He just went ashore at the first landing and trotted back to us.

In the fall of 1898, Steve and I went up the Yukon on the last free-flowing water before the yearly freeze. This time we were bound for Stewart River. On our way, we met two men who needed an extra dog. They took a fancy to Spot, and we agreed to trade the dog for two much-needed sacks of flour.

We went our way with happy hearts. The men who took Spot were going in a different direction. This time we were rid of that Spot for sure.*

COMPREHENSION CHECK

(F) 1. _____ As the story begins, where are we standing? (on the river bank)

(F) 2. _____ What happened every time Spot was put on a steamboat? (He went ashore at the first stop and came back)

(I) 3. _____ What do you suppose happened to the Yukon River in the winter? (The water got frozen and didn't flow freely or didn't flow at all)

(V) 4. _____ What does "they took a fancy to Spot" mean? (that they liked him)

(F) 5. _____ What was Spot finally traded for? (two sacks of flour)

(F) 6. _____ Which way were Spot's new owners going? (in a different direction from his old owners)

(I) 7. _____ Why were the sacks of flour probably "much needed"? (After the river froze over, supplies would be hard to get—they were running low and would not be able to buy more until after the river thawed)

(I) 8. _____ In the phrase, "We went our way with happy hearts," what does "happy hearts" mean? (glad)

(M) 9. _____ What were Steve and his companion trying to do in the story? (get rid of the dog, Spot)

(I) 10. _____ Why were the men having such trouble getting rid of Spot? (because the dog would always manage to get back, because too many people had heard about him, etc.)

SCORING GUIDE: LEVEL 4

WR ERRORS		COMP ERRORS	
IND	0–8½	IND	0–1
INSTR	9–17	INSTR	2–3
FRUST	17½ +	FRUST	4+

*Excerpted from "That Spot," in Jack London, BROWN WOLF AND OTHER STORIES (New York: Macmillan Publishing Co., Inc., 1963), pp. 314–15.

SILENT FORM—Level 4 (151 words)

MOTIVATION: This tells about an unusual sled race in Hawaii between two boys,
Ahele and Umi. The sled slides on a smooth stone path instead of
snow. One boy does something unusual to win the race.

Ahele knew it. He was a good rider, but he was nervous
as the thundering sled behind him crept closer and
closer. He knew he had tried hard, but he had also tried
to cheat. He felt he could not expect fair play after he
had been such a poor sport himself. He waited fearfully
for the touch of Umi's sled against his own fast-moving
sled. He knew the sudden move would unseat him.
They were nearly at the bottom now. Then Ahele heard
a cry of warning. He felt rather than saw a shadow
streak by overhead. Umi's sled, answering the sudden
backward pull of his body, left the track to rise in a
perfect arc. It cleared Ahele and his sled by a space no
larger than a man's hand. Umi's sled touched the
ground again on the smooth grass at the base of the
slide.*

COMPREHENSION CHECK

(F)   1. _____ What was Ahele riding on? (a sled)

(I)   2. _____ How was Ahele a poor sport? (he tried to cheat)

(I)   3. _____ Why do you suppose Ahele was nervous? (he was afraid that Umi might
not play fair or that Umi might win)

(F)   4. _____ What was Ahele fearfully waiting for? (for Umi's sled to touch his; for
Umi to catch up—½ credit)

(F)   5. _____ What was the shadow that streaked over Ahele's head? (Umi and his
sled)

(F)   6. _____ How close did Umi's sled come to Ahele as it passed over? (a space no
larger than a man's hand)

(I)   7. _____ Who do you think won the race? (Umi)

(V)   8. _____ Why do you suppose that the author describes the sled as "thundering"?
(It made a noise that sounded loud like thunder.)

* Adapted from "The Royal Race," in THE MAGIC WORD, Grade 4, Level 12, *The Macmillan Reading Program*—Albert J. Harris, Senior Author, pp. 364–65. Copyright © 1974
Macmillan Publishing Co., Inc.

(V)   9. _____ In the phrase, "left the track to rise in a perfect arc," what does "arc" mean? (curved path, circle)

(M)   10. _____ What do you think would be a good title for this story? ("An Exciting Sled Race", etc.)

SCORING GUIDE: LEVEL 4

COMP ERRORS

IND   0–1
INSTR   1½–3
FRUST   3½ +

ORAL FORM—Level 5 (195 words)

MOTIVATION: How many of you have gotten up in the middle of the night and dressed to go on an exciting trip with your father? This story that you are going to read tells of such an adventure.

Father pulled on his pants and boots and heavy jacket and lit his lantern. By the time he'd done that, I had my things on, too. My mother was up then and objecting, but my father shushed her. So I went with him. The late moon was up and we could see our way easy. I stayed in the shack with the operator and my father went off to set his signal and tend his switch. Sure enough, in about twenty minutes the train came along, swung into the second line of track and stopped. The telegraph operator stepped out and started talking to a brakeman. I was scared stiff. I stood in the shack door-way and looked at the train and I was shaking inside like I had some kind of fever. It wasn't much of a train. Just an engine and little fuel car and four old coaches. I mean the railroad wasn't wasting any good equipment or any extra men on this train, and it was being shoved along slow between other trains. Except for the wheezing engine, the train was a tired and sleeping or dead thing on the track. *

COMPREHENSION CHECK

(F)   1. _____ What three items of clothing did Father put on? (his pants, boots, and heavy jacket—give ½ credit for 2 items)

*Adapted from "Jacob," in Jack Schaefer, THE PLAINSMEN (Boston: Houghton-Mifflin, 1954), pp. 243–44. Copyright © 1954 by Jack Schaefer, copyright © renewed 1982. Reprinted by permission of the Harold Matson Co., Inc.

(I)   2. _____ Why do you think the child's mother objected to his going out with his father? (The child had already been undressed for the night. It was dark outside.)

(V)   3. _____ What does "Father shushed her" mean? (Father told her to be quiet, shut up, etc.—½ credit for told her not to worry)

(F)   4. _____ What were the men doing? (switching the train onto the second track)

(F)   5. _____ How many coaches did the train have? (four)

(F)   6. _____ Where did the child stay when Father went to set his signal? (in the shack with the operator)

(I)   7. _____ Was it night or day when Father and the child went out from home? How do you know? (at night. Father lit his lantern, and on their way to the track the late moon was up)

(I)   8. _____ Why do you think the child was shaking inside? (He was scared, nervous, afraid, or excited)

(M)   9. _____ Give this story a title. ("A Trip to the Track During the Night," etc.)

(I)   10. _____ Why did the train seem "a tired and sleeping or dead thing on the track"? (the coaches were old, it seemed abandoned, it moved slowly, etc.)

SCORING GUIDE: LEVEL 5

WR ERRORS		*COMP ERRORS*	
IND	0–9½	IND	0–1
INSTR	10–19½	INSTR	1½–3
FRUST	20 +	FRUST	3½ +

SILENT FORM—Level 5 (118 words)

MOTIVATION: Have you ever had so much of something that you thought it would never finish? The story we are about to read tells how the first settlers in North America had so many trees they felt they would never finish and they could use them any way they liked.

The forests made America the richest and most fertile country on earth. There was abundant wood for buildings. The rich earth could be farmed when the trees had been felled. There were more than one billon acres of untouched forest—enough wood, everyone thought, to last forever.

Trees were slashed and land was cleared for farming without a thought for the future. Great stretches of forest were fired and burned to clear the land for farms. Logs were used to build homes and schools, barns, churches, bridges, and forts. After the early settlers came the loggers.

It was during the days of the Gold Rush, in the middle 1800's, that cutting timber for profit became a really big business. *

COMPREHENSION CHECK

(F) 1. _____ What made America the richest and most fertile country on Earth? (the forests)

(V) 2. _____ What does "abundant wood" mean? (plenty of wood—or—more than enough wood)

(V) 3. _____ What does "trees were slashed" mean? (trees were cut down)

(F) 4. _____ Why were the forests cut down and fired? (to clear land for farms—½ credit for making homes)

(F) 5. _____ Name three things the story says that the early settlers built from wood. (homes, schools, barns, churches, forts, bridges—give half credit for two correct answers)

(F) 6. _____ Who came after the early settlers? (loggers)

(I) 7. _____ Why do you think a particular period of time was referred to as the days of the "Gold Rush"? (people were rushing for gold in that period)

(F) 8. _____ About when was the Gold Rush? (100–125 years ago—or—middle 1800's)

(I) 9. _____ What could have been done during the time the trees were cut down to make sure that the forests remain? (Young trees could have been planted; seeds could have been sown in their place)

(M) 10. _____ Give the story a title. ("The Early Settlers Wasted the Forests," etc.)

SCORING GUIDE: LEVEL 5

COMP ERRORS

IND   0–1
INSTR   1½–3
FRUST   3½ +

*Adapted from THE FRIENDLY FORESTS by Alma Chesnut Moore. Copyright © 1954 by Alma Chesnut Moore. Copyright © renewed 1982. Reprinted by permission of Viking Penguin Inc.

ORAL FORM—Level 6 (239 words)

MOTIVATION: To be a successful scientist, one must be able to think and act in an organized step fashion based on the facts one knows about a certain situation or experiment. Let's see how a scientist's thinking can be applied to a fishing trip.

What is the "scientific method" of thinking? An example will answer a number of questions about it.

Suppose you have been out trout fishing, using worms for bait, and after several hours you have not even had a nibble. You saw another fisherman bring home a day's limit of trout the day before from the same place you have been fishing. You wonder why he caught so many and you none at all.

Puzzled, you stop fishing and just watch the stream for a while. Presently you see fish breaking the surface of the water. Why? What makes them jump up to the surface this way? Perhaps they are coming up for air, or just feeling playful. Or possibly the light attracts them.

Another idea seems more likely. Maybe these trout like insects to eat, and leap up to strike when they see one near the surface of the water.

This seems like a good lead, so you decide to test your idea. You just slapped a mosquito that lit on your arm; now you toss it onto the surface of the water. You see a swirl, and the mosquito is gone. In fact, you find that every time you toss a mosquito onto the surface of the water, a fish strikes at it. After a few tests in this fashion you come to a conclusion; these trout do not like worms, but they seem to find mosquitos irresistible. *

COMPREHENSION CHECK

(F)   1. _____ What kind of fish were you trying to catch? (trout)

(I)   2. _____ What kind of bait was the successful fisherman using in an attempt to catch fish? (insects or mosquitos)

(F)   3. _____ What fact in the story caused you to stop fishing and just observe the surroundings? (the fact that he wasn't catching any fish—or—that another fisherman was having luck where he was not)

(F)   4. _____ What reasons did you first think of for the fishs' behavior? (coming up for air, feeling playful, attracted to light, like insects—any two of these count for full credit)

* Adapted and abridged from SO YOU WANT TO BE A SCIENTIST by Alan E. Nourse, M.D., p. 61. Copyright © 1960 by Alan Edward Nourse. By permission of Harper & Row, Publishers, Inc.

(F)   5. _____ What did you throw into the water that the trout seemed to like? (mosquitos)

(F)   6. _____ What conclusion was formed at the end of this story about the eating habits of the trout? (the trout did not like worms, but they found mosquitos irresistible—must include both halves for full credit)

(V)   7. _____ In the phrase, "slapped a mosquito that lit on your arm," what does the word "lit" mean? (landed or came to rest)

(F)   8. _____ What do you see just before the mosquito disappears? (a swirl)

(M)   9. _____ Explain what the scientific method of thinking is. (any logical answer which states that you find a problem, think of solutions, test them, and arrive at conclusions)

(M) 10. _____ Give this passage a title. ("A Successful Method to Catch Trout," or title which indicates that the writer learned the method used to catch trout)

SCORING GUIDE: LEVEL 6

WR ERRORS		COMP ERRORS	
IND	0–11½	IND	0–1
INSTR	12–23½	INSTR	1½–3
FRUST	24 +	FRUST	3½ +

SILENT FORM—Level 6 (231 words)

MOTIVATION: A naturalist is a person who studies animal behavior and plant life in their natural settings in order to gain more of an understanding of nature. One such man observed a pond for a long time to gain knowledge on one particular creature. Let's read the following passage to see what creature held the observer's interest.

This was the day: I knew it. For a month I had been watching, brooding over this pond, and now I knew. I felt a stirring of the pulse of things that the coldhearted turtles could no more escape than could the clouds and I.

Leaving my horse unhitched, as if he too understood, I slipped eagerly into my hidden nook for a look at the pond. As I did so, a large fish ploughed a furrow through the still pond water. And in his wake rose the head of an enormous turtle. Swinging slowly around, the creature headed straight for the shore, and without a pause scrambled out on the sand.

She was about the size of a big scoop shovel. But that was not what excited me so much as her manner and the gait at which she moved. For I could see there was method in it, and fixed purpose. On she came, shuffling over the sand toward the higher open fields. She had a hurried, determined seesaw motion that was taking her somewhere in particular, and that was bound to get her there on time.

I held my breath.

Over the strip of sand, without a stop, she paddled. Up a narrow cowpath into the high grass along a fence she went. Then up the narrow cowpath, on all fours, just like another turtle, I paddled, and into the high wet grass along the fence. *

COMPREHENSION CHECK

(F) 1. _____ What creature in the story was the man so interested in? (turtle)

(I) 2. _____ How long had the man been watching and brooding over the pond? (for a month; 30–31 days)

(F) 3. _____ What creature in the story ploughed a furrow through the water? (a fish)

(F) 4. _____ To what object was the size of the turtle compared? (scoop shovel)

(F) 5. _____ What about the turtle excited the man most? (Her manner and the gait at which she moved)

(V) 6. _____ If the turtle is "enormous," what do we know about it? (very big, large)

(V) 7. _____ What is meant by the word "nook" in the following phrase: "I slipped eagerly into my hidden nook for a look at the pond"? (hiding place—or—secluded place)

(I) 8. _____ What method of transportation did the man use to get to the pond? (a horse)

(I) 9. _____ Why was it necessary for the man to follow the turtle on all fours? (so the turtle wouldn't notice that he was there)

(M) 10. _____ Give this story a title. ("Learning about a Turtle"—or any title that seems logical)

SCORING GUIDE: LEVEL 6

COMP ERRORS

IND   0–1
INSTR   2–3
FRUST   4 +

* Excerpted from Dallas Lore Sharp, "Turtle Eggs for Agassiz," in THE ATLANTIC MONTHLY (November 1932).

ORAL FORM—Level 7 (218 words)

MOTIVATION: Have you ever had a relative stay with you while your parents were away? Let's read a story about some children who didn't enjoy their aunt's visit.

After we moved to Montclair, Aunt Anne came to stay with us for several days while Mother and Dad were away on a lecture tour. She made it plain from the start that she was not a guest, but the temporary commander-in-chief. She even used the front stairs, leading from the front hall to the second floor, instead of the back stairs, which led from the kitchen to a hallway near the girls' bathroom. None of us was allowed to use the front stairs, because Dad wanted to keep the varnish on them looking nice.

"Daddy will be furious if he comes home and finds you've been using his front stairs," we told Aunt Anne.

"Nonsense," she cut us off. "The back stairs are narrow and steep, and I for one don't propose to use them. As long as I'm here, I'll use any stairs I have a mind to. Now rest your features and mind your business."

She sat at Dad's place at the foot of the table, and we resented this, too. Ordinarily, Frank, as the oldest boy, sat in Dad's place, and Anne, as the oldest girl, sat at Mother's. We also disapproved of Aunt Anne's blunt criticism of how we kept our bedrooms, and some of the changes she made in the family routine.*

COMPREHENSION CHECK

(F)   1. _____ Why did Aunt Anne come to stay? (to watch the children while Mother and Dad were away on a lecture tour)

(F)   2. _____ What stairway did Aunt Anne always use? (the front stairs)

(F)   3. _____ Why weren't the children allowed the use the front stairs? (because Dad wanted to keep the varnish on them looking nice)

(I)   4. _____ What did Aunt Anne mean when she said, "Now rest your features"? (relax, don't worry, any comparable answer)

(V)   5. _____ What does the word "propose" mean in the phrase "I for one don't propose to use them?" (intend, plan, etc.)

*From CHEAPER BY THE DOZEN by Frank B. Gilbreth, Jr., and Ernestine Gilbreth Carey (New York: Thomas Y. Crowell Co., 1948), pp. 175–76. Copyright © 1948, 1963 by Frank B. Gilbreth, Jr., and Ernestine Gilbreth Carey. By permission of Harper & Row, Publishers, Inc., and Heinemann Ltd.

(I)   6. _____ Were Frank and Anne the only children in the family? (No) How do you know? (The passage said that Frank was the oldest of the *boys* and Anne was the oldest of the *girls*)

(F)   7. _____ Where did Aunt Anne sit at the table? (in Dad's place—or—at the foot of the table)

(I)   8. _____ Why did Frank and Anne resent Aunt Anne choosing to sit where she did at the table? (because being the oldest generally meant that they could sit in Mother and Dad's places when they were away)

(I)   9. _____ How did Aunt Anne feel about the way the children kept their bedrooms? (She didn't like it—says that she gave blunt criticism)

(M)   10. _____ Why did the children resent Aunt Anne? (Because she changed things that seemed important to them, etc.)

SCORING GUIDE: LEVEL 7

WR ERRORS		COMP ERRORS	
IND	0–10½	IND	0–1
INSTR	11–21½	INSTR	2–3
FRUST	22 +	FRUST	4 +

SILENT FORM—Level 7 (201 words)

MOTIVATION: Have you ever watched the way various animals behave in the zoo? In some cases, it is necessary to observe animals in their natural settings in order to really understand them. Let's read a story about such an expedition.

Now the larger and commoner creatures from most parts of the world are well represented in nearly all zoological collections, and quite a lot is known about them. So it was the smaller and rarer beasts, about which we know so little, that I wanted to collect. It is about them that I am going to write.

From many points of view it is sometimes the small animals in a country that influence man more than the large ones. At home, for instance, the brown rat does more damage every year than any of the larger creatures. It was for this reason that I concentrated during my collecting trips on the smaller forms of life. For my first expedition I chose the Cameroons, since it is a small, almost forgotten corner of Africa, which is more or less as it was before the advent of the white man. Here, in the gigantic rain forests, the animals live their lives as they have done for thousands of years.

It is of great value to get to know and study these wild creatures before they are influenced by civilization, for wild animals can be affected just as much by change as people.*

COMPREHENSION CHECK

(F) 1. _____ What kinds of creatures are well represented in most zoos? (larger and commoner ones—need both answers for full credit)

(F) 2. _____ What animal does more damage every year than any of the larger animals, back at home? (the brown rat)

(I) 3. _____ Why do you suppose he concentrated on the smaller forms of life during his collecting trips? (little research has been done on them—or any logical answer)

(F) 4. _____ Where did he choose to go on his first expedition? (the Cameroons—or—Africa)

(F) 5. _____ Where are the Cameroons? (in a small, almost forgotten corner of Africa)

(V) 6. _____ What does the word "expedition" mean in the phrase "For my first expedition I chose the Cameroons"?

(F) 7. _____ What kind of region are the Cameroons in? (rain forest)

(F) 8. _____ How do the animals live in the Cameroons? (as they have for 1000 years)

(I) 9. _____ Why is it important to study wild animals before they are put into zoos? (so we can see how they act and live, without disturbing their nature and habitat)

(M) 10. _____ What title would you give this story? (Learning about rare creatures—or—any other appropriate title)

SCORING GUIDE: LEVEL 7

COMP ERRORS

IND	0–1
INSTR	1½–3
FRUST	3½ +

---

*Excerpted from "Collecting in the Cameroons," in Gerald Durrell, THE NEW NOAH (New York: Viking Penguin Inc., 1967).

ORAL FORM—Level 8 (247 words)

MOTIVATION: You've probably seen many wild west movies on TV. You know that eventually the Indians lost. Have you ever thought about what reasons, other than the soldiers' guns, caused the Indians to lose? Read the story to find out why Jacob was actually defeated when the government sent an expedition to go after him.

They chased Jacob farthest and almost penned him a few times and killed a lot of braves and got wind of where his women and their kids were hidden, and forced him to move them farther into the mountains with them getting out just in time, not being able to carry much with them. But that wasn't catching Jacob and stopping him and his braves from carrying on their hop-skip-and-jump war against all whites in general and these troops in particular. Then a second general went in and about a thousand more soldiers with them and they had hard fighting off and on over a couple hundred miles and more, and the days drove on into deep winter and Jacob was licked. Not by the government and its soldiers and their guns. By the winter. He and his braves, what was left of them, had kept two generals and up to two thousand troops busy for four months fighting through parts of three states and then the winter licked him. He came to the second general under truce in what remained of his chief's rig and took off his headdress and laid it on the ground and spoke. His children were scattered in the mountains, he said, and the cold bit sharp and they had few blankets and no food. Several of the small ones had been found frozen to death. From the moment the sun passed overhead that day he would fight no more. *

COMPREHENSION CHECK

(I)   1. _____ Who was Jacob? (the chief of the Indian tribe)

(V)   2. _____ What are "braves" in the phrase "they killed a lot of braves"? (North American Indian warriors)

(I)   3. _____ Why do you suppose they were called "braves"? (the word brave means showing courage or not afraid and warriors should possess these qualities—½ credit for they were fighters)

(F)   4. _____ Who or what was Jacob and his braves hop-skip-and-jump war aimed against? (all whites in general and the troops in particular)

*Adapted from "Jacob," in Jack Schaefer, THE PLAINSMEN (Boston: Houghton-Mifflin, 1954), pp. 243–44. Copyright © 1954 by Jack Schaefer, copyright © renewed 1982. Reprinted by permission of the Harold Matson Co., Inc.

(F) 5. _____ How did the soldiers' discovery of the hiding place of the Indian women and children hurt the Indians? (They were forced to move, and had to leave behind supplies)

(F) 6. _____ How long did Jacob keep fighting before giving up? (four months)

(I) 7. _____ The second general gained an unexpected advantage, what was it? (The Indians were not prepared for the hardships of winter)

(F) 8. _____ What happened to several of Jacob's small children? (they were found frozen to death)

(I) 9. _____ Why do you suppose Jacob took off his headdress and laid it on the ground before he spoke to the second general? (to show that he surrendered)

(M) 10. _____ What title could you give this story? ("How Jacob was Finally Captured," etc.)

SCORING GUIDE: LEVEL 8

WR ERRORS		COMP ERRORS	
IND	0–12	IND	0–1
INSTR	12½–24½	INSTR	1½–3
FRUST	25+	FRUST	3½+

SILENT FORM—Level 8 (245 words)

MOTIVATION: Most of us take the ability to walk for granted. Let's read a story about a boy who lost that ability as a result of having polio, a crippling disease.

The massages were continued. I lay in bed most of the time. Each day I tried to walk a bit. The weakness in my legs gradually disappeared. My feet would flop a bit; the muscles of my knees would twitch; curious numb sensations would come and go. But before many months I relearned to walk, and the frailty which the disease had caused seemed to pass. Someone said that the salt water and massages had effected wonders. Mother was silent awhile and then said, "So did my prayers."

But the ordeal had left its scars. Mother believed the doctor implicitly, and was convinced that the sand would fast run out of my glass. So she set about to guard my health, to protect me against physical strain, to do all sorts of favors designed to save my energy. I was waited on, hand and foot. Worse than that, I began to hear what Mother was saying to others: "he's not as strong as other boys; he has to be careful what he does—you know, his legs were almost paralyzed."

This solicitiousness set up a severe reaction. It seemed to me I was being publicly recognized as a puny person—a weakling. Thus there began to grow in me a great rebellion. I protested against Mother's descriptions of me. But I believe my rebellion was not so much against her as it was against the kind of person I thought I was coming to be. *

COMPREHENSION CHECK

(F)   1. _____ What did the boy do most of the time? (lay in bed)

(F)   2. _____ What did he feel as the weakness gradually went out of his legs? (feet flopping a bit; knee muscles twitching; numb sensations coming and going—should give at least 2)

(F)   3. _____ What did Mother think helped him improve? (her prayers)

(I)   4. _____ Why did Mother work so hard to save his energy? (Because she believed he wouldn't survive long and wanted to protect him for as long as she could)

(I)   5. _____ What treatment aided the boy's recovery? (salt water, massages, rest—name 1 for full credit)

(F)   6. _____ What was Mother saying to other people? (he's not as strong as other boys; he has to be careful what he does)

(I)   7. _____ Why did Mother's actions and statements upset the boy? (Because he believed them—or—because he felt publicly humiliated or embarrassed)

(V)   8. _____ What does "solicitousness" mean in the sentence "This solicitousness set up a severe reaction"? (helpfulness, protectiveness, waiting on, etc.)

(F)   9. _____ What was the boy rebelling against more than his mother? (the kind of person he thought he was becoming)

(M) 10. _____ What lesson can be learned from this story? (Certain kinds of help can do more harm than good—or—Faith is the best healer, etc.)

SCORING GUIDE: LEVEL 8

COMP ERRORS

IND   0–1
INSTR 1½–3
FRUST 3½ +

INDICES

NAME INDEX

SUBJECT INDEX

TEST INDEX